I0438957

Perspectives Gained From the Individual Plant Examination of External Events (IPEEE) Program

Final Report

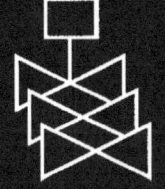

U.S. Nuclear Regulatory Commission
Office of Nuclear Regulatory Research
Washington, DC 20555-0001

AVAILABILITY OF REFERENCE MATERIALS
IN NRC PUBLICATIONS

NUREG-1742
Vol. 1

Perspectives Gained From the Individual Plant Examination of External Events (IPEEE) Program

Final Report

Manuscript Completed: September 2001
Date Published: April 2002

Division of Risk Analysis and Applications
Office of Nuclear Regulatory Research
U.S. Nuclear Regulatory Commission
Washington, DC 20555-0001

ABSTRACT

On June 28, 1991, the U.S. Nuclear Regulatory Commission (NRC) issued Supplement 4 to Generic Letter (GL) 88-20, "Individual Plant Examination of External Events (IPEEE) for Severe Accident Vulnerabilities, 10 CFR 50.54(f)," and NUREG-1407, "Procedure and Submittal Guidance for the Individual Plant Examination of External Events (IPEEE) for Severe Accident Vulnerabilities." Supplement 4 to GL 88-20 specifically requested that each licensee identify and report to the NRC all plant-specific vulnerabilities to severe accidents caused by external events. The external events to be considered in the IPEEE were seismic events; internal fires; and high winds, floods, and other (HFO) external initiating events, including accidents related to transportation or nearby facilities and plant-unique hazards. All currently operating U.S. nuclear power plants have completed their assessments and submitted them for NRC review. Acts of sabotage or terrorism were not included in the set of events considered.

The objective of the NRC's IPEEE submittal reviews was to ascertain whether the licensees' IPEEE processes were capable of identifying severe accident vulnerabilities to such external events and implementing cost-effective safety improvements to either eliminate or reduce the impact of those vulnerabilities. However, the reviews did not attempt to validate or verify the licensees' IPEEE results.

The primary purpose of this report is to document the perspectives derived from the technical reviews of the IPEEE submittals. The report describes the overall IPEEE process and findings; discusses the dominant risk contributors for the major areas of evaluation (i.e., seismic events, fires, and HFO events); lists plant improvements made by licensees as a result of the IPEEE program; summarizes the overall strengths and weaknesses in the licensees' implementation of the IPEEE evaluation methodologies; and assesses licensees' overall effectiveness in meeting the IPEEE objectives, including the extent to which licensees have met the intent of Supplement 4 to Generic Letter 88-20. Volume 1 presents general IPEEE perspectives. Volume 2 contains tables with plant-specific information from the IPEEE program.

Table of Contents

List of Figures

List of Tables

Summary

Introduction

On June 28, 1991, the U.S. Nuclear Regulatory Commission (NRC) issued Supplement 4 to Generic Letter (GL) 88-20, "Individual Plant Examination of External Events (IPEEE) for Severe Accident Vulnerabilities, 10 CFR 50.54(f)." This GL requested that "each licensee perform an individual plant examination of external events to identify vulnerabilities, if any, to severe accidents and report the results together with any licensee-determined improvements and corrective actions to the Commission." The external events considered in the IPEEE program include seismic events; internal fires; and high winds, floods, and other (HFO) external initiating events involving accidents related to transportation and nearby facilities.[1] Acts of sabotage or terrorism were not included in the set of events considered.

Consistent with the intent of GL 88-20, the primary goal of the IPEEE program has been for each licensee to identify plant-specific vulnerabilities to severe accidents, if any, and to report the results together with any licensee-determined improvements and corrective actions to the NRC. Supplement 4 to GL 88-20 identified the following four supporting IPEEE objectives for each licensee:

- develop an appreciation of severe accident behavior,

- understand the most likely severe accident sequences that could occur at the licensee's plant under full-power operating conditions,

- gain a qualitative understanding of the overall likelihood of core damage and fission product releases, and

- reduce, if necessary, the overall likelihood of core damage and radioactive material releases by modifying, where appropriate, hardware and procedures that would help prevent or mitigate severe accidents.

In June 1991, about the same time the NRC issued Supplement 4 to GL 88-20, the NRC issued NUREG-1407, "Procedure and Submittal Guidance for the Individual Plant Examination of External Events (IPEEE) for Severe Accident Vulnerabilities," which provided guidelines for conducting IPEEEs. On September 8, 1995, the NRC issued Supplement 5 to GL 88-20 to notify licensees of modifications to the recommended scope of the seismic portion of the IPEEE for certain plant sites in the Eastern United States.

The NRC received 70 IPEEE submittals covering all operating U.S. nuclear reactors. (Some submittals covered more than one unit at multi-unit sites with similar or almost identical plant designs.) The staff of the NRC's Office of Nuclear Regulatory Research (RES) completed Staff Evaluation Reports (SERs) to document the staff's overall conclusions for each of the IPEEE reviews. Additional details on the plant-

---

[1]On November 23, 1988, the NRC issued GL 88-20, "Individual Plant Examination for Severe Accident Vulnerabilities, 10 CFR 50.54(f)," to licensees of nuclear power plants. GL 88-20 outlined the objectives and overall logistics of the Individual Plant Examination (IPE) program, which addresses only internally initiated events (including internal flooding).

specific IPEEE review findings are presented in Technical Evaluation Reports (TERs) prepared by RES staff and contractors for each of the IPEEE submittals.[2] Each TER discusses the strengths and weaknesses of the licensee's IPEEE submittal, particularly with reference to the guidelines established in NUREG-1407. The TERs also present (1) an overview of the licensee's IPEEE process and insights; (2) the review process employed for evaluation of the seismic, fire, and HFO events; (3) the dominant contributors to core damage frequency for fire, seismic, and HFO events; (4) licensee-identified vulnerabilities; (5) plant improvements made or planned as a result of the licensee's IPEEE process; and (6) an overall evaluation of the strengths and weaknesses of the IPEEE submittal.

In addition to performing technical reviews of the IPEEE submittals, the NRC's Office of Nuclear Regulatory Research (RES) instituted a program to identify and document general perspectives and significant safety insights resulting from the IPEEE program. This program was based on a compilation of the reviews of all 70 IPEEE submittals. The objectives of this program were to provide:

- a description of the overall IPEEE process, findings, and impacts of the major areas of evaluation for external initiators (seismic events, internal fires, and HFOs),

- an overview of plant improvements related to the IPEEE program, with a description of their beneficial impact on reactor safety,

- an overview of the IPEEE review process describing the site-specific hazards, plant-specific design and operational features, and modeling and screening assumptions that affect the understanding of a plant's severe accident behavior and containment performance to assure that the IPEEE process is capable of identifying potential plant vulnerabilities to severe accidents from external events,

- a description of the overall strengths and weaknesses in the implementation of evaluation methodologies, including the implications of assumptions consistently made in IPEEEs, and

- an assessment of the overall effectiveness in meeting the IPEEE objectives, including a summary of the extent to which the licensees have met the intent of Supplement 4 to GL 88-20.

This report documents the results of this program.

Organization of Report

In developing this report, the staff sought to address each distinct, significant topic considered in NUREG-1407, including seismic events, fires, and HFOs, as well as the relevant IPEEE-related aspects of generic safety issues (GSIs) and unresolved safety issues (USIs). Volume 1 of this report contains general IPEEE perspectives, while Volume 2 contains tables of plant-specific information relevant to the IPEEE program.

---

[2] Each plant-specific IPEEE SER and TER was transmitted to the respective licensee for their plant. Readers interested in specific plants can obtain the plant-specific SERs and TERs through the NRC's Agencywide Documents Access and Management System (ADAMS). (Include the plant name and "IPEEE" in the Title Contains block of the ADAMS Find window.) SERs that were issued prior to November 1999 are available to the public, for a fee, by contacting the NRC's Public Document Room (PDR) librarian at (800) 397-4209 or via e-mail to pdr@nrc.gov.

In Volume 1, Chapter 1 covers the general background and objectives of the IPEEE program. Chapters 2 and 3 discuss the perspectives derived from the seismic and fire portions of the IPEEE submittals, respectively. Chapter 4 presents findings derived from the HFO portion of the IPEEE submittals. Each major category of HFO initiator is discussed, including high winds and tornadoes, external floods, and accidents related to transportation or nearby facilities. Chapters 2 through 4 each summarize walkdown findings, human action perspectives, containment performance perspectives, plant improvements, generic versus plant-specific perspectives, and observations of specific strengths and weaknesses in the evaluation of each type of external initiator. Chapter 5 describes each of the external-event-related unresolved and generic safety issues and provides the staff's conclusions regarding the verification of these issues for each plant.

Volume 2 of this report, containing plant-specific tables, is organized as follows: Chapter 1 is a brief introduction; Chapter 2 covers seismic events; Chapter 3 fire; Chapter 4 high winds, floods and other external events; and Chapter 5 IPEEE-related unresolved safety issues and generic safety issues.

The following discussion describes the NRC's review process and a number of general limitations with the IPEEE submittals as a whole. This discussion provides context to the remainder of the summary, which presents the major perspectives, results, and conclusions for the various aspects of the IPEEE program (i.e., seismic, fire, and HFO events, and USIs and GSIs).

NRC's Technical Review of IPEEE Submittals

The primary objective of the NRC's technical review process was to ascertain the extent to which the licensees' IPEEE submittals have achieved the intent of GL 88-20, satisfied the four principal IPEEE objectives listed in the introduction section above, and followed the guidance in NUREG-1407. The reviews focused on verifying that the critical elements of acceptable IPEEE analyses in the fire, seismic, and HFO areas were performed in accordance with the guidelines in NUREG-1407. The reviews were not intended to validate or verify the licensee's IPEEE analyses or results (i.e., an in-depth evaluation of the various inputs, assumptions, and calculations was not performed). Rather, methods, approaches, assumptions, and results were reviewed for reasonableness. If inconsistencies were found, they were reported in the plant-specific IPEEE TERs.

The review process was comprised of a Step 1 (screening) review of each submittal, with follow-on Step 2 reviews of individual submittals on an as-needed basis. The Step 1 reviews considered only the submittal itself; none of the underlying or supporting (second-tier) documents were examined. Step 1 reviews also included interactions with licensees in the form of requests for additional information (RAIs) and/or conference calls. The objective of these interactions was to obtain clarification on unclear or questionable points in a given submittal. These RAIs were generally limited to items considered to be of sufficient importance that the insights or findings of the IPEEE, or the reviewers' understanding of those findings and insights, might be significantly impacted by the licensee's responses.

If, at the end of the Step 1 review, the reviewers could not conclude that a submittal met the intent of the IPEEE process, or if the submittal reported unusual results (e.g., extremely high or low core damage frequencies (CDFs) or high confidence of low probability of failure (HCLPF) values), a Step 2 review was undertaken. A Step 2 review involved further interactions with the licensee to resolve the identified concerns. Step 2 reviews, which were conducted for four plants, included plant visits, reviews of supporting documents, interviews with plant personnel, and plant walkdowns.

The NRC also convened a senior review board (SRB) to oversee the technical aspects of the review process. The objectives of the SRB were to provide additional assurance that (1) the scope of the review met the objectives of the program, and (2) critical issues that have the potential to mask vulnerabilities were not overlooked. The SRB included NRC staff members and contractors who are experts in the field of general risk assessment and the specific areas addressed by the IPEEE analyses (seismic events, internal fires, and HFOs).

Scope, Limitations, and General Comments

IPEEE studies have been limited to the consideration of plant behavior under full-power operating conditions. The perspectives documented in this report are somewhat limited for the following reasons: (a) IPEEEs are intended to yield predominantly qualitative perspectives, rather than quantitative findings; (b) IPEEEs address several different types of initiators of varying importance (for a given plant) and, therefore, require different methods of analysis with varying levels of detail and accuracy; and (c) the procedures and methods used by the various licensees to conduct their IPEEEs have also varied considerably, even for the same type of external event initiator. Therefore, prior to using the IPEEE findings for specific risk-informed activities, factors such as the IPEEE objectives, level of modeling detail, and assumptions needs to be considered in relation to the potential risk-informed applications.

Additionally, the IPEEE submittals used various sources of information, such as seismic hazard curves derived from different sources (e.g., Lawrence Livermore National Laboratory (LLNL) [NUREG/CR-1488 and NUREG/CR-5250]; Electric Power Research Institute [EPRI, 1989]; and site-specific studies). Some licensees applied simplified conservative methods in some studies while others used more realistic approaches. These differences make it difficult to compare analysis results between plants. Comparisons of IPEEE results among plants and among the various types of external hazards are also limited because of variations in the quality of submittals. Hence, the staff made no attempt in this report to compare IPEEE results among the various categories of external initiators for individual plants. For the most part, then, discussions in this report are kept distinct for seismic events, internal fires, and HFO initiators.

The qualitative perspectives in this report include a summary of the licensees' findings on severe accident issues and the identification of plant improvements, a summary of the staff's observations on licensees' methods and findings, and assessments of the consistency and potential usefulness of the IPEEE results. Among the quantitative results discussed are licensees' estimates of CDFs and plant capability.

It should be noted that the IPEEEs were typically performed with the state-of-the-art as of the early 1990s. Since then, the techniques used have been improving, and research is continuing. For example, knowledge of the potential impacts of fires on cable failure modes has been improved. Also, the American Nuclear Society is developing standards for risk assessments of external hazards. In the arena of human error probabilities, the NRC's Office of Nuclear Regulatory Research is actively pursuing research activities on estimating the probabilities under accident conditions, including fires. The staff currently has no information indicating that use of current state-of-the-art information would lead to the identification of new or different plant vulnerabilities.

Although not required, many licensees have chosen to keep their IPEs updated (living) and have used them in prioritizing plant work and as part of the basis for requested NRC actions. In the same manner, it could be beneficial for licensees that have performed their IPEEE with PRA techniques to maintain their IPEEE as a living document. Although not required by the NRC, licensees are encouraged to maintain their IPEEE as a living document.

Seismic Events

As requested in NUREG-1407, licensees used one of two methods to conduct their seismic IPEEEs. The first was a seismic probabilistic risk assessment (SPRA) consisting of at least a Level 1 analysis and a qualitative containment performance analysis. The second method was a seismic margins assessment (SMA), including a qualitative containment performance analysis. Both methods satisfy the objectives of the seismic IPEEE in that they both include a systematic, comprehensive walkdown of important components and are capable of identifying plant vulnerabilities. The scope of the seismic examination for a particular plant depends on the location of the plant, with higher hazard sites undertaking more extensive investigations. Therefore, plants fell into the following categories: reduced-scope, focused-scope, full-scope, and committed to perform an SPRA.

Almost all licensees reported in their IPEEE submittals that no plant vulnerabilities were identified with respect to seismic risk (the use of the term "vulnerability" varied widely among the IPEEE submittals). However, most licensees did report at least some seismic "anomalies," "outliers," and/or other concerns. In the few submittals which identified a seismic vulnerability, the concerns were comparable to concerns identified as outliers or anomalies in other submittals.

Quantitative findings and perspectives

- With respect to SPRA analyses, (including both LLNL and EPRI hazard curves) the largest group of plants reported seismic CDFs between 1E-5 and 1E-4 per reactor-year (ry), with the next largest group falling between 1E-6 and 1E-5/ry. Only a few plants had CDFs higher than 1E-4/ry or less than 1E-6/ry. For operating plants, the point-estimate seismic CDFs obtained from the analyses with the EPRI hazard curves vary from about 2E-7/ry to 6E-5/ry.

- The results obtained from the SPRA analyses also indicate that the CDFs of newer plants (i.e., those designed and built to later seismic standards) are similar to the CDFs of older plants built before some of the later design criteria were in place. These data suggest that seismic backfit programs for older plants have successfully brought their CDF estimates in line with those of the newer plants.

- With respect to SMA results, plant HCLPF capacities for the 36 submittals in the full and focused-scope categories of NUREG-1407 that performed SMAs are between 0.12g and 0.3g. Fourteen licensees reported plant HCLPFs of at least 0.3g, ten plants fell between 0.25 and 0.3g, nine plants were between 0.2 and 0.25g, and two plants were between 0.15 and 0.2g. One plant reported a HCLPF value of 0.12g. As with the SPRA results, the seismic margins of older plants built before some of the later design criteria were in place are similar to the seismic margins of the newer plants.

- Taking the proposed improvements into account, the SMA results indicate that the HCLPF value for all plants is never below the safe shutdown earthquake (SSE) and generally exceeds the SSE. The SMA studies are generally effective in demonstrating a level of seismic margin beyond the design basis for these plants.

- Dominant contributors from SPRAs for seismic failure involve the failure of the electrical systems, including the failure of offsite power (17% of all contributors); the failure of various components of the electrical system (17%), such as motor control centers (MCCs), switchgear, and relays; the failure of the emergency diesel generator (EDG) (8%); and the failure of the dc batteries (5%). Building and structural failures also contribute significantly (30% of all contributors). Other structures whose failure could cause core damage include block walls, pump house/pump intake structures, dams, and stacks. Failures of front line and support systems (28% of all contributors) and tank failures (11%) also contribute to core damage frequency.

- Generally, the weak link components identified in the SMA analyses were similar to the structures, systems, and components (SSCs) listed as dominant contributors in the SPRAs. The components identified as outliers in the SMAs included many electrical components and their anchorages, various tanks, residual heat removal (RHR) heat exchangers, and structures like the turbine and auxiliary buildings. Many licensees identified block walls located near safety-significant equipment as weak link structures.

Qualitative findings and perspectives

- The common denominator of acceptable seismic IPEEE evaluations is a well-conducted, detailed walkdown to find as-designed, as-built, and as-operated seismic weaknesses in plants. Regardless of the specific approach used, all licensees conducted detailed seismic plant walkdowns, gaining many insights. Often the walkdowns identified seismic concerns whose correction proved to be relatively simple and cost effective. For sites where the seismic hazard is low (i.e., where a reduced-scope seismic margins method is considered adequate), the detailed walkdowns were the most significant aspect of the IPEEE process to identify seismic weak links.

- Low-ruggedness relays were identified in several seismic IPEEE analyses. Since many relay concerns were identified and verified under USI A-46, "Verification of Seismic Adequacy of Equipment in Operating Plants," when low ruggedness relays were identified solely in the seismic analysis of the IPEEE program, licensees often determined that the chatter of these relays would have no adverse consequences.

- Most submittals for plants founded on soil provided some level of discussions on liquefaction. For earthquakes beyond the design basis, a potential for liquefaction-related failures was identified as a contributor to risk at a few sites.

- All of the IPEEE submittals provided some treatment or discussion of non-seismic failures and human actions. However, licensees used a wide variety of approaches to model the seismic impacts on operator error rates. In some instances, licensees developed simplified operator error fragilities. In other instances, licensees applied scaling factors (in relation to the importance of the human action) to internal event error rates or used other means to account for seismically related performance shaping factors.

- All licensees qualitatively examined seismic-fire interaction and seismic-flood issues, and in many of the IPEEE submittals, the seismic-fire and/or seismic-flood interaction evaluations revealed concerns. In a number of instances, the examination resulted in significant plant improvements. Some of the relevant improvements include strengthening component anchorages, replacing vulnerable (e.g., mercury) relays and switches, restraining gas cylinders, waterproofing, replacing sight glass tubes, and implementing procedures to properly secure transient fire protection equipment.

- All licensees performed walkdowns of their containments. Licensees did not report any anomalous conditions with respect to containment structural integrity. However, in a few instances, they identified outliers pertaining to containment penetrations and containment cooling.

Plant improvements

Most licensees identified a number of improvements to enhance the seismic ruggedness of their plants. In some cases these plant improvements were only proposed in the submittals (sometimes without a firm commitment for implementation), while other submittals indicated the improvements were already implemented. The improvements fell into three categories: hardware modifications, improved procedures and training, and enhanced maintenance and housekeeping. In keeping with the expectation of GL 88-20, the majority of the implemented or proposed improvements enhance the plants' resistance to a seismic event, but do not involve significant cost. The major findings related to seismic improvements are as follows.

- Seventy percent of the plants proposed improvements as a result of their seismic IPEEE analyses.

- Of plants that proposed plant improvements, 84% proposed some form of hardware changes, often adding new anchorages or supports or strengthening existing ones. Many of the modifications carried out were similar to ones carried out under the USI A-46 program, but they involved more SSCs under the IPEEE, since the scope of the IPEEEs was broader than that of USI A-46.

- Block walls were identified in many IPEEEs either as significant contributors to CDF or as controlling elements for plant HCLPF capacity.

- About 60% of the plants that proposed plant improvements included maintenance/housekeeping improvements, including the improvement of maintenance conduct and training; the correction of housekeeping errors; the issuance of new housekeeping standards; other corrective actions, such as restraining gas bottles, scaffolding, and ladders; corrective actions to address loose or missing fasteners, bolts, and clamps; and rust protection measures.

- About 20% of plants that proposed plant improvements proposed revising or adding new procedures and training for seismic events.

Perspectives on seismic evaluation methods

The review of the IPEEE results, especially the SPRA results, indicates that the broad plant-to-plant variability probably results from a combination of many factors, including differences in methods and analytical assumptions, as well as variations in plant designs and locations. In general, the assumptions and procedures were more consistent for HCLPF calculations in the SMAs than for the fragility calculations and other analyses in the SPRAs.

The following are some of the more important variations and observations identified in the reviews:

- Licensees used a variety of hazard results to calculate CDFs. In many cases, the spectral shape used in evaluating fragilities and the hazard curve used for quantifying CDF were not derived from a consistent set of hazard results. For example, the uniform hazard spectrum (UHS) derived from the 1989 LLNL hazard analysis was typically used to define the SPRA spectral shape, whereas the seismic hazard curve derived from the 1989 EPRI or 1994 LLNL hazard analyses was typically used to quantify CDF.

- Seismic fragility evaluations for the subset of components selected for risk quantification (components not screened) were carried out using various methods, including fragility analysis, generic information, and testing. In general, SPRAs liberally employed various forms of simplified fragility analyses, in contrast to the detailed conventional fragility analyses in past SPRAs. The use of simplified fragilities raises the possibility that in some cases the relative importance of the dominant contributors to the seismic CDF may be overstated or understated.

- A limited review of selected fragility calculations suggests that the analyst's prior experience in conducting such calculations is a significant factor in the quality of the component fragility calculations. Of the calculations reviewed, some were of good quality, while other calculations lacked material documentation and, in some cases, used unrealistic estimates of uncertainties.

- In calculating plant HCLPFs, the licensees have made significant efforts to reduce inherent conservatism in the seismic demand calculations. Many of the plants performed new seismic analyses, and plant sites founded on soil usually considered soil-structure interaction (SSI) effects. As a result, many have demonstrated significant reductions in the seismic demands on plant components. Therefore, the HCLPF values computed are more realistic plant seismic capacities than conveyed by the design basis SSE capacities of the plants.

- For the plants that performed new SSI analyses, the seismic analyses often resulted in much lower review-level earthquake (RLE) in-structure response spectra (IRS) demand than the design basis SSE IRS. Therefore, comparisons of the component seismic fragility/HCLPF values for two plants using the two different approaches (scaling versus new SSI calculations) could be misleading. The different approaches to estimating building and component seismic responses can significantly affect the magnitude of the reported fragility (or CDF) or HCLPF values. Hence, comparison of the seismic capacities should be made mainly among plants which were analyzed using similar methods.

- In some EPRI SMA IPEEE submittals, licensees did not entirely follow the criteria for success path development, or the submittal did not contain sufficient information to permit verification of appropriate application of the criteria. Although all SMAs included two success paths, the success paths varied in redundancy and diversity. The lack of redundancy or diversity was due either to the actual limitations of the systems available at the plant or to the system selection process used by the analyst.

- The licensees of some plants in the Eastern United States (EUS), when conducting their component fragility calculations, used UHS whose shapes differed from the conventional spectrum shapes derived from observed earthquakes. The energy content of these UHS appears to be reduced from that of the respective design basis SSE spectra in the frequency range that is typically considered to have the greatest impact on the SSC responses to seismic motions. The seismic analyses using the UHS as input resulted in significant reduction in seismic demand, compared to the corresponding design basis calculations.

- To date, an adequately detailed investigation of the implications of using the surrogate element[3] in the IPEEEs has not been undertaken. No regulatory guidelines have been developed concerning its use (particularly with respect to sensitivities in plant logic modeling). If the surrogate element is found to be only a minor contributor to seismic CDF, then its use is probably reasonable. Since a surrogate element represents more than one component, those studies that identified the surrogate element as a dominant risk contributor cannot determine which specific component among the surrogates is the risk contributor.

- The possibility of failures due to soil liquefaction may be difficult to fully preclude in a cost-effective manner. Currently, there is no general guidance (or even a consensus) on the best approach to estimating liquefaction-induced soil displacement. Therefore, a significant amount of uncertainty still exists with respect to these liquefaction studies performed for the IPEEE program.

- Human actions were treated in SPRAs using a wide variety of approaches. In most SPRAs, human error probabilities were based on the values developed for the IPE models, usually modified with some simplified means to account for seismic-related performance shaping factors, but without strong technical bases for the values chosen. For SMAs, the timing and location of human actions was usually reported, along with qualitative comments on their reliability.

Fires

Summary of vulnerabilities and plant improvements

Out of all the IPEEE submittals, only two licensees, representing three nuclear power plant units, identified fire vulnerabilities. In one case (Quad Cities), the vulnerabilities were identified in the licensee's original IPEEE submittal. However, a subsequent detailed reanalysis by the licensee showed that the original analysis did not provide sufficient credit for existing equipment and for operator recovery actions. Even though the licensee concluded that the originally identified fire vulnerabilities did not exist, the licensee did make plant improvements as a result of the insights gained in the original IPEEE analysis and credited some of those improvements in the reanalysis. In the second case (Millstone 2), two fire vulnerabilities were identified, and the licensee implemented plant improvements involving rerouting of control cables in the turbine building to address these vulnerabilities. For both Quad Cities and Millstone 2, the vulnerabilities included fire safety issues in the turbine building, which housed important safety-related cables and equipment needed for safe shutdown. The turbine building also presented substantial fire sources. In both cases, postulated large fires in the turbine building led to identification of fire vulnerabilities. Turbine building areas were also identified by many other licensees as important CDF contributors.

---

[3] A surrogate element is an element used in a seismic PRA (SPRA) to account for the effects of the components that are screened out during the walkdown and screening phase of the SPRA. A surrogate element represents the failures of several screened components by the failure of a single surrogate element.

Although the vast majority of licensees did not identify fire-related vulnerabilities, most licensees (over 60%) did identify and/or implement plant improvements to reduce fire risk. A total of approximately 240 fire-related plant improvements were identified by licensees. The majority of the cited plant improvements (about 60%) were associated with various plant procedures (operating procedures, maintenance procedures, combustible controls, enhancements to operator training, enhanced fire brigade training, etc.). The remaining improvements (about 40%) involved plant modifications and hardware changes (general plant system design changes, enhancements to fire protection features, relocation of critical cables, and upgrading of fire barriers).

Quantitative findings and perspectives

One of the primary objectives of the IPEEE process was to identify potential plant vulnerabilities. For fires, this goal could be achieved using a screening analysis method such as the EPRI Fire-Induced Vulnerability Evaluation (FIVE) methodology [EPRI, 1992]. However, the vast majority of the IPEEE fire analyses included PRA-based quantification of unscreened fire scenarios and reported the total plant fire-induced CDF values. The reported values range from approximately 4E-8 to 2E-4 per reactor-year. Most licensees reported fire CDF that exceed 10% of the internal events CDF as reported in the corresponding IPE. For about 25% of the submittals, the reported fire CDF exceeds the internal events CDF as reported in the corresponding IPE. Many of the IPEEE submittals cited a low degree of confidence in their estimates of fire-induced CDF, and several explicitly stated that the estimated fire CDFs were considered conservative. However, the relative CDF values reported in the IPE and IPEEE fire analyses nominally indicate that fire can be a potentially important contributor to overall plant CDF. The IPEEEs provide no basis for discounting the importance of potential fires in a nuclear power plant.

In the vast majority of cases, licensees concluded that the dominant fire CDF contributors were areas that held both significant fire sources and important equipment and cables. Hence, it appears that spatial factors (e.g., the location of the fire source and targets) were more significant in determining fire risk than were plant system design features. Areas devoid of either fire sources or important targets were generally screened.

Overall, the two fire analysis zones found most often to be the single highest fire CDF contributors were switchgear areas and main control rooms (MCRs). The next most commonly identified areas were the turbine building and the cable spreading room (for plants that have only one cable spreading room). Other commonly reported areas were electrical equipment rooms, diesel generator rooms, cable vault and tunnel areas, and battery/charger rooms. A range of other areas were identified as important on a plant-specific basis.

In the case of the MCR, fire CDF was dominated by the abandonment scenarios; that is, unsuppressed fires leading to MCR abandonment. In this case, fire CDF estimates were driven largely by two factors, namely, the assumed conditional probability of MCR abandonment and the reliability of human actions associated with plant shutdown using the remote shutdown capability.

Fire sources considered in the fire assessments included both fixed sources (e.g., electrical panels, pumps, transformers, and electrical cables) and transient combustibles. Electrical panel fires were the most significant fire CDF contributors in most submittals. In a minority of submittals, transient combustible fires were also found to be significant.

Fire-induced transients were found to be the most important accident sequences. These transients included loss of feedwater and main steam isolation valve (MSIV) closure transients, loss of offsite power (LOOP) events, and loss of support system initiators. Loss-of-coolant accidents (LOCAs) induced by spurious opening of power-operated relief valves (PORVs) or safety relief valves (SRVs) were generally not identified as significant contributors to the fire-related CDF. However, fire scenarios resulting in reactor coolant pump (RCP) seal LOCAs were important for many Westinghouse pressurized water reactors (PWRs).

Most licensees screened all scenarios involving propagation of a fire from one zone to another. Of the submittals that provided some quantitative assessment of the CDF contribution from multizone fire scenarios, 80% concluded that these scenarios were not significant (i.e., the scenarios were screened). The rest reported CDF contributions ranging from 1% to 30% of the overall fire-induced CDF.

The fire-induced CDFs reported by the newer plants (i.e., those licensed to operate after January 1, 1979) and older plants (those to which the Appendix R backfit requirements applied) showed considerable variability but no clear trend with respect to plant age. One possible interpretation of this result is that fire protection backfit programs for older plants have successfully brought their fire-induced CDFs in line with those of the newer plants. However, the level of review given to the IPEEEs cannot support a definitive explanation of this observation.

With respect to containment performance, all licensees concluded that fires did not lead to any new or unique containment failure modes not identified in the internal event IPE results. Relatively few licensees included a Level 2 PRA quantification of fire-induced containment failure scenarios. The few who did perform a Level 2 analysis concluded that fire-induced early containment bypass scenarios were of low likelihood in comparison to similar scenarios analyzed in the IPEs.

Fire methodology perspectives

For the IPEEE fire assessments, all licensees utilized probabilistic analysis methods in one form or another. By far the most commonly cited analysis approach was the EPRI Fire-Induced Vulnerability Evaluation (FIVE) methodology [EPRI, 1992]. The FIVE methodology was cited as being used to support about 80% of the licensees' IPEEE submittals. However, most of these submittals also went beyond the FIVE approach and applied PRA methods as a supplement to the FIVE method. Of the licensees who utilized FIVE, 75% went on to quantify unscreened fire scenarios using supplemental PRA methods. About 20% of the licensees chose to directly implement fire PRA without reference to FIVE.

The selected methodology did have some impact on the final estimates of fire CDF, but ultimately appeared to have little impact on the overall findings of the IPEEE studies (e.g., identification of dominant areas contributing to fire CDF). Since FIVE is primarily a screening method, those licensees who stopped with FIVE screening generally obtained higher total CDF estimates than those who continued with more detailed fire PRA-based quantification of unscreened zones.

Plant walkdowns were important sources of information for the licensees' fire evaluations. Virtually all of the submittals cited at least one, and many cited several, plant walkdowns focused on fire safety. Typically, at least one walkdown was performed to address seismic-fire interactions. Most licensees cited that plant walkdowns as used to support a range of IPEEE analysis needs, including defining IPEEE fire analysis zones, identifying fire sources, mapping the location of important cables and equipment, developing input parameters for fire modeling, reviewing fire protection systems, and screening fire source/target combinations based on the results of fire modeling.

There was significant variation among the submittals in the methods and assumptions used to support particular aspects of the fire assessments. The impacts of individual modeling choices on the fire CDFs cannot, in general, be isolated from the other modeling factors and from plant design differences. Areas of methodological variability included the following.

- Only a small number of licensees provided an explicit treatment of the potential variation in fire size in their evaluation of the CDF for each fire area. The majority of submittals were based on the analysis of those fire intensities considered representative of the most likely fires. When fire size was explicitly treated, the greatest CDF contribution generally derived from larger fires, although these fires were assumed to be less likely.

- Electrical panel fires were identified as key contributors to the fire-induced CDF at most plants. However, the methods of analysis varied substantially with regard to the assumed fire intensity, the potential for spread and/or damage outside a panel, the fire duration, the effectiveness of fire suppression, the application of severity factors, and the extent of damage in the panel.

- Self-ignited cable fires were generally assumed possible only for plants that did not use Institute of Electrical and Electronic Engineers 383 standard (IEEE-383) or equivalent low-flame-spread cables (consistent with the FIVE approach). The majority of licensees either cited use of IEEE-383 qualified cables in construction or back-qualification of the cables used at the plant to the IEEE-383 flame spread test or an equivalent test after construction had been completed. In these cases, self-ignited cable fires were not considered. In the other cases, cable-initiated fires were found to be important only in a few cases. These generally involved areas without other fixed ignition sources, areas where risk-important cables converged, and area that had some limitation to the fire suppression capability.

- Many of the submittals included the application of severity factors for CDF quantification. This approach utilized industry-wide experience-based statistics in lieu of scenario-specific analyses. A wide variety of severity factor approaches were used in the fire analyses.

High Winds, Floods, and Other External Events

The following types of events were included in the high winds, floods and other (HFO) external events category:

- high winds, including tornadoes, tornado missiles, and hurricanes,

- external floods, including intense rainfall resulting in site flooding and roof ponding; flooding from nearby bodies of water, including wave runup from rivers, lakes, and the ocean; and potential flooding from postulated dam failures,

- accidents related to transportation or nearby industrial facilities, and

- other types of external events such as onsite hazardous material spills, hydrogen line breaks, effects of low-temperature conditions such as icing and blockage of cooling water intake lines, blockage of drains and intakes by debris, and any other plant-unique hazard.

Guidance for conducting HFO analyses

As discussed in Section 5 of NUREG-1407, the guidance for conducting HFO analyses for the IPEEEs follows a progressive screening approach to identify potential HFO-related vulnerabilities. This progressive screening approach, summarized below, follows a series of steps or analyses in increasing level of detail and effort.

- Review the plant-specific hazard data and licensing basis and determine whether there were any significant changes since the issuance of the operating license that could affect the IPEEE.

- Determine whether the plant conforms to the guidance in the NRC's 1975 Standard Review Plan (SRP), NUREG-0800, and perform a plant walkdown.

- If the plant does not conform to the 1975 SRP guidance, perform one or more of the following steps:

    – Determine if the hazard frequency of the original design is acceptably low (i.e., less than 1E-5 per year).

    – If the event cannot be screened out based on hazard frequency, perform a bounding analysis to show that the hazard would not result in a CDF contribution of 1E-6 per reactor-year (ry).

    – Perform a PRA.

Summary of results and perspectives

Most licensees screened out HFO events on the basis of qualitative assessments, consistent with one of the accepted approaches given in NUREG-1407. A qualitative assessment typically involved demonstrating conformance with the 1975 SRP criteria and performing a plant walkdown. The purpose of the walkdown was to identify any changes in the plant configuration from the original design basis that might affect the IPEEE evaluation.

Most of the HFO-related IPEEE studies (approximately 80%) used the qualitative screening method, roughly 15% performed a PRA (both fully and partially bounding PRAs), and less than 5% used the initiating event hazard frequency method.

None of the 70 IPEEE submittals identified any HFO-related vulnerabilities; however, 34 submittals reported that they had either made, or were considering, a total of 64 HFO-related plant improvements. Sixteen plants cited more than one HFO-related improvement, and one plant (Turkey Point) considered making five improvements. These improvements are summarized in Tables 4.4 through 4.8 in Volume 1 and on a plant-by-plant basis in Table 4.1 of Volume 2. Thirty-six plants reported no HFO-related improvements.

All HFO evaluations screened out accidents involving transportation and nearby facilities, and they all screened out other plant-unique hazards that licensees identified for site-specific evaluations.

Of the 70 IPEEE submittals, most indicated that some type of walkdown was performed for HFO events during the IPEEE. However, the submittals usually did not provide detailed descriptions of the walkdown procedures and results.

For those cases where the licensees performed PRAs or CDF bounding analyses for their HFO analysis, the estimated CDF results varied from plant to plant as follows.

- For high winds and tornadoes, the plant-specific CDF results varied from less than 2E-7/ry to 6E-5/ry.

- For external flood events, the plant-specific CDF results varied from 2E-8/ry to about 7E-6/ry.

- For transportation and nearby facility accidents, all reported plant-specific CDF results from PRA studies or bounding analyses were below the NUREG-1407 screening criterion of 1E-6/ry.

- One submittal (Haddam Neck) reported bounding analysis CDF results of 8E-6/ry for lightning events and 7E-6/ry for snow and ice.

- One submittal (South Texas) reported CDF results of 8E-6/ry for a chemical release from a nearby chemical facility.

- One submittal (Salem) reported a plant modification that resulted in an external events CDF reduction of three orders of magnitude from approximately 1E-4/ry to approximately 1E-7/ry. The plant modification cited was the improvement of door penetration seals between the service and auxiliary buildings to protect against external flooding.

The licensees' evaluations of HFO events did not identify any vulnerabilities to these types of events. The licensees' documentation of their HFO evaluations and the list of HFO-related plant improvements suggest that these evaluations have contributed significantly to the licensees' understanding of, and preparation for, potential HFO events.

IPEEE-Related Unresolved Safety Issues and Generic Safety Issues

The IPEEE program covers a number of unresolved safety issues (USIs) and generic safety issues (GSIs). In accordance with Supplement 4 to Generic Letter 88-20 and the associated guidance in NUREG-1407, licensees were requested to provide information to address the following issues:

- USI A-45, "Shutdown Decay Heat Removal Requirements,"
- GSI-103, "Design for Probable Maximum Precipitation,"
- GSI-131, "Potential Seismic Interaction Involving Movable In-Core Flux Mapping System Used in Westinghouse Plants,"
- GSI-57, "Effects of Fire Protection System Actuation on Safety-Related Equipment," and
- Sandia Fire Risk Scoping Study (FRSS) issues [U.S.NRC, 1989].

Four additional GSIs having external event aspects were not specifically identified as issues to be verified under the IPEEE program and, therefore, were not explicitly discussed in Supplement 4 to GL 88-20 or NUREG-1407. After the issuance of the generic letter, the NRC evaluated the scope and the specific information requested in the generic letter and the associated IPEEE guidance. The NRC concluded that the plant-specific analyses being requested in the IPEEE program could also be used to evaluate and verify the external event aspects of the following safety issues:

- GSI-147, "Fire-Induced Alternate Shutdown/Control Room Panel Interactions,"
- GSI-148, "Smoke Control and Manual Fire-Fighting Effectiveness,"
- GSI-156, "Systematic Evaluation Program (SEP)," and
- GSI-172, "Multiple System Responses Program" (MSRP).

Although most of these issues are within the IPEEE scope, aspects of a number of issues (and sub-issues) were related to internal events and covered in the IPE program. Only the external events aspects are covered in the IPEEE program. Section 5.4 of this report describes each of these issues and discusses the findings and plant modifications related to these issues. Detailed plant-specific tables on these USIs and GSIs are provided in Section 5 of Volume 2 of this report.

The assessment of the verification of each USI and GSI was based on the following criteria.

- The licensee's IPEEE covers the scope of each USI and GSI, and is capable of identifying plant vulnerabilities related to these issues.

- The licensee's assessment demonstrates an in-depth knowledge of the external events aspects and plant characteristics relevant to the issues discussed.

- The licensee's assessment results are reasonable for the design, location, features, and operating history of the plant.

In concert with the above criteria, an issue is considered verified if no potential vulnerabilities associated with its related concerns were identified in the submittal or if plant-specific improvements to eliminate or mitigate the identified potential vulnerabilities were implemented or planned at the plant.

One of the important results of the IPEEE program was that most plants verified a large majority of these generic issues. A total of 31 IPEEE-related unresolved safety issues and generic safety issues and sub-issues (including 5 FRSS issues, 9 SEP issues under GSI-156, and 11 MSRP issues under GSI-172) are discussed in Chapter 5 of this report. Licensees provided sufficient information in 44 submittals to verify all 31 USIs and GSIs. The remaining submittals had one or more generic issues open or only partially verified.[4] The following issues were fully verified for all plants: USI A-45, GSI-131, and GSI-156 (9 SEP issues). Of the other generic issues, GSI-57, GSI-103, and GSI-147 were verified for approximately 95% of the plants. GSI-172 and the FRSS issues were verified for almost 80% of the plants.[5] The issue that was most commonly open, GSI-148, was verified for 70% of the plants. Not surprisingly, those issues that were explicitly

---

[4] If a generic issue was not addressed in the licensee's submittal, but a potential vulnerability was not missed, the NRC's Staff Evaluation Report for that plant would identify that as a weakness in the submittal. In that case, the submittal would still meet the intent of the IPEEE program, but the GSI may not be "verified" for that plant. For those issues that have not been completely verified, the NRC staff will determine if any additional actions or assessments are needed for these GSIs. This followup will be done separately from the IPEEE program.

[5] GSI-172 (MSRP) comprises 11 separate issues, and there are 5 FRSS issues. All plants verified at least some of the FRSS and MSRP issues. If one or more individual MSRP or FRSS issues were not verified for a plant, the issue is considered "partially verified" for that plant.

identified in Supplement 4 to GL 88-20 or NUREG-1407 had a higher percentage of verification then those that were not explicitly identified, but even those issues that were not identified in the GL or NUREG-1407 were verified for most of the plants.

Uses of IPEEE Information

Information from the IPEEE program has been, and can be, used in NRC and industry activities in a variety of ways (some of which are beyond the stated objectives of the IPEEE program). Examples of such activities include:

- implementing plant improvements (procedural and/or hardware changes) in one or more of the seismic, fire, or HFO areas,[6]

- verifying certain generic safety issues (see Chapter 5 of this report),

- identifying topics and providing the basis to prioritize some of the topics for the fire risk research program (e.g., importance of turbine building fires),

- prioritizing areas for plant inspections (e.g., fire protection, seismic),

- providing insights on the risk importance of inspection findings (i.e., significant determination process for the reactor oversight program),

- incorporating lessons learned into the "Performance-Based Standard for Fire Protection for Light Water Reactor Electric Generating Plants" [NFPA, 1998],

- incorporating fire risk insights into Regulatory Guide 1.189, "Fire Protection for Operating Nuclear Power Plants,"

- assessing the cumulative effect of exemptions to Appendix R fire protection requirements on fire core damage frequency, and

- prioritizing research needs for age-degraded structures and passive components by using risk insights from the IPEEE program and aging data from operating plants.

When the IPEEE information is used in risk-informed regulatory applications, careful consideration needs to be given to the basis for the IPEEE information being used on a case-by-case basis. While some of the seismic analyses and most of the fire analyses were based on PRAs, most of the seismic, and high wind, flood, and other external event assessments were not based on PRAs. Whether the analysis was performed with a PRA or screening approach, the IPEEE results may be useful, albeit to a variable extent and in a quantitative or qualitative manner, to risk-informed decision making. Each IPEEE submittal had different strengths and weaknesses, which are documented in plant-specific SERs and TERs. These weaknesses or limitations are partly due to the screening, bounding, seismic margins methods used, or limitations in the PRA practices that were state-of-the-art in the early 1990s. Many of the plant-specific risk insights derived from

---

[6] Over 90% of licensees have implemented or proposed modifications as a result of their IPEEE.

the IPEEE are valid and, therefore, relevant to the risk-informed approach. However, applications must be carefully reviewed on a case-by-case basis to take into account the nature, quality, and completeness of the licensee's IPEEE analysis to ensure that the analysis is suitable, reasonable, and sufficiently robust for the intended risk-informed application.

Overall Conclusions and Observations

Some of the major findings and observations derived from the review of the IPEEE submittals are summarized below.

- Over 90% of the licensees have identified and implemented or proposed plant improvements to address concerns revealed through the IPEEE program. These improvements led to enhanced plant capability to respond to external events that might lead to severe accidents. In some cases licensees had already implemented relevant plant improvements before the IPEEE program began.

- Many of the IPEEE submittals (70%) have reported or proposed seismic-related plant improvements; almost as many (over 60%) have reported or proposed fire-related plant improvements; and about 50% have reported or proposed improvements pertaining to high winds and external flooding. These improvements involve changes to existing procedures, development of new procedures, or plant modifications. None of the IPEEE submittals reported improvements pertaining to transportation and nearby facility accidents or other (e.g., plant-unique) external hazards.

- In some cases, the IPEEEs referenced plant improvements that had been proposed or implemented before the IPEEE program began, since those improvements had a beneficial effect on plant safety for seismic, fire, and/or HFO events. For example, at one plant, the addition of diesel generators was identified as a plant improvement in the IPE, and was correspondingly reported in the IPEEE since it reduced the risk of station blackout for seismic, fire, and HFO events.

- Seismic and fire events have been found to be important contributors to CDF for a majority of plants. In fact, CDF contribution from seismic or fire events can, in some cases, approach (or even exceed) that from internal events. Core damage frequency estimates varied over several orders of magnitude. For example, seismic CDF results for operating plants (using the EPRI hazard curves) ranged from about 2E-7 to 6E-5 per reactor-year (ry); fire CDFs ranged from 4E-8 to 2E-4/ry. For high winds and tornadoes, the plant-specific CDF results ranged from less than 2E-7 to 6E-5/ry.

- The most commonly reported dominant contributors to seismic CDF were failures of offsite power; failure of various components of the electrical system such as motor control centers, switchgear, and relays; failure of the emergency diesel generator; failure of dc batteries; failure of various tanks; and failures of structures such as block walls located near safety-related equipment. The ranking of dominant CDF contributors was insensitive to the use of different seismic hazard curves.

- The most commonly reported risk-dominant fire areas were the main control room, switchgear rooms, turbine building, and cable spreading rooms. Other commonly reported areas were the electric equipment rooms, diesel generator rooms, cable vault and tunnel areas, and battery charger rooms. Other areas were identified as important on a plant-specific basis.

- As a whole, licensees have expended significant effort in developing their IPEEEs. As a result, they have acquired relevant knowledge concerning their plants, and have taken meaningful steps to improve plant safety, operations, and configuration.

Based on the reviews of the IPEEE submittals, the NRC staff has concluded that the IPEEE program has been successful in meeting the overall intent of GL 88-20. The following paragraphs summarize the overall effectiveness of licensees' IPEEEs in achieving each of the four identified IPEEE objectives.

Objective 1:   *Develop an appreciation of severe accident behavior*

The review of the IPEEE submittals reveals that the IPEEE program has increased licensees' overall appreciation of severe accident behavior attributed to external events at their plants. As requested in NUREG-1407, each licensee has performed evaluations of seismic events, internal fires, and HFO events. These evaluations have assessed the potential for externally initiated severe accidents, and have considered plant-specific behavior in response to potential severe accidents.

For the most part, licensees have been involved in both the management and the preparation of their IPEEEs. Licensees have sponsored training of their personnel in specific aspects of IPEEE analysis (e.g., seismic IPEEE training) to develop or enhance their personnel's appreciation of severe accident issues and of relevant plant behavior. In accordance with the request of NUREG-1407, licensees have undertaken peer reviews of their IPEEEs.

Objective 2:   *Understand the most likely severe accident sequences that can occur at the plant under full-power operating conditions*

Through the IPEEE program, licensees gained a qualitative understanding of the most likely severe accident sequences that may occur as a result of external events. Licensees identified (at least qualitatively) the relative importance or risk significance of the various external events. For each external event that was not screened out, licensees have generally identified the important initiators, critical plant components, operator actions, and plant areas. Thus, licensees have acquired an understanding of such effects on plant systems and safety.

Consistent with the guidance of NUREG-1407, the emphasis in the IPEEE program was to obtain predominantly qualitative (as opposed to predominantly quantitative) understanding. Therefore, the IPEEEs generally do not report a quantitative ranking of the risk significance of severe accident sequences or their dominant risk contributors. Overall, by means of screening analyses, supplemented by systems modeling where relevant, licensees have obtained a greater awareness of the most important externally initiated potential severe accident sequences and external event initiators.

Objective 3:   *Gain a qualitative understanding of the overall likelihood of core damage and fission product releases*

By means of the IPEEE program, licensees have generally been able to ascertain whether the risk of core damage associated with each external initiator is comparatively negligible (i.e., falling below the 1E-6 per reactor-year screening criterion in NUREG-1407), low, moderate, or high. In some cases, this understanding arose through direct quantification of core damage frequency (CDF). In other cases, this understanding resulted from increased knowledge of the given hazard in conjunction (where necessary) with an assessment of the plant's ability to withstand that hazard.

Each IPEEE submittal has reported the findings of a qualitative evaluation of containment performance in response to seismic events. Some IPEEE submittals have also reported quantitative estimates of the frequency of seismically induced early or large releases. For internal fire events, NUREG-1407 requests a containment analysis only if there are containment failure modes that differ significantly from those identified in the IPE. For HFO events, NUREG-1407 does not specifically request an assessment of containment performance, unless the licensee predicts or identifies a substantially unique situation. Licensees have generally followed the NUREG-1407 guidance in this regard.

The accuracy of licensees' estimates of CDF may be limited due to simplifying assumptions and approximations employed in the analyses. Hence, the results in such cases serve only as general indicators of risk (suitable for qualitative categorization), and they should not be viewed as being well established. In other cases, however, it appears that the quantitative CDF assessment methods have been rigorously applied and have produced realistic numerical estimates.

Objective 4:   *Reduce, if necessary, the overall likelihood of core damage and radioactive material releases by modifying, where appropriate, hardware and procedures that would help prevent or mitigate severe accidents.*

Overall, as a result of the IPEEE program, licensees have implemented or proposed plant modifications that have a beneficial effect on plant safety in response to external events. The modifications involved hardware changes, procedural changes, performance improvement requests, and the implementation of severe accident management guidelines. Because of the qualitative nature of the IPEEE program, most licensees did not quantitatively estimate the risk reductions achieved by these modifications. However, some licensees have employed probabilistic risk assessment (PRA) in their IPEEEs as a means of (a) determining the risk reduction associated with proposed plant improvements, or (b) determining whether plant modifications are warranted on a cost-benefit basis. In response to easily corrected observed anomalies having unknown safety impact (often encountered in seismic walkdowns), licensees readily undertook various simple fixes.

Foreword

This report provides information on the results of licensees' analyses of nuclear power plant potential vulnerabilities to severe accident as a result of external events (seismic events; fires; and high winds, floods, and other external initiating events involving accidents relating to transportation and nearby facilities, but excluding acts of sabotage or terrorism). The insights in this report were gleaned from the reviews of 70 Individual Plant Examination of External Events (IPEEE) submittals by licensees to the U.S. Nuclear Regulatory Commission (NRC). The submittals covered all the operating nuclear power plants in the United States. The report complements a previous study on potential severe accident vulnerabilities to internal events that was published in December 1997 as NUREG-1560, "Individual Plant Examination Program: Perspectives on Reactor Safety and Plant Performance."

The report was issued as a draft for public comment in April 2001. This final version takes the comments received into consideration. It does not contain any new requirements for the nuclear industry in general or for individual nuclear power plants.

We anticipate that this report will be useful to the NRC, industry, and the general public. Volume 1 provides general perspectives and observations on external event risks (e.g., the licensees' success in meeting the objectives of the IPEEE program, the dominant contributors to risk from various external events, and the strengths and weaknesses of methodologies used for the IPEEE analyses). Volume 2 consists of tabular information on plant-specific results from the IPEEE program. The perspectives and insights gained from this program are expected to be particularly useful in (1) NRC and industry risk-informed regulatory initiatives and activities, (2) guidance for future external event standards and probabilistic risk analyses, and (3) prioritization of research to improve risk analysis methods.

Scott F. Newberry, Director
Division of Risk Analysis and Applications
Office of Nuclear Regulatory Research

Acknowledgments

This report presents perspectives derived from reviewing the Individual Plant Examination of External Events (IPEEE) submittals that licensees prepared in response to Supplement 4 to Generic Letter 88-20. A large number of NRC staff and contractors supported various aspects of the IPEEE program, as shown below. The contributions from these people are greatly appreciated.

Overall management of the project was provided by A.M. Rubin of the U.S. Nuclear Regulatory Commission (NRC), Office of Nuclear Regulatory Research (RES).

The following individuals served as the principal authors of this report:

J. Chen	Formerly with NRC/RES
V. Dandini	Sandia National Laboratories (SNL)
J. Forester	SNL
W.H. Hardin	NRC/RES
M. Kazarians	Kazarians and Associates*
M. Khatib-Rahbar	Energy Research, Inc. (ERI)
J. LaChance	SNL
J. Lehner	Brookhaven National Laboratory (BNL)
C.C. Lin	BNL
S.P. Nowlen	SNL
J.N. Ridgely	NRC/RES
A.M. Rubin	NRC/RES
R.T. Sewell	Consultant* (formerly with ERI)
J. Xu	BNL

The following individuals served as the primary IPEEE reviewers in the seismic area:

R.J. Budnitz	Future Resources Associates, Inc.*
H. Esmaili	ERI
M.V. Frank	Safety Factor Associates, Inc.*
C.C. Lin	BNL
R. Morante	BNL
Z. Musicki	Formerly with BNL
Y. Park	Formerly with BNL
R.T. Sewell	Consultant* (formerly with ERI)
S. Sholly	Formerly with Beta Corporation International*
J. Xu	BNL

.

* Consultant/Subcontractor to Energy Research, Inc.

xxxix

The following individuals served as the primary IPEEE reviewers in the fire area:

M.V. Frank	Safety Factor Associates, Inc.*
J. Gregory	SNL
M. Kazarians	Kazarians and Associates*
J. LaChance	SNL
J.A. Lambright	Consultant*
D. Mitchell	Formerly with SNL
R. Pepping	SNL
S. Ross	Battelle Memorial Institute

The following individuals served as the primary IPEEE reviewers in the high winds, floods and other (HFO) external events area:

D.A. Bidwell	ERIN Engineering* (formerly with PLG, Inc.)
A. Buslik	NRC/RES
E. Chelliah	NRC/RES
J. Chen	Formerly with NRC/RES
E. Chow	NRC/RES
K.N. Fleming	ERIN Engineering* (formerly with PLG, Inc.)
M.V. Frank	Safety Factor Associates, Inc.*
W. Hardin	NRC/RES
J.A. Lambright	Consultant*
M. Modarres	University of Maryland*
A. Mosleh	University of Maryland*
J.N. Ridgely	NRC/RES
R.T. Sewell	Consultant* (formerly with ERI)
R. Vijaykumar	Formerly with ERI

The following individuals were the principal NRC reviewers who prepared IPEEE staff evaluation reports (SERs):

A. Buslik	NRC/RES
E. Chelliah	NRC/RES
J. Chen	Formerly with NRC/RES
E. Chow	NRC/RES
A. El-Bassioni	Formerly on detail to NRC/RES (currently with NRC/NRR)
W. Hardin	NRC/RES
A.S. Kuritzky	NRC/RES
J.N. Ridgely	NRC/RES

* Consultant/Subcontractor to Energy Research, Inc.

The following individuals served as members of the IPEEE Senior Review Board (SRB):

M.P. Bohn   SNL (seismic and HFO)
T.Y. Chang   NRC/RES (seismic)
J. Chen   Formerly with NRC/RES (seismic)
N.C. Chokshi   NRC/RES (seismic)
E. Connell   NRC/NRR (fire)
D. Jeng   NRC/NRR (seismic)
R. Kornasiewicz   Formerly with NRC/RES (HFO)
S.P. Nowlen   Sandia National Laboratories (fire)
N. Siu   NRC/RES (fire)

The following provided technical guidance and support and/or management and oversight for the IPEEE reviews:

G. Bagchi   NRC/NRR
M.A. Cunningham   NRC/RES
M. Drouin   NRC/RES
M.W. Hodges   NRC/RES
T.L. King   NRC/RES
R. Rothman   NRC/RES
H. VanderMolen   NRC/RES
W.C. Chang   SNL
T. Sype   SNL
T. Wheeler   SNL

Coordination and preparation of the camera-ready copy for publication was prepared by J.N. Ridgely, NRC/RES.

Secretarial support was provided by P. Nielsen, NRC/RES.

Abbreviations

ACRS	Advisory Committee on Reactor Safeguards
ACU	air cooling unit
ADS	automatic depressurization system
ADV	automatic depressurization valve
AEER	auxiliary electrical equipment room
AFW	auxiliary feedwater
ANO	Arkansas Nuclear One
AOP	abnormal operating procedures
AOV	air-operated valve
ASD	alternate shutdown
ATWS	anticipated transients without scram
BNL	Brookhaven National Laboratory
BR	battery room
BTP	Branch Technical Position
BWR	boiling water reactor
CACS	containment air circulation system
CCDP	conditional core damage probability
CCFP	conditional containment failure probability
CCW	component cooling water
CDF	core damage frequency
CDFM	conservative deterministic failure margin
CFR	*Code of Federal Regulations*
CP	construction permit
CRDS	control rod drive system
CS	containment spray
CSR	cable spreading room
CSS	core spray system
CST	condensate storage tank
CUS	Central United States
CV	cable vault
CVCS	chemical and volume control system
CWS	circulating water system
DBE	design basis event
DG	diesel generator
DGR	diesel generator room
DHR	decay heat removal
ECCS	emergency core cooling system
ECS	emergency condenser system
EDG	emergency diesel generator
EER	electrical equipment room
EFWST	emergency feedwater storage tank
EOP	emergency operating procedure
EP	emergency procedures
EPG	emergency procedure guidelines

EPRI	Electric Power Research Institute
ERCW	essential raw cooling water
ERI	Energy Research, Inc.
ESF	engineered safety feature
ESSW	essential station service water
ESW	emergency service water
EUS	Eastern United States
FCIA	fire compartment interaction analysis
FIVE	fire-induced vulnerability evaluation method
FPRAIG	fire PRA implementation guide
FPS	fire protection system
FRSS	fire risk scoping study
FSAR	final safety analysis report
GDC	general design criteria
GERS	generic equipment ruggedness spectrum
GI	generic issue
GIP	generic implementation procedure
GL	generic letter
GSI	generic safety issue
HCLPF	high confidence of low probability of failure
HEP	human error probability
HFO	high winds, floods, and other (external initiating events)
HHSI	high head safety injection
HLF	heat loss factor
HMR	hydrometeorological report
HPCI	high pressure coolant injection
HPCS	high pressure core spray
HPI	high pressure injection
HPSI	high pressure safety injection
HRA	human reliability analysis
HRR	heat release rate (from a fire)
HVAC	heating, ventilation, and air conditioning
ICFM	in-core flux mapping
IEB	Inspection and Enforcement Bulletin
IEEE	Institute of Electrical and Electronic Engineers
IN	information notice
IPE	individual plant examination
IPEEE	individual plant examination of external events
IRS	in-structure response spectra
IRT	independent review team
ISLOCA	interfacing systems loss-of-coolant accident
LLNL	Lawrence Livermore National Laboratory
LCO	limiting condition of operation
LOCA	loss-of-coolant accident
LOOP	loss of offsite power
LTSP	long-term seismic program
MCC	motor control center

MCR	main control room
MDAFW	motor-driven auxiliary feedwater
MEER	miscellaneous electrical equipment room
MFW	main feedwater
MOV	motor-operated valve
MSIV	main steam isolation valve
MSRP	multiple system responses program
NEI	Nuclear Energy Institute (formerly the Nuclear Management and Resource Council)
NFPA	National Fire Protection Association
NOAA	National Oceanic and Atmospheric Administration
NPP	nuclear power plant
NRC	U.S. Nuclear Regulatory Commission
NRR	NRC Office of Nuclear Reactor Regulation
NSAC	Nuclear Safety Analysis Center
NSSS	nuclear steam supply system
NUMARC	Nuclear Management and Resources Council (now the Nuclear Energy Institute)
NWS	National Weather Service
OL	operating license
PA	penetration area
PDS	plant damage state
PGA	peak ground acceleration
PMF	probable maximum flood
PMP	probable maximum precipitation
PORV	power-operated relief valve
PRA	probabilistic risk assessment
PSA	probabilistic safety assessment
PSF	performance shaping factor
PWR	pressurized water reactor
RAI	request for additional information
RB	reactor building
RBCCW	reactor building closed cooling water
RCIC	reactor core isolation cooling
RCP	reactor coolant pump
RCS	reactor coolant system
RDS	reactor depressurization system
RES	NRC Office of Nuclear Regulatory Research
RG	regulatory guide
RHR	residual heat removal
RHRSW	residual heat removal service water
RLE	review-level earthquake
RPS	reactor protection system
RSP	remote shutdown panel
RV	relief valve
RWST	refueling water storage tank
ry	reactor-year
SAMG	severe accident management guidelines
SBLOCA	small break loss-of-coolant accident

SBO	station blackout
SCBA	self-contained breathing apparatus
SEP	systematic evaluation program
SER	staff evaluation report
SFP	spent fuel pool
SGTR	steam generator tube rupture
SISBO	self-induced station blackout
SISIP	seismically induced systems interaction program
SMA	seismic margins assessment
SME	seismic margin earthquake
SMM	seismic margin methodology
SNL	Sandia National Laboratories
SOP	station operating procedure
SORV	stuck open relief valve
SP	suppression pool
SPC	suppression pool cooling
SPEL	success path equipment list
SPLD	success path logic diagram
SPRA	seismic probabilistic risk assessment
SPSA	seismic probabilistic safety assessment
SQUG	Seismic Qualification Utilities Group
SRB	senior review board
SRP	Standard Review Plan [NUREG-0800]
SRT	seismic review team
SRV	safety relief valve
SSC	structure, system, or component
SSE	safe shutdown earthquake
SSEL	safe shutdown equipment list
SSER	supplemental safety evaluation report
SSF	safe shutdown facility
SSI	soil-structure interaction
SSMRP	Seismic Safety Margins Research Program
SSRAP	Senior Seismic Review and Advisory Panel
SW	service water
SWGR	switchgear room
TB	turbine building
TDAFW	turbine-driven auxiliary feedwater
TER	technical evaluation report
UCSR	upper cable spreading room
USAR	updated safety analysis report (updated FSAR)
UHS	uniform hazard spectrum
USI	unresolved safety issue
U.S.NRC	U.S. Nuclear Regulatory Commission
WUS	Western United States
ZPGA	zero period ground acceleration

1. INTRODUCTION

1.1   Background

On November 23, 1988, the U.S. Nuclear Regulatory Commission (NRC) issued Generic Letter (GL) 88-20 [U.S.NRC, 1988], "Individual Plant Examination for Severe Accident Vulnerabilities, 10 CFR 50.54(f)," to licensees of nuclear power plants. Specifically, GL 88-20 requested that the licensees "perform a systematic evaluation of existing plants to identify any plant-specific vulnerabilities to severe accidents, and report the results to the Commission." GL 88-20 also outlined the objectives and overall logistics of the Individual Plant Examination (IPE) program, which solely addresses internally initiated events (including internal flooding).

On June 28, 1991, the NRC issued Supplement 4 to GL 88-20, "Individual Plant Examination of External Events (IPEEE) for Severe Accident Vulnerabilities, 10 CFR 50.54(f)." That supplement described the objectives and overall logistics of the Individual Plant Examination of External Events (IPEEE) program, which addresses externally initiated events. In particular, the external events considered in the IPEEE program include seismic events; internal fires; and high winds, floods, and other (HFO) external initiating events involving accidents related to transportation and nearby facilities. The Commission formulated both the IPE and IPEEE programs in response to the NRC's "Policy Statement on Severe Accidents Regarding Future Designs and Existing Plants," issued in August 1985. In particular, these programs were intended as a means for licensees to identify potential vulnerabilities to severe accidents, and to conceive cost-effective improvements to ensure that plants do not pose any undue risk to public health and safety. The impetus for this policy statement came from perspectives developed from early probabilistic risk assessments (PRAs). This impetus was further strengthened by the general finding that systematic examinations have been beneficial in identifying plant-specific vulnerabilities to severe accidents that could be fixed with low-cost improvements.

Along with Supplement 4 to GL 88-20, the NRC issued NUREG-1407, "Procedure and Submittal Guidance for the Individual Plant Examination of External Events (IPEEE) for Severe Accident Vulnerabilities," in June 1991. In NUREG-1407 [U.S.NRC, 1991], the NRC provided guidelines for conducting IPEEEs. Specifically, the guidance pertained to evaluations concerning the following external initiators: seismic events; internal fires; and HFO external events including accidents related to transportation or nearby facilities and plant-unique hazards. Subsequent to the publication of NUREG-1407, the NRC issued Supplement 5 to GL 88-20 on September 8, 1995, to notify licensees of modifications to the recommended scope of the seismic portion of the IPEEE for certain plant sites in the Eastern United States (EUS).

The NRC received 70 IPEEE submittals covering all operating U.S. nuclear reactors. (Some submittals covered more than one unit at multi-unit sites with similar or almost identical plant designs.) The staff of the NRC's Office of Nuclear Regulatory Research (RES) completed 69 Staff Evaluation Reports (SERs) to document the staff's overall conclusions for each of the IPEEE reviews.[1] Additional details on the plant-specific IPEEE review findings are presented in Technical Evaluation Reports (TERs) for each of the 69

---

[1] One plant, Haddam Neck, was permanently shut down, so the staff suspended work on reviewing that plant's IPEEE submittal.

IPEEE submittals.[2] Each TER discusses the strengths and weaknesses of the licensee's IPEEE submittal, particularly with reference to the guidelines established in NUREG-1407. The TERs also typically present (1) an overview of the licensee's IPEEE process and insights; (2) the review process employed for evaluation of the seismic, fire, and HFO events; (3) the dominant contributors to core damage frequency for fire, seismic, and HFO events; (4) licensee-identified vulnerabilities; (5) plant improvements made or planned as a result of the licensee's IPEEE process; and (6) an overall evaluation of the strengths and weaknesses of the IPEEE submittal. This report provides insights and perspectives gleaned from the reviews of all of the licensees' submittals.

1.2 Objectives

The following subsections discuss the objectives of (1) the IPEEE program itself, (2) NRC's technical review of the IPEEE submittals, and (3) the overall IPEEE perspectives program.

1.2.1 IPEEE Program

Consistent with the intent of GL 88-20, the primary goal of the IPEEE program has been for each licensee to identify plant-specific vulnerabilities to severe accidents, if any, and to report the results together with any licensee-determined improvements and corrective actions to the NRC. More specifically, Supplement 4 to GL 88-20 identified the following four supporting IPEEE objectives for each licensee:

- develop an appreciation of severe accident behavior,

- understand the most likely severe accident sequences that could occur at the licensee's plant under full-power operating conditions,

- gain a qualitative understanding of the overall likelihood of core damage and fission product releases, and

- reduce, if necessary, the overall likelihood of core damage and radioactive material releases by modifying, where appropriate, hardware and procedures that would help prevent or mitigate severe accidents.

---

[2] Each plant-specific IPEEE SER and TER was transmitted to the respective licensee for their plant. The TERs in the seismic and fire areas were written by NRC contractors (i.e., Energy Research, Inc. (ERI), Brookhaven National Laboratory (BNL), and Sandia National Laboratories (SNL)). TERs in the HFO area were written by ERI (26 submittals) and RES staff (the balance of the submittals). Readers interested in specific plants can obtain the plant-specific SERs and TERs through the NRC's Agencywide Documents Access and Management System (ADAMS). (Include the plant name and "IPEEE" in the Title Contains block of the ADAMS Find window.) SERs that were issued prior to November 1999 are available to the public, for a fee, by contacting the NRC's Public Document Room (PDR) librarian at (800) 397-4209 or via e-mail to pdr@nrc.gov.

1.2.2   NRC's Technical Review of IPEEE Submittals

The primary objective of the NRC's technical review process was to ascertain the extent to which the licensees' IPEEE submittals have achieved the intent of GL 88-20, satisfied the four principal IPEEE objectives listed above, and followed the recommended guidance in NUREG-1407. The reviews focused on verifying that the critical elements of acceptable IPEEE analyses in the fire, seismic, and HFO areas were performed in accordance with the guidelines in NUREG-1407. However, the reviews were not intended to validate or verify the licensee's IPEEE analyses or results (i.e., an in-depth evaluation of the various inputs, assumptions, and calculations was not performed). Rather, methods, approaches, assumptions, and results were reviewed for reasonableness. If inconsistencies were encountered, they were reported in the plant-specific IPEEE TERs.

The review process was comprised of a "Step 1" (screening) review of each submittal, with follow-on "Step 2" reviews of individual submittals on an "as needed" basis. The Step 1 reviews considered only the submittal itself, and none of the underlying or supporting (second-tier) documents were examined. Step 1 reviews also included interactions with licensees in the form of requests for additional information (RAIs) and/or conference calls. The objective of these interactions was to obtain clarification regarding specific points in a given submittal that were either unclear or of questionable basis. These RAIs were generally limited to items considered to be of sufficient importance that the insights or findings of the IPEEE, or the reviewers' understanding of those findings and insights, might be significantly impacted by the licensee's responses. (Appendix A to this report provides additional information regarding the guidance developed by the staff for issuing RAIs.)

If, at the end of the Step 1 review, the reviewers could not conclude that a given submittal met the intent of the IPEEE process, or if the submittal reported unusual results (i.e., extremely high or low core damage frequencies (CDFs) or high confidence of low probability of failure (HCLPF) values), a Step 2 review was undertaken. A Step 2 review included further licensee interactions to resolve the identified concerns. Step 2 reviews, which were conducted for four plants, included plant visits, reviews of supporting second-tier documents, interviews with plant personnel, and plant walkdowns.

The NRC also convened a senior review board (SRB) to oversee the technical aspects of the review process. The objectives of the SRB were to provide additional assurance that (1) the scope of the review met the objectives of the program, and (2) critical issues that have the potential to mask vulnerabilities were not overlooked. The SRB included NRC staff members and contractors who are experts in the field of general risk assessment and the specific areas addressed by the IPEEE analyses (seismic events, internal fires, and HFOs). The SRB members also performed abbreviated reviews of each IPEEE submittal and held regular meetings at which the reviewers with primary responsibility for a given plant submittal presented their findings, insights, and recommendations. The SRB then commented on the completeness of the review, whether the reviewers' technical findings were of sufficient importance to warrant an RAI, and whether the submittal met the IPEEE intent. The SRB participated in all aspects of the Step 1 and Step 2 reviews.

1.2.3   IPEEE Perspectives Program

In addition to performing technical reviews of the IPEEE submittals, the NRC's Office of Nuclear Regulatory Research (RES) instituted a program to identify and document general perspectives and significant safety insights resulting from the IPEEE program. This program was based on a compilation of the reviews of all 70 IPEEE submittals.[3] The objectives of this program were to provide:

- a description of the overall IPEEE process, findings, and impacts of the findings in major areas of evaluation for external initiators (seismic events, internal fires, and HFOs),

- an overview of plant improvements related to the IPEEE program, with a description of their beneficial impact on reactor safety,

- an overview of the IPEEE review process describing the site-specific hazards, plant-specific design and operational features, and modeling and screening assumptions that affect the understanding of a plant's severe-accident behavior and containment performance to assure that the IPEEE process is capable of identifying potential plant vulnerabilities to severe accidents from external events,

- a description of the overall strengths and weaknesses in the implementation of evaluation methodologies, including the implications of assumptions consistently made in IPEEEs, and

- an assessment of the overall effectiveness in meeting the IPEEE objectives, including a summary of the extent to which the licensees have met the intent of Supplement 4 to GL 88-20.

This report documents the above perspectives gleaned from the technical reviews of the IPEEE submittals.

1.3   Scope, Limitations, and General Comments

IPEEE studies have been limited to the consideration of plant behavior under full-power operating conditions, and the results have been influenced by a wide spectrum of factors. These factors include the basic plant characteristics, such as plant type (boiling-water reactor (BWR) or pressurized-water reactor (PWR)), plant layout, and so forth. Other related factors include frequencies of external initiating events, including earthquakes, high winds, floods, and other plant-unique natural hazards; and proximity to sources of man-made hazards (such as transportation routes and industrial facilities).

The perspectives documented in this report are somewhat limited for the following reasons: (a) IPEEEs are intended to yield predominantly qualitative perspectives, rather than more quantitative findings; (b) IPEEEs address several different types of initiators of varying importance (for a given plant) and, therefore, require the implementation of different methods of analysis offering varying levels of detail and accuracy; and (c) even for a given type of external initiator, the procedures and methods used by the various licensees to conduct their IPEEEs have also varied considerably.

Additionally, the IPEEE submittals used various sources of information, such as seismic hazard curves derived from different sources (e.g., Lawrence Livermore National Laboratory (NUREG/CR-1488 and NUREG/CR-5250); Electric Power Research Institute [EPRI, 1989]; and site-specific studies), or applied simplified conservative methods, or used more realistic approaches. These differences make it difficult to

---

[3] Twenty-six of the IPEEE submittal reviews were performed by ERI, under contract to RES. The remaining reviews were performed by SNL (fires), BNL (seismic events), and RES staff (HFO events).

draw plant-to-plant comparisons of analysis results. Comparisons of IPEEE results among plants and among the various types of external hazards are also limited because of variations in the quality of submittals. Hence, the staff made no attempt in this report to compare IPEEE results among the various categories of external initiators for individual plants. For the most part, then, discussions in this report are kept distinct for seismic events, internal fires, and HFO initiators.

In particular, the qualitative perspectives addressed in this report include a summary of the licensees' findings pertaining to their investigations of severe accident issues, including identification of plant improvements. In addition, the qualitative perspectives include a summary of the staff's observations concerning the validity of licensees' methodologies and findings, as well as assessments of the consistency and potential usefulness (or limitations) of the IPEEE results. The quantitative results discussed include licensees' estimates of CDFs and plant capability.

It should be noted that the IPEEEs were typically performed with the state-of-the-art as of the early 1990s. Since then, the techniques used have been improving, and research is continuing. For example, knowledge of the potential impacts of fires on cable failure modes has been improved. Also, the American Nuclear Society is developing standards for risk assessments of external hazards. In the arena of human error probabilities, the NRC's Office of Nuclear Regulatory Research is actively pursuing research activities on estimating the probabilities under accident conditions, including fires. The staff currently has no information indicating that use of current state-of-the-art information would lead to the identification of new or different plant vulnerabilities.

Although not required, many licensees have chosen to keep their IPEs updated (living) and have used them in prioritizing plant work and as part of the basis for requested NRC actions. In the same manner, it could be beneficial for licensees that have performed their IPEEE with PRA techniques to maintain their IPEEE as a living document. Although not required by the NRC, licensees are encouraged to maintain their IPEEE as a living document.

1.4   Uses of IPEEE Information

Information from the IPEEE program has been, and can be, used in NRC and industry activities in a variety of ways (some of which are beyond the stated objectives of the IPEEE program). Examples of such activities include:

- implementing plant improvements (procedural and/or hardware changes) in one or more of the seismic, fire, or HFO areas,[4]

- verifying certain generic safety issues (see Chapter 5 of this report),

- identifying topics and providing the basis to prioritize some of the topics for the fire risk research program (e.g., importance of turbine building fires),

- prioritizing areas for plant inspections (e.g., fire protection, seismic),

---

[4] Over 90% of licensees have implemented or proposed modifications as a result of their IPEEE.

- providing insights on the risk importance of inspection findings (i.e., significant determination process for the reactor oversight program),

- incorporating lessons learned into the "Performance-Based Standard for Fire Protection for Light Water Reactor Electric Generating Plants" [NFPA, 1998],

- incorporating fire risk insights into Regulatory Guide 1.189, "Fire Protection for Operating Nuclear Power Plants,"

- assessing the cumulative effect of exemptions to Appendix R fire protection requirements on fire core damage frequency, and

- prioritizing research needs for age-degraded structures and passive components by using risk insights from the IPEEE program and aging data from operating plants.

When the IPEEE information is used in risk-informed regulatory applications, careful consideration needs to be given to the basis for the IPEEE information being used on a case-by-case basis. While some of the seismic analyses and most of the fire analyses were based on PRAs, most of the seismic, and high wind, flood, and other external event assessments were not based on PRAs. Whether the analysis was performed with a PRA or screening approach, the IPEEE results may be useful, albeit to a variable extent and in a quantitative or qualitative manner, to risk-informed decision making. Each IPEEE submittal had different strengths and weaknesses, which are documented in plant-specific SERs and TERs. These weaknesses or limitations are partly due to the screening, bounding, seismic margins methods used, or limitations in the PRA practices that were state-of-the-art in the early 1990s. Many of the plant-specific risk insights derived from the IPEEE are valid and, therefore, relevant to the risk-informed approach. However, applications must be carefully reviewed on a case-by-case basis to take into account the nature, quality, and completeness of the licensee's IPEEE analysis to ensure that the analysis is suitable, reasonable, and sufficiently robust for the intended risk-informed application.

1.5   Report Organization

In developing this report, the staff sought to address each distinct, significant topic considered in NUREG-1407, including seismic events, fires, and HFOs, as well as the relevant IPEEE-related aspects of generic safety issues (GSIs) and unresolved safety issues (USIs). Volume 1 of this report includes general IPEEE perspectives, while Volume 2 includes detailed tables with plant-specific information relevant to the IPEEE program.

In Volume 1, Chapter 1 covers the general background and objectives of the IPEEE program, while Chapter 2 discusses the perspectives derived from the seismic portion of the IPEEE submittals, and includes comments regarding licensees' seismic probabilistic risk assessments (PRAs) and seismic margin assessments (SMAs). It also discusses information provided in seismic IPEEE submittals relevant to specific GSIs and USIs.

Chapter 3 discusses the perspectives derived from the fire portion of the IPEEE submittals, and includes comments regarding licensees' fire PRAs and fire-induced vulnerability evaluation (FIVE) studies. It also discusses fire-related findings concerning specific GSIs and USIs, as well as issues arising from the fire risk scoping study conducted by SNL.

Chapter 4 presents findings derived from the HFO portion of the IPEEE submittals. Each major category of HFO initiator is discussed, including high winds and tornadoes, external floods, and accidents related to transportation or nearby facilities. It also discusses HFO-related findings concerning specific GSIs and USIs.

Chapters 2 through 4 each provide summaries of applicable walkdown findings, human action perspectives, containment performance perspectives, plant improvements, generic versus plant-specific perspectives, as well as observations of specific strengths and weaknesses relevant to the evaluation of each particular type of external initiator.

Chapter 5 describes each of the external-event-related unresolved and generic safety issues and provides the staff's conclusions regarding the verification of these issues for each plant.

The staff anticipates that this report will be used by many different readers with different backgrounds. Some terms used in this report may have different definitions depending on the technical context in which they are used. Therefore, a glossary is provided at the end of Volume 1 to aid the reader in understanding the specific meaning of each term used in this report.

Volume 2 of this report, which includes detailed plant-specific tables, is organized as follows: Chapter 1 is a brief introduction; Chapter 2 covers seismic events; Chapter 3 fire; Chapter 4 high winds, floods and other external events; and Chapter 5 IPEEE-related unresolved safety issues and generic safety issues.

2. SEISMIC INSIGHTS

2.1　Introduction

As noted in Chapter 1 of this report, licensees for every operating commercial nuclear power reactor in the United States have performed an assessment of severe accident risk due to seismic events, as part of the NRC's IPEEE program. Most of these analyses have developed estimates of seismic risk or seismic capacity, have identified the dominant seismic risk contributors or components controlling plant capacity, and have resulted in plant improvements to reduce risk and/or increase plant capacity. This chapter presents perspectives and insights gained from the licensees' seismic IPEEE submittals. The seismic perspectives discussed in this chapter are drawn from 71 seismic IPEEE submittals.[1]

This first section of this chapter describes the objectives of the seismic portion of the IPEEE perspectives program, provides background information on the seismic IPEEE program, and outlines the organization of Chapter 2.

2.1.1　Objectives

The objectives of the overall IPEEE perspectives program are stated in Section 1.2.3. This chapter addresses those objectives as they apply to the seismic analyses performed for the IPEEE. Seismic perspectives are collectively derived from the review of the seismic portion of the IPEEE submittals. More specifically, the objective of this program is to provide perspectives in the following areas:

- description of the overall seismic IPEEE process, findings, and impacts,

- overview of plant improvements related to the seismic portion of the IPEEE program, with a description of their beneficial impact on reactor safety,

- identification and assessment of the impacts of site-specific seismic hazards, plant-specific design and operational features, and modeling and screening assumptions that affect the understanding of a plant's severe-accident behavior and containment performance in response to a seismic event,

- description of the overall strengths and weaknesses in the implementation of seismic evaluation methodologies, including the implications of assumptions made in the IPEEEs, and

- summary of the extent to which the licensees have met the intent of Supplement 4 to GL 88-20 [U.S. NRC, 1988] as it pertains to seismic analyses.

It should be noted at the outset that the perspectives presented in this chapter are based on reviews for which the goal was to verify that a licensee's IPEEE process was capable of identifying seismic vulnerabilities and

---

[1] This number differs from the 70 submittals mentioned elsewhere in this report because the licensee for Arkansas Nuclear One (ANO) submitted separate seismic submittals for ANO 1 and ANO 2 but treated other external hazards in a single submittal for both units.

cost-effective safety improvements. However, the reviews did not attempt to validate the results of the licensees' submittals.

2.1.2 Organization

Perspectives and insights gained from the reviews of the seismic portion of the IPEEE submittals are presented in five major sections as follows:

Section 2.2 provides an overview of the impact that the IPEEE process has made on reactor safety. This includes discussion of seismic weaknesses or vulnerabilities identified, as well as discussion of modifications and improvements proposed or implemented as a result of the IPEEE seismic analyses.

Section 2.3 presents a summary of the seismic analyses results as reported by the licensees, and some of the perspectives which can be derived from these results. Results common to both analyses methodologies are discussed first, then results from seismic probabilistic risk analyses (SPRAs) are presented, and finally results derived from seismic margin assessments (SMAs).

Section 2.4 discusses specific methodological issues identified in the seismic reviews, as well as perspectives related to those issues.

Section 2.5 summarizes information in the seismic portion of the IPEEE submittals pertinent to a number of seismic-related generic safety issues (GSIs) and unresolved safety issues (USIs).

Section 2.6 summarizes the perspectives of Chapter 2, and presents a number of conclusions.

2.1.3 Background

2.1.3.1 Historical Perspectives on the Seismic Concerns and Regulatory Programs for U.S. Commercial Nuclear Power Plants

The primary regulatory basis governing the seismic design of nuclear power plants is contained in Title 10 of the *Code of Federal Regulations*, Part 50 (10 CFR Part 50), Appendix A, "General Design Criteria for Nuclear Power Plants," General Design Criterion (GDC) 2 defines design basis requirements for protection against natural phenomena. Specifically, GDC 2 states the performance criterion that "structures, systems, and components important to safety shall be designed to withstand the effects of natural phenomena such as earthquakes ... without loss of capability to perform their safety functions... ." Consequently, seismic issues have played a major role in determining site suitability; plant layout; and design of systems, structures and components (SSCs) that are important to safety for U.S. commercial nuclear power plants.

During the late 1960s and early 1970s, a seismic design philosophy evolved as the licensing of the earlier commercial nuclear plants was in progress. The concept of the safe shutdown earthquake (SSE) emerged and was codified into the Federal regulations with the publication in December 1973 of Appendix A, "Seismic and Geologic Siting Criteria for Nuclear Power Plants," to 10 CFR Part 100, "Reactor Site Criteria." Appendix A provides detailed criteria to evaluate the suitability of proposed sites and the suitability of the plant design basis established in consideration of the seismic and geologic characteristics of the proposed sites.

In 1975, the NRC published the Standard Review Plan (SRP), which provides standardized review criteria to assist the staff in evaluation of Safety Analysis Reports submitted by license applicants. Since its first publication, the SRP has undergone several revisions [U.S.NRC, 1989] to incorporate new developments in seismic design/analysis technology. The NRC has also published a series of Regulatory Guides (Regulatory Guides 1.29, "Seismic Design Classification," 1.60, "Design Response Spectra for Seismic Design of Nuclear Power Plants," 1.61, "Damping Values for Seismic Design of Nuclear Power Reactors," 1.92, "Combining Modal Responses and Spatial Components in Seismic Response Analysis," 1.100, "Seismic Qualification of Electric and Mechanical Equipment for Nuclear Power Plants," and 1.122, "Development of Floor Design Response Spectra for Seismic Design of Floor—Supported Equipment or Components") which are periodically updated to reflect the current state of knowledge in defining acceptable methods for seismic design/analysis.

Over the years, a number of major initiatives, concerned with ensuring the ability of nuclear plants to adequately cope with seismic hazards, have been undertaken by the NRC and the domestic nuclear industry. These major initiatives are discussed below.

The Systematic Evaluation Program (SEP) was initiated in the mid-1970s. This program recognized that many safety criteria, including seismic ones, had rapidly evolved since the time of initial licensing of the earliest nuclear power plants. The purpose of the SEP was to develop a documented basis for the safety of these older facilities by comparing them to then current criteria. Phase I of the SEP developed a list of 137 topics of safety significance which collectively affect the plant's capability to respond to various design basis events (DBEs). One of the most significant topics was assessment of seismic safety. In October 1977, the Nuclear Regulatory Commission approved initiation of Phase II of the SEP, which consisted of a plant-specific reassessment of the safety of 11 older operating nuclear reactors which received construction permits between 1956 and 1967. Seismic design procedures had evolved significantly during and after this period through publication of the regulations in Appendix A to 10 CFR Part 50, Appendix A to 10 CFR Part 100, and the Standard Review Plan. As a result, the original seismic design bases of these 11 older facilities differed in varying degrees from the accepted seismic standards at the time of the SEP initiation (i.e., the mid-1970s). The design bases of these plants varied from the considerations of the Uniform Building Code (static analysis) up through and approaching then-current standards (dynamic analysis). Recognizing that these plants were designed to criteria that were less rigorous than current plants, the NRC staff utilized for its SEP plant seismic assessment the criteria in NUREG/CR-0098, "Development of Criteria for Seismic Review of Selected Nuclear Power Plants" [U.S.NRC, 1978].

In 1980, the NRC issued Inspection and Enforcement Bulletin (IEB) 80-11, "Masonry Walls," after a specific seismic issue surfaced concerning the design basis for masonry walls in operating plants. It was recognized that the potential for failure of masonry walls due to seismic loads may not have been adequately addressed during initial design. This created the possibility that safety-related structures, systems, and components (SSCs) might be damaged by masonry wall collapse. All operating plants were required to conduct a systematic program to identify, evaluate, and resolve issues for all masonry walls whose failure had the potential to damage safety-related SSCs. The program established a seismic evaluation basis for all identified masonry walls which ensured that no unacceptable consequences would result from the plant-specific SSE. This program was completed in the late 1980s.

During the assessment of the SEP plants, a seismic safety issue surfaced which was applicable to a much larger group of plants. Equipment in nuclear plants for which construction permit (CP) applications had been docketed before about 1972 had not been reviewed according to the then-current (1980–1981) licensing criteria for seismic qualification of equipment (i.e., Regulatory Guide 1.100; Institute of Electrical and Electronics Engineers Standard 344-1975, and Standard Review Plan Section 3.10). Therefore, the seismic adequacy of the equipment in these older plants to survive and function in the event of a safe shutdown earthquake (SSE) was questionable. Equipment in plants with a CP application docketed after about 1972 was qualified according to the then-current licensing criteria and license compliance had been audited by the NRC staff. In December 1980, the NRC designated "Seismic Qualification of Equipment in Operating Plants" as an unresolved safety issue. Subsequently, the NRC issued Generic Letter (GL) 87-02, "Verification of Seismic Adequacy of Mechanical and Electrical Equipment in Operating Reactors, Unresolved Safety Issue (USI) A-46." All operating plants for which seismic qualification of equipment could not be verified as meeting the intent of then-current licensing criteria were requested to implement the provisions outlined in the GL. In anticipation of an NRC directive to develop a seismic qualification basis, affected utilities formed the Seismic Qualification Utility Group (SQUG) in 1982. In 1983, the SQUG proposed the formation of a panel of consultants, the Senior Seismic Review and Advisory Panel (SSRAP), to independently assess and review the viability of using earthquake experience data and test data to demonstrate equipment ruggedness, and to provide expert advice and consultation. The SQUG subsequently developed the "Generic Implementation Procedure (GIP) for Seismic Verification of Nuclear Plant Equipment" for its members' use. The SQUG completed the final version of the GIP, Revision 2, in February 1992 (GIP-2). The NRC staff completed its review and issued Supplemental Safety Evaluation Report (SSER) No. 2 on May 22, 1996. The supplement superseded all previous NRC staff safety evaluations on this subject. The USI A-46 program was recently completed. Because of similarities between the requirements of the USI A-46 program and the activities necessary to conduct the seismic part of the IPEEE, licensees of A-46 plants typically combined the implementation of both programs to the extent practical. This was encouraged in the guidance document for the IPEEE, to reduce the burden on licensees (see NUREG-1407 [U.S.NRC, 1991], Paragraph 6.3.3.3). While the IPEEE and A-46 programs have many elements in common, their objectives are different. The A-46 program has licensing implications for plant operation. The scenario considered in the A-46 program is an SSE-level earthquake and a possible loss of power as a result of the earthquake. The concern is to establish at least one success path under these conditions, using seismically adequate SSCs, by which the plant can be brought to safe shutdown and maintained so for at least 72 hours. The seismic IPEEE program seeks to identify the limiting SSCs when the plant is subjected to an earthquake generally more severe than the SSE.

Another NRC-initiated program to confirm the adequacy of the seismic design basis of nuclear power plants is the Seismic Safety Margins Research Program (SSMRP) which predated the formalization of regulatory requirements and guidance. In 1982, the U.S. Geological Survey sent a letter to the NRC pointing out the possibility that large, damaging earthquakes have some likelihood of occurring at locations that had not been considered in licensing decisions. This was initially referred to as the Charleston Earthquake Issue and is now called the EUS Seismicity Issue. The NRC initiated the Seismic Hazard Characterization Project at Lawrence Livermore National Laboratory (LLNL) to develop probabilistic seismic hazard estimates for all nuclear power plant sites east of the Rocky Mountains. A similar project was carried out by the Electric Power Research Institute (EPRI) for the electric utility industry. The results of these programs and related follow-on programs have helped shape the seismic IPEEE guidelines: acceptable methodologies for conducting seismic PRAs (SPRAs); development of component fragilities; screening guidelines for seismically rugged SSCs; probabilistic-based and deterministic-based seismic margin methods; and the development of appropriate review-level earthquakes (RLEs) and probabilistic seismic input to SPRAs for EUS plants. As discussed in Section 6.2.2.1 of NUREG-1407, licensee submittals for the seismic IPEEE would resolve the EUS seismicity issue, without requiring additional analyses or documentation.

Verification of a number of other unresolved seismic safety issues was subsumed under either the USI A-46 program or the seismic IPEEE. One of the issues identified in USI A-17, "System Interactions in Nuclear Power Plants," was spatial system interaction due to safe shutdown earthquake (SSE) loads. The verification of this issue has been included in USI A-46. One of the issues identified in USI A-40, "Seismic Design Criteria," was a concern for the seismic capacity of safety-related above-ground tanks. The verification of this issue has also been included in USI A-46. USI A-45, "Shutdown Decay Heat Removal Requirements," addresses the adequacy of shutdown decay heat removal at operating plants; the internal event-related aspects of this issue was subsumed in the Individual Plant Examination (IPE) program, and the external event aspects, including seismic adequacy, was subsumed in the IPEEE program. GSI-131, "Potential Seismic Interaction Involving the Movable In-Core Flux Mapping System Used in Westinghouse Plants," identified a potential seismic issue related to the movable in-core flux mapping system used in Westinghouse plants. Verification of this issue has also been subsumed in the seismic IPEEE program.

The development of the IPEEE program itself is discussed in Section 1.1 of this report: the NRC, as part of its policy on severe accidents, recognized, based on experience with plant-specific probabilistic risk assessments, that systematic examinations are beneficial in identifying plant-specific vulnerabilities to severe accidents that could be fixed with low-cost improvements. Generic Letter 88-20 [U.S.NRC, 1988] requested such an examination, and Supplement 4 to the GL, issued on June 28, 1991 [U.S.NRC, 1991], extended the examination to external events, including seismic events. Supplement 4 identified seismic probabilistic risk assessments (SPRAs) and seismic margins methods as acceptable methodologies for performing a seismic IPEEE. Although other licensing programs had been conducted over the years to address various aspects of seismic design and analysis, the seismic IPEEE program was the first attempt by the NRC and the nuclear industry to provide a systematic and comprehensive evaluation of the seismic hazard and its effects on the safe operation of commercial nuclear power plants in the U.S. The IPEEE has provided valuable qualitative or quantitative assessments of the seismic margins that may exist over the original seismic design bases of U.S. nuclear plants.

2.1.3.2 Seismic Analysis Methods Used for the IPEEE

Subsequent to Supplement 4 to GL 88-20, the NRC published two additional documents pertinent for carrying out the IPEEE seismic analyses. On June 28, 1991, the NRC issued NUREG-1407, "Procedural and Submittal Guidance for the Individual Plant Examination of External Events (IPEEE) for Severe Accident Vulnerabilities" [U.S. NRC, 1991]. In NUREG-1407, the NRC provided guidance for conducting an IPEEE for external initiators, including seismic initiators. Four years later the NRC issued Supplement 5 to GL 88-20 [U.S. NRC, 1995] on September 8, 1995, to notify licensees of permissible modifications to the recommended scope of the seismic analysis portion of the IPEEE for certain plant sites in the EUS.

In NUREG-1407 two methodologies are considered acceptable for the purpose of performing an IPEEE to identify potential seismic vulnerabilities at nuclear power plants. The first is a seismic probabilistic risk assessment (SPRA) consisting of at least a Level 1 analysis and a qualitative containment performance analysis. The second is a seismic margins method, with two types of margin analyses, one developed under NRC sponsorship and the other under EPRI sponsorship, being permissible, as per NUREG-1407. The SMAs also need to include a qualitative containment performance analysis. IPEEE guidance was developed recognizing the fact that the SPRA approach can differ substantially from the SMA approaches in terms of procedures, objectives, results, and the format used to present major findings. However, in terms of satisfying the objectives of the seismic IPEEE, the SPRA and SMA approaches (a) both involve a systematic, comprehensive walkdown of important components, and (b) are both capable of identifying plant vulnerabilities.

The objective of a Level 1 SPRA is to provide a measure of seismic risk by estimating the core damage frequency (CDF) resulting from seismic initiators. First, a seismic hazard estimate is made by defining the annual frequency of exceedance in terms of levels of a ground motion quantity, such as peak acceleration, which can be correlated with the damage of critical structures, systems, and components (SSCs) being considered. For each SSC, a seismic fragility curve is then estimated in terms of the same ground motion quantity with which the hazard estimate was defined. Conditional failure probabilities of SSCs for various ground motion levels are then used in the Boolean logic of the accident sequence analysis to obtain conditional core damage probabilities or a core damage fragility curve. This result is then convolved with the exceedance frequency of the hazard estimate to obtain a seismic core damage frequency estimate. This process can be carried out for mean values, or the process can use probability distributions of the variables at each step, to include uncertainty.

The objective of an SMA is to describe the additional seismic margin plants have, by virtue of their conservative design, to withstand earthquakes larger than the design basis earthquake (i.e., larger than the SSE). This margin may be defined in terms of the high confidence of low probability of failure (HCLPF) capacity of each critical SSC and the overall HCLPF of the plant. One definition of the HCLPF capacity is that it corresponds to the 1% probability of failure point on the mean (composite) fragility curve. This point can be computed from a fragility curve estimated as for an SPRA, or it can be deterministically approximated by the conservative deterministic failure margin (CDFM) method [EPRI, 1991]. The plant damage state and plant HCLPF can then be developed by either an event/fault tree approach to delineate accident sequences as described in the NRC's approach [U.S.NRC, 1985] or by a systems "success paths" approach developed by EPRI [EPRI, 1991]. An EPRI SMA involves identifying success paths, and finding the weakest links along each success path. The components having lowest HCLPF capacity comprise the weak links, and they determine the plant-level HCLPF capacity. In an NRC SMA, systems modeling is performed in a manner similar to an SPRA, whereas evaluation of component HCLPF capacities may involve a deterministic or probabilistic assessment. The plant-level HCLPF capacity in an NRC SMA is determined from component-level HCLPFs using a Boolean expression for core damage and a simple min-max approach (minimum HCLPF among "OR" events, and maximum HCLPF among "AND" events).

The principal products of an SPRA are an estimate of seismic CDF, a list of dominant contributors to the seismic CDF, and a probabilistic plant-level capacity (i.e., fragility curve). The principal products of an SMA are a list of component capacities and an estimate of the HCLPF capacity of the plant. Although a plant-level HCLPF capacity can also be determined from an SPRA study, the HCLPF capacities resulting from the SPRA approach should not generally be compared with the HCLPF capacities reported from SMA studies, primarily due to the fact that each evaluation approach uses a different type of input spectrum, and each approach is based on different procedures, assumptions, and objectives.

While an SPRA provides a quantitative assessment of the seismic risk, the SMA has been more popular among the industry practitioners, chiefly because (1) it is a more engineering-oriented approach, (2) it is a straightforward way to demonstrate the seismic margin, and (3) implementation can be combined with the verification of USI A-46.

The scope of the seismic margins analyses discussed in NUREG-1407 for a particular plant depends on the location of the plant (i.e., the seismic hazard associated with the plant site). The scope of an acceptable analysis varies (as defined in NUREG-1407) with higher hazard sites designated for more extensive investigation.

Based on seismic hazard as well as the seismic design basis, NUREG-1407 separates plant sites into the following seismic review categories:

- Plant Sites East of the Rocky Mountains

  1. Reduced-scope
  2. 0.3g Focused-scope
  3. 0.3g Full-scope
  4. Committed to perform an SPRA

- Plant Sites in the Western United States

  5. 0.3g Full-scope
  6. 0.5g Full-scope
  7. Must perform an SPRA

These seismic categories have been established primarily on the basis of relative comparisons of plant-to-plant seismic hazard. The following paragraphs briefly describe the applicability, scope, and procedures for each of these seismic categories.

- Reduced-Scope: This evaluation, appropriate for the lowest hazard sites in the EUS, involves a detailed plant walkdown with capacity of equipment evaluated against the plant's design basis earthquake. (Equipment with capacity below desired levels is termed an "outlier.") The equipment list for the selected success paths is developed in accordance with the guidance described in EPRI's seismic margin assessment (SMA). This list is expanded to include equipment needed for successful containment performance in preventing large early releases. No evaluation of soil failures is required in a reduced-scope evaluation.

- Focused-Scope: This evaluation, appropriate for intermediate-hazard EUS sites, also involves a detailed plant walkdown. In this case, however, equipment capacity is evaluated against a review-level earthquake (RLE), defined by a ground motion with a peak ground acceleration (PGA) of 0.3g and a median spectral shape defined in accordance with NUREG/CR-0098 for the relevant soil condition. The equipment list, expanded to include containment performance in preventing large early releases, may be developed in accordance with the guidance described in either NRC's or EPRI's seismic margin assessment (SMA) methodology. An evaluation of low-ruggedness relays is required, as is an evaluation of the effects of soil failures. Seismic capacities for those components/outliers expected to control plant capacity, and the plant's high-confidence of low probability of failure (HCLPF) capacity are developed and are among the principal results of the SMA.

- Full-Scope: This evaluation is appropriate for the higher hazard EUS sites and some Western United States (WUS) sites. It involves a detailed plant walkdown with outliers evaluated against a review-level earthquake (RLE) of 0.3g or 0.5g PGA and a median NUREG/CR-0098 spectral shape. As in the focused-scope evaluation, the equipment list is expanded to include containment

2 - 7

performance in preventing large early releases and may be developed in accordance with the guidance described in either NRC's or EPRI's SMA procedures. A full-scope, detailed relay chatter evaluation is required, as is a full evaluation of soil failures. In addition, seismic capacities are assessed for all identified outliers, and a plant-level HCLPF capacity is obtained.

- Seismic PRA: This evaluation includes a Level 1 SPRA with specified enhancements in plant walkdowns, relay chatter evaluation, and analysis of liquefaction and other potential soil failure modes, as appropriate. In addition, an SPRA evaluation should also include a qualitative assessment of containment performance (as in a full-scope analysis) or an analysis of the sequences involving containment, containment functions, and containment systems with seismic failure modes or timing that are significantly different from those found in the Individual Plant Examination (IPE) for internal events.

In addition to these recommended evaluation approaches, Supplement 5 to GL 88-20 makes provision for modifications to seismic evaluation requirements for EUS plants. The modifications derive from the staff's acceptance of revised LLNL hazard results [LLNL, 1994] for use in IPEEE studies. In the case of an SPRA, a licensee can use the higher of the mean (arithmetic) seismic hazard estimates in the revised LLNL study and the EPRI hazard study [EPRI, 1989]. Modifications to focused-scope and full-scope studies generally take the form of permissible relaxation in evaluation requirements, relative to the NUREG-1407 guidance for these analyses. These procedural adjustments reflect the general finding that the LLNL revised mean seismic hazard results are typically lower than the corresponding original (1989) LLNL mean hazard results [LLNL, 1989].

As indicated in GL 88-20, Supplement 5, the principal adjustments in the modified evaluations include the following.

- Modified Focused-scope: The seismic capacities for reactor internals and soil-related failures need not be evaluated. Relay chatter evaluation is still required, and HCLPF evaluations should still be performed for critical components, including masonry walls, flat-bottomed tanks, adverse physical interactions, and items deemed by the licensee's seismic review team (SRT) to be significant.

- Modified Full-scope: The seismic capacity for reactor internals need not be evaluated. Soil-related failures should still be evaluated, but only for safety-related supporting systems and equipment that are founded on soil whose function might be affected by soil liquefaction or instability. For assessing the potential and consequences of postulated soil failures, a review of appropriate design and construction records is considered to be adequate.

NUREG-1407 indicates that a licensee may also propose an alternative seismic evaluation approach, which the NRC would consider with regard to acceptability for IPEEE purposes.

Figure 2.1 identifies the NUREG-1407 seismic IPEEE category designated for each of the plants included in this study. These designations define a minimum recommended level of evaluation, as described in NUREG-1407, for each plant site. Figure 2.1 also identifies the seismic analysis methods that were actually implemented for each of the plants IPEEE analyses.

Licensees could, of course, conduct a more extensive evaluation than the minimum recommended level for their site, and, as Figure 2.1 indicates, a number of plants designated for margin analyses opted to carry out an SPRA instead. In addition, as also indicated in Figure 2.1, some licensees chose to implement a reduced-scope evaluation even though their plant had been assigned to the focused-scope category in NUREG-1407. Some of these licensees may have had the option of implementing the modified focused-scope procedures provided in GL 88-20 Supplement 5, but initially interpreted this option as allowing a reduced-scope evaluation. In these cases, additional information was typically provided by the licensee subsequent to the submittal, through responses to RAIs or phone conferences, and often indicated that the licensee had essentially satisfied the criteria of a modified focused-scope assessment, or had provided acceptable justification for implementing a reduced-scope evaluation.

As can be seen from Figure 2.1, about 40% of the submittals used SPRAs versus about 60% that used SMAs. One plant (Nine Mile Point, Unit 2) conducted both an SPRA and a focused-scope SMA; hence, the total number of actual IPEEE analyses in Figure 2.1 is 72 while the NUREG-1407 designation total is 71 analyses.

Table 2.1 of Volume 2 of this report presents the seismic review categories and evaluation approaches for the individual plants.

2.2   Vulnerabilities and Plant Improvements

As noted in Section 1.2 of this report, consistent with the intent of GL 88-20, the primary goal of the IPEEE program was for licensees to "identify plant-specific vulnerabilities to severe accidents that could be fixed with low-cost improvements." Supplement 4 to GL 88-20 identified four supporting objectives for each licensee. One of these is to reduce, if necessary, the overall likelihood of core damage and radioactive material releases by modifying, where appropriate, hardware and procedures to help to prevent or mitigate severe accidents.

2.2.1   Seismic Vulnerabilities

Although GL 88-20 asked for the identification of plant-specific severe accident vulnerabilities, the generic letter said that licensees should provide discussion on how a vulnerability is defined for each external event evaluated. Neither the Generic Letter nor any of its supplements or associated documents provided guidance in this area.

As a result, the use of the term vulnerability varied widely among the IPEEE submittals in general and in the seismic analyses in particular. Some licensees avoided the term altogether, others stated that no vulnerabilities existed at their plant without defining the word, and still others provided a definition of vulnerability along with a discussion of their findings.

In those submittals where vulnerability was defined, a number of different definitions were used. Licensees that submitted SPRA analyses sometimes defined a vulnerability in terms of the overall core damage frequency or early release frequency at their plant, compared with results from studies of other similar plants. In some other cases, they defined a vulnerability as a scenario which contributes inordinately to core damage frequency. Most licensees who submitted an SMA did not define vulnerability. When definitions were provided in SMA submittals, they sometimes related a vulnerability to a component needed in a success path whose seismic ruggedness fell below the RLE level.

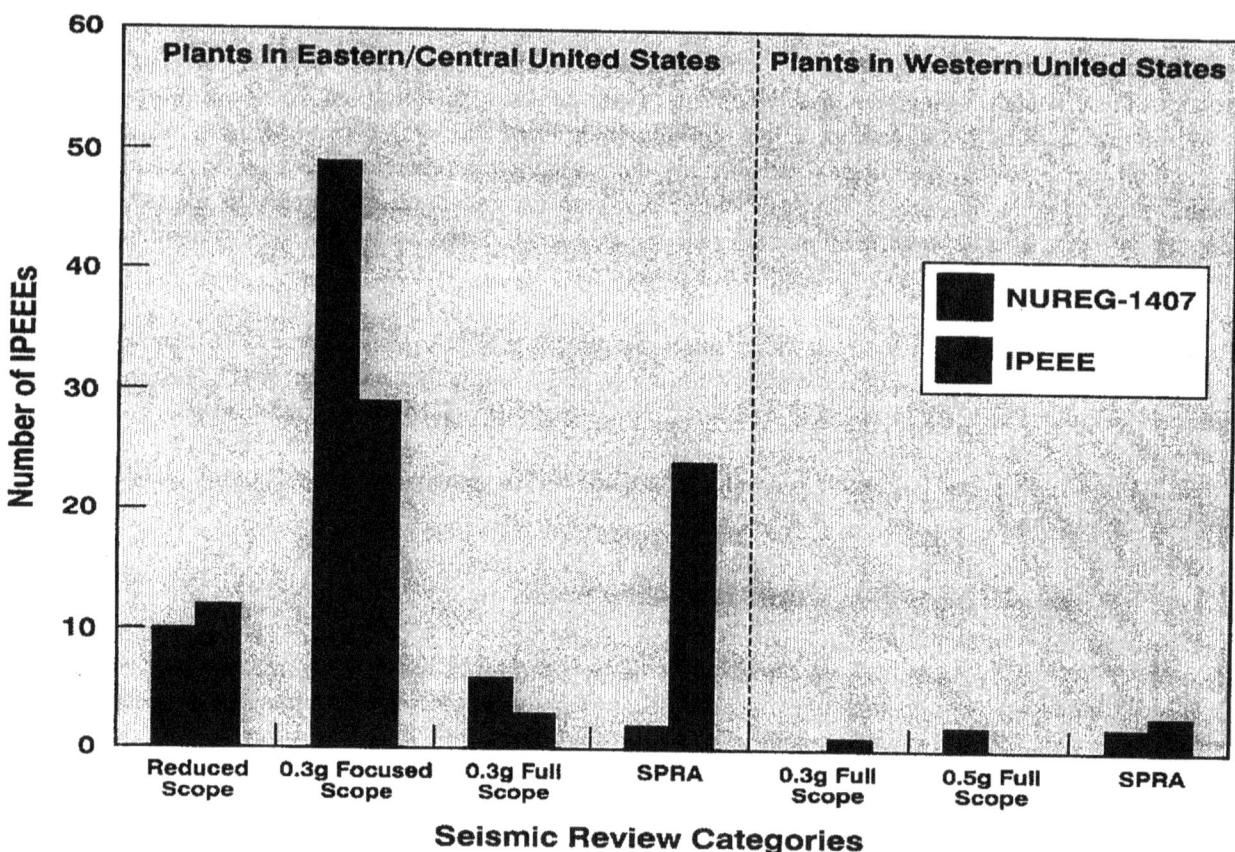

Figure 2.1 Evaluation approaches

Almost all licensees reported in their IPEEE submittals that no plant "vulnerabilities" were identified with respect to seismic risk. However, most licensees did report at least some seismic "anomalies," "outliers," and/or other concerns. The term "outlier" was usually used in the submittals to designate a component that could not be screened out (i.e., eliminated from further consideration) because a condition was encountered, in a seismic walkdown or documentation review, that violated one or more screening criteria. The term "anomaly" often referred to an obvious plant condition that deviated from a normal configuration. However, these and others, like "open issue," were often used in the seismic submittals to characterize similar items, and it was not possible to make a clear distinction between them.

As indicated by the following examples, in some submittals which identified a seismic "vulnerability," the concerns identified as vulnerabilities were comparable to concerns identified as outliers or anomalies in other submittals. One submittal identified a "seismic vulnerability" as a seismic event which induces a spurious actuation of the emergency diesel generator (EDG) room CO_2 system and subsequent shutdown of the EDG ventilation system. Another submittal identified a number of conditions, including poor anchorage/support and interaction concerns, as seismic vulnerabilities. A third submittal, in the 0.3g focused-scope category, listed a number of SSCs with seismic capacity less than 0.3g (but equal or greater than 0.25g) as "vulnerabilities"/outliers. A fourth submittal lists the grouted condition of a penetration of the standby service water system, which could induce significantly high seismic stresses in this piping system, as a potential vulnerability. Similar concerns have been identified as outliers or anomalies in other submittals.

It is important to note that of the 71 plants whose seismic submittals are discussed in this report, 45 were also USI A-46 plants (i.e., they were subject to the implementation provisions outlined in GL 87-02, "Verification of Seismic Adequacy of Mechanical and Electrical Equipment in Operating Reactors, Unresolved Safety Issue (USI) A-46"). Most of these plants performed the seismic part of their IPEEE in conjunction with their A-46 effort. As a result, numerous seismic weaknesses or vulnerabilities were identified and rectified under the A-46 program, and thus were not raised as an IPEEE concern.

2.2.2 Plant Modifications and Improvements

Just as many licensees identified outliers, anomalies or other seismic concerns resulting from their IPEEE, most also identified a number of improvements to enhance the seismic ruggedness of their plants. In some cases these plant improvements were only proposed in the submittals (sometimes without firm commitment for implementation), while in others the submittals indicated the improvements were already implemented as a result of the seismic IPEEE. Proposed/implemented plant improvements varied from simple housekeeping enhancements to more elaborated plant design modifications. In keeping with the expectation of GL 88-20, the majority of the implemented/proposed improvements, while enhancing the plants' resistance to a seismic event, did not involve significant cost.

Of the 20 IPEEEs that did not report any seismic IPEEE-related improvement, about half are USI A-46 plants and plant improvements were identified and made under the verification of that program. For the rest of these plants, improvements were not required (for relatively new plants), improvements have been made recently under other programs, or improvement opportunities were identified, but deemed not needed because of low seismic CDF estimates.

Improvements can generally be grouped into the three general categories of (1) hardware modifications, (2) improved procedures and training, and (3) enhanced maintenance and housekeeping. The distinction between hardware modifications, procedures and training, and maintenance or housekeeping issues was not always the same among various licensees.

Figure 2.2 provides an overview of the seismic plant improvements resulting from the IPEEEs. The figure indicates the approximate number of plants making improvements in each of the three general categories, and also breaks these general categories into more specific type of improvements, again indicating how many plants identified each improvement type. Details on the improvements presented by the 51 plants that proposed improvements as a result of the seismic IPEEE are provided in the sections below.

As can be surmised from all these improvements, the seismic IPEEE program has had a notable impact on improving plant safety. At the time the licensees submitted their IPEEEs, some of these improvements had already been implemented, some improvements were planned, and some were still under consideration.

2.2.2.1 Hardware/Structural Modifications

Of all plants that proposed plant improvements as a result of the IPEEE, 84% included some form of hardware changes. As Figure 2.2 shows, the most common type of proposed/implemented hardware modification was to add new anchorages or supports or strengthen existing ones. This was followed by eliminating spatial interactions and tying or bolting adjacent cabinets, instrument racks, or panels together. Other hardware/structural modifications include carrying out design or field modification of some equipment, tying loose items to adjacent structures, replacing low-ruggedness relays, fixing control room ceilings and/or

2 - 11

fixtures, strengthening masonry walls, and addressing conduit and raceway issues. These modifications are similar to the ones carried out under the USI A-46 program, but were extended to more SSCs under the IPEEE, since the IPEEE program scope was broader than that of USI A-46.

The adding or strengthening of anchorages and supports includes the addition or replacement of anchorages for motor control centers (MCCs), inverters, instrument racks/panels, various pipes, air dryers, the raw water system, the component cooling water (CCW) surge tank, the CCW heat exchanger, the chilled water surge tank, the reactor building closed cooling water (RBCCW) surge tank, residual heat removal (RHR) heat exchangers, isolation valves, station blackout (SBO) diesel mufflers, fire system standpipes, battery racks, cable trays and conduits, and various cabinets.

In many cases the MCCs, instrument and control cabinets and relay panels were tied together to remove interaction concerns or the potential for relay chatter. Other improvements on interaction issues include adequate clearance for valves, for motor-operated valve (MOV) handwheels, for conduit routing, and between MCCs and cable tray supports; spacers installed on batteries/racks; improvement to remove the potential failure of a main transformer bushing and adjacent lightning arrester, and the potential interactions between the diesel generators and crane controller; removal of a floor grating surrounding the auxiliary feedwater (AFW) valve actuators; and providing additional flexibility for a taut power cable.

Equipment modifications include design modifications for the valve operators that exceed GIP limits on height and weight; upgrade of electric pumps, diesel pumps, and the water storage tanks for the fire suppression system; modification of pipe support at penetrations to coincide with a design basis piping analysis assumption; installation of new actuation control panels; and other field modification of tanks and pipes.

The strengthening of the block walls in the EDG building and in switchgear rooms was an important modification in a number of plants.

2.2.2.2 Procedural Modifications and Training

About 20% of plants that proposed plant improvements included the addition of new or revised procedures and training for seismic events as part of the improvements.

Examples of procedure improvements for seismic events include developing procedures to (1) cope with sustained loss of offsite power as well as the emergency power supply, (2) improve control room ventilation in case smoke from a fire enters the control room, (3) establish alternate long-term room ventilation and power sources, (4) open the condenser waterbox vacuum breaker to conserve intake canal inventory, (5) deal with spurious alarms in a seismic event, and (6) close combustible gas lines.

Additional operator training to handle seismic-induced scenarios was identified in a number of cases as well.

Procedural modifications include those related to maintenance and housekeeping enhancements and those related to improved plant procedures and training. The distinction between hardware modifications and maintenance or housekeeping issues was not always the same among various licensees.

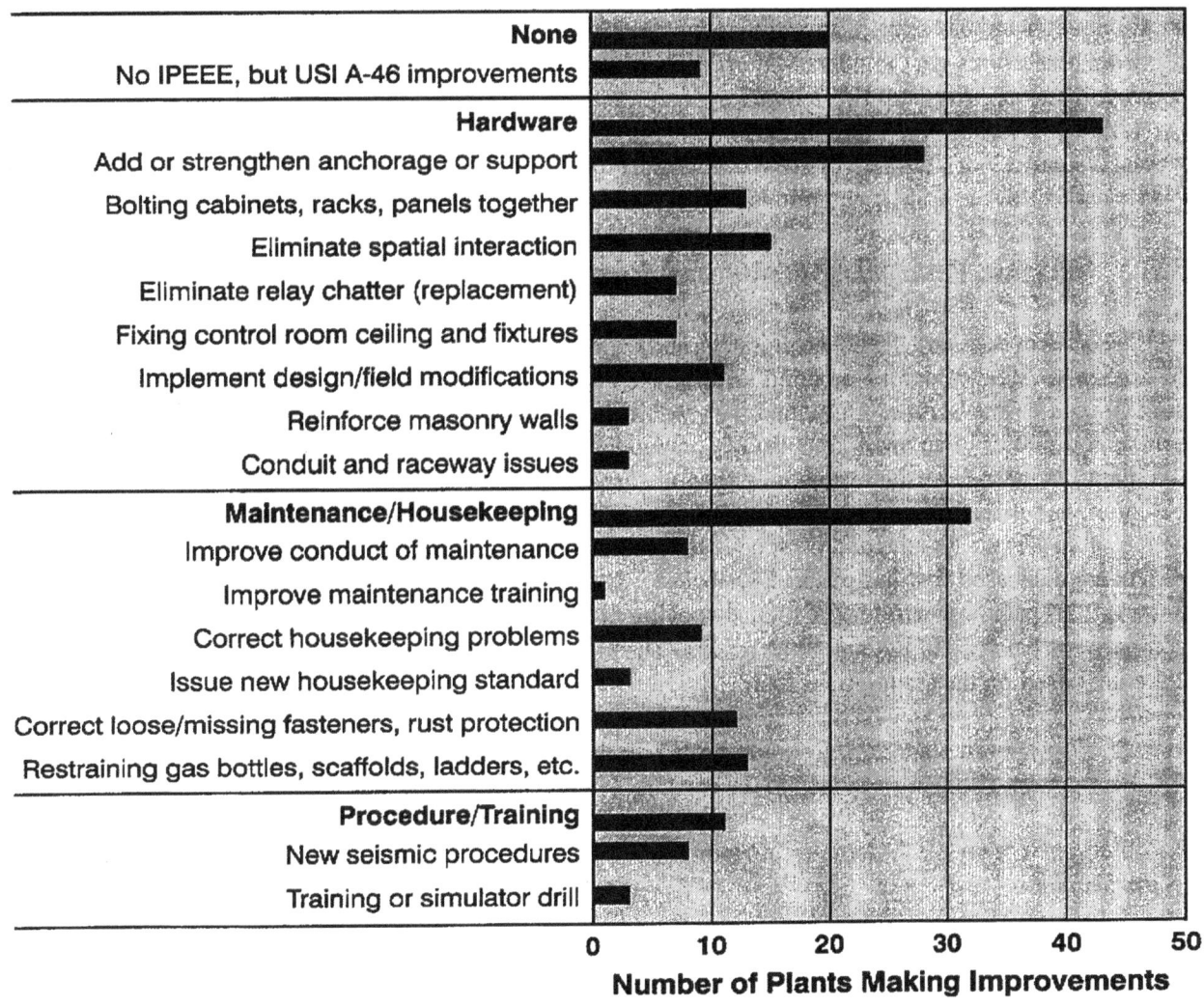

Figure 2.2 Number and type of IPEEE-related plant improvements

2.2.2.3 Maintenance and Housekeeping Issues

About 60% of the plants that proposed plant improvements included maintenance/housekeeping as part of the improvements. These include the improvement of maintenance conduct and training; the correction of housekeeping errors; the issuance of new housekeeping standards; and other corrective actions such as the restraining of gas bottles, scaffolding, and ladders, and taking corrective actions to address loose or missing fasteners/bolts/clamps and rust protection.

Maintenance/housekeeping measures included procedures and signs for storage of transient equipment, and for securing a chain hoist; a new standard to address seismic housekeeping issues; and development of guidance for dealing with movable equipment.

In many of the IPEEE submittals, the seismic-fire and/or seismic-flood interaction evaluations also revealed concerns and, in a number of instances, resulted in significant plant improvements. Some of the relevant

2 - 13

improvements include strengthening component anchorages, replacing vulnerable (e.g., mercury) relays and switches, restraining gas cylinders, waterproofing, replacing sight glass tubes, and implementing procedures to properly secure transient fire-protection equipment.

Tables 2.4 and 2.7 of Volume 2 of this report present the seismic outliers and improvements for the individual plants with SPRA and SMA submittals, respectively.

2.3   Seismic Analysis Results and Perspectives

As discussed in Section 2.1.3.2, the products, and therefore the findings, of an SPRA are different from those of an SMA. The principal products of an SPRA are an estimate of seismic CDF, a list of dominant contributors to the seismic CDF, and a probabilistic plant-level capacity (i.e., fragility estimate). The principal products of an SMA are a list of component capacities and an estimate of the HCLPF capacity of the plant. Nonetheless, the evaluations used to carry out an SPRA and an SMA have several features in common, and therefore a number of steps in the seismic IPEEE proceed in the same manner for either an SPRA or an SMA. Results and perspectives drawn from the common elements of the IPEEE SPRAs and SMAs are discussed first in Section 2.3.1 below. SPRA specific results and perspectives are addressed in Section 2.3.2, while specific SMA-related ones are discussed in Section 2.3.3. Section 2.3.4 provides some comparisons between SPRA and SMA results. The numerical results presented in Sections 2.3.2, 2.3.3, and 2.3.4 are based on the assumptions that:

- all proposed plant improvements have been implemented, and
- the improvements will lead to the capacity levels assumed by the licensee.

As noted in Section 2.2.2, some improvements are planned, sometimes without a firm commitment for implementation.

2.3.1   Results and Perspectives Common to All Seismic IPEEEs

Common elements found in both SPRA and SMA IPEEE evaluations are screening of SSCs, conduct of plant walkdowns, identification of dominant contributors or weak link components controlling seismic capacity, evaluation of electric relays, soil evaluation, consideration of non-seismic failures and human actions, seismic-fire and seismic-flood evaluations, and qualitative containment performance assessment.

2.3.1.1 Screening Assumptions and Methods

Seismic capacity screening of structures, systems, and components (SSCs) represented a major effort in the seismic IPEEE program for both SPRA and SMA evaluations. The purpose of the screening is to confirm the seismic ruggedness of those SSCs which meet certain screening criteria and to remove them from further consideration in risk quantifications, so that the work load can be significantly reduced in both SPRA and SMA evaluation processes. SSCs are screened based on their importance to safety and seismic capacity.

In applying the SMA, once a licensee has generated an equipment list, the components are evaluated against screening criteria. Such screening typically involves a documentation review and seismic walkdowns (if a component is accessible). An outlier is identified as any component that does not satisfy screening criteria or a check of anchorage capacity. For the SMA evaluations, the licensees applied the screening criteria guidance outlined in EPRI NP-6041. The methodology utilizes two review or screening levels geared to peak ground accelerations of 0.3g and 0.5g (0.8g and 1.2g, 2-10 Hz average spectral acceleration), depending on the RLE. In areas of low to moderate seismic hazard, most plants that have been evaluated using SPRAs or seismic margin studies have been shown to have high confidence of low probability of failure (HCLPF) values at or below 0.3g. Past experience indicates that, at the 0.3g screening level, a small number of "weak links" are likely to be identified, efficiently defining the components controlling plant HCLPF capacity.

In the screening process used with the seismic portion of the IPEEEs, the majority of plants applied screening criteria based on the g level of the review-level earthquake (RLE) level assigned to them. For their IPEEE analysis, licensees made no attempt to assess the SSC seismic capacities beyond the assigned RLE, since this was not requested under the IPEEE program. This means that, for newer plants with seismic capacities that may exceed the assigned RLE, no insights can be gained with respect to plant seismic margins beyond the RLE. However, the majority of the plants were binned in either the focused or full-scope categories in which the assigned RLE is considerably higher than the respective design basis SSE. Therefore, the SMA evaluations are still capable of providing insights with respect to seismic margins beyond the respective design basis SSE for these plants.

The criteria used for the SSC screening vary considerably among plants that performed SPRA evaluations. For SPRA plants, the different screening criteria applied for component selections can be grouped in three categories: (a) plant uniform hazard spectrum (UHS) shape anchored to a PGA higher than the assigned RLE; (b) the EPRI NP-6041 screening guidance in conjunction with UHS or site-specific spectra; and (c) the EPRI NP-6041 screening guidance in conjunction with the NUREG/CR-0098 spectrum. Table 2.1 presents the breakdown of screening categories among the SPRA plants.

Table 2.1: Breakdown of screening criteria used in IPEEE SPRA

Screening criteria applied	Number of plants
UHS shape anchored to a PGA higher than assigned RLE	4
EPRI NP-6041 screening requirements in conjunction with UHS or site-specific spectra	10
EPRI NP-6041 screening requirements in conjunction with NUREG/CR-0098 spectrum	13

Because of the considerable difference in the UHS shapes, it is difficult to make comparisons between the screening levels of plants. However, it should be noted that many UHS shapes developed for the EUS plants appear to have substantially reduced energy content in the frequency range of 1.0 to 10 Hz, compared to the respective design basis SSE spectra. Because these frequencies are more closely related to seismic events that could cause damage at nuclear power plants, the use of the UHS for screening is most likely to lead to lower seismic demand than the design basis and, therefore, could result in premature component screening. This is further substantiated by the results reported for some IPEEE SPRAs, where surrogate elements (see below) had been found among the dominant risk contributing components.

When screening is used in conjunction with an SPRA, a surrogate element can be added to the cutsets to replace all the components which have been screened out from the analysis. However, this practice was not correctly followed in all SPRA IPEEEs. When a surrogate element has a significant contribution to the computed seismic risk, risk contributions from individual SSCs can be masked. Therefore, the screening level should be chosen to avoid a significant risk contribution from the surrogate element. A few plants applied higher screening criteria than the RLE; their justification was that the components being screened out in this manner should have an insignificant contribution to the seismic CDF, even if failures of these components could lead directly to the core damage, i.e., that the HCLPF level chosen for screening corresponded to a suitably low frequency of component failure, even if this single failure led to core damage. Beaver Valley (a 0.3g focused-scope plant), which used 0.5g HCLPF as a screening threshold, is an example of such plant. In another IPEEE SPRA (Seabrook), the rather stringent criteria of 2.0g median and 1.2g HCLPF capacities were applied as the screening threshold.

It can be seen from the above table that most of the SPRAs applied very aggressive screening, which may have affected the quality of the SPRA analyses from the risk quantification viewpoint. As noted above, if plants apply the RLE for component screening with their SPRA, without proper justification, there is a potential for overlooking certain seismic initiators and the affected sequences. In one example (Oyster Creek) where the licensee applied the RLE for component screening and was asked for justification, the licensee performed a sensitivity study by incorporating into the SPRA model a seismic generic fragility representing the screened out components in a manner similar to a surrogate element. The seismic CDF result showed a 22% increase. Such an approach does not provide the analysts with an opportunity to identify additional seismic initiators among the screened out components and corresponding accident sequences.

However, because all SPRAs have identified numerous components with seismic capacity lower than the screening threshold, and many of them end up being the dominant risk contributors, it is not believed that these screening practices have compromised the identification of dominant risk contributors and their rankings in most cases. Therefore, from a qualitative standpoint, these SPRAs still satisfied the intent of GL 88-20, despite carrying out the less stringent screening in their SPRA processes.

The use of UHS and surrogate elements in the IPEEEs is further discussed in Section 2.4 of this report. Tables 2.4 and 2.7 of Volume 2 of this report present the screening levels used for the individual plants with SPRA and SMA submittals, respectively.

2.3.1.2 Walkdown Procedures and Findings

The common denominator for the seismic IPEEE evaluations is a well-conducted, detailed walkdown to find as-designed, as-built, and as-operated seismic weaknesses in plants. Regardless of the specific approach used, all plants performed a detailed seismic walkdown, and many of the insights gained by licensees resulted from the walkdowns.

The principal elements of a seismic walkdown are the same, regardless of whether an SPRA or SMA is conducted. Specifically, these elements include (1) determining seismic capacity versus seismic demand, (2) looking for caveats based on earthquake experience and generic testing databases, (3) checking anchorage adequacy, and (4) identifying seismic-spatial interaction with nearby equipment, systems, and structures.

For both SPRA and SMA IPEEEs, seismic walkdowns have been performed by trained and qualified personnel. Licensees have often indicated that personnel received Seismic Qualification Utility Group

(SQUG) training, as well as the "add-on" seismic IPEEE training. All IPEEE submittals for USI A-46 plants also referenced the use of the walkdown procedures and criteria described in the Generic Implementation Procedure (GIP) [SQUG, 1992].

Most of the IPEEEs referenced use of EPRI NP-6041-SL [EPRI, 1991] or EPRI NP-6041 [EPRI, 1988] procedures for performing the seismic screening and walkdowns. The few exceptions also have some (albeit limited) similarities with these procedures.

Based on the results of walkdowns, licensees have reported outliers and anomalous conditions at many plants pertaining to the following general issues:

- adequacy of equipment anchorage,
- functional adequacy of equipment,
- physical interactions, and
- seismic maintenance and housekeeping.

In the past, well-conducted, detailed walkdowns have been demonstrated to be a most important and effective tool for identifying seismic weak links, and the IPEEEs have reinforced this view. Often the walkdowns have identified seismic concerns whose correction proved to be relatively simple and cost effective, in part because a well-organized walkdown team and a properly planned walkdown enabled many issues to be addressed at the same time. For sites where the seismic hazard is low (i.e., where a reduced-scope seismic margins method is considered adequate), the detailed walkdowns were the most significant product of the IPEEE process.

Tables 2.4 and 2.7 of Volume 2 of this report present the walkdown findings for the individual plants with SPRA and SMA submittals, respectively.

2.3.1.3 Dominant Contributors From the SPRAs and Weak Links From the SMAs

As previously noted in this report, one of the principal products of an SPRA is a list of dominant contributors to the seismic CDF, and NUREG-1407 requests that licensees who perform an SPRA for their IPEEE report the dominant functional and/or systemic sequences leading to core damage. An SMA is not intended to explicitly determine core damage frequency and dominant risk contributors, and thus it is generally not possible to draw conclusions regarding risk from an SMA that are as definitive as the findings of an SPRA study.

Nevertheless, the underlying seismic analysis procedures are essentially the same for the seismic probabilistic risk assessment and the seismic margins methodology. In each case, the SSC capacity is combined with the seismic demand in order to obtain the component failure probability or HCLPF value in terms of ground motion quantity, usually peak ground acceleration. The component capacity analyses appeared to have been performed in a consistent manner in most of the IPEEE seismic submittals, although with varying degrees of quality. In an SMA, the components having the lowest HCLPF capacity are the weak links, and the plant-level HCLPF capacity is determined either directly from the weak link components (EPRI method) or from component-level HCLPFs using a Boolean expression for core damage and a simple min-max approach (NRC method). Therefore, some insights as to dominant contributors can also be gained from seismic margin analyses if the weak link components identified in an SMA are looked upon as the likely leading contributors to plant risk.

The discussion below first focuses on dominant contributors identified in the SPRAs, and then reviews insights based on weak links identified in the SMAs.

Table 2.2 summarizes the most significant CDF contributors reported in the SPRA IPEEEs that have been included in this study. The contributors are listed approximately in order of decreasing frequency of occurrence.

About half of the contributors listed in Table 2.2 for seismic failure involve the failure of the electrical systems, which includes the failure of the offsite power (17% of all contributors listed in Table 2.2); the failure of various components of the electrical system (17%), such as MCCs, load centers, switchgear, and relays; the failure of the emergency diesel generator (EDG) (8%); and the failure of the dc batteries (5%). The failure of the EDG can be caused by the failure of the EDG itself, or the failure of its support systems, such as the battery, the oil tank, the oil cooler, and controls. The failure of the dc battery can be caused by the failure of the battery itself or by the failure of the battery room fans or inverter.

Besides the electrical system, building and structural failures also contribute significantly (30% of all contributors in Table 2.2). Major buildings whose failure causes core damage include the auxiliary building, the turbine building, the control building, the reactor building, and the EDG building. Other structures whose failure causes core damage include block walls, pump house/pump intake structures, dams, and stacks.

The front line and support systems whose failure could contribute to core damage (28% of all contributors) primarily include the service water system (pump failure, valve relay chatter), the component cooling water (CCW) system (heat exchanger and pump failure), the auxiliary feedwater system (pipe and storage tank failure), the decay heat removal system (pump, heat exchanger), and the compressed air system (containment instrument air, nitrogen accumulator). Other front line and support systems that also contribute to core damage include the high pressure injection system, the ice condenser, main steam isolation valves (MSIVs) (interaction), main feedwater system (heater), control rods, containment air circulation system, fire protection system (diesel fire pump, day tank, control panel), and emergency sump valve bellows.

The failure of some major tanks also contributes to core damage (11%). The tanks involved are the CCW surge tank, the condensate storage tank (CST), the refueling water storage tank (RWST), and the chiller tank for the emergency chillers.

In some SPRAs another major contributor to CDF is the surrogate element (8%). Of the SPRAs that considered the screened out components in the risk quantification, the majority used a single surrogate element to represent all the screened out components, while others applied more than one surrogate element. For example, in one IPEEE, one surrogate element is used to represent all screened out components in the auxiliary building and another surrogate element is used to represent all screened out components in the safe shutdown facility. As noted elsewhere in this report, when a surrogate element has a significant contribution to the computed seismic risk, risk contributions from individual SSCs can be masked.

Table 2.2: Dominant contributors to CDF from SPRAs

Seismic Failures		
Most Frequently Observed	Frequently Observed	Observed
• Offsite power • Electrical system components (panels, MCCs, load centers, switchgear, etc.) • Emergency diesel generators (EDG failure due to failure of EDG or components such as battery, oil tank, control panel, cooler, etc.) • Surrogate elements • DC batteries (due to failure of battery, fans, inverters)	• Auxiliary building • Block walls • Service water (SW) system • Turbine building • CCW system • CST • Pump house/pump intake structure • Control building/room • Auxiliary feedwater system • RHR system	• Emergency chiller • Cable tray • Dam • Fire system • Reactor building • EDG building • Superheater stack • High pressure injection system • Emergency sump valve bellows • Ice condenser • MSIV interaction • Main feedwater system • Control rod • Containment Air circulation system • RWST
Random Failures		
Most Frequently Observed	Frequently Observed	Observed
• Diesel generators	• Relief valves • Auxiliary feedwater pumps • Long-term heat removal	• Diesel generator supports • Chillers • CCW pumps • High pressure safety injection pumps • Class 1E ac power train
Operator Action Errors		
Most Frequently Observed	Frequently Observed	Observed
• Align for AFW flow	• Initiate cooling/recirculation • Diesel generator operation • Station units crosstie • Reset relays	• Reduce CCW heat loads • Shutdown from remote shutdown panel • Station blackout diesel procedure • Manual recovery action of instrumentation panels • Manual alignment SW source • Alignment of fire protection system to isolation condenser makeup • Offsite power recovery via combustion turbines • Establish alternate emergency shutdown facility room ventilation

Figure 2.3 presents the information on seismic failures in Table 2.2 grouped by SSC type and indicates the number of times the SSC was identified as a dominant contributor (i.e., shown as "number of occurrences" in Figure 2.3).

Besides seismic failures, random failures and operator errors are also presented in the IPEEE submittals. They are listed in Table 2.2, along with the seismic failures.

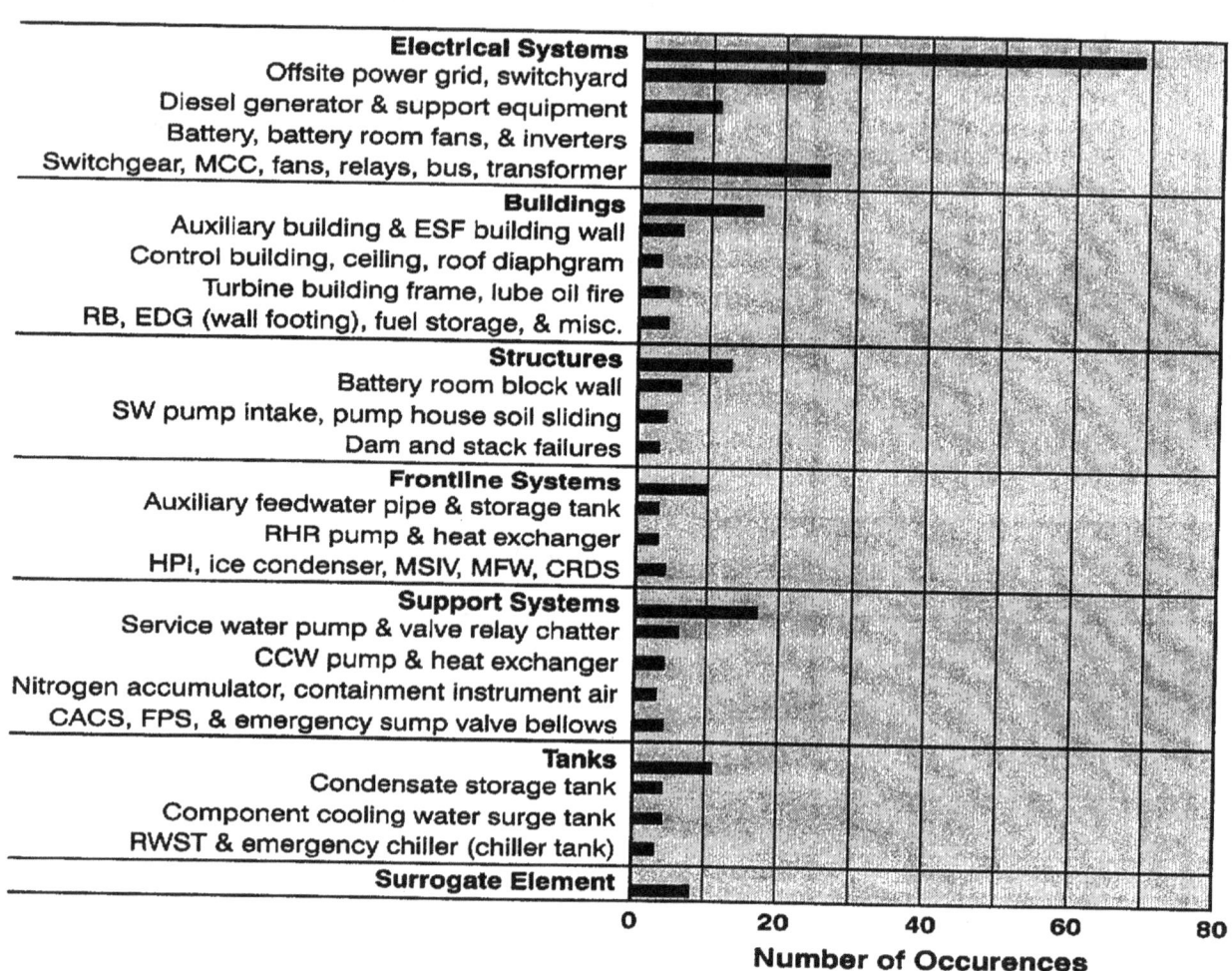

Figure 2.3 Dominant contributors from SPRAs

For PWRs, it is not surprising that diesel generators and alignment for AFW flow are the most frequently observed random failures and human errors, respectively. Most seismic scenarios are accompanied by a loss of offsite power (LOOP), with the associated dominant core damage sequences involving common cause failure of diesel generators coupled with failure to align and initiate the steam-driven AFW pump.

For the six BWRs with SPRAs, diesel generator failure was also the most observed random failure, and manual actions designed to recover power involved the most observed human errors.

The weak link components identified in the SMA analyses in general were similar to the SSCs listed as dominant contributors in the SPRAs. Components identified as outliers in the SMAs included many electrical components and their anchorages, various tanks, RHR heat exchangers, and structures like the turbine and auxiliary buildings. Many licensees identified block walls located in the proximity of safety-significant equipment as weak link structures. Figure 2.4 shows SSCs identified in SMA analyses as having HCLPF values below 0.3g after plant modifications, grouped by component type (i.e., shown as "number of occurrences" in Figure 2.4).

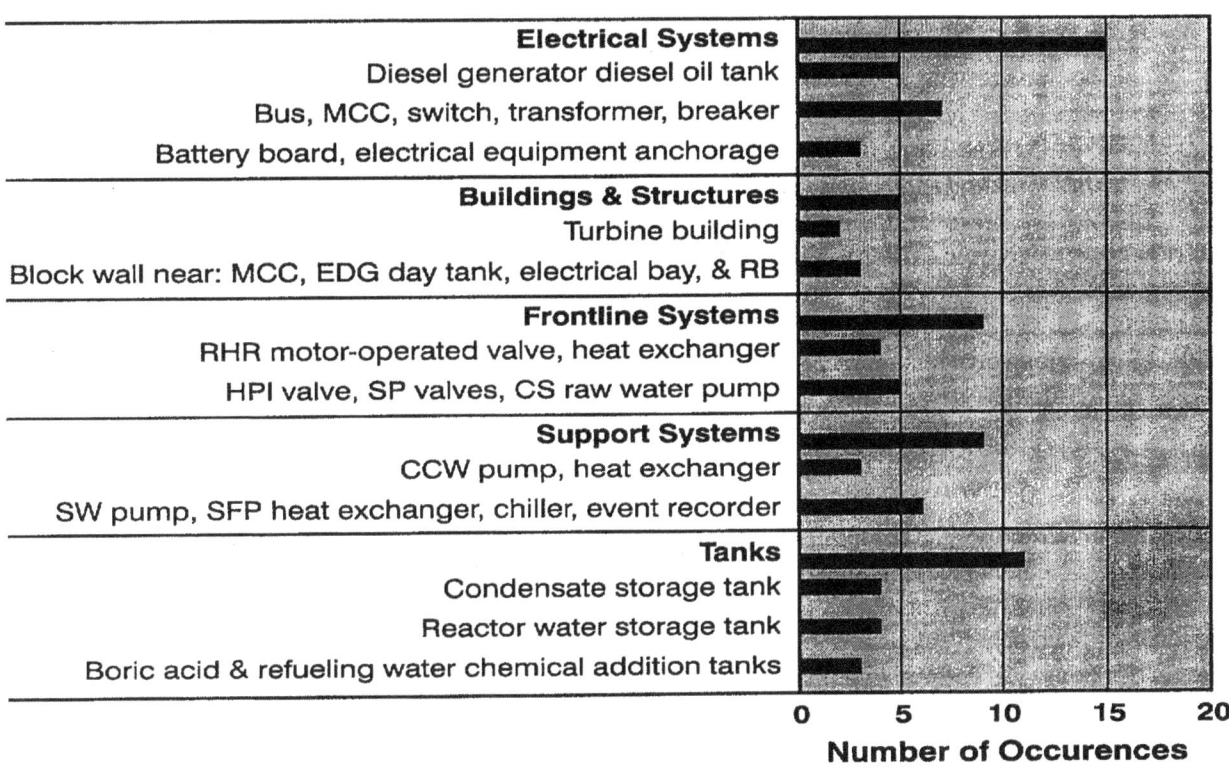

Figure 2.4 Low HCLPF components from SMAs

As the above discussion indicates, masonry walls were identified in many IPEEEs either as significant contributors to CDF or as controlling elements for plant HCLPF capacity. This finding is not surprising for the following reasons.

- Although all operating plants were required to assess the seismic adequacy of safety-significant masonry walls for the plant-specific seismic design basis in response to Inspection Enforcement Bulletin (IEB) 80-11, this was a backfit evaluation of existing masonry walls, and many of the resolutions targeted and documented only minimal capacity above the plant-specific seismic design basis.

- In a seismic margins assessment, at a higher seismic demand, masonry walls are automatically considered outliers requiring further evaluation. It is not possible to generically screen masonry walls because of (a) the wide variation in geometry and construction detail, and (b) the limited capability to absorb energy without failure, particularly in the case of unreinforced walls.

- The IEB 80-11 program addressed interactions with safety-related SSCs; whereas USI A-46 and the IPEEE allowed the use of non-safety SSCs in defining the success paths. The assessment of spatial interactions (seismic II/I)[2] for the items on the safe shutdown equipment list (SSEL) in some cases identified masonry walls not previously evaluated in the 80-11 program.

- In contrast to the cost of increasing the seismic capacity of low-HCLPF equipment anchorages, which accounted for many of the reported plant improvements and often effectively eliminated anchorage as a controlling structural element, the cost of structural modifications to masonry walls is likely to be significant.

For plants with relatively high design basis peak ground accelerations (PGAs) and conservative design basis in-structure response spectra, HCLPF capacities at least equal to the 0.3g RLE were demonstrated for many masonry walls by scaling and/or by use of analysis methods and acceptance criteria documented in EPRI NP-6041. In one case, however, the licensee identified the plant HCLPF capacity as the seismic design basis, controlled by the seismic capacity of masonry walls. The licensee made no attempt to demonstrate margin, and indicated that plant improvements would not be cost-effective.

Table 2.3 of Volume 2 of this report presents the dominant risk contributors reported for the individual plants with SPRA. Table 2.7 of Volume 2 lists controlling outliers reported in individual SMA submittals.

2.3.1.4 Relay Evaluation

NUREG-1407 describes the recommended procedures for relay evaluation in performing the seismic part of the IPEEEs. The actual recommendations depend on the scope of the seismic evaluation, and whether or not the plant is a USI A-46 plant. Relay evaluations performed under the USI A-46 program have revealed the existence of "bad actor" relays at a significant number of plants. "Bad actor" relays are seismically low-ruggedness relays, as defined in guidance and procedures pertaining to USI A-46 and the SQUG. Relay concerns identified under the USI A-46 program, were typically resolved under that program.

As a consequence, few significant low-ruggedness relays were identified solely as a result of the IPEEE program since almost all of the important low-ruggedness relays were typically fixed under the USI A-46 program. When bad actor relays were evaluated solely in the seismic analysis of the IPEEE program, they were often been found by licensees to be of low seismic significance for a number of reasons: they exist only in alarm circuitry, the effects of relay chatter were found to have negligible consequence, or the licensee has assumed that operator actions would provide for effective reset of the relays. In only limited instances, therefore, have licensees actually proposed replacing relays based specifically on the analysis conducted for the IPEEE evaluation.

The treatment of relays in the SPRA models varied. Fourteen of the 27 SPRAs conducted for the IPEEE included relays in their models. For the 13 others, analysts performed separate evaluations to determine the ruggedness of relays. When relays were explicitly modeled in the SPRA, the effect of low-ruggedness relay

---

[2] The seismic II/I criteria states that any seismic Category II (i.e., non-seismic Category I) structure, system, or component that is installed over a seismic Category I structure, system, or component will not fail in such a manner as to adversely affect the seismic Category I structure, system, or component; however, the seismic Category II structure, system, or component may no longer be functional.

chatter on accident sequences was clearly identified and quantified. Some of the SPRAs credited recovery actions with respect to relays in their logic model.

Information on this issue for individual plants can be found in Table 2.9 of Volume 2 of this report.

2.3.1.5 Soil Evaluation

Of the 71 plants for which seismic analyses were performed for the IPEEE, 12 plants performed a reduced-scope analysis and thus did not perform a soil evaluation. Forty-one of the remaining plants are located on soil (as opposed to rock) sites. Most SPRA submittals provided some level of discussion on liquefaction, if the plants examined were founded on soil. For SMA plants, the plants in the full-scope category provided some qualitative discussion on soil-related failures. Most of the focused-scope plants did not perform such evaluations, and instead referred to the modified seismic IPEEE guidelines described in Supplement 5 to GL 88-20, which exempted some plants from soil evaluation. Some rock sites may have potential soil-related concerns (e.g., due to buried piping, ducts, and tanks) and some submittals for rock sites considered these potential concerns.

Plants which performed soil analyses addressed various concerns of soil failure, including: (1) the potential for, and effects of, liquefaction, (2) slope instability, (3) settlement, (4) displacement, and (5) stresses in buried piping. Some licensees performed analyses of liquefaction-induced slope instability and soil displacement, using a variety of approaches, some of which apparently have not yet been reviewed or approved by the NRC. The potential for liquefaction-related failures was identified as a significant contributor or causing a low HCLPF at some sites. It should be noted that currently there are no general recommendations (or even a consensus) on the best approach to estimating liquefaction-induced soil displacement. Therefore, a significant amount of uncertainty still exists with respect to these liquefaction studies performed for the IPEEE program.

A number of interesting findings resulted from the soil evaluations: One licensee found that the evaluation indicated that liquefaction is likely to occur below the RLE, but above the SSE at their plant. At another plant (Calvert Cliffs), the liquefaction potential has been identified as a potential concern. However, upon further evaluation, the licensee concluded that although liquefaction would likely occur at low PGA, the seismically induced settlement would be negligibly small and would not cause a realistic hazard. Seismic slope instability at the RLE was also identified for two plants, but the magnitude of slope deformations was assessed by these licensees as minor. With regard to settlement, the submittals have generally reported that seismically induced differential soil settlement has only minor impact.

The principal insight from these soil evaluations is that the possibility of soil failures is a concern at some plants, but it may be difficult to fully rectify the potential for such failures in a cost-effective manner (particularly if the problem is not isolated to a few specific locations on the plant site). Although soil improvements may not be cost-effective, the IPEEE findings regarding soil failures provide useful information concerning the expected plant response.

Information on this issue for individual plants can be found in Table 2.10 of Volume 2 of this report.

2.3.1.6 Non-Seismic Failures and Human Actions

All of the 71 IPEEE submittals provided some treatment or discussion of non-seismic failures and human actions. For SPRAs, these effects were introduced in seismic event-tree and fault-tree models, which generally reflect the plant logic as constructed for internal events. However, among the IPEEEs reviewed, the seismic impacts on operator error rates were modeled with a wide variety of approaches. In some instances, licensees developed simplified operator error fragilities. In other instances, licensees applied judgemental scaling factors (in relation to the importance of the human action) to internal event error rates, or used other means to account for seismic-related performance shaping factors.

In most SPRAs, human error probabilities (HEPs) were based on the values developed for the IPE models. In a few, the IPE values were used without modification, but in most IPEEE SPRAs multipliers that depended either on (1) seismic level or (2) the HEP values themselves were applied to the values used for internal events. For multipliers that depended on seismic levels, usually a multiplier of 1 (i.e., the IPE value) was used for low seismic levels (e.g., less, or slightly higher, than the SSE value), a multiplier of 5 to 10 was used for intermediate seismic values, and a HEP value of 1 was used for high seismic levels (e.g., greater than three times the SSE, or greater than 0.5 to 1.0 g). For multipliers that depended on the HEP values themselves, a multiplier of 2 or 3 was used for HEP values greater than 0.1, a multiplier of 5 was used for the HEP values between 0.01 and 0.1, and a multiplier of 10 was used for HEP values less than 0.01. Although in some cases the submittals stated that HEP-dependent factors were based on previous seismic PRAs and were thus judged to be appropriate for the assessment, no strong technical basis was provided for the values chosen. Nonetheless, most IPEEE SPRA analyses showed an effort to judgementally assess the effects of an earthquake on operator actions, and the values arrived at are generally consistent with adjustment factors used in other seismic SPRA studies.

Effects of location of the action and its timing were considered in the determination of HEP values in some IPEEEs. For example, a higher HEP value, or a value of unity, was usually assumed for operator actions outside the control room, while the IPE HEP values were used if actions were not required until more than 1 hour after event initiation.

Seismic-specific human actions were also considered in some SPRAs. Most of them are related to the recovery of relay chatter. Other seismic-specific actions considered include the response to seismic failure of upstream dams, actions to conserve intake canal inventory in order to save service water, and alignment of water from fire trucks to CCW makeup, given failure of the primary makeup tank. For seismic-specific human actions, the failure probabilities were assigned in ways varying from using a human reliability analysis (HRA) method, such as the Accident Sequence Evaluation Program (NUREG/CR-4772) [U.S.NRC, 1987] method, to simply assigning very conservative values.

With regard to the treatment of human actions in SMA IPEEEs, there was little documentation in the submittals on whether or how the licensees attempted to evaluate seismic impacts on operator error rates. This was a relatively consistent finding. Also, there was only one case among the SMA IPEEEs where the licensee applied quantitative screening criteria with respect to random failure rates and human error rates. The other SMA IPEEE submittals took the qualitative approach of relying on those success paths that are most familiar to plant operators and that use the most reliable equipment. However, in response to RAIs issued as part of the reviews, licensees generally reported on the timing and locations of the required human actions, and commented qualitatively on their reliability.

2 - 24

Table 2.11 of Volume 2 summarizes the findings for individual plants pertaining to non-seismic failures, operator errors, and the licensees' treatment of such potential failures. This table also indicates that many submittals have considered operator actions required to reset relays.

2.3.1.7 Seismic-Fire and Seismic-Flood Evaluations

All licensees qualitatively examined seismic-fire interaction issues as part of their assessment of fire risk. To varying degrees, such examinations have included the potential for, and effects of, seismically initiated fires, seismic actuation of fire suppression systems, and degradation of fire suppression systems from seismic events. Some licensees undertook quantitative assessments of component capacities related to seismic-fire and seismic-flood interactions. A few licensees performed some form of SPRA study for seismic-fire and/or seismic-flood initiating events and documented it in their submittal.

In most of the submittals, licensees included seismic-fire and seismic-flood considerations within the scope of their overall seismic walkdown effort. The seismically induced fire interactions were generally addressed by first identifying combustion sources (e.g., hydrogen lines, oil tanks) and then performing walkdowns to evaluate whether these sources are both significant hazards and seismically vulnerable. Some of the seismic-fire interaction evaluations have led to a number of fixes, such as restraining gas cylinders, strengthening anchorages for fuel oil tanks, and, where feasible, relocating combustion sources away from safety equipment. The most consistent strong points of these evaluations appear to be the treatment of inadvertent actuation of fire suppression systems and the identification of potential interaction concerns involving safety equipment. However, the scope, and detail of efforts to address seismic-fire and seismic-flood issues have varied significantly among the IPEEE submittals. Some licensees did not include any seismic-fire or seismic-flood evaluation in their submittal, but provided some information on these topics in RAI responses. In most cases, licensees have limited their seismic-fire and seismic-flood evaluations exclusively to assessing direct impacts on safe shutdown equipment, and some submittals did not consider the potential for seismically induced loss of fire suppression systems.

Some licensees have sought to include all relevant plant areas and equipment in their evaluations of the potential and effects of seismic-fire and seismic-flood events. Such relevant items include, for instance, fire suppression system components and non-safety piping and tanks, which may not be part of the seismic plant model or safe shutdown equipment list, but are nonetheless important and/or may have indirect effects on safety equipment.

In many of the IPEEE submittals, the seismic-fire and/or seismic-flood interaction evaluations revealed concerns and, in a number of instances, resulted in significant plant improvements. Some of the relevant improvements include strengthening component anchorages, replacing vulnerable (e.g., mercury) relays and switches, restraining gas cylinders, waterproofing, replacing sight glass tubes, and implementing procedures to properly secure transient fire-protection equipment.

In one instance, the licensee evaluated the potential for seismically induced toxic chemical release, as part of its seismic-interactions walkdown. As a result, the licensee identified a plant-specific improvement related to strengthening the anchorage of an ammonia storage tank.

Information on this issue for individual plants can be found in Table 2.12 of Volume 2 of this report.

2.3.1.8 Containment Performance Under Seismic Conditions

The primary purpose of a containment performance evaluation for a seismic event is to identify vulnerabilities that might cause early failure of containment functions. This includes an evaluation of containment integrity, containment isolation, prevention of containment bypass, and some specific systems depending on a containment design (e.g., igniters, suppression pools, ice baskets). The containment performance issues could be addressed either qualitatively by a systematic examination of the performance of the various containment functions under the review-level seismic condition, or, quantitatively, by a Level 2 PRA.

All SMA submittals contained qualitative assessments of seismic containment performance, as did most SPRA submittals. Of the 27 SPRA IPEEE submittals, 9 included a quantitative assessment of seismic containment performance. The relevant NUREG-1407 guidance for SPRA quantitative containment performance analyses focuses on the assessment of containment failure modes that are significantly different from those encountered in the IPE. In some instances, the quantitative results provided in the IPEEE submittals are presented as frequencies of small and large releases (small and large are usually defined based on a release fraction of volatiles less than or greater than 10% of core inventory, respectively). In other cases, they are presented in the form of frequencies of small and large containment failures. (A definition of small and large failure was not provided in most cases. In one case, it was based on containment leakage less than or greater than that from a 3-inch diameter hole.) At least one SPRA IPEEE submittal (Kewaunee) also reported a containment HCLPF capacity for preventing large early releases.

The frequencies of early large release (or early release if the size of the release is not provided) obtained from the SPRA Level 2 analyses vary from less than 1E-7 to 1.6E-5/ry. As a percentage of total seismic CDF, they vary from about 1% to more than 90%. Two of the nine plants have an early large release frequency greater than 1.0E-6/ry. One plant, Pilgrim, is a BWR with a Mark I containment with a total frequency of early release determined as 1.6E-5/ry, or about 27% of the seismic CDF. The dominant contributors to the early release frequency were identified in the submittal as: drywell liner melt-through, containment structural failure before core damage, and containment isolation failure. The other plant, Point Beach 1 and 2, is a PWR that has a large early release frequency of 1.3E-5/ry, or more than 90% of total seismic CDF. This high release frequency resulted from the assumption that most core damage sequences would also result in the failure of the automatic containment isolation function, a potential seismic vulnerability. However, the licensee effectively invalidated this finding by assuming that the containment would be isolated manually by the operators at least 90% of the time in the event of core damage where automatic isolation failed. A qualitative assessment was also performed for this plant. This involved an examination of the containment safeguards systems significant to early large release, including containment integrity, mechanical penetrations, containment isolation, and containment cooling. The evaluation led the licensee to conclude that the containment and the system designed to ensure containment isolation are seismically sound, having no vulnerabilities.

Qualitative assessment of containment performance was essentially carried out the same way for analyses using either SPRA or SMA methods. These IPEEEs generally implemented a qualitative assessment of containment performance involving screening and/or walkdown examination of the following items:

- containment structural integrity,
- containment penetrations, hatches, and seals, and
- containment cooling systems.

All licensees performed walkdowns of their containments. Licensees did not report any anomalous conditions with respect to containment structural integrity. However, in a few instances, they identified outliers pertaining to containment penetrations and containment cooling.

Most licensees did not encounter any significant findings regarding containment performance during the conduct of their IPEEEs. In one submittal, the licensee initially noted a concern with a potential interfacing systems LOCA occurring inside the containment, and considered the possibility of implementing a relevant severe accident management guideline. In a subsequent Step 2 review for this plant, however, the licensee presented calculations demonstrating that for this scenario the HCLPF capacity exceeded the RLE.

Table 2.5 of Volume 2 presents both qualitative and quantitative findings associated with containment performance for the 27 individual plants with SPRA submittals, while Table 2.8 summarizes the individual plant findings on seismic containment performance from the SMA IPEEEs.

2.3.1.9 Independent Peer Review Process

All IPEEEs underwent a peer review process, as called for in NUREG-1407, and, to a varying degree, all licensees provided some level of discussion in their submittals on the role of independent peer reviews in the context of the overall IPEEE process. The purpose of the peer review was to confirm that the IPEEE conformed with GL 88-20, Supplement 4, and to ensure the overall quality of the IPEEE process. Most licensees provided details of the peer review, while a few others merely provided a statement that the peer review was performed.

Details provided by those licensees who elaborated on the role of the peer reviews included:

- a list of the peer reviewers,
- the qualifications of the peer reviewers,
- a description of the peer review walkdowns,
- the peer review evaluation letter report, or a summary of the peer review findings, and
- verification of potential concerns/issues identified by the peer review.

Based on the information in the submittals regarding the peer reviews carried out, the peer review process was generally carried out successfully.

2.3.2 SPRA Results and Perspectives

This section summarizes qualitative and quantitative results and perspectives obtained from the IPEEEs that performed SPRAs.

The following analytical elements are necessary for the quantification of seismic CDF in an IPEEE:

- seismic hazard curves,
- seismic fragility curves for components (equipment and structures),
- seismic plant logic models, and
- numerical analysis to quantify accident sequence frequencies.

In general, licensees used seismic hazard curves from one or more of the following sources:

- 1989 EPRI seismic hazard study,
- 1989 LLNL seismic hazard study,
- 1994 (revised) LLNL seismic hazard study, or
- a site-specific seismic hazard study.

EPRI hazard results are available for many, but not all, EUS plants. Licensees have employed site-specific seismic hazard results for WUS plants. A few EUS plants chose to conduct a site-specific study. Some submittals used a spectral shape taken from seismic hazard results developed for a different (e.g., the closest) plant. For many submittals, licensees performed sensitivity studies to examine effects related to seismic hazards. In particular, these studies focused on the impact of the type of hazard results (EPRI, LLNL, or site-specific) on seismic CDF, the ranking of dominant CDF contributors, and the impact of the truncation of ground motion on CDF.

Seismic hazard results are used in two principal, related ways in SPRAs. The first way is to develop seismic initiating event frequencies based on a seismic hazard curve, or (where plant/sequence-level fragility curves are developed) to convolve conditional accident sequence probabilities with the hazard curve to obtain an annual frequency of seismically induced CDF. The second way is to characterize the ground motion response spectrum for use as input to component seismic fragility calculations.

Licensees have used a variety of hazard results (or a combination of hazard results) to calculate CDFs. In many cases, the spectral shape used in evaluating fragilities and the hazard curve used for quantifying CDF were not derived from a consistent set of hazard results. For example, the uniform hazard spectrum (UHS) derived from the 1989 LLNL hazard analysis has typically been used to define the SPRA spectral shape, whereas the seismic hazard curve derived from the 1989 EPRI or 1994 LLNL hazard analyses has typically been used to quantify CDF. Further discussion regarding the use of the UHS can be found in Section 2.4.1.

Seismic fragility evaluations for the subset of components selected for risk quantification (components not screened) were carried out using various methods. These methods include fragility analysis, generic information, and testing. In general, SPRAs carried out for the IPEEEs have liberally employed various forms of simplified fragility analyses, in contrast to the predominance of detailed, conventional fragility analyses in past SPRAs. The use of simplified fragilities raises the possibility that in some cases the relative importance of the dominant contributors to the seismic CDF may be overstated or understated.

In general, licensees developed plant logic models for SPRAs directly from the IPE event trees and fault trees. Modifications were generally made to include seismic structural failures and failures of passive equipment (tanks, piping, ductwork, etc.) and to incorporate specific seismic failure correlations within the plant model. The specific initiating events typically considered included loss of offsite power (LOOP), small loss-of-coolant accidents (small LOCAs), and general transients. In some cases, licensees also included certain seismic-specific failures (usually building failures) as additional initiating events or as events leading directly to core damage. Typically, licensees developed a seismic event tree to map the seismic initiating events (in some cases defined as occurrence of an earthquake, and in other cases defined as occurrence of a particular level of ground motion) to the relevant IPE initiators. In some cases, licensees' plant seismic models also included an initiating event category unique to seismic events. Some of these unique initiators included seismically induced internal floods, external flooding attributable to seismically induced dam breaks, and seismically induced fires.

Licensees generally modified their IPE fault trees to include unique common cause effects related to earthquakes, including failure dependencies and the effects of passive component failures. In most cases, the mission times for the seismic analyses remained the same as those used for the IPEs. In addition, licensees' seismic plant logic models sometimes included recovery from seismically induced relay chatter. Licensees accomplished their quantification of accident sequences in general (e.g., for seismic CDF and sequence frequencies) either by (a) directly quantifying event-tree sequences, or by (b) developing relevant fragility curves that were subsequently convolved with the given seismic hazard curve.

2.3.2.1 CDF Results

Figure 2.5 indicates the number of plants having total estimated seismic CDF values for different ranges (orders of magnitude) of CDF. The figure also breaks up the results by hazard spectrum used. In 15 SPRAs, licensees have evaluated seismic CDF results using both EPRI and LLNL seismic hazard data. Most licensees treated the results from using the EPRI hazard data as their base case, and the results from using the LLNL data as a sensitivity calculation. Only two SPRAs (Calvert Cliffs and Palisades) evaluated the seismic CDF based solely on LLNL hazard data.

Figure 2.5 shows that the most plants reported seismic CDFs between 1E-5 and 1E-4 per reactor-year (/ry), with the next most common group falling between 1E-6 and 1E-5/ry. Only a small fraction of plants had CDFs higher than 1E-4/ry or less than 1E-6/ry. The point-estimate seismic CDFs obtained from the analyses with the EPRI hazard curves vary from about 1.9E-7/ry to 5.9E-5/ry. (This excludes a permanently shutdown plant, Haddam Neck, which had a CDF of 2.3E-4/ry.) Figure 2.5 indicates that the broad variability in these results cannot be attributed to the selection of seismic hazards (e.g., LLNL versus EPRI). Rather, the broad plant-to-plant variability probably results from a combination of many factors (e.g., differences in seismic plant capacities, differences in the levels of seismic hazard, and differences in methods and analytical assumptions).

Figure 2.6 shows the CDF range obtained for SPRAs conducted for EUS and Central United States (CUS) plants versus WUS plants. (Base case results are shown.) The highest CDF value for the EUS/CUS group comes from a plant which is now permanently shut down. With this point excluded, there are a few EUS/CUS plants with CDFs comparable to the WUS plants, but most EUS/CUS core damage frequency values fall well below those of the WUS plants. This result is in line with the relative seismic hazard for these locations, but, of course, many other factors, such as plant design and construction, and analysis assumptions and methods also come into play.

For individual plants, the seismic CDF, type of hazard curve used, spectral shape used, and indication of surrogate element use is provided in Table 2.2 of Volume 2 of this report. Dominant contributors for individual SPRA plants are provided in Table 2.3 of Volume 2.

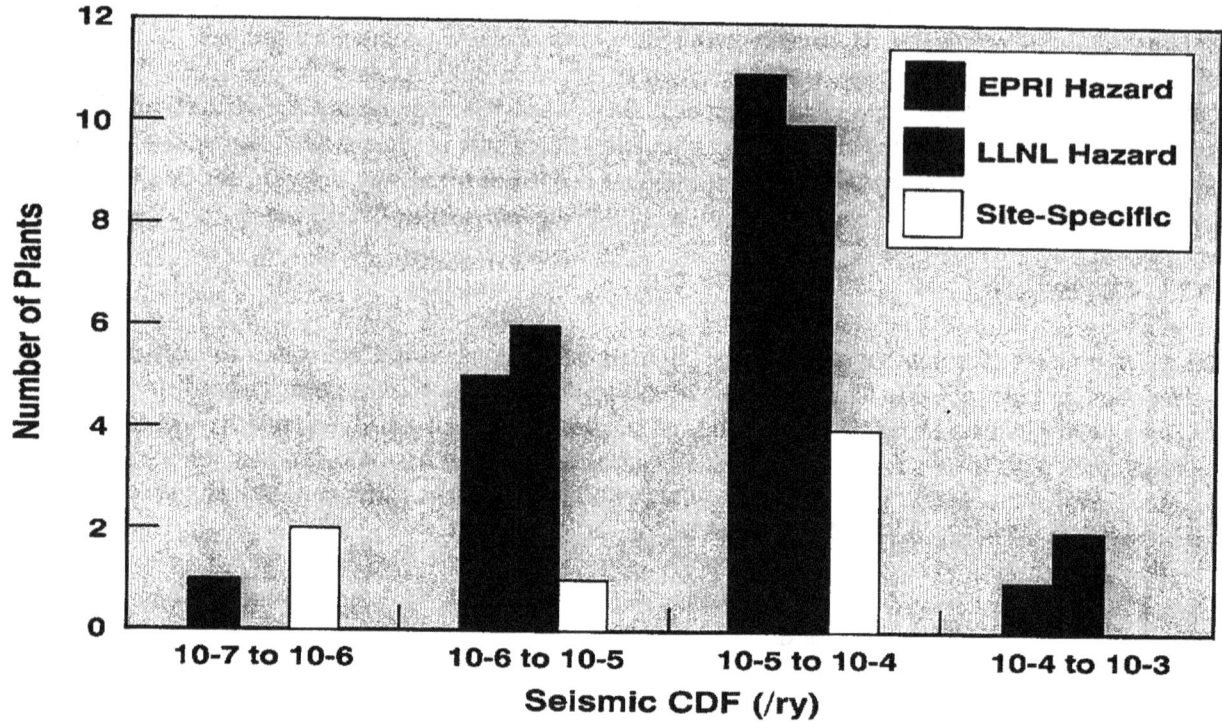

Figure 2.5 CDF results

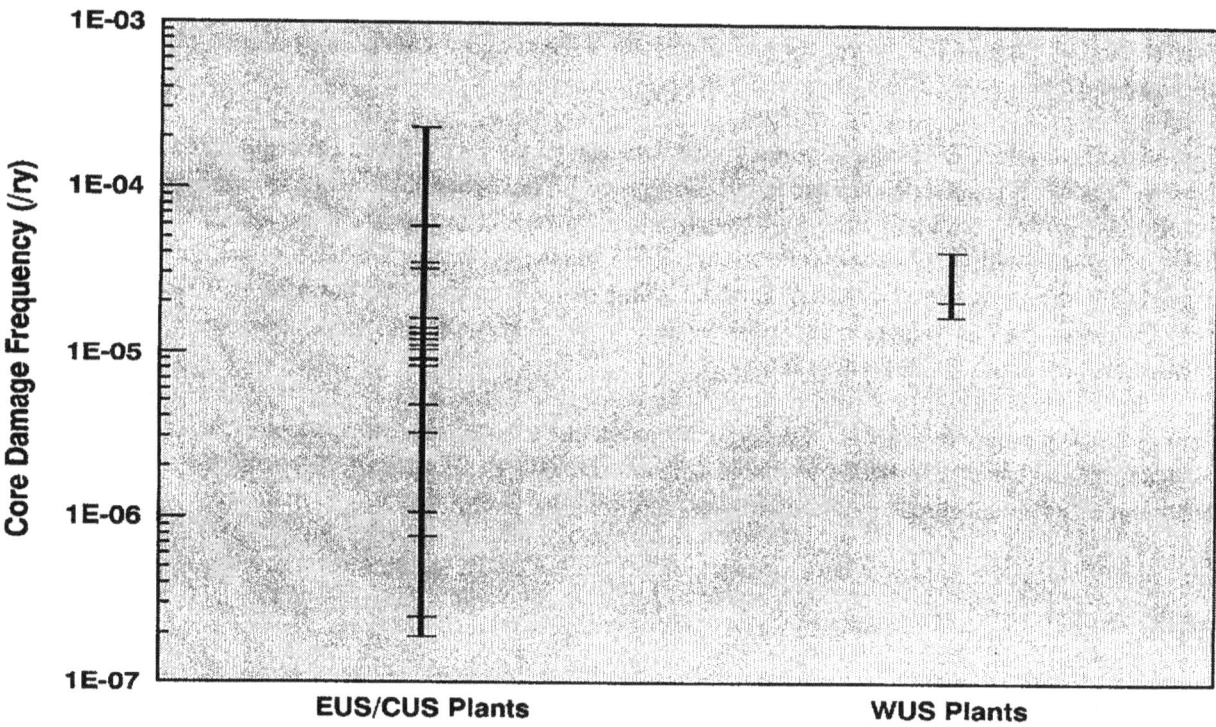

Figure 2.6 Range of CDF values for EUS/CUS plants versus WUS plants

2.3.2.2 SPRA Insights

The results obtained from the SPRA analyses performed for the IPEEEs, and indicated in Figure 2.5, are for the most part within the range of CDF estimates obtained in other SPRAs for U.S. plants. A point of interest with respect to seismic risk is whether newer plants (i.e., those designed and built to later seismic standards) show different CDFs than older plants built before some of the later design criteria were in place. In Figure 2.7 plant seismic CDF is shown versus the date the plant went into commercial operation. (Only the CDF obtained with the EPRI hazard curve is plotted for plants reporting both EPRI and LLNL hazard curve CDFs.)

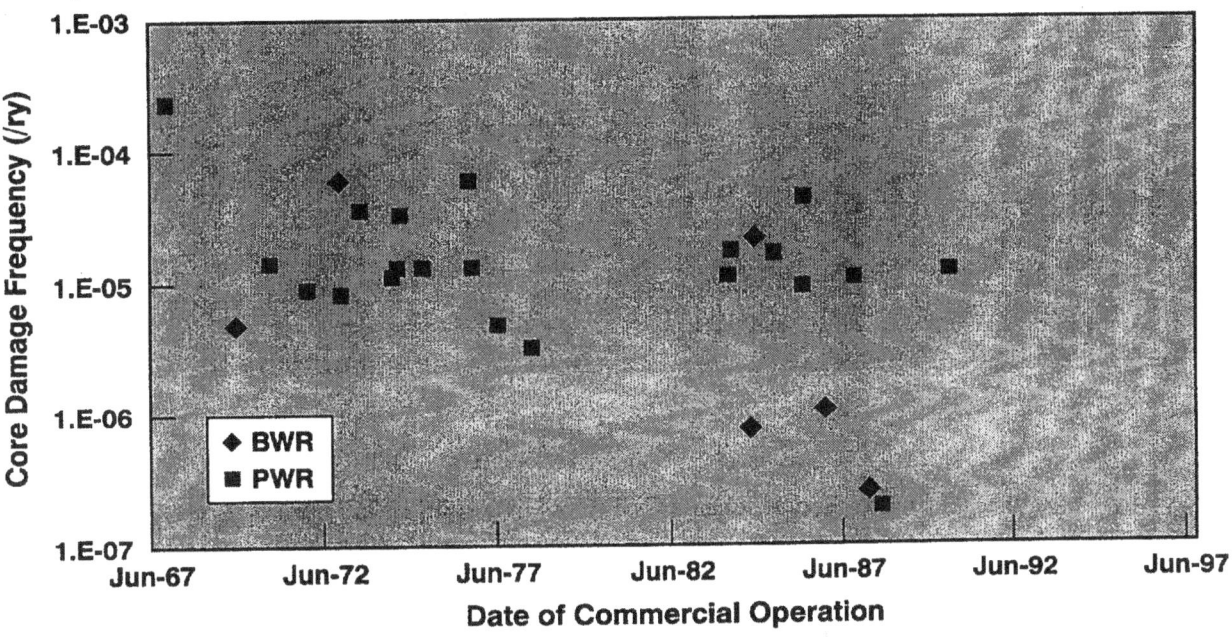

Figure 2.7 Seismic CDF values versus date of commercial operation

The figure indicates a slight downward trend, mainly due to the four low CDF values among the newer plants. Otherwise the range of CDF values does not change dramatically from the older to the newer plants. Disregarding for a moment factors such as analysis assumptions and methods, one way this data could be interpreted is that seismic backfit programs for older plants have successfully brought their CDF estimates in line with those of the newer plants.

Figure 2.5 suggests that use of the EPRI versus LLNL hazard curves did not significantly influence the CDF estimates obtained. To confirm this perspective, the CDFs generated by the EPRI and LLNL hazard curves are plotted side by side, for the 15 plants that computed both, in Figure 2.8. The figure indicates that, with one exception, the results were within an order of magnitude, and for most plants the results were almost the same. Figure 2.9 makes the same point by plotting the plant seismic CDF based on the LLNL hazard curves versus the seismic CDF based on the EPRI hazard.

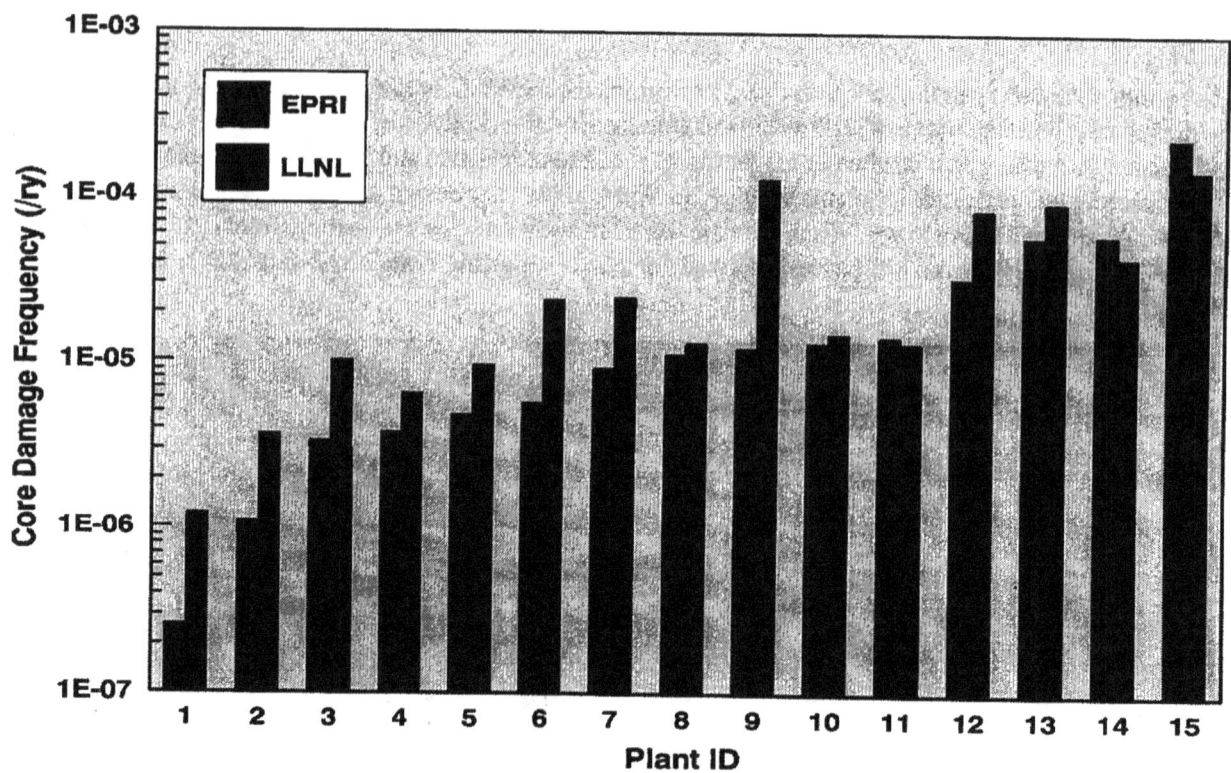

Figure 2.8 Comparison of seismic CDFs with EPRI and LNLL hazard curves

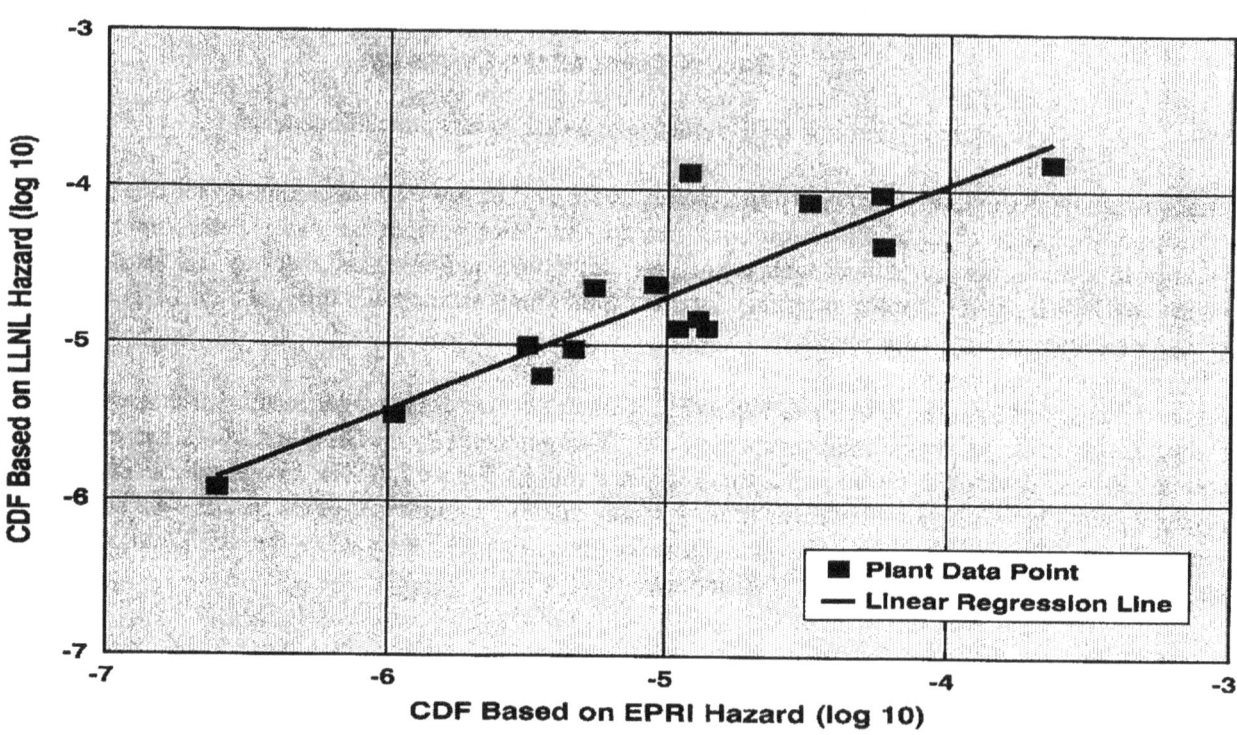

Figure 2.9 Correlation of CDFs obtained with EPRI and LNLL hazard curves

In addition, none of the SPRAs reported that the list of dominant contributors is significantly altered by the hazard curve used for seismic CDF quantification. That is, the set of dominant contributors is substantially the same, regardless of which hazard curve (LLNL or EPRI) is used. Additionally, the SPRA IPEEEs revealed only isolated minor changes in the ranking of dominant risk contributors using different hazard curves.

Additional study would be needed to explain why the use of the EPRI versus the LLNL hazard curves did not make a significant difference to the CDF despite the significant difference in the curves. However, as noted below, the ranking and relative contributions of the dominant seismic sequences were also virtually the same when both LLNL (original 1989 estimates) and EPRI hazard estimates were used for Surry and Peach Bottom in the NUREG-1150 studies (although CDF magnitudes were substantially higher with the 1989 LLNL curves than with the EPRI curves). NUREG-1407 notes that this equivalence is apparently due to the fact that the slopes of the seismic hazard curves are not significantly different over those ground motion levels that, in conjunction with the fragilities, control the relative distribution of seismically induced core damage frequencies.

When the IPEEE SPRA results are compared to those of past SPRAs, such as the NUREG-1150 studies of Surry and Peach Bottom, the dominant contributors to CDF are quite similar. Just as in the IPEEEs, seismic induced loss of offsite power transients are the major contributors in the NUREG-1150 studies, along with seismic failures of the diesel generators and various electric components, such as insulators and relays. One interesting difference between the NUREG-1150 study for Peach Bottom and the IPEEEs for BWRs is that the NUREG-1150 study identified a large LOCA sequence resulting from a seismically induced failure of the support on the recirculation pumps as an important contributor to CDF. The IPEEE submittals and RAI responses indicate that this sequence was not found important and that support failure of these pumps was very unlikely.

The NUREG-1150 studies also obtained results with both EPRI and LLNL hazard curves, but, because of the time frame of the NUREG-1150 work, the LLNL hazard curves used were the ones from the original (1989) LLNL report. The difference in the mean and median CDFs obtained in NUREG-1150 with these two sets of hazard curves was in general much more pronounced than the differences obtained for the point estimates in the IPEEEs (Figures 2.8 and 2.9) with the EPRI and revised LLNL hazard curves. However, the ranking and relative contribution of the seismic sequences were very similar with both sets of curves. It should also be noted that while the NUREG-1150 studies made use of the EPRI and LLNL data, they did not use the UHS estimates provided by these studies. In NUREG-1150 earthquake time histories from real earthquake records were used to determine the vibratory motion within the plant.

Another difference between the IPEEE SPRAs and the NUREG-1150 studies is the treatment of uncertainty. In NUREG-1150 Monte Carlo techniques were used to propagate frequency distributions of seismic parameters through the accident sequences and plant damage states to total core damage. Therefore, distributions were obtained at each step. In other words, a complete uncertainty analysis was carried out. In contrast, in keeping with the IPEEE guidelines, the IPEEE SPRAs contained some sensitivity calculations, but very little on uncertainty estimates.

In general the IPEEE SPRAs, while based on very extensive and thorough walkdowns, often used more simplified analysis techniques than previous SPRAs, as mentioned above with regard to fragility calculations and HRA approaches. In addition, the screening for the IPEEE SPRAs generally was carried out at lower values (i.e., usually at the RLE level) than the screening in previous seismic studies.

2.3.3 Seismic Margins Analysis

This section summarizes qualitative and quantitative results and perspectives obtained from the IPEEEs that performed SMAs.

To quantify a plant's seismic margin for the IPEEE, licensees must address the following principal elements in the analysis:

- success path development (EPRI SMA) [EPRI, 1991] or plant logic analysis (NRC SMA) [U.S.NRC, 1985],
- seismic screening and outlier identification,
- evaluation of component HCLPF capacities, and
- assessment of plant HCLPF capacity.

In an EPRI SMA, two alternative success paths are developed to take the plant to a stable shutdown condition and maintain that condition for at least 72 hours. At least one of the alternative success paths must involve mitigation of the effects of a small LOCA. The principal functions considered when developing the success paths include reactivity control, reactor pressure control, reactor coolant inventory control, and decay heat removal. The product of the success path development is a safe shutdown equipment list (SSEL) or success path equipment list (SPEL) that identifies the components to be evaluated, as well as the random failures and operator actions that could impact the integrity of the success paths. As discussed below, in some IPEEEs where the EPRI margin analysis was used, licensees have not entirely followed the criteria for success path development, or the submittal has not contained sufficient information to permit verification of appropriate application of the criteria. In an NRC SMA, a seismic plant logic model is developed in a manner similar to an SPRA. The initiating events examined must include loss-of-offsite power transients and the small LOCA.

Once a licensee has generated an equipment list, the components are evaluated against screening criteria. As discussed in Section 2.3.1.1 of this report, such screening typically involves a documentation review and seismic walkdown (if a component is accessible). Outliers are identified as any component that does not satisfy screening criteria or a check of anchorage capacity.

HCLPF capacities are determined for components identified as outliers either by calculation or by engineering judgements of the seismic capacity engineers. In an EPRI SMA, the CDFM methodology [EPRI, 1991] is typically used to assess HCLPF capacities. In an NRC SMA, licensees may employ either the CDFM methodology or a probabilistic fragility analysis.

In an EPRI SMA, the plant-level capacity is assessed as the lowest component HCLPF capacity in both the transient and small LOCA success paths. By contrast, in an NRC SMA, the plant-level HCLPF capacity is evaluated by inspecting a core damage Boolean expression, or is determined directly from a plant-level fragility curve. Only two licensees (FitzPatrick and Fort Calhoun) performed an NRC SMA.

2.3.3.1 HCLPF Results

For the 36 plants in the full- and focused-scope categories of NUREG-1407 that carried out an SMA for the IPEEE, Figure 2.10 indicates the range of HCLPF results obtained, and the number of plants falling in each range of results. All of these SMAs have been performed for plants located east of the Rocky Mountains. The plant HCLPF capacities for these plants are between 0.12g and 0.3g. One plant (Quad Cities) originally reported a HCLPF capacity of 0.09g but the licensee proposed USI A-46 improvements that would raise the plant HCLPF capacity to at least the SSE level (0.24g).

It should also be noted that if a plant performed a reduced-scope evaluation, this evaluation was performed using input from the plant's seismic design basis (SSE spectra). Therefore, a reduced-scope evaluation does not convey the degree of seismic margin (i.e., does not produce a plant HCLPF). However, six of the plants whose HCLPFs are included in Figure 2.10, although in the focused- or full-scope category of NUREG-1407, performed only modified reduced-scope analyses. Therefore, their HCLPF values are limited to their SSE level. There are 10 plants that were placed in the reduced-scope category in NUREG-1407, and these were not asked to report plant HCLPF results. However, by successfully completing the IPEEE program, these 10 licensees have demonstrated that the plants' HCLPF capacities are close to or equal to the plant's design basis SSE.

All HCLPF values presented in Figure 2.10 for focused- and full-scope plant categories have been derived based on a NUREG/CR-0098 spectral shape for rock or soil (depending on the site conditions at the plant). For reduced-scope plants, the plant's design basis spectral shapes are used, which are mostly Housner or Newmark types, similar to the NUREG/C-0098 median spectrum shape.

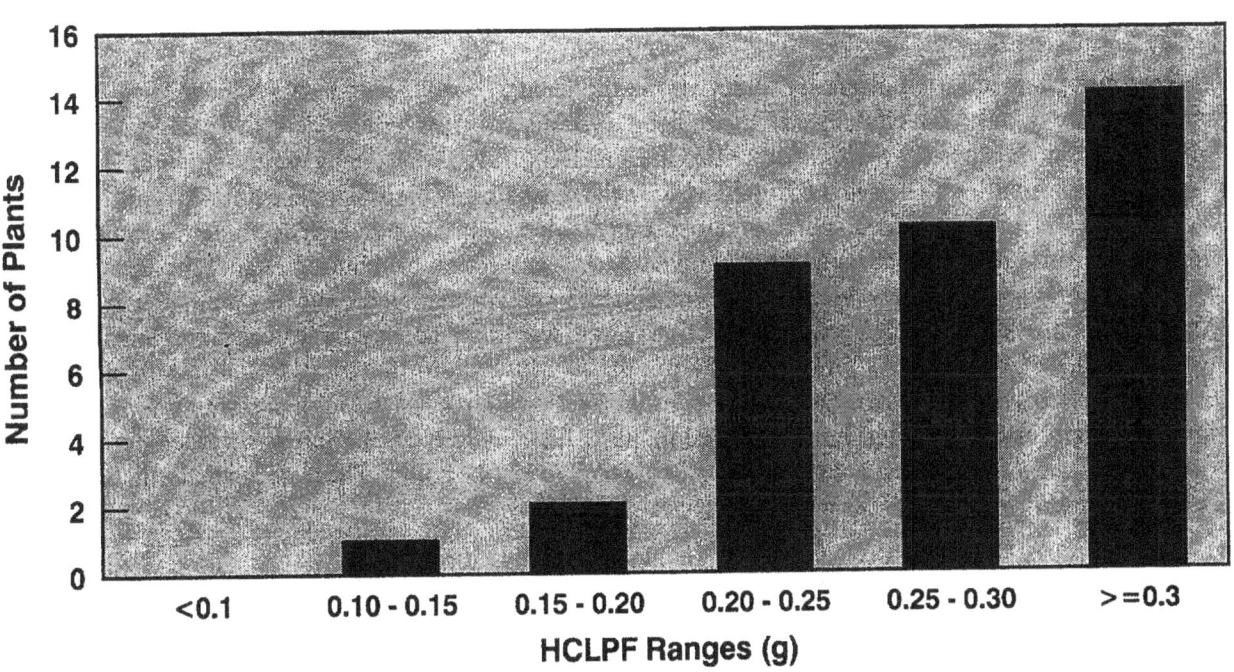

Figure 2.10 HCLPF results

Table 2.6 of Volume 2 of this report presents the HCLPF capacities and the spectral shape used in the analyses for the individual plants with SMA submittals.

2.3.3.2 SMA Insights

Perspectives on two elements of an SMA are considered below. First, insights regarding the development of the success paths are discussed, and then insights with respect to the plant HCLPF results obtained are treated.

Most of the IPEEEs that use the EPRI methodology follow the procedure prescribed in EPRI NP-6041, at least the minimum requirements. (Only two licensees performed an NRC SMA.) This procedure involves the development of success path logic diagrams (SPLDs), which depict, in a block diagram form, the sets of systems that represent the potential paths of success for satisfying the needed safety functions. The SPLD provides a logic diagram for a structured evaluation of the systems required to accomplish the four safety functions, and can be used to identify any "weak links" which might limit the plant's shutdown capability. With very few exceptions, SPLDs are used in the IPEEEs that performed an EPRI SMA.

The value of using an SPLD for system analysis can be demonstrated with the example of one IPEEE, which, rather than using an SPLD to define the scope of the review, included all safety-related components in the plant for a seismic assessment. Although this approach seems to provide a bigger equipment list, it cannot provide the valuable insights a structured evaluation using success paths can provide. For example, the impact of the failure of some of the systems that are included in the outliers list cannot be assessed without the help of success paths. Because of the potential failure of these systems under an RLE, a success path for a small LOCA condition could not be established. This problem was pointed out to the licensee in an RAI, and the problem was subsequently resolved.

The success paths are used primarily to determine the front line systems that are required to perform the safety functions. The development of the support systems for front line system and support-system-to-support-system dependency tables is described in EPRI NP-6041. Dependency tables are provided in about half of the submittals which used the EPRI SMA. In the remaining submittals, the plant PRA, performed for the plant IPE, is referred to for a source of dependency tables. Although system dependency evaluations in the IPEEEs were usually thorough, there were cases where the lack of required support components was found during submittal review to lead to the unavailability of a system in the success path. For example, in one IPEEE, one train of the high pressure injection system was found not available because an injection valve was not included in the SSEL. In another IPEEE, the success path for the small LOCA case did not work because the low pressure system, which provides the suction source for the high pressure injection system for sump recirculation cooling, is not included in the SSEL. Sump recirculation was needed because there was not sufficient water in the borated water storage tank to last 72 hours. These deficiencies in the success paths were rectified by licensees in response to RAIs.

In some EPRI SMA IPEEE submittals, licensees have not entirely followed the criteria for success path development, or the submittal has not contained sufficient information to permit verification of appropriate application of the criteria. Although all SMA IPEEEs include two success paths, with at least one success path capable of mitigating a small LOCA, they vary in terms of redundancy and diversity. The lack of redundancy or diversity is either due to the limitation of the actual systems available at the plant or due to the system selection process. For example, for a few PWR plants, pressurizer PORVs are not available, and the high pressure injection system does not have enough head to discharge into the reactor coolant system

(RCS) without depressurization. As a consequence, feed-and-bleed cooling cannot be performed in these plants, and RCS depressurization must rely on secondary-side cooling. The auxiliary feedwater system is therefore required for both success paths, presenting an obvious lack of diversity. In another example, both pressurizer PORVs and steam generator PORVs (or atmospheric dump valves) are not included in the SSEL because of their dependency on instrument air, which is assumed to be unavailable in a seismic event, and because of some anchorage problem for the steam generator PORV accumulators. The lack of these valves takes away the plant's capability of rapid RCS depressurization for RCS inventory control via the high pressure injection system.

Often the fewest systems possible are selected to construct a success path. In PWRs where the charging pumps of the chemical and volume control system (CVCS) have enough capacity and enough head to discharge into the RCS without RCS depressurization, these pumps are selected in the SSEL. Although some of these plants also have a separate high pressure safety injection system that operates at intermediate pressure, this system is not selected in the SSEL in most of the plants that have both systems. But other PWRs, where the pumps of the CVCS do not have enough capacity, must rely on the high pressure safety injection system operating at intermediate pressure for RCS inventory control. This means that RCS depressurization using the pressurizer PORV is also required for feed-and-bleed cooling.

Most BWRs have two high pressure systems that can be used for reactor system inventory control. Specifically, these include the reactor core isolation cooling (RCIC) system and the high pressure coolant injection (HPCI) system, or the high pressure core spray (HPCS) system. In most of the BWR IPEEEs that use the high pressure injection (HPI) system in a success path, both of these systems were selected in the SSEL to address a non-seismic failure concern raised in EPRI NP-6041. For some early BWR plants (BWR 2 or BWR 3) that are equipped with isolation condensers, there is either none, or only one, high pressure injection system. In one of these plants, only the low pressure system was selected in the SSEL. Although two success paths are identified in this submittal, they consist of redundant trains of the same system and really represent only one success path. The licensee stated that there is not sufficient justification to spend additional resources on an alternate path, and that the selected path would be more rugged than the alternate path that could be added to the seismic assessment.

A few other BWR plants, despite the availability of two high pressure systems, chose to use only low pressure systems in the success paths. This does not seem to be consistent with EPRI NP-6041, which states that "in general, the selected path for performing the safety functions to shutdown (sic) the reactor will be the one consisting of the front line systems (and their necessary support systems) that were provided as a 'first line of defense,' and designed to respond automatically (at least in the short time during and after the seismic margins earthquake) to the types of transients and/or accidents that might be induced by a margin earthquake." Based on this criterion, the HPI systems (i.e., HPCI and RCIC) seem to provide a better choice for coolant injection. In these analyses, the decision to select only low pressure systems is based on reasons that include concern regarding the reliability of the high pressure system, the desire to minimize the number of components to be evaluated (the low pressure system is required anyway), and the desire to include the automatic depressurization system (ADS) in the SSEL. In general, both low pressure systems (i.e., core spray and low pressure coolant injection) are included in the SSEL. In order to use the low pressure systems, operator initiated depressurization is required, and motive power to the relief valves (RVs) may be a concern.

In calculating plant HCLPFs, licensees have made significant efforts to reduce inherent conservatism in the seismic demand calculations. A majority of the plants performed new seismic analyses, and for soil sites, soil-structure interaction (SSI) effects are usually considered. As a result, many have achieved significant reductions in the seismic demands on the plant components. Therefore, the HCLPF capacities computed represent more realistic plant seismic capacities than conveyed by the design basis SSE capacities of the plants.

As with the SPRA results, a point of interest also for SMA plants is whether those designed and built to later seismic standards show different seismic margins than older plants built before some of the later design criteria were in place. In Figure 2.11 minimum plant HCLPF values are shown versus the date the plant went into commercial operation. It is important to remember when interpreting this figure that the 0.3g HCLPF value represents an upper limit due to the way the margin analyses were conducted. Since plants screened at the 0.3g level, they cannot claim a higher plant HCLPF, even though in some cases the actual HCLPF for the plant may be higher.

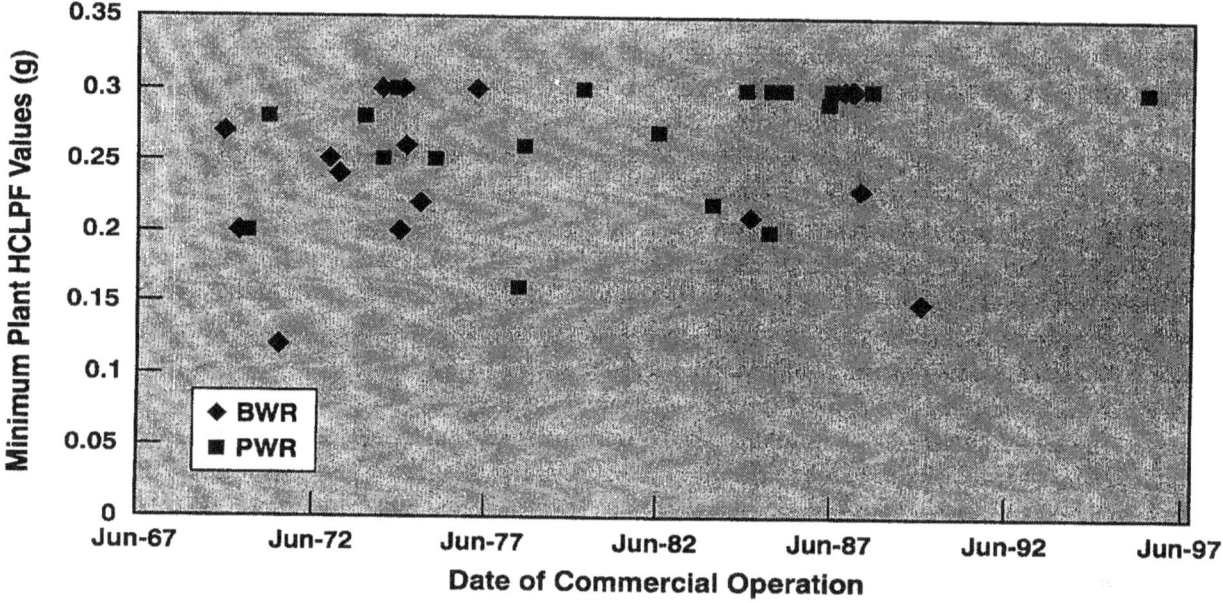

Figure 2.11 Plant HCLPF values versus date of commercial operation

The figure indicates that, with some exceptions, older plants have, in general, seismic margins similar to newer plants. It would be interesting to see if the HCLPF values for newer plants would increase if actual plant HCLPFs were obtained, not limited by the screening level of 0.3g, mentioned above. While some early plants have HCLPF values that are quite low, on the whole, most older plants show reasonably high HCLPF levels. As discussed above for SPRAs, this data gives reason to conclude that seismic backfit programs for older plants have, for the most part, successfully brought the plants' seismic margins up to those of the newer plants. It should be noted that, in general, a greater level of consistency has been observed in assumptions and procedures implemented for HCLPF calculations in the SMAs than for the fragility calculations performed for SPRAs. In other words, differences in analyses assumptions and methods were not as great for the SMAs and, therefore, can be assumed to have been less of a contributor to the variation in results obtained here than is true for the SPRA results.

To assess the seismic margins above the design basis for plants, based on their IPEEE margin findings, Figure 2.12 plots the minimum plant HCLPF value against the plant SSE level. As the figure indicates, the HCLPF is never below the SSE and generally exceeds the SSE for the given plants. With the exception of six plants where the HCLPF value is equal to the SSE level, the SMA studies are generally effective in demonstrating a level of seismic margin beyond the design basis.

The HCLPF values reported in the SMA submittals generally fall into one of three categories.

- A reported plant HCLPF at least equal to the 0.3g RLE. In most cases this required some physical improvements of lower capacity components.

- A plant HCLPF capacity less than the 0.3g RLE but greater than or equal to the SSE PGA. In some cases this required physical improvement of some low-capacity components, in others it did not.

- A reported seismic capacity equal to the design basis SSE, mostly as a result of a reduced-scope assessment.

As previously noted, a number of licensees conducted what amounts to a reduced-scope assessment even though their plants were binned into the 0.3g focused-scope category, according to NUREG-1407. In these cases attempts were made to elicit, through requests for additional information (RAIs), the HCLPF information. Where this was unsuccessful, or where the licensee indicated that their improvements would only raise the plant HCLPF value to the design basis earthquake level, the plant HCLPF capacity has been assigned a value equal to the design basis SSE in Figures 2.10 through 2.14. This is the case with the six plants whose value is equal to the SSE in Figure 2.12. For some of these plants it is likely that the real plant HCLPF capacity is somewhat higher than the design basis SSE.

No licensee reported a plant HCLPF capacity lower than the SSE PGA. Individual component HCLPF capacities below the SSE PGA were always identified for verification in the submittals.

The reported plant HCLPF capacities are based on the licensees' submittals, sometimes augmented by responses to the RAIs. It should be pointed out that concerns about the quality of reported component HCLPF capacities are documented in the NRC staff evaluations of the individual plant submittals. A concern which surfaced in a number of evaluations was the calculation of the HCLPF capacity of unreinforced masonry walls. Review of several calculations identified the use of excessive damping values (6 to 7%), which likely resulted in optimistic HCLPF capacities.

Figure 2.12 also differentiates between those plants which obtained HCLPF values based on a new structural analysis and those which based the HCLPF on scaling of the SSE analysis results. (The use of new structural analyses versus the use of scaling is discussed further in Section 2.4 of this report.) It is interesting to note that the HCLPF values for the plants using a new structural analysis are clustered more or less in two bands, one in the upper range of values (i.e., near 0.3g) and the other along or close to the SSE level. On the other hand, the HCLPF values based on scaling are scattered throughout the range of values. However, as discussed in Section 2.4 of this report, comparisons of the component seismic fragility/HCLPF values for plants using the two different approaches could be misleading.

In Figure 2.13 the same data is presented in a slightly different way: The ratio of the plant HCLPF value to the SSE value is plotted against the plant SSE level. This gives a better idea of the size of the margin involved. Again, the figure differentiates between those plants which obtained HCLPF values based on a new structural analysis and those which based the HCLPF on scaling of the SSE analysis results.

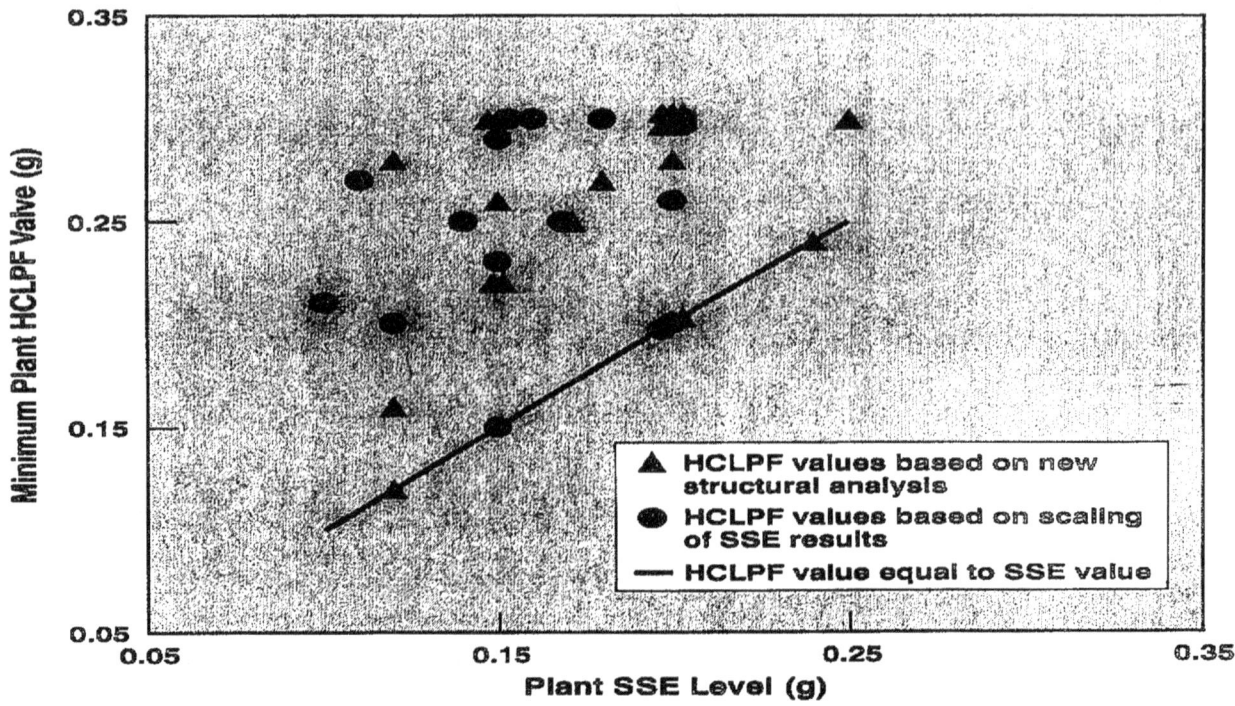

Figure 2.12 Minium plant HCLPF values versus plant SSE level

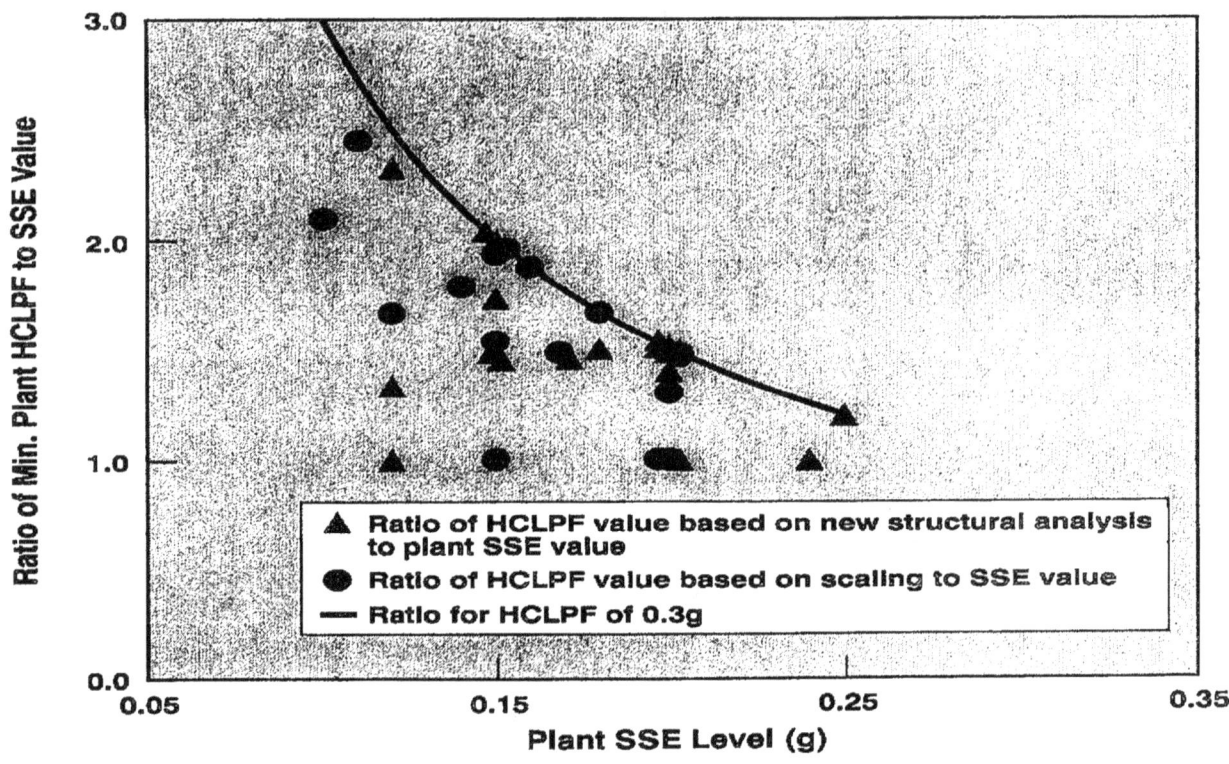

Figure 2.13 Ratio of plant HCLPF to SSE level versus SSE level

2.3.4 SPRA Compared to SMA

Important distinctions between perspectives drawn from SPRAs and those derived from SMAs pertain to the manner and effectiveness of demonstrating plant risk, impacts of non-seismic failures (i.e., random and operator failures), and plant seismic margin.

An SMA study does not convey a quantitative measure of seismic risk (i.e., seismic core damage frequency), and an EPRI SMA does not quantitatively account for the effects of non-seismic failures and operator errors. On the other hand, while a plant-level HCLPF can be derived from intermediate results developed in any SPRA, NUREG-1407 did not request such results as part of the IPEEE submittal and, hence, few of the IPEEE SPRA submittals contained an explicit quantitative measure of a plant's seismic margin beyond the design basis.

In reference to the IPEEE results from SMA studies, only qualitative perspectives should be developed regarding risk. In other words, for plants having plant-level HCLPF capacities significantly greater than their design basis (e.g., close to, or exceeding, the plant's RLE), it can be qualitatively expected that the seismic risk will be low, since the IPEEE review procedures for SMAs have roughly accounted for (a) the various levels of seismic hazard at plants, and (b) qualitative screening of non-seismic failures.

In reference to the IPEEE results from SPRA studies, only qualitative perspectives should be developed regarding seismic margin beyond the design basis. In other words, for plants found to have a low core damage frequency, it may be qualitatively anticipated that the plant has useful margin beyond the design basis, since (a) the IPEEE procedures for SPRAs include an appropriate screening evaluation and detailed plant walkdown, and (b) SPRAs are generally performed for plants where the seismic hazard is, comparatively speaking, not low.

Based on these qualitative arguments, it may be inferred from the results of the IPEEE program that, with some noteworthy exceptions, plants generally have low seismic risk (this can be qualitatively concluded even for those plants evaluated by means of SMA), and plants generally have significant seismic margin beyond the design basis.

In estimating the seismic CDF, some licensees have developed plant-level fragility curves in their IPEEE submittals. In such instances, the licensees reported plant-level HCLPF capacities. In other SPRA submittals, however, the licensees did not provide plant-level fragility curves but, in some of these cases, approximations to the plant-level fragility and HCLPF capacities may be inferred from the results presented in the submittal. As previously noted, although a plant-level HCLPF capacity can be determined from an SPRA study, the HCLPF capacities resulting from the SPRA approach should not generally be compared with the HCLPF capacities reported from SMA studies, primarily due to the fact that each evaluation approach uses a different type of input spectrum, and each approach is based on different procedures, assumptions, and objectives. Keeping in mind these caveats, Figure 2.14 plots plant HCLPFs against seismic CDF for 10 plants that reported both. The figure illustrates that there is a reasonable correlation between the two different measures (i.e., the higher the plant HCLPF, the smaller the seismic CDF).

Table 2.2 of Volume 2 of this report lists the HCLPF values provided for the individual plants with SPRA SPRA submittals, for which this value was available.

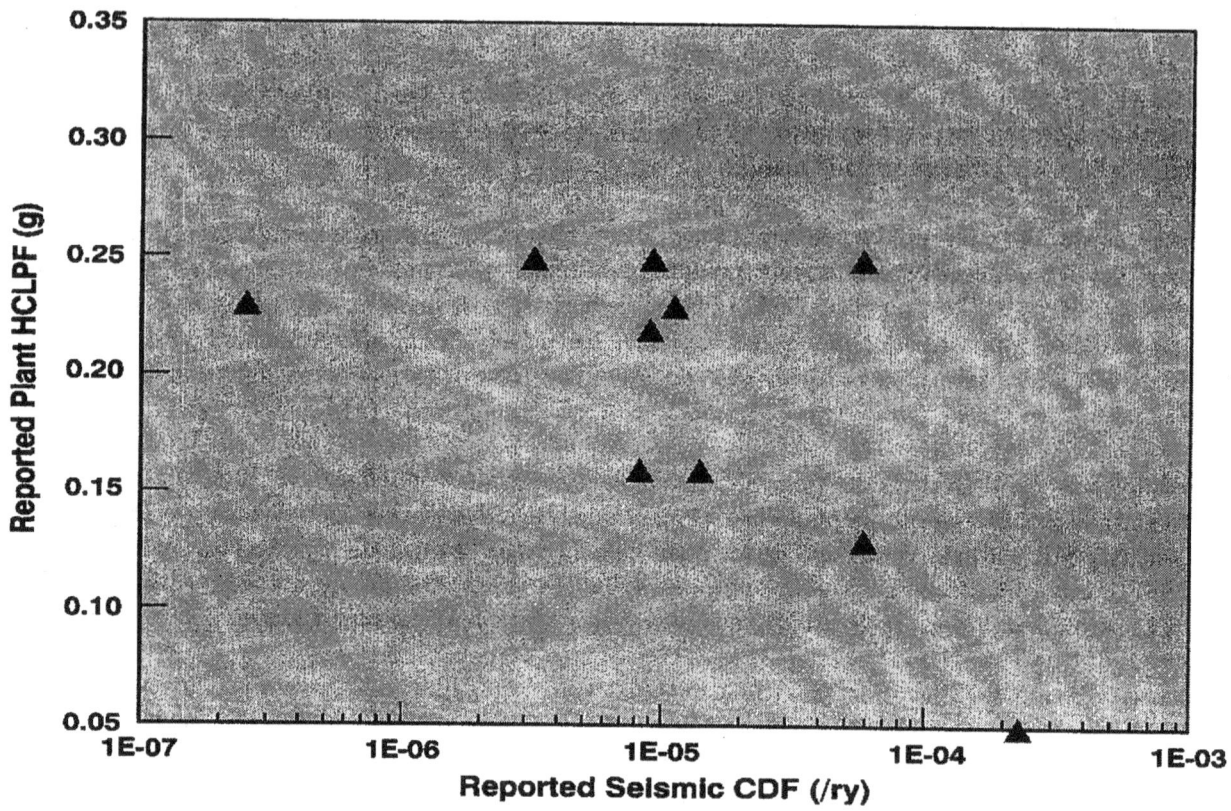

Figure 2.14 Correlation between HCLPF values and CDF for 10 plants

2.4   Methodological Issues

The review of the IPEEE seismic submittals identified a number of issues related to the varying methods used by the licensees to conduct their examination. A number of issues which appeared to have a significant influence on the results obtained are discussed below.

2.4.1   Use of the Uniform Hazard Spectrum (UHS)

The licensees of some plants in the EUS, when conducting their component fragility calculations, used UHS whose shapes differed from the conventional spectrum shapes derived from observed earthquakes. The energy content of these UHS appear to be reduced from that of the respective design basis SSE spectra, in the frequency range that is typically considered to have the greatest impact on the SSC responses to seismic motions. The seismic analyses using the UHS as input resulted in significant reduction (50% to about 70%) in seismic demand, compared to the corresponding design basis calculations.

Furthermore, since there was no consistent guidance provided for anchoring the UHS to the zero peak ground acceleration (ZPGA), the licensees in their SPRA analyses applied their engineering judgement for the anchorage of the UHS. For instance, one licensee anchored the UHS at 25 Hz, which the licensee believed to be the cutoff frequency for the plant SSC amplified responses to seismic motions (only rigid response exists). However, anchoring the UHS in such a manner is inconsistent with the method for establishing seismic initiating event frequencies and the subsequent SPRA quantification model and, therefore, may potentially underestimate the component seismic fragilities. This SPRA was subsequently revised in response to an NRC RAI. The UHS anchorage was changed from 25 Hz and 0.151g to 50 Hz and 0.096g (which was taken directly from the site hazard curve), and the licensee revised the fragility calculations and the final CDF estimate accordingly. The revised results showed a reduction in the seismic fragility calculations by 36%, and an increase in the final seismic CDF value by 41% for one unit and 93% for the other unit. The lack of guidance on the UHS anchorage appeared to have measurable impacts on the quality of the seismic fragility calculations and the seismic CDF quantification.

2.4.2   Use of a Surrogate Element in SPRAs

The basis and approach for surrogate element modeling are discussed in EPRI TR-103959 [EPRI, 1993]. The overall concept of the surrogate element is to account quantitatively (albeit approximately) for the risk contribution of components that are screened out during the walkdown and screening phase of an SPRA. Hence, the failure of a single surrogate element represents the potential failures of several components that might normally be excluded from the SPRA model. Use of the surrogate element helps to ensure that the SPRA does not overlook a potentially significant portion of the seismic CDF. Use of a surrogate element represents acceptable SPRA practice when (1) screening is performed at a sufficiently high threshold, (2) the capacity of the surrogate element is appropriately assessed to be consistent with the screening threshold, and (3) the surrogate element is appropriately included in the seismic plant logic model. Otherwise, the usefulness and validity of SPRA findings may be compromised.

If the surrogate element is used to represent a low screening threshold, resulting in relatively few components having lower capacity than the surrogate element, dominant risk contributors can be masked, and the ranking of dominant sequences may be misleading. If the surrogate element is applied to represent a reasonably high screening threshold, but is not used appropriately in the seismic plant logic model, then a fraction of the seismic CDF may be missed in quantification. Such undesirable cases are more related to pitfalls associated with improper application of the surrogate element, rather than flaws in the conceptual basis for the surrogate element itself. Therefore, the use and implications of the findings and perspectives derived from some of the SPRA IPEEEs that have applied the surrogate element approach need to be treated carefully.

Table 2.2 in Volume 2 of this report identifies the plants where the surrogate elements were employed. Of the 27 SPRA studies, 12 made use of a surrogate element in one form or another.

To date, an adequately detailed investigation of the implications of using the surrogate element in IPEEEs has not been undertaken. No regulatory guidelines have been developed concerning its use (particularly with respect to sensitivities in plant logic modeling). However, in most circumstances, if failure of the surrogate element is modeled as leading to core damage, and if the surrogate element is found to be only a minor contributor to seismic CDF, then its use is probably reasonable.

From Table 2.3 of Volume 2 of this report, it can be observed that 7 of the 27 SPRA studies reported the undesirable situation that the surrogate element was identified as a dominant CDF contributor. This is a small, but noteworthy fraction of all submittals (10%).

When examined individually, the plant-specific findings of those submittals that identified the surrogate element as a dominant contributor may be limited, to varying degrees, with respect to producing robust SPRA-type insights. Although undesirable, this situation may not be as serious as might be initially thought, since the studies are usually still capable of (a) identifying outliers, (b) producing substantially legitimate

SMA-type insights, and (c) reasonably demonstrating that the seismic CDF is expected to be low. Points a and b are apparent when considering that (1) the surrogate/screening levels for the noted plants are at least equal to the RLE values designated in NUREG-1407, (2) thorough seismic screening walkdowns have been performed, and (3) generally appropriate HCLPF capacities (or fragilities) have been computed for all unscreened components. Point c is apparent by examining the approximate seismic CDF estimates for these plants in Table 2.2 in Volume 2 of this report, and noting that these values are typically small. Although the seismic CDF results for these plants are somewhat questionable, they may have meaning as first order approximations. Hence, the most serious problem with those studies that have identified the surrogate element as a dominant risk contributor is the compromised insights into the identification and ranking of dominant risk contributors.

2.4.3 The Use of New Soil-Structure Interaction Calculations Versus the Use of Scaling

Two approaches were used in the IPEEEs for developing the RLE in-structure response spectra (IRS). The first approach is associated with scaling the existing design basis SSE IRS to the RLE IRS, following the procedure as outlined in EPRI NP-6041. While this approach was applied mostly by the plants founded on rock, which is appropriate under the guideline given in EPRI NP-6041, it should be noted that a few plants founded on soil also performed this scaling. The application of the scaling method for structures founded on soil was often justified by the licensees by stating that (1) the shapes of the RLE and SSE design ground spectra are relatively similar and the SSE IRS used for the scaling are broadened spectra. Therefore, if there is any shift in frequency due to the soil effect, it should be small and its effect on the scaling should be negligible, and (2) the damping applied in the scaling is much smaller than the damping associated with the radiation damping if the soil effects were considered. Therefore, scaling was felt to still produce conservative RLE IRS.

The second approach used in IPEEEs requires the performance of a new seismic analysis, including the soil effect, or the soil-structure interaction (SSI) effect and the detailed structural modeling. This approach was utilized by the majority of plants founded on soil for the RLE IRS development. Many of the licensees performed detailed seismic analyses, using either the direct method (FLUSH) [Lysmer, 1975] or the substructure method (SASSI [Lysmer, 1981] or CLASSI [Wong, 1980]), and followed closely the guidelines given in EPRI NP-6041 for the consideration of the uncertainties in soils. One plant performed a simplified seismic analysis, which included direct comparisons of the free field motions at the surface and foundation level, and comparisons of the IRS using the simple analysis with a lumped mass stick model. Regardless of the methods applied, it was noted that the new seismic analyses achieved substantial, across-the-board reductions in the RLE IRS compared to the SSE IRS, when the SSI effects were introduced in the seismic analysis. It was also noted that in many cases, especially for deep soil sites, the deconvolution analysis often produced much higher reduction of the free field motion from the ground surface to the basemat than would be permissible in the design process.

When the scaling was used, the fragility/HCLPF computations inherited the conservatisms that existed in the design basis analyses, whereas new SSI analyses usually remove as much conservatism as allowed, sometimes going well beyond what would be permissible in design practice. It was observed that for the plants using the scaling, the scaled RLE IRS is generally higher than the corresponding SSE IRS, whereas for those plants that performed new SSI analyses, the seismic analyses often resulted in much lower RLE IRS demand than the design basis SSE IRS. Therefore, comparisons of the component seismic fragility/HCLPF values for two plants using the two different approaches could be misleading. The different approaches to estimating building and component seismic responses (scaling versus new SSI calculations) can significantly affect the magnitude of the reported fragility (or CDF) or HCLPF values. Hence, comparison of the seismic capacities should be made mainly among plants which were analyzed using similar methods.

2.4.4 Reliance on Structures for Which the Original Design Documentation Is No Longer Available

Some plants identified dams designed by other agencies (Corps of Engineers, Bureau of Reclamation, etc.) as critical SSCs for providing emergency cooling water or ac power. In one case, although the dam is not under the quality assurance program and control of the licensee, it has been reviewed by the licensee and its consultant and found to be able to successfully withstand the RLE without catastrophic failure. The availability of lake water to support the plant's service water system is thus not jeopardized.

In another plant, a dam failure was identified as leading to the depletion of the water supply to the containment cooling service water, which provides cooling water to the low pressure coolant injection for decay heat removal. This limited the plant's capability to perform an orderly safe shutdown following a seismic event. However, since this dam was designed by other agencies, in this particular case no documentation of the original design was available for review. Therefore, the seismic capacity of the dam could not be determined. This type of weak link, resulting from an SSC outside the plant boundary and not under plant control, could not be resolved and documented without coordination and consultation with the relevant agencies involved.

2.4.5 Importance of the Analyst's Expertise in Component Fragility/HCLPF Assessments

While a complete, detailed examination of a licensee's component fragility/HCLPF assessments was beyond the scope of the IPEEE review, selected fragility calculations were requested from licensees for certain components that were reported in the IPEEE submittals as having unusually higher capacity than expected from past SPRA experiences.

A limited review of selected fragility calculations suggests that the analyst's expertise in component fragility/HCLPF assessments and his (her) prior experience in conducting such calculations is a significant factor in the quality of the component fragility calculations. Some calculations reviewed represented good quality fragility/HCLPF assessments, which followed very closely past SPRA practice in the nuclear industry, and reflected the analyst's expertise in the fragility estimates.

Other calculations lacked material documentation and, in some cases, used unrealistic estimates of uncertainties. In one instance, the licensee acknowledged the misuse of certain design information in the fragility calculation. In another case involving a structure with the failure mode controlled by soil liquefaction, the structural fragility was presented with a randomness uncertainty equal to 0.14 due to soil liquefaction. This is very low considering the highly probabilistic nature of soil liquefaction.

2.5 Unresolved Safety Issues and Generic Safety Issues

Most of the seismic IPEEE submittals reviewed for this report have included information regarding (where applicable) many of the following unresolved safety issues (USIs) and generic safety issues (GSIs):

- USI A-46, "Verification of Seismic Adequacy of Equipment in Operating Plants,"
- USI A-40, "Seismic Design Criteria,"
- USI A-17, "Seismic Interactions in Nuclear Power Plants,"
- USI A-45, "Shutdown Decay Heat Removal Requirements,"
- GSI-131, "Potential Systems Interactions Involving the Movable In-Core Flux Mapping System in Westinghouse Plants," and
- Eastern U.S. Seismicity Issue (i.e., Charleston Earthquake Issue).

In addition, the seismic IPEEE submittals have provided information related to the following generic safety issues (GSIs):

- GSI-156, "Systematic Evaluation Program (SEP)," and
- GSI-172, "Multiple System Responses Program (MSRP)."

USI A-46 has been verified separately from the seismic IPEEEs, and, hence, is not extensively addressed in the IPEEE submittal reviews. USIs A-40 and A-17 are subsumed as part of the licensees' USI A-46 programs. As indicated in NUREG-1407, the Eastern U.S. seismicity issue is resolved with the submittal of a satisfactory IPEEE. Thus, the following subsections focus on discussions related to USI A-45, GSI-131, GSI-156, and GSI-172.

2.5.1 USI A-45, "Shutdown Decay Heat Removal Requirements"

Whether a licensee uses an SPRA or an SMA for the seismic IPEEE, the capability of decay heat removal (DHR) functions is directly included by definition. Thus, any findings encountered in the IPEEE with respect to seismic capability of DHR functions are also applicable to USI A-45. In other words, for seismic events, USI A-45 perspectives are a subset of the IPEEE perspectives. Consequently, the IPEEE submittals have generally reiterated those seismic IPEEE findings pertaining to DHR capability as the basis for verification of USI A-45. Such an approach is valid.

However, any weaknesses in the seismic IPEEE with respect to the assessment of DHR functions will be mirrored as weaknesses in the treatment of USI A-45. As a result of the IPEEE screening efforts, licensees have encountered some significant seismic outliers related to the capability of the DHR function at their plant (e.g., weak anchorage of RHR heat exchangers), and these outliers are listed in Tables 2.4 and 2.7 of Volume 2 of this report. For additional discussion of USI A-45, see Section 5.4.1 of this report.

2.5.2 GSI-131, "Potential Systems Interactions Involving the Movable In-Core Flux Mapping System in Westinghouse Plants"

GSI-131 applies only to Westinghouse plants that have a movable in-core flux mapping system. For 39 of the 69 plants, GSI-131 is not relevant. For 3 of the 30 Westinghouse plants, the flux mapping cart is in an immobile configuration. For 19 of the remaining 27 cases, licensees had previously addressed this issue through specific plant improvements or analyses, and the issue was considered by those licensees as being verified. For the remaining plants, the licensees have performed reviews on the movable in-core flux mapping system restraints and found them to be seismically adequate.

In some cases, the licensees undertook a walkdown to verify the installation of a previous improvement as part of the seismic IPEEE. Some plants implemented hardware improvements related to GSI-131 by either replacing the flux mapping system cart hold down bolts or installing stiffener and anchor assemblies for the mapping carts. A few submittals (at least 13 of 30) indicated that licensees evaluated the capability of the flux mapping system for RLE loads. In one case, the licensee implemented an administrative procedure to help eliminate the potential for an interaction hazard involving an overhead chain hoist. In another submittal, the existing configuration of the movable flux mapping system was found to be adequate provided operators reinstalled bolts connecting the cart frame to its supporting beams whenever the cart was moved into position above the seal table.

Overall, licensees have generally undertaken appropriate actions, either preceding the IPEEE program or as part of the seismic IPEEE, to address GSI-131. The treatment of this issue by individual plants is presented in Table 2.13 of Volume 2 of this report. For additional discussion of GSI-131, see Section 5.4.4 of this report.

2.5.3   GSI-156, "Systematic Evaluation Program (SEP)"

Regarding GSI-156, the seismic IPEEE submittals for applicable plants provided relevant information concerning some or all of the following seismic-related issues:

- settlement of foundations and buried equipment,
- dam integrity and site flooding,
- design codes, criteria, and load combinations, and
- seismic design of structures, systems, and components.

The NRC and the IPEEE guidance documents have not explicitly requested that licensees discuss GSI-156 in their IPEEE submittals. Nonetheless, relevant information has been found in the licensees' submittals that is useful in verifying the related issues listed above for each applicable plant. For additional discussion of GSI-156, see Section 5.4.7 of this report.

2.5.4   GSI-172, "Multiple System Responses Program (MSRP)"

Regarding GSI-172, the seismic IPEEE submittals for applicable plants provided relevant information concerning some or all of the following seismic-related issues:

- seismically induced spatial and functional interactions,
- seismically induced fires,
- seismically induced fire suppression system actuation,
- seismically induced flooding,
- seismically induced relay chatter,
- evaluation of earthquake magnitudes greater than the safe shutdown earthquake, and effects of hydrogen line ruptures, and
- failures related to human errors.

The NRC and IPEEE guidance documents have not explicitly requested that licensees discuss GSI-172 in their IPEEE submittals. Nonetheless, relevant information has been found in the licensees' submittals that may be useful in verifying the related issues listed above for each applicable plant. For additional discussion of GSI-172, see Section 5.4.8 of this report.

2.6   Summary and Conclusions

Seismic perspectives were derived in this chapter with the objective to provide perspectives in the following areas:

- description of the overall IPEEE seismic process, findings, and impacts,
- overview of plant improvements related to the seismic portion of the IPEEE program, with a description of their beneficial impact on reactor safety,
- summary of the extent to which the licensees have met the intent of Supplement 4 to GL 88-20, as it pertains to seismic analyses,
- identification and assessment of the impacts of site-specific seismic hazards, plant-specific design and operational features, and modeling and screening assumptions that affect the understanding of a plant's severe accident behavior and containment performance in response to a seismic event, and
- description of the overall strengths and weaknesses in the implementation of seismic evaluation methodologies, including the implications of assumptions made in the IPEEEs.

2.6.1   Seismic Process, Findings, and Impacts

As requested in NUREG-1407, licensees used one of two methodologies to conduct their seismic IPEEEs. The first is a seismic probabilistic risk assessment (SPRA) consisting of at least a Level 1 analysis and a qualitative containment performance analysis. The second is a seismic margins method, including a qualitative containment performance analysis. Both methods satisfy the objectives of the seismic IPEEE, in that they both include a systematic, comprehensive walkdown of important components, and are both capable of identifying plant vulnerabilities. The scope of the seismic examination for a particular plant depends on the location of the plant, with higher hazard sites undertaking more extensive investigations. Therefore, plants fell into the following categories: reduced-scope, focused-scope, full-scope, or committed to perform an SPRA.

Almost all licensees reported in their IPEEE submittals that no plant "vulnerabilities" were identified with respect to seismic risk (the use of the term vulnerability varied widely among the IPEEE submittals). However, most licensees did report at least some seismic "anomalies," "outliers," and/or other concerns. In the few submittals which identified a seismic "vulnerability," the concerns identified were comparable to concerns identified as outliers or anomalies in other submittals.

Quantitative findings of the examinations and associated insights are discussed below.

- With respect to SPRA analyses, assuming proposed improvements are in place (including both LLNL and EPRI hazard curves), the largest group of plants reported seismic CDFs between 1E-5 and 1E-4 per reactor-year (/ry), with the next largest group falling between 1E-6 and 1E-5/ry. Only a small fraction of plants had CDFs higher than 1E-4/ry or less than 1E-6/ry. The point-estimate seismic

CDFs obtained from the analyses with the EPRI hazard curves vary from about 1.9E-7/ry to 5.9E-5/ry.

- The results obtained from the SPRA analyses also indicate that newer plants (i.e., those designed and built to later seismic standards) show CDFs similar to those of older plants built before some of the later design criteria were in place. This data gives reason to conclude that seismic backfit programs for older plants have successfully brought their plants' CDF estimates in line with those of the newer plants.

- With respect to SMA results, plant HCLPF capacities for the 36 plants in the full- and focused-scope category of NUREG-1407 that performed SMAs are between 0.12g and 0.3g. These results assume proposed improvements are in place. Fourteen licensees reported plant HCLPFs of at least 0.3g (due to the screening levels used, no plant could claim a HCLPF greater than 0.3g), 10 plants fell between 0.25 and 0.3g, 9 plants were between 0.2 and 0.25g, and 2 plants were between 0.15 and 0.2g. One plant reported a HCLPF value of 0.12g.

- As with the SPRA results, the seismic margins of older plants built before some of the later design criteria were in place are similar to the margins of the newer plants. Again, it must be remembered that since components were screened at 0.3g, no plants could claim a HCLPF greater than 0.3g, even if calculated HCLPF values for unscreened components exceeded 0.3g.

- With the proposed improvements taken into account, SMA results indicate that for all plants the HCLPF is never below the SSE and generally exceeds the SSE. The SMA studies are generally effective in demonstrating a level of seismic margin beyond the design basis for these plants.

- Dominant contributors from SPRAs for seismic failure involve the failure of the electrical systems, which includes the failure of the offsite power (17% of all contributors); the failure of the various components of the electrical system (17%), such as the MCCs, the load centers, switchgear, and relays; the failure of the emergency diesel generator (EDG) (8%); and the failure of the dc batteries (5%). Building and structural failures also contribute significantly (30% of all contributors). Other structures of whose failure could cause core damage include block walls, pump house/pump intake structures, dams, and stacks. Front line and support systems (28% of all contributors), as well as tank failures (11%), also contribute to core damage.

- The weak link components identified in the SMA analyses in general were similar to the SSCs listed as dominant contributors in the SPRAs. Components identified as outliers in the SMAs included many electrical components and their anchorages, various tanks, RHR heat exchangers, and structures like the turbine and auxiliary buildings. Many licensees identified block walls located in the proximity of safety-significant equipment as weak link structures.

Other qualitative findings and associated insights are as follows.

- The common denominator for the seismic IPEEE evaluations was a well-conducted, detailed walkdown to find as-designed, as-built, and as-operated seismic weaknesses in plants. Regardless of the specific approach used, all plants performed a detailed seismic walkdown, and many of the insights gained by licensees resulted from the walkdowns. Seismic walkdowns have been performed by trained and qualified personnel. Often the walkdowns identified seismic concerns whose correction proved to be relatively simple and cost effective. For sites where the seismic hazard is low (i.e., where a reduced-scope seismic margins method is considered adequate), the detailed walkdowns were the most significant product of the IPEEE process.

- Low-ruggedness relays were identified in several seismic IPEEE analyses. Since many relay concerns were identified and verified under the A-46 program, when low-ruggedness relays were identified solely in the seismic analysis of the IPEEE program, licensees often determined that the chatter of these relays would have no adverse consequences.

- Most submittals provided some level of discussions on liquefaction, if the plants examined were founded on soil. For earthquakes beyond the design basis, a potential for liquefaction-related failures was identified as a contributor to risk at a few sites.

- All of the IPEEE submittals provided some treatment or discussion of non-seismic failures and human actions. However, the seismic impacts on operator error rates were modeled with a wide variety of approaches. In some instances, licensees developed simplified operator error fragilities. In other instances, licensees applied scaling factors (in relation to the importance of the human action) to internal event error rates, or used other means to account for seismic-related performance shaping factors.

- All licensees qualitatively examined seismic-fire interaction and seismic-flood issues and in many of the IPEEE submittals, the seismic-fire and/or seismic-flood interaction evaluations revealed concerns. In a number of instances, the examination resulted in significant plant improvements. Some of the relevant improvements include strengthening component anchorages, replacing vulnerable (e.g., mercury) relays and switches, restraining gas cylinders, waterproofing, replacing sight glass tubes, and implementing procedures to properly secure transient fire-protection equipment.

- All licensees performed walkdowns of their containments. Licensees did not report any anomalous conditions with respect to containment structural integrity. However, in a few instances, they identified outliers pertaining to containment penetrations and containment cooling.

- All IPEEEs underwent a peer review process to confirm that the IPEEE conformed with GL 88-20, Supplement 4, and to ensure the overall quality of the IPEEE process. Based on the information in the submittals it appears that the seismic part of the peer review process was generally carried out successfully.

Most of the seismic IPEEE submittals also included information on the following USIs and GSIs:

- USI A-45, "Shutdown Decay Heat Removal Requirements,"
- GSI-131, "Potential Systems Interactions Involving the Movable In-Core Flux Mapping System in Westinghouse Plants,"
- GSI-156, "Systematic Evaluation Program (SEP)," and
- GSI-172, "Multiple System Responses Program (MSRP)."

2.6.2   Plant Improvements

Most licensees identified a number of improvements to enhance the seismic ruggedness of their plants. In some cases these plant improvements were only proposed in the submittals, while in others the submittals indicated the improvements were already implemented. Improvements vary from simple housekeeping enhancements to more elaborate plant design modifications and can generally be grouped into three general categories: hardware modifications, improved procedures and training, and enhanced maintenance and housekeeping. In keeping with the expectation of GL 88-20, the majority of the implemented/proposed improvements, while enhancing the plants' resistance to a seismic event, do not involve significant cost. Relevant insights were as follows.

- Seventy percent of the plants proposed improvements as a result of their seismic IPEEE analyses.

- Of plants that proposed plant improvements, 84% included some form of hardware changes, often involving the addition of new anchorages or supports, or strengthening existing ones. Many of the modifications carried out were similar to ones carried out under the USI A-46 program, but were extended to more SSCs under the IPEEE, since the IPEEE scope was broader than that of USI A-46.

- Block walls were identified in many IPEEEs either as significant contributors to CDF or as controlling elements for plant HCLPF capacity.

- About 60% of the plants that proposed plant improvements included maintenance/housekeeping as part of the improvements, including the improvement of maintenance conduct and training, the correction of housekeeping errors; the issuance of new housekeeping standards; other corrective actions, such as the restraining of gas bottles, scaffolding, and ladders; corrective actions to address loose or missing fasteners, bolts, and clamps; and actions for rust protection.

- About 20% of plants that proposed plant improvements included the addition of new or revised procedures and training for seismic events as part of the improvements.

- Based on the improvements described by licensees it is clear that the seismic IPEEE program has had a notable impact on improving plant safety. At the time the licensees submitted their IPEEEs, some of these improvements had already been implemented, some improvements were planned, and some were still under consideration.

2.6.3   Meeting the Intent of Supplement 4 to GL 88-20

Based on results of the IPEEE submittal reviews, whose goal was to verify that a licensee's IPEEE process was capable of identifying seismic vulnerabilities and cost-effective safety improvements, the IPEEE program has been successful in meeting the overall intent of GL 88-20, Supplement 4, for the following reasons.

- As a result of the program, licensees have obtained an increased appreciation of severe accident behavior at their individual plants resulting from seismic initiators. Licensees have participated in the plant walkdowns and analyses related to estimating seismic risk.

- Licensees have gained a qualitative, and in some cases a quantitative, understanding of the most likely severe accidents that may occur as a result of a seismic initiator. This includes an understanding of the dominant contributors to seismic risk and/or the weak links in successfully avoiding or mitigating that risk.

- A qualitative understanding of the likelihood of core damage and fission product release at their plants has been generally attained by licensees. Licensees have searched for vulnerabilities and outliers related to potential core damage accidents stemming from seismic initiators.

- Licensees have carried out numerous modifications to reduce the likelihood of core damage and fission product releases. The IPEEE program clearly has had a notable impact on improving plant safety, based on the improvements made by licensees in response to the program.

The degree of success achieved by licensees varied, depending on the methods and assumptions used.

2.6.4 Seismic Evaluation Methods and Strengths and Weaknesses

Review of the IPEEE results, especially the SPRA results, indicates that the broad variability in these results cannot be attributed only to variation in plant design and location. Rather, the broad plant-to-plant variability probably results from a combination of many factors, including differences in methods and analytical assumptions. It should be noted that, in general, a greater level of consistency has been observed in assumptions and procedures implemented for HCLPF calculations in the SMAs than for the fragility calculations and other analyses performed for SPRAs.

Some of the more important variations identified in the reviews were as follows.

- Licensees have used a variety of hazard results (or a combination of hazard results) to calculate CDFs. In many cases, the spectral shape used in evaluating fragilities and the hazard curve used for quantifying CDF were not derived from a consistent set of hazard results. For example, the uniform hazard spectrum (UHS) derived from the 1989 LLNL hazard analysis has typically been used to define the SPRA spectral shape, whereas the seismic hazard curve derived from the 1989 EPRI or 1994 LLNL hazard analyses has typically been used to quantify CDF.

- Seismic fragility evaluations for the subset of components selected for risk quantification (components not screened) were carried out using various methods. These methods include fragility analysis, generic information, and testing. In general, SPRAs liberally employed various forms of simplified fragility analyses, in contrast to the predominance of detailed, conventional fragility analyses in past SPRAs. The use of simplified fragilities raises the possibility that in some cases the relative importance of the dominant contributors to the seismic CDF may be overstated or understated.

- A limited review of selected fragility calculations suggests that the analyst's prior experience in conducting such calculations is a significant factor in the quality of the component fragility calculations. Of the calculations reviewed, some were of good quality, while other calculations lacked material documentation and, in some cases, used unrealistic estimates of uncertainties.

- In calculating plant HCLPFs, significant efforts have been made by the licensees to reduce inherent conservatism in the seismic demand calculations. Many of the plants performed new seismic analyses, and for soil sites, soil-structure interaction (SSI) effects were usually considered. As a result, many have achieved significant reductions in the seismic demands on the plant components. Therefore, the HCLPF capacities computed represent more realistic plant seismic capacities than conveyed by the design basis SSE capacities of the plants.

- For the plants that performed new SSI analyses, the seismic analyses often resulted in much lower RLE IRS demand than the design basis SSE IRS. Therefore, comparisons of the component seismic fragility/HCLPF values for two plants using the two different approaches (scaling versus new SSI calculations) could be misleading. The different approaches to estimating building and component seismic responses can significantly affect the magnitude of the reported fragility (or CDF) or HCLPF values. Hence, comparison of the seismic capacities should be made mainly among plants which were analyzed using similar methods.

- In some EPRI SMA IPEEE submittals, licensees have not entirely followed the criteria for success path development, or the submittal has not contained sufficient information to permit verification of appropriate application of the criteria. Although all SMAs include two success paths, the success paths vary in terms of redundancy and diversity. The lack of redundancy or diversity is due either to the actual limitation of the systems available at the plant or to the system selection process.

- The licensees of some plants in the EUS, when conducting their component fragility calculations, used UHS whose shapes differed from the conventional spectrum shapes derived from observed earthquakes. The energy content of these UHS appears to be reduced from that of the respective design basis SSE spectra, in the frequency range that is typically considered to have the greatest impact on the SSC responses to seismic motions. The seismic analyses using the UHS as input resulted in significant reduction in seismic demand, compared to the corresponding design basis calculations.

- To date, an adequately detailed investigation of the implications of using the surrogate element in the IPEEEs has not been undertaken. No regulatory guidelines have been developed concerning its use (particularly with respect to sensitivities in plant logic modeling). If the surrogate element is found to be only a minor contributor to seismic CDF, then its use is probably reasonable. The most serious problem with those studies that have identified the surrogate element as a dominant risk contributor is the compromised insights into the identification and ranking of dominant risk contributors.

- The possibility of soil failures as the result of earthquakes beyond the design basis is a potential concern at some plants. It may be difficult to provide a significant enhancement over the plant's current capability in a cost-effective manner. It should be noted that currently there are no general recommendations (or even a consensus) on the best approach to estimating liquefaction-induced soil displacement. Therefore, a significant amount of uncertainty still exists with respect to these liquefaction studies performed for the IPEEE program.

- Human actions were treated in SPRAs using a wide variety of approaches. In most SPRAs, human error probabilities were based on the values developed for the IPE models, usually modified with some simplified means for accounting for seismic-related performance shaping factors, and without strong technical bases for the values chosen. For SMAs, the timing and location of human actions was usually reported, along with qualitative comments on their reliability.

3. FIRE INSIGHTS

3.1 Introduction

3.1.1 Objectives

The objectives of this chapter are to discuss the results and findings presented in licensees' IPEEE fire analysis submittals, and to identify fire risk insights gained as a result of those analyses.

3.1.2 Organization

This chapter deals exclusively with the IPEEE fire analyses. The discussions focus on licensee-reported fire vulnerabilities, fire safety plant improvements identified through the IPEEE process, fire-induced severe accident results, and methodological insights gained through the IPEEE process. These discussions are organized in three major sections as follows.

- Section 3.2 discusses the impact that the IPEEE process has had on reactor safety. This includes a discussion of fire vulnerabilities, plant modifications, and fire safety improvements identified in the IPEEE fire analyses.

- Section 3.3 summarizes the direct results of the IPEEE fire analyses, as reported by licensees. These results are presented in various contexts, generally focusing on the fire-induced core damage frequency (CDF) as the measure of fire risk.

- Section 3.4 discusses specific methodological aspects and related insights of the fire analyses performed by licensees. Section 3.4 itself is organized based on the general steps undertaken in performing a fire risk analysis.

3.1.3 Background

This section provides a brief historical overview of U.S. nuclear power plant (NPP) fire protection strategies and regulation. The information presented here is largely based on the discussions presented in Draft Regulatory Guide (DG) 1097 [U.S. NRC, 2000]. This historical perspective is considered important to understanding the results and insights gained through the IPEEE process. This section also provides a context for later discussions regarding issues such as trends in the fire risk results based on plant vintage.

During the early stages of nuclear power plant construction and licensing, fire protection was implemented based on the performance objectives of General Design Criterion (GDC) 3 in Appendix A to 10 CFR Part 50. GDC 3 set general goals for the fire protection program, but did not provide specific implementation guidance. Hence, fire protection was largely based on compliance with local fire codes and with the requirements of insurance underwriters. As a result, fire protection was based largely on best practices as established for other industrial facilities including, in particular, fossil fuel power plants.

In March 1975, a fire occurred at Browns Ferry NPP Unit 1. This fire led to fundamental changes in the regulatory approach to NPP fire protection. The fire damaged multiple safety systems, and operator-initiated repairs were required to achieve safe shutdown of the reactor. The NRC investigations into this event identified significant fire protection deficiencies, and ultimately led to the development of a new set of fire protection guidelines and requirements.

The first new guidelines appeared in Branch Technical Position (BTP) APCSB 9.5-1. These guidelines applied to plants that were issued a construction permit after July 1, 1976, and established the "defense in depth" concept for fire protection. In November 1980, the U.S. NRC published a new set of fire protection requirements as 10 CFR 50.48 and Appendix R to 10 CFR Part 50. Additional guidance has been provided via a number of generic letters (GLs) including GL 77-002, GL 81-12, GL 83-33, GL-85-01, GL 86-10, and GL 88-12. Additional guidance was also provided in Section 9.5.1 of the NRC's "Standard Review Plan" (NUREG-0800) [U.S.NRC, 1987]. Taken together, the "fire protection requirements and guidelines consist of a multitude of rules, generic communications, staff guidance, and other related documents" [U.S. NRC, 2000]. The NRC is currently developing a comprehensive guide to fire protection regulations and guidance.

One point to be taken from this discussion is that fire protection for the U.S. nuclear power industry is not currently governed by a uniform set of requirements. Rather, while the requirements are similar, they do vary from plant to plant. One significant factor in determining which specific requirements apply to a given plant is the vintage of that plant (in particular, the dates of the construction permit and operating license). Even given the same fire protection requirements, the fire protection strategies and approaches taken to meet the requirements vary substantially from plant to plant. Another factor is that those plants that were already in operation or nearing the completion of construction nominally faced greater challenges in implementing the new requirements than did those plants that were still under construction or just entering the construction phase. That is, the options for fire protection implementation would generally be somewhat more limited and more difficult to implement for a plant that is already completed than for one that is still under construction. For example, design decisions related to separation of redundant equipment are more easily implemented before the concrete is poured. Given these observations, one would nominally anticipate that plant fire risk might also vary substantially from plant to plant, and that plant vintage might be a factor in this variation (see Section 3.3.1 for further discussion).

A second point is that for most plants in the United Sates today, the current fire protection requirements (i.e., Appendix R to 10 CFR Part 50) were imposed as a backfit, rather than as an integral part of plant design. At the time of the issuance of Appendix R to 10 CFR Part 50, most of the current U.S. nuclear power reactors were already in operation or under construction.

Implementing fire protection requirements for existing plants is a challenge. Indeed, the U.S. NRC granted a large number of case-by-case exemptions to licensees during the initial implementation process. Nonetheless, many studies have concluded that implementation of the requirements specified in Appendix R to 10 CFR Part 50 resulted in a substantial and measurable risk reduction (see, for example, NUREG/CR-5088). However, there is still some risk from fires associated with the operation of nuclear power plants. The IPEEE fire assessments have, in part, helped to assess this risk.

3.2 Vulnerabilities and Plant Improvements

Two of the objectives of the IPEEE process were for licensees to identify potential severe accident vulnerabilities, and to identify cost-effective opportunities for plant improvements that might reduce severe accident risk. This section discusses licensees' findings related to these two objectives of the IPEEE process.

3.2.1 Vulnerabilities

3.2.1.1 Defining a Vulnerability

The U.S. NRC IPEEE guidance documents did not specify a definition of what constituted a severe accident vulnerability. This was left to licensees. In approximately 45% of the IPEEEs (47 of 108 units), licensees did not provide an explicit definition of what constituted a vulnerability either in the general context of the IPEEE or in the specific context of the fire assessment. (See Table 3.4 in Volume 2 for a listing of vulnerability definitions used by licensees.) For the other 55% of the submittals, a range of vulnerability definitions were applied as follows:

- vulnerability assessments were based on application of the "Severe Accident Issue Closure Guidelines" [NUMARC, 1991] (18 units),

- the assessment of vulnerabilities was based on a general assessment of the magnitude of fire CDF and the distribution of CDF contributors (i.e., risk was low and/or evenly distributed across fire areas) (15 units),

- a vulnerability was defined as any area where the CDF "significantly exceeded" or was "well above" the fire area[1] quantitative screening criterion (typically 1E-6/ry, see Section 3.4.2.3) (13 units),[2]

- the assessment of vulnerabilities was based on a comparison of the risk profile to those cited in other PRA studies (8 units),

- any scenario with a CDF greater than 1E-4/ry or an early release frequency of 1E-6/ry was considered a vulnerability (4 units), and

- a vulnerability was defined as any fire scenario leading directly to core damage (i.e., any fire scenario leading to core damage without at least one independent/random failure in addition to the postulated fire damage) (3 units).

---

[1] This report refers to fire areas, fire analysis zones, fire zones, and fire compartments. The term "fire area" is used strictly in the context of fire areas as defined in the plant fire protection program (e.g., Appendix R fire areas). The terms "fire analysis zone," "fire zone," and "compartment" refer to those subdivisions of the plant that were used as the basis for the analysis of fire hazards. This may include full fire areas or subsets of such areas. In a few cases, a zone may actually represent a combination of fire areas. (See Section 3.4.2.1 for further discussion of plant partitioning.)

[2] Note that in one of these cases (Cooper), in one section of the IPEEE submittal, the licensee states that any unscreened fire area constituted a fire vulnerability. Several plant areas did survive screening. However, in the cover letter provided with the IPEEE submittal, the licensee concluded that "No significant vulnerabilities were discovered during the CNS IPEEE evaluation."

3.2.1.2 Identification of Fire Vulnerabilities

The licensees for three units at two separate plant sites did report fire vulnerabilities in their IPEEE submittals. All other licensees indicated that no vulnerabilities were identified based on their IPEEE fire analyses.

In one case, a two-unit plant site (Quad Cities) initially concluded that fire vulnerabilities existed, but later revised this conclusion based on a re-analysis of the plant. The initially identified vulnerabilities were primarily associated with large oil fires in the turbine building that might compromise the capability to safely shut down the plant. Factors contributing to this assessment were the concentration of safety-related cables routed through certain areas of the turbine building, the proximity of large oil spill sources to these cables, and the proximity of the remote shutdown panels to significant fire sources that might lead to a demand for safe shutdown from those panels. Upon identification of the fire vulnerabilities, the licensee began an effort to resolve the identified issues. The licensee also chose to re-quantify its fire CDF, and ultimately submitted a revised IPEEE fire analysis. This later analysis concluded that the original analysis had been excessively conservative, and that the fire CDF was substantially lower than had been estimated in the original analysis. A number of plant improvements were implemented to further reduce the fire-induced CDF, and many of these improvements were credited in the revised analysis. Ultimately, the licensee concluded that there were no fire vulnerabilities at the plant.

In the second case, a licensee (Millstone Unit 2) initially determined that one fire outlier/vulnerability had been identified in the IPEEE.[3] A second vulnerability was identified during the IPEEE review process. These two vulnerabilities are summarized as follows.

- In the initial analysis, the licensee concluded that the accumulation of significant quantities of transient combustibles (protective clothing) in the vicinity of a large concentration of safety-related cables was an outlier/vulnerability. At the time of the submittal, the licensee was considering three options to resolve the vulnerability. Specifically, these included reducing the quantity of materials, storing the materials in "fire-related lockers," or removing the materials from the area.

- In the original analysis, the licensee acknowledged that "the turbine building ... is very important to safe shutdown." However, the licensee's original analysis concluded that the CDF contribution was no more than about 2E-6/ry. Hence, the turbine building was initially found to be an insignificant CDF contributor. However, the approach to quantification used in the turbine building assessment was questioned during the NRC review process. In response to a request for additional information (RAI) from the NRC, the licensee re-examined their treatment of the turbine building fire scenarios, and provided a re-analysis. As a result, the licensee concluded that "a vulnerability was discovered." The identified vulnerability involved two fire initiators (scenarios) with potential conditional core damage probability (CCDP) values of 0.1. In contrast, the original analysis indicated that the licensee expected the CCDP for these scenarios to be on the order of 0.002. The critical element of each scenario was loss of the turbine-driven auxiliary feedwater system. Based on the assumptions of the original analysis, the CDF for each of these two scenarios was estimated at about 2E-8/ry. A

---

[3] In this case, Chapter 7 of the IPEEE submittal discussed risk scenario "outliers" that were to be addressed by the plant. The summary section of the submittal equates the "outliers" with "vulnerabilities."

"very conservative" re-quantification of the "as found" conditions provided in response to the NRC questions estimated that each scenario's CDF contribution is approximately 5E-4/ry. The licensee implemented plant improvements to address these two scenarios and, as a result, the CDF contributions were reduced to approximately 2E-8/ry and 2E-7/ry for these two scenarios.

It is interesting to note that all three of the NPP units that identified fire vulnerabilities identified these vulnerabilities in the turbine building. By contrast, many past fire PRAs concluded that the turbine building is not risk significant. The turbine building does present some of the most severe fire hazards at an NPP in terms of fire severity and duration. Indeed, many of the most severe NPP fires from the classical fire protection perspective have occurred in the turbine building [Kazarians, 2000]. However, at many plants, the turbine building is exclusively (or nearly so) related to the secondary (power generation) side of the plant. For these plants, little or no safety-related equipment is housed there. Hence, while severe fires are possible, the consequences of such fires would be minimal.

In contrast, these cases illustrate that while the general perception is that turbine building fires are not significant contributors to CDF, exceptions do exist. In these cases, substantial safety-related equipment was housed in the turbine building. At Quad Cities, for example, most of the plant's safety-related cables are routed from the control/auxiliary building, through the turbine building to the reactor buildings. This co-location of significant safety-related equipment and potentially severe fire sources led to risk-dominant fire scenarios. Based on this insight, future fire safety and fire risk assessments should pay particular attention to turbine building fires. For future fire PRAs, it will be important to ensure that the turbine building fires are not prematurely screened (see Section 3.3.2.1.5 for further discussion).

In the second vulnerability case at Millstone, the fire scenario is in many ways reminiscent of the classical fire PRA dominant fire risk scenario; that is, a concentration of safety-related cables in proximity to a significant fire source. Scenarios such as this have dominated many past NPP fire risk assessments. Scenarios involving the fire exposure of cable "pinch points" are common in the early fire PRAs in particular. In the case at Millstone, the fire source was classified as a transient fuel source (protective clothing). However, based on the IPEEE, it would appear that the fuel was in fact a relatively permanent fixture in the plant.

3.2.2 Plant Improvements

As a part of their IPEEE documentation, 44 plants (representing 62 NPP units) identified plant improvements intended to reduce fire risk and/or to take advantage of insights gained through the IPEEE process.[4] A listing of the plant improvements identified by each licensee is provided in Table 3.5 in Volume 2. These improvements fall into three broad categories. The first category, *Operational Procedures*, includes improvements in emergency procedures, operator training, fire brigade training, and other miscellaneous procedural improvements directly related to dealing with fires. The second category, *Maintenance Procedures*, includes routine maintenance procedures that are applicable to fire-related issues. These include

---

[4] Note that the discussion of plant improvements includes certain licensees that are not included in other sections of this report. In particular, other sections of this report have excluded Maine Yankee, Millstone Unit 1, Big Rock Point, and Zion because these plants are permanently shutdown, and full IPEEE reviews were not completed for these units. However, this discussion includes plant improvements reported by these plants.

transient fuel load monitoring and control, general housekeeping, and equipment maintenance. The third category, *Physical Design Change*, deals with actual changes to either plant safety and support systems or fire protection systems and structures.

A total of 242 fire-related improvements were identified. They are summarized by general category in Table 3.1 below, and by specific type within each general category in Table 3.2.

By far, most improvements involved changes to emergency procedures. The 71 changes and additions to the plant emergency response procedures represent 65% of the operational procedures improvements and 29% of all identified plant improvements. The emergency procedures and training types in the *Operational Procedures* category are self-explanatory. Examples of "other" operational procedure changes include actions such as improved inspections of fire protection systems, improved approaches to systems control, and new administrative controls on fire doors and barriers.

Table 3.1: Fire-related plant improvements by general category

Improvement category	Number of improvements	Percent of total
Operational procedures	110	45
Maintenance procedures	28	12
Physical design changes	104	43

Examples of "other" improvements for *Maintenance Procedures* include enhanced identification of fire barriers to ensure appropriate inspections, better mounting of storage units for flammable materials, and increased frequency of inspections.

"Physical Design Changes" covers changes to systems other than fire protection systems. These changes include redesigning circuits to provide circuit redundancy, including additional water supplies for service water systems, and adding redundant switches to provide redundant control of certain valves. "General Equipment Modifications" in the *Physical Design Change* category made as a result of the IPEEE studies include improvements such as adding shields and sealing gaps, installing dampers in large vents, replacing one type of instrument air compressor with another, and replacing wooden scaffolding with metal scaffolding. Other physical design changes included modifications such as adding battery-powered emergency lighting units.

Plants that identified five or more improvements account for 70% (169) of the total improvements identified by all licensees. There are 19 such plant sites (representing 31 units), and their improvements are enumerated by category in Table 3.3.

With emergency procedures and system design changes comprising the bulk of improvements, some discussion of these improvements is appropriate. These are discussed in the subsections that follow.

Table 3.2: Fire-related plant improvements by specific type

Improvement type	Number of improvements	Percent of category	Percent of total
Operational procedures			
Emergency procedures	71	65	29
Operator training	17	15	7
Fire brigade training	16	15	7
Other	6	5	2
Maintenance procedures			
General maintenance procedures	23	82	10
Technical specifications	0	0	0
Other	5	18	2
Physical design changes			
General equipment modifications	25	24	10
Relocate equipment/cables	17	16	7
Fire protection system modifications	19	18	8
Barrier change/upgrade	19	19	8
Plant system design change	19	19	8
Other	5	5	2

Generally, with very few exceptions, it was not possible to quantify how plant improvements reduced the fire CDF. In the vast majority of cases, the licensees have provided only a single fire CDF quantification, rather than a "before and after" quantification of CDF. In most cases, it appears that the cited plant improvements were credited in the fire analysis. In some cases improvements that were still under consideration were not credited in the fire analysis. In other cases, it was not clear whether or not the cited improvements had been credited in the analysis. In a few cases, the staff questioned licensees as to the status of plant improvements where it appeared that a particular plant improvement credited in the analysis had a significant impact on fire CDF. In all such cases, licensees cited that the improvements had been, or were currently being, implemented.

3.2.2.1 Emergency Procedures

A large number of the procedural improvements take the form of enhancements and/or changes to existing emergency procedures. Other improvements involved the development of new procedures as a result of the "opportunities for improvement" that were identified during the IPEEE process.

During the course of the IPEEE effort, close scrutiny of emergency procedures indicated that changes (often minor) to certain procedures often enhanced the likelihood of accomplishing their safe shutdown goals. One general example is the actuation of certain valves earlier in the procedure to ensure their proper alignment before a fire might deprive them of electrical power. Another is the use of selective and sequenced load shedding from certain buses rather than the wholesale dropping of loads (see Section 3.4.8.2). This ensures that necessary electric power remains available for as long as possible.

Several procedural additions and changes concerned the maintenance of the emergency core cooling system (ECCS) and addressed the potential isolation of reactor core isolation cooling (RCIC) and high pressure safety injection (HPSI). In one case, an interesting circuit anomaly was found as a result of a simulator exercise, which demonstrated that, during a loss of offsite power (LOOP) event, a false high RCIC room temperature signal would be generated. As a result, the inboard ac-powered RCIC isolation valve would be instructed to close. However, the valve could not respond to the close signal due to the lack of ac power, but the close signal would remain active. Upon restoration of ac power, the relay associated with the false high-temperature signal would energize (activating the close action) before the loss-of-power contact would open

Table 3.3: Plants with five or more improvements

Plant	Operational procedures	Maintenance procedures	Physical design changes
Beaver Valley			10
Big Rock Point	4	1	6
Duane Arnold		3	3
Haddam Neck	3	1	8
J. M. Farley	5		
Limerick	2	2	1
Maine Yankee	5		
Millstone		1	5
Nine Mile Point	2	2	2
North Anna	10	2	5
Oconee	5	1	7
Oyster Creek	2	1	5
Palo Verde	3		2
Peach Bottom	18	2	5
Prairie Island	6		4
Quad Cities	2		7
R.E. Ginna	2	1	4
Summer	5		
Vermont Yankee	2	2	5

(inhibiting the close action). As a result, the RCIC isolation valve would close before the control system sensed a loss of power. Analysis showed that this could happen during station blackout (SBO), LOOP, or loss of an ac power train. An improvement was implemented to address this finding.

Several other improvements addressed the availability of necessary electrical power. These included procedures to deal with the coincident loss of two collocated dc buses, a new procedure to bring an emergency diesel generator (EDG) on line (the examination had indicated a relatively high diesel generator (DG) unavailability), and procedures for switching to alternate power supplies. Other improvements in emergency procedures deal with control room habitability, switchgear and cable spreading room ventilation, cooling in pump rooms, and maintaining reactor coolant pump (RCP) seal cooling.

3.2.2.2 Fire Protection System Changes

Several of the improvements to fire protection systems involved installing detection and suppression equipment in areas that previously had none. Other improvements involved system modifications of varying degrees. Some were as simple as replacing valves and switches with different types of the same components. Some of these cases appeared to be related to seismic-fire interactions. For example, in one case a wet pipe sprinkler system was redesigned as a dry pipe system. In another case, a carbon dioxide system had an auto-actuation capability added to it in order to increase reliability and speed of operation. Perhaps the most interesting "improvement" was a change in sprinkler head orientation. A walkdown inspection found that some of the heads had been installed upside-down. The improvement turned the heads right-side-up.

3.2.2.3 Other System Changes

The following changes deal with modifications to systems other than the fire protection system. For the most part they impact core cooling systems:

- addition of diverse water sources for a service water system,
- installation of alternate shutdown systems,
- addition of extra switches to facilitate certain valve operations,
- replacement of oil-filled transformers with dry transformers to reduce the potential for transformer fires,
- improved logic for auto-isolation of certain plant areas,
- addition of dedicated DG to ensure RCP seal injection cooling, and
- addition of battery-powered lighting to improve visibility in certain plant areas.

3.3   Fire-Induced Core Damage Frequency Perspectives

This section discusses the fire-induced CDFs reported in the IPEEE submittals. As noted below, most (but not all) submittals provided quantified fire-induced CDFs, whereas almost none of the submittals quantitatively assessed fire-induced containment failure, offsite releases, or long-term consequences. Hence, CDF is the primary measure of fire-induced plant risk that emerges from the IPEEE fire analyses.

This section makes various comparisons of the reported fire-induced CDF values to illustrate how a number of potential factors may have impacted those results. As noted in Section 1.3 of this report, because of differences in methodologies and assumptions used in the IPEEE submittals, comparisons of quantitative

CDF results should be done with caution. The intent of the comparisons presented here is to illustrate how the total population of U.S. nuclear power plants compares in various key areas. For example, the fire-induced CDF is compared to the internal events CDFs industry-wide to illustrate the relative importance of fire versus internal events accident initiators, given the IPE and IPEEE analyses. However, in making this comparison, and others like it, the authors have avoided direct numerical comparisons of the results for individual plants. The only exception is a general discussion of the ratio of fire CDF to internal CDF for the overall plant population.

Within the subject of fire-induced CDF results, some comparisons have been made to assess the relative importance of certain plant zones in comparison to other commonly considered plant zones. In this case, the comparison of one zone to another should be self-consistent for any given submittal, since each analysis was nominally performed on a self-consistent basis. It is observed that some licensees did not carry the risk calculations as far as was possible, but rather stopped at a level of analysis equivalent to a detailed screening. Hence, even these comparisons are subject to some uncertainty. For this reason, the authors have, again, avoided direct comparisons of actual CDF values, in particular between individual plants and, rather, have focused on the relative ranking of fire zone contributions and the range of actual CDF values reported by the total plant population.

The reported CDF results are discussed for both boiling water reactors (BWRs) and pressurized water reactors (PWRs). In addition, the results have been reviewed to determine if there is any correlation between the plant type or vintage and the fire-induced CDF. This section also provides an in-depth discussion of the perspectives gained from the fire-induced CDF evaluations reported in the IPEEE submittals. The key design and operational features that affect the fire-induced CDF and the impact of methods and assumptions on the CDF results are discussed. Since the major design factor impacting the CDFs is the spatial layout of equipment and cables, the dominant fire zones have been identified, along with the factors that lead to their importance and important fire sources (e.g., equipment, cables, and transient ignition sources) and scenarios. The important types of accident sequences (e.g., station blackouts, loss-of-coolant accidents, and general transients) resulting from the fires modeled in the IPEEEs are also discussed.

The results and perspectives presented below are based on the IPEEE submittals and responses to requests for additional information (RAIs) that were received by the NRC. A few licensees completely revised their fire assessments after submitting their IPEEEs to the NRC, while others revised their analyses in specific areas in response to RAIs. In such cases, the CDF results, conclusions, and findings presented in this report reflect all such revisions to the IPEEE submittals.

3.3.1 Plant-Wide Fire-Induced CDF Results

This section discusses the total fire-induced CDFs from the submittals. The results are sorted according to plant type and vintage. Note that in some cases the total fire CDF estimates have been inferred by summing the CDF contributors reported by licensees (i.e., cases where a licensee reported individual fire zone CDFs but did not report a total plant fire CDF). The availability of different types and numbers of accident mitigating systems is generally a function of the plant type. This factor contributed to the variation of the internal event CDFs reported in the Individual Plant Examination (IPE) submittals. Thus, some of the variation in the fire-induced CDFs could be related to the plant types. This potential is explored in Sections 3.3.1.1 and 3.3.1.2. However, the reasons for any plant type variations are difficult to identify for several reasons. First, based on the findings of past fire PRAs, it is generally expected that the impact of a fire is primarily determined by the equipment and cables located in the area affected by the fire. Thus, the availability of redundant accident mitigating systems can be negated by the location of related cables and equipment. Perspectives related to spatial location of equipment are discussed in Section 3.3.2.1. Secondly, the licensees used their IPE models in their fire assessments. The IPE models reflected the variations both in the available mitigating systems and in the modeling assumptions. Thus, these modeling assumptions could also impact the fire-induced CDF assessments. However, no attempt has been made to assess the impact of IPE model variations on the fire-induced CDF. Instead, the focus of the insights obtained from the fire assessments is restricted to fire-specific modeling variations.

As discussed in Section 3.1.3.1, a fire at Browns Ferry Unit 1 in 1975 was a pivotal event that brought about fundamental changes in the fire protection requirements at nuclear power plants. New regulations and regulatory guidance were generated to address the insights that were identified as a result of the investigation of this fire. These included requirements that both new plants under construction and existing plants provide an analysis that divided the plant into fire areas and demonstrated that redundant success paths of equipment required to achieve safe shutdown were adequately protected from fire damage.

As noted in Section 3.1.3.1, the implementation of the post-Browns Ferry fire protection requirements presented a greater challenge at older plants (those for which construction was already completed) than it did at newer plants (those either just entering, or early into, the construction phase). Furthermore, while the fire protection requirements are similar for all plants, there is some variation in those requirements related in part to plant vintage. Given these observations, some variation might be expected in the fire-induced CDFs based on the vintage of the plant. This potential is explored in Section 3.3.1.3.

Many of the plants were granted case-specific exemptions to the fire protection requirements based on implementation of alternative measures taken to meet the regulatory compliance criteria. A limited review of the impact of the granted exemptions at nine plants on the fire-induced CDF has been performed. The review is summarized in Section 3.3.1.4.

3.3.1.1 Fire-Induced CDF Results

One of the primary objectives of the IPEEE process was to identify potential plant vulnerabilities. For fires, this goal could be achieved using a screening analysis method such as EPRI's Fire-Induced Vulnerability Evaluation (FIVE) [EPRI, 1992]. However, the vast majority of the IPEEE fire analyses included PRA-based quantification of unscreened fire scenarios and reported the total plant fire-induced CDF values. The fire-induced CDFs reported by licensees are shown in Figure 3.1. For BWRs, licensees reported unit fire CDF values that ranged from 3.6E-8/ry to 8.1E-5/ry. For PWRs, licensees reported fire CDF values that ranged from 5.1E-7/ry to 1.9E-4/ry. Figure 3.1 also compares the reported fire CDFs industry-wide for both BWR and PWR plants to the internal events CDFs reported in the IPEs. (See Table 3.2 in Volume 2 for comparison of the CDFs for each plant.) This figure indicates that the CDFs from accidents initiated by fires are of the same order of magnitude as those from other internal events for the industry taken as a whole. In fact, the range of fire-induced CDFs for the BWRs is very similar to the range of CDFs for the BWR internal events. However, for the PWRs, the fire-induced CDFs are generally lower than the CDFs for the PWR internal events.

The relative importance of fire compared to internal events at each plant was also analyzed. Approximately 25% of the plants reported fire-induced CDFs that are larger than the IPE internal events CDFs. The large majority of the plants (approximately 75%) reported fire-induced CDFs that were within an order of magnitude (either higher or lower) of the internal events CDFs. Four BWRs reported fire-induced CDFs that

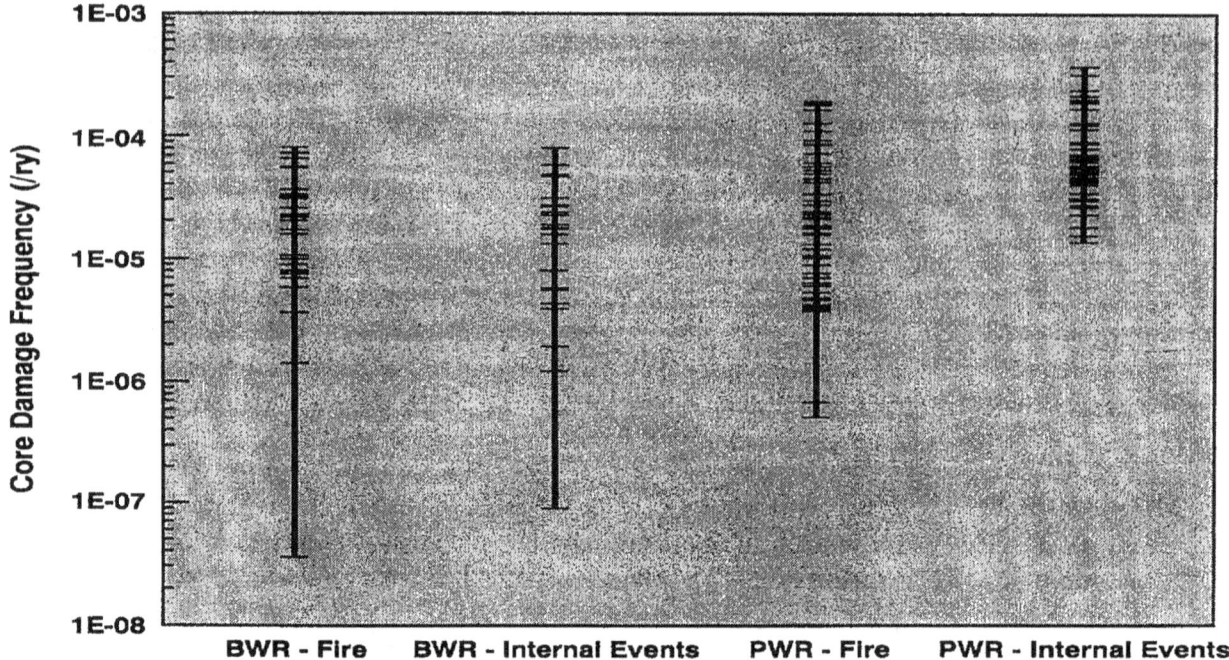

Figure 3.1 Fire CDFs versus internal events for the entire U.S. nuclear power plant population

were significantly higher (i.e., more than an order of magnitude) than their corresponding internal events CDFs. The fire-induced CDFs for these plants are within the range of most of the BWR CDFs. Thus, the higher ratio for these four BWRs is attributable to the relatively low internal events CDFs documented in their IPE submittals. Twenty plants reported fire-induced CDFs that were significantly lower (i.e., more than an order of magnitude) than their corresponding internal events CDFs. On an absolute scale, the fire-induced CDFs for all 20 of these plants were significantly below the average value reported by other licensees. Many of the IPEEE submittals cited a low degree of confidence in their estimates of fire-induced CDF, and several explicitly stated that the cited fire CDFs were considered conservative. However, the relative CDF values reported in the IPE and IPEEE fire analyses indicate that fire can be a potentially important contributor to overall plant CDF. The IPEEE's provide no basis for discounting the importance of potential fires in a nuclear power plant.

For the population of U.S. nuclear power plants, it was found that the average fire-induced CDF for BWR plants is less than that for the PWR plants. This trend is consistent with the internal event CDFs reported in the IPEs. The lower CDFs for the BWRs provided in the IPE submittals are partly attributable to the fact they have more coolant injection systems than PWRs. In addition, the susceptibility of some PWRs to reactor coolant pump (RCP) seal LOCAs is a major contributor to the higher PWR CDFs reported in the IPEs. These factors account for some of the differences in the fire-induced CDFs for BWRs and PWRs. Specifically, the availability of more systems in BWRs results in relatively lower conditional probabilities of core damage from fire scenarios (i.e., more components must fail in BWRs due to either the fire or from random causes). In addition, many PWR licensees identified important scenarios where fire impacts coupled with random failures resulted in the failure of cooling water system(s) that resulted in RCP seal failure and the failure of needed coolant injection systems.

The range in the fire-induced CDFs for BWRs is very similar to the range in the internal event CDFs for this same group of plants. However, the minimum fire-induced CDF for PWRs is a factor of 20 lower than the minimum reported internal event CDF. For most plants, while a variety of damage targets were considered (e.g., pumps, motors, instrument and control components, and cables), the dominant fire sequences generally involved fires that damaged electrical cables. Hence, the most important factor in the variation in the fire-induced CDF results, both for fire zones within a given plant and from plant to plant, appears to be the spatial location of important cables. Cable separation/convergence strongly influenced the CDF contribution of specific fire zones, which, in turn, influenced the total calculated plant-wide fire-induced CDF. Differences in the fire PRA methodology and assumptions also contribute to the variation in the calculated fire-induced CDFs. These and other factors that contribute to the variation in the fire-induced CDFs are discussed in more detail in Section 3.4 of this report.

The variability in the fire-induced CDFs is also likely affected by other factors that have not been assessed in the IPEEE review process. These factors include plant design differences (e.g., in the ECCS, decay heat removal, and support systems), the safe shutdown method used by the plant, and differences in the IPE models used in the fire assessments. The IPE model variations that could impact the fire-induced CDF estimates include modeling assumptions and data values (both component failure probabilities and human error probabilities) used in the model evaluation. The importance of these factors for the internal event CDF was discussed in the IPE insights report, NUREG-1560. However, the documentation of the plant models provided in the submittals was generally limited, and the discussion of the fire assessment results did not generally focus on the importance of these factors. Therefore, the insights related to the calculated fire-induced CDFs focus primarily on the areas in the plants that are most likely to result in fire-induced core damage, the important fire ignition sources and scenarios, and the types of accident sequences that might be induced by the fires. In addition, the impact of factors related to the fire PRA methodology on the calculated CDFs is also assessed. These factors include the treatment of fire sources, the modeling of fire growth, the modeling of fire detection and suppression, and the modeling of fire impacts on operator actions.

3.3.1.2 Plant Vintage Impacts on Fire-Induced CDF

As the use of nuclear power has grown, the lessons learned from the older plants have been used to improve upon the design, operation, and maintenance of newer plants. In addition, the occurrences of abnormal events or accidents have led to new regulations that are designed to prevent recurrence of such events and improve the safety of both existing and future plants. The most important incident that has impacted fire protection and its regulation in the U.S. nuclear power industry is the 1975 fire at Browns Ferry Unit 1. The investigation that followed the fire identified significant deficiencies in both the design of fire protection features and the procedures for responding to a fire. The most notable conclusion of the investigation was that the fire protection concerns did not sufficiently encompass nuclear safety issues, especially with regard to protecting redundant trains of equipment that are required to safely shut down the reactor. To address these deficiencies, the fire investigators recommended that the U.S. NRC develop detailed guidance on implementing an improved fire protection program. Such guidance was initially provided through Branch Technical Position (BTP) APCSB 9.5-1. The guidelines in APCSB 9.5-1 were only applied to those licensees that filed for a construction permit after July 1, 1976. For existing plants that were already operating or well into the construction phase, the U.S. NRC issued Appendix A to APCSB 9.5-1, which provided acceptable alternatives for meeting the fire protection requirements for cases where strict compliance would require significant modifications to the plants.

Subsequently, in 1980, the NRC published the "Fire Protection Rule" in 10 CFR 50.48 and Appendix R to 10 CFR Part 50, "Fire Protection Program for Nuclear Power Facilities Operating Prior to January 1, 1979." All reactors that were licensed to operate before January 1, 1979, were required to comply with three items addressed in this rule (other items applied to plants on a case-by-case basis). Specifically, these items included fire protection for the safe shutdown capability of the plant (including alternate, dedicated, or backup shutdown systems), emergency lighting, and the reactor coolant pump oil collection systems. The U.S. NRC approved approximately 800 exemptions to the fire protection requirements (i.e., alternate methods for achieving the underlying purpose of the regulation).

This brief history indicates that, while the fire protection requirements for all plants are similar, there are variations in the fire protection requirements. More importantly, perhaps, there are variations in the methods and approaches used to meet those requirements. As discussed in Section 3.1.3.1, these variations might be expected to contribute to variations in plant fire CDF, and one factor in this variability may be plant vintage. For this reason, the fire-induced CDFs were examined to determine if the vintage of the plant may be an important factor in fire CDF. (See the tables in Volume 2 for a listing of fire-induced CDFs and dates operating licensees were issued for each plant.)

Figure 3.2 indicates that there is a wide range in calculated CDFs for plants granted operating licenses both before and after January 1, 1979 (pre- and post-Appendix R plants respectively). However, the overall spread in CDF results does not illustrate any consistent or pronounced trends with respect to plant vintage. For the PWRs, the average CDF for the older plants is a factor of two higher than for the newer plants, a very modest difference given the uncertainties of fire PRA. For BWRs the averages for the pre- and post-Appendix R plants are virtually identical.

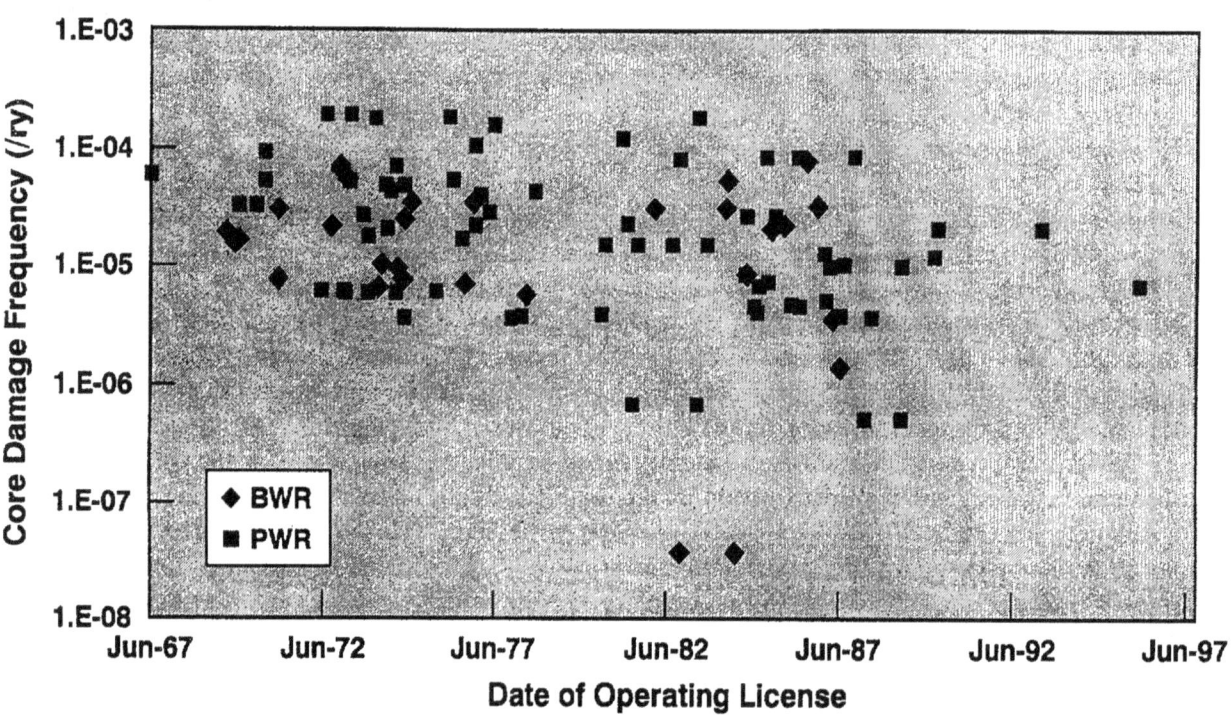

Figure 3.2 Fire-induced CDFs versus date of operating license

3 - 14

Several BWRs and PWRs licensed after January 1, 1979, had significantly lower fire CDFs than the other plants. In addition, there appear to be proportionately fewer plants with relatively high fire CDFs. These observations would reflect a combination of both improvements in general plant design and implementation of the lessons learned from the Browns Ferry fire. It is not, however, possible to clearly distinguish the CDF impact between these factors, given the IPEEE results and the level of technical review performed.

3.3.1.3 Impact of Appendix R Exemptions on CDF

As a part of the IPEEE review process, a subset of the IPEEE fire analyses was examined for insights relating to the impact of Appendix R exemptions on plant fire CDF [U.S. NRC, 1999].[5] The study considered a sample of nine licensee IPEEE submittals representing 13 individual units. These submittals were chosen because the reported fire-induced CDF values ranked among the highest values reported by licensees at the time of the study.

For each unit in the sample group fire protection regulatory exemptions were identified using information made available by the U.S. NRC Office of Nuclear Reactor Regulation (NRR). Each exemption was characterized with regard to the general nature of the exemption and the impacted fire areas. The IPEEE treatment of each impacted fire area was then examined. An assessment was made as to the nominal importance of the exemption to the CDF estimate provided in the IPEEE. Attempts were made to quantify the potential impact for exemptions that appeared to have had some notable impact on the CDF estimates.

The study considered a total of 169 exemptions impacting the 13 units in the sample group. The number of exemptions impacting an individual unit ranged from two to 54. It was found that the vast majority of the exemptions reviewed had little or no discernible impact on the fire CDF estimates. Only five of the exemptions were found to be potentially risk-significant (as measured by the potential CDF impact of each exemption). Of the remaining 164 exemptions, 143 (85% of the sample group) were found to have a small or very small impact on fire CDF. The remaining 21 exemptions were found to have an indeterminate CDF impact because insufficient information was available in the IPEEE to fully assess the exemption's impact.

The results of this study also showed that a simple count of the number of exemptions at a given plant provides little or no direct insight into the potential risk significance of exemptions at that plant. Similarly, a comparison of the number of exemptions between plants does not provide a reliable indication of the relative risk significance of exemptions at each plant.

The cumulative risk impact, again as measured by the potential impact on CDF, of all exemptions at each individual plant in the sample group was also examined. It was found that the cumulative risk impact could be potentially significant for three of the nine plants in the sample group. However, the risk significance of one or more exemptions could not be determined. Hence, the cumulative impact of the exemptions could also not be explicitly determined.

The overall conclusions of the exemption study are considered robust. However, the findings relating to the risk importance of specific exemptions are considered preliminary given the nature of this limited scope study. In particular, the IPEEE studies were not originally intended for use in such an exercise. Inherent

---

[5] It should be noted that the licensees were not asked to address this topic in their IPEEEs and, in general, did not.

limitations in the available IPEEE documentation made a concise assessment of individual exemptions difficult in some cases.

The NRC staff is following up to obtain additional information from those licensees that had exemptions that were initially determined to be potentially risk significant. This follow-up activity is being done separately from the IPEEE program and was not yet fully completed at the time this report was being prepared. A preliminary review by the staff indicates that the exemptions granted to those plants do not represent a significant risk. In particular, two licensees have revised their fire analyses, and the revised CDFs were substantially lower than the original CDFs as the result of improved fire risk models. The reduction of the CDFs in the revised fire analyses also substantially reduced the impact of the exemptions.

Another licensee stated that the two exemptions that the NRC staff considered initially to be potentially risk significant (i.e., lack of 1-hour rated fire barrier and lack of an automatic fire suppression system in an electrical penetration room) were no longer required. At the time these exemptions had been submitted, a fire in either of the electrical penetration rooms could have affected redundant safe shutdown equipment. Since that time, the licensee took actions including rerouting cables for redundant safe shutdown equipment, removing power from some equipment, and implementing operator actions. As a result of these actions, there is no longer a requirement for the 1-hour rated barriers or the automatic fire suppression system in these areas. Therefore, the licensee requested that these two exemptions be withdrawn.

3.3.2 Dominant Contributors to Fire-Induced CDF

The fire areas/zones in each plant are diverse in content and name. However, there are several fire zone classifications that are common to most plants. These include the main control room, cable spreading rooms, switchgear rooms, cable vaults and chases, electrical penetration areas, battery rooms, the turbine building, and diesel generator rooms. The CDFs calculated for these common zones that could clearly be identified from the submittals are shown in Figure 3.3. Some of the CDFs shown in this figure are the result of screening assessments while the rest are the product of detailed analysis. For the majority of the areas listed above, there are generally more than one of these areas in each plant. (For example, most plants have more than one switchgear room.) The values shown in the figure are the CDFs for each area, not the cumulative CDF for each type of area. As indicated in the figure, there is a significant range in the reported values for these areas. The factors that contribute to this variability are identified in Section 3.3.2.1.

The important fire sources and scenarios for each of these fire areas are also identified in Section 3.3.2.1. In addition, the contribution of fire scenarios involving more than one area is identified in Section 3.3.2.2. The types of accident sequences initiated by fires (e.g., station blackout, LOCAs, and transients) and their relative contribution to the total fire-induced CDF are discussed in Section 3.3.2.3.

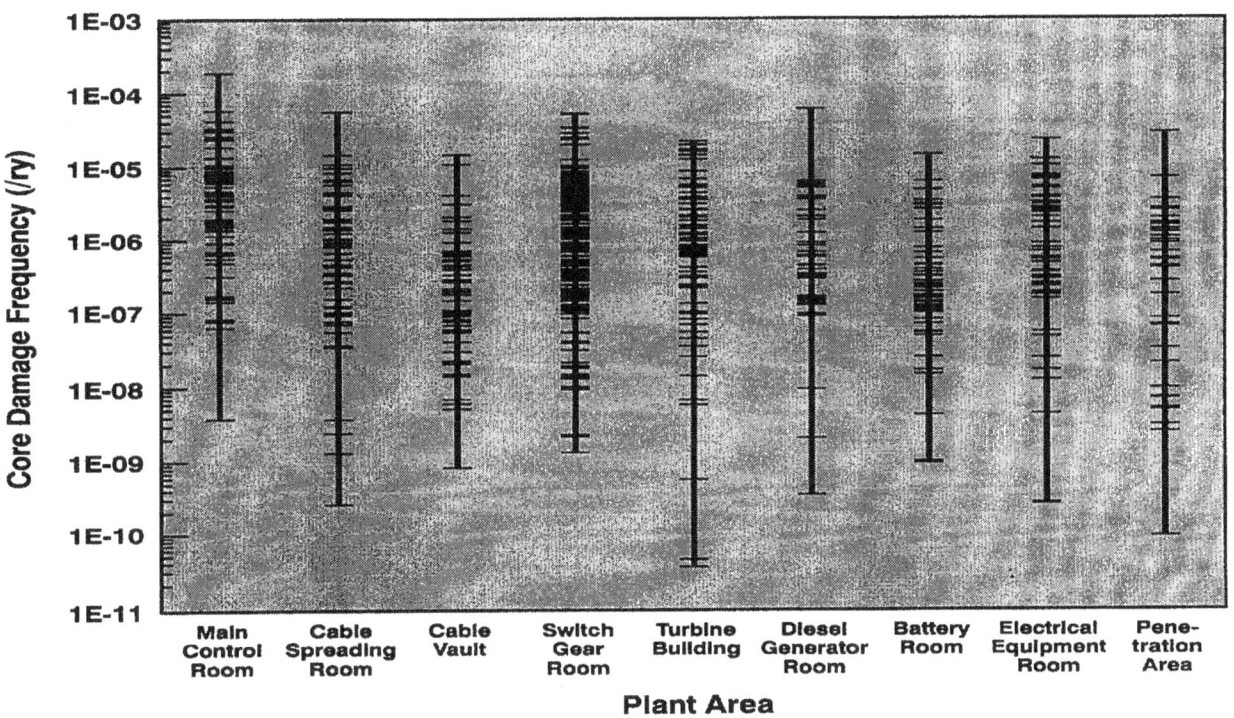

Figure 3.3 Reported fire-induced CDFs for commonly identified plant fire analysis zones

3.3.2.1 Dominant Fire Zones

The IPEEEs indicate that, by and large, the plant-wide fire-induced CDF is made up of relatively important contributions from several fire scenarios in different fire zones rather than being dominated by a single scenario or single fire zone. The fire zone that is the largest contributor to the fire-induced CDF, and the factors contributing to the importance of a fire zone, vary considerably among the plants. (A listing of the significant fire areas for each plant is provided in Table 3.3 in Volume 2.) Table 3.4 identifies the common plant zones that are among the dominant fire zones identified by the licensees. The table identifies the number of plants that rate each zone as one of the top five contributors to fire-induced CDF and how frequently each of these common zones was ranked at a given relative contributor ranking (e.g., how often the main control room (MCR) was ranked as the single most significant CDF contributor). The zones identified have typically been reported in past fire PRAs as being dominant fire risk contributors; they include the MCR, cable spreading room (CSR), cable vault (CV) and tunnel areas, and emergency switchgear rooms (SWGRs). In addition, other fire zones, such as the turbine building (TB), were also found to be important at some plants.

The percent contribution to the total plant fire CDF from each of these common zones is provided in Figure 3.4. The figure indicates that the relative contribution from each of these commonly identified fire zones varies significantly. Some of the zones contribute a large percentage of the plant's total fire-induced CDF. In particular, a number of plants reported that the MCR, CSR, switchgear rooms, and the turbine hall fire zones represented over half of the total plant fire-induced CDF. An analysis of the reported CDF confirms that the zones identified above, on average, are significant contributors to fire-induced core damage. The factors contributing to the variability in the calculated CDFs for these dominant zones are discussed in the following subsections. Factors that contribute to the importance of other unique zones in the plants are also discussed.

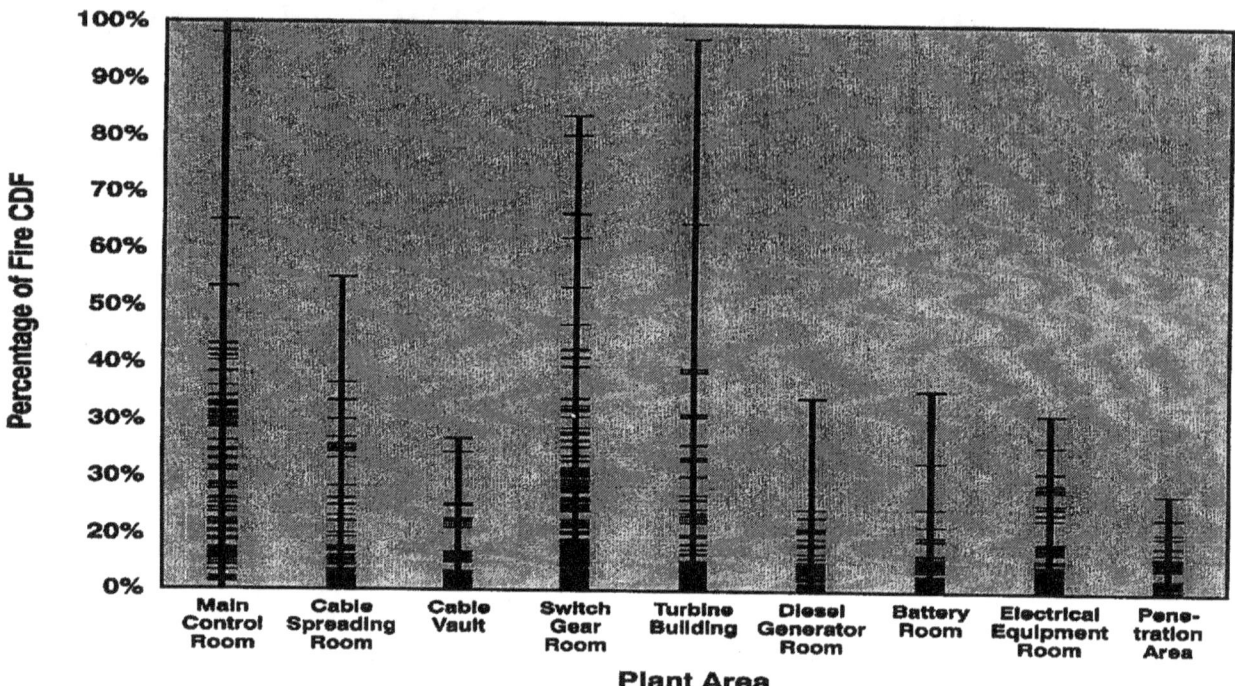

Figure 3.4 Plant zone contribution to fire-induced core damage

Table 3.4: Number of common fire zones ranked as important contributors to fire-induced CDF

Fire zone[1]	Number of zones reported in each relative CDF ranking						
	Top 5 ranking positions					Total ranked in top 5	Plants with no identified contribution[2]
	1	2	3	4	5		
Main control room	35	18	13	9	10	85	14
Switchgear rooms	21	29	20	27	15	112	9
Turbine building	12	5	14	3	6	40	30
Cable spreading rooms	7	9	4	8	7	35	34
Electrical equipment rooms	4	5	8	3	5	25	67
Diesel generator rooms	1	4	7	2	2	16	80
Cable vault/tunnel/chase zones	3	8	2	1	2	16	59
Battery/charger rooms	2	2	0	2	3	9	78

1. Not all plants have fire zones that can be categorized into one of these groups while other plants may have multiple fire zones that fit into a category (e.g., multiple switchgear rooms).
2. This includes plants that may have screened the zones and plants where no zone of this type was identified from the zone names provided in the submittals.

3.3.2.1.1 Control Room

Of all plant fire zones, the main control room was most often cited as the most significant fire risk contributor. Furthermore, the main control room was found to be among the top five contributors in 80% of the plants. A total of 54 plants reported MCR fire CDFs greater than 1E-6/ry. Of these 54, 24 plants reported fire CDFs greater than 1E-5/ry. Two plants reported control room fire CDFs greater than 1E-4/ry.

Fire scenarios leading to MCR abandonment were included in the assessment of control room fire CDF. These abandonment scenarios commonly ranked among the top contributors to the total MCR CDF. Approximately 13% of the submittals either screened the main control room or did not report a risk contribution. In a very few cases, licensees simply acknowledged the importance of the main control room without quantifying the actual CDF contribution.

The MCR CDF at most plants generally included contributions from two types of scenarios, both deriving from electrical cabinet fires in the MCR. One scenario involved fires that are not quickly suppressed (e.g., fires that lasted greater than 15 minutes) leading to control room abandonment and reliance on alternative shutdown. The second scenario involved fires that are suppressed quickly enough to prevent a forced abandonment of the control room (e.g., fires of 15 minutes duration or less), but that still require a reactor shutdown given the loss of some subset of the instrument and control functions. In general, the contribution from the non-abandonment scenarios is significantly less than the contribution from abandonment scenarios. For the non-abandonment scenarios, damage was generally assumed to be limited to the equipment located in the cabinet of fire origin. In some cases where controls for multiple trains of equipment were located on the same (or adjacent) cabinet(s), severity factors were used to differentiate between scenarios that only impacted one train versus those that would impact more than one train (see Section 3.4.10.2). The non-abandonment scenarios were further limited by an assumption that the fire would not propagate to, nor damage equipment in, an adjacent cabinet if there were metal partitions and an intervening air gap between the cabinets. In some submittals, fires in long, open control boards and cabinets were also assumed to have limited zones of influence based on the assumption that rapid horizontal fire propagation in cabinets is not likely, and that fires would be suppressed before such propagation would occur. Where fire propagation was considered, either between two cabinets or within a larger cabinet, detailed fire modeling of the fire propagation process was not performed. Instead, severity factors were typically used to quantify the likelihood of cabinet-to-cabinet or section-to-section fire propagation. Only a few plants have in-cabinet suppression systems; therefore, fire suppression is largely dependent on manual fire suppression. The Halon system at one plant (Oyster Creek) was noted as reducing the frequency of core damage from MCR cabinet fires.

The partitioning of the MCR fire frequency is another factor that impacted the calculated CDFs. The generic frequency of electrical cabinet fires was generally partitioned equally among all of the electrical cabinets located in the control room. In most cases, the frequency of an individual cabinet fire was less than 1/100 of the total MCR frequency, and only the failure of a small portion of the cabinets was identified as contributing to core damage. A factor in the low MCR contributions to the fire-induced CDF calculated for the two plants (Byron and Braidwood) is the fact that many of the cabinets typically located in the MCR are located in a separate auxiliary electrical equipment room at each plant. Thus, a major portion of the frequency of the MCR cabinet fires was attributed to this location. The CDF contribution from these zones was approximately 1E-7/ry at each plant as compared to the MCR contribution of 6E-8/ry to 8E-8/ry.

Control room abandonment scenarios were generally modeled very simplistically. Fires that were not suppressed within an assumed time were assumed to require abandonment either due to smoke/heat buildup (habitability) or fire-induced loss of MCR control function (controllability) issues. Once the control room is abandoned, the potential for core damage was assumed to be dominated by operator failure to control the plant from the remote shutdown panel(s). The probability for non-suppression of the fire and failure to remotely shut down the plant are, thus, the most important modeling factors contributing to the MCR CDF.

Most licensees assumed that 15 minutes would be available after detection of a fire and before smoke or heat would require control room abandonment, and used a conditional probability of 3.4E-3 from the Electric Power Research Institute (EPRI) "Fire PRA Implementation Guide" (FPRAIG) [EPRI, 1995] for non-suppression of the fire within that time frame. The smoke filling time was based on detection time data obtained in electrical cabinet fire experiments where there were in-cabinet detectors. Most licensees used the corresponding conditional abandonment probability value regardless of whether or not their plant has in-cabinet detectors, arguing that human detection would be as reliable as an optimally placed in-cabinet detector. However, some licensees used more conservative non-suppression probabilities. Some assumed that only 10 minutes would be available to suppress the fire; this translates to a non-suppression probability of 2.2E-2 using the FPRAIG suppression probability curves. Others used EPRI's FIVE guidance that a manual suppression probability should not exceed 0.1 in evaluating the control room. Generally, those licensees that used higher non-suppression probabilities for control room fires had larger MCR CDFs. It should be noted that many licensees argued in their original IPEEE submittals that large fires in the control room requiring abandonment were unlikely and, therefore, were not analyzed. However, in response to RAIs issued during the IPEEE review process, these licensees generally provided an assessment of control room abandonment scenarios.

Following the failure to suppress a control room fire, the operators would be forced to abandon the control room and initiate control from the remote shutdown panel(s). In most cases, the licensees argued that failure to control the plant from the remote shutdown panel was dominated by operator error and, thus, did not include any control system failures in their assessment. The remote shutdown capability varies substantially from one plant to the next in several aspects, all of which could impact the potential for operator success. The first is in the ability to isolate the remote shutdown panel from the control room. At most plants, that isolation is accomplished by transfer switches. The number of switches and their locations can vary. Secondly, the remote shutdown capability is not always located in a single location, especially at older plants. Finally, the required operator actions can vary significantly. Of particular interest are those plants that impose a self-induced station blackout (SISBO) in order to prevent inadvertent spurious component operations. It was not clear from the majority of the submittals how factors such as these were accounted for in evaluating the human error probability for this action. The modeling of the operator errors to remotely shut down the plant is discussed in detail in Section 3.4.8.

The human error probabilities for failing to shut down the plant following control room abandonment range from 0.1 to 1E-3. In general, those that used the lower values had insignificant CDF contributions from control room abandonment scenarios. However, use of the higher values (generally screening values) did not always result in relatively high MCR CDFs. In fact, it was typical for licensees to use the 3.4E-3 non-suppression probability in conjunction with a 0.1 remote shutdown failure probability. The combination of the values used for these two parameters contributed to the plants with both the highest and the lowest reported MCR CDFs. The plants with the highest reported MCR CDFs (Turkey Point 3 & 4 and St. Lucie 1 & 2) both used relatively high probabilities for non-suppression of the fire (0.05 or 0.1) and relatively high human error probabilities (HEPs) for failing to shutdown the plant remotely (0.1). Several of the plants with the lowest reported MCR CDFs (Braidwood 1 & 2 and Byron 1 & 2) used 3.4E-3 for the non-suppression probability and 1.2E-2 (when offsite power is available) or 1.8E-2 (when offsite power is not available) for the remote shutdown failure probability. In the specific cases of Byron and Braidwood, partitioning of the MCR fire frequency to an alternate fire zone was a quantification factor that was not observed in other submittals.

3.3.2.1.2 Switchgear Rooms

Switchgear rooms were also identified as important contributors to fire-induced CDF for many plants, a finding that confirms previous fire PRA results. Fire zones classified as switchgear rooms were quantified by 90% of the plants as specific (unscreened) contributors to the fire-induced CDF. Nearly half of the submittals ranked switchgear zones among the top five risk-significant fire zones. There were over 100 such zones identified as having CDF contributions greater than 1E-6/ry. Of these, 11 were reported that have CDFs greater than 1E-5/ry.

The most commonly cited fire scenarios involved a fire starting in a switchgear panel that then damaged overhead cables. Most licensees assumed fire heat release rates of less than 100 kW for such fires (see Section 3.4.3.1.1), although many assumed that switchgear fires would damage cables above the initiating panel regardless of the assumed fire size. It was noted during the review process that virtually all of the IPEEE analyses treated switchgear fires in the same manner as other fire sources. That is, the analyses did not explicitly treat energetic electrical faults (that have been observed in actual experience) as a unique fire threat (a point that also holds true for the treatment of oil-filled transformers).

The final CDF contribution was largely dependent on the functions lost due to cable damage, the fire severity assumed, and the conditional probability assumed for suppression of the fire before critical damage occurred. For example, several of the plants with large CDF contributions from switchgear rooms identified scenarios that resulted in loss of offsite power or cooling water systems led to RCP seal failures. One licensee (Haddam Neck) identified switchgear fires that could damage cables for multiple electrical divisions. The fact that the operators would be required to shut down the reactor from outside the control room contributed to the importance of these scenarios. Plants with low CDF contributions tended to have credited separation between trains of equipment and cables. The separation could be a rated barrier or a 20-foot combustible free zone. Fire suppression often was credited to prevent propagation in cases where two divisions were located in the same zone.

3.3.2.1.3 Cable Spreading Rooms

In comparison to other fire zones and to the findings of earlier fire PRAs, CSRs tended to rank somewhat less commonly among the top fire CDF contributors. Approximately 25% of the submittals identified CSRs among the top five fire zones, and only about 15% of the submittals ranked them among the top two contributors. Approximately 30 CSRs were identified that had CDFs greater than 1E-6/ry and, of these, 3 CSRs were reported to have CDFs greater than 1E-5/ry. Many submittals cited a lack of fixed fire sources in the CSR; hence, the fire frequency was assumed to be low. Overall, approximately 30% of the plants either screened the CSR or did not report a specific CDF contribution for the CSR, implying that the zones were screened.

One factor affecting the contribution of cable spreading rooms to the fire-induced CDF is the number of cable spreading rooms the plant utilizes. A fraction of the plant designs have two (or more) CSRs. A review of the reported CDF contributions indicated generally lower values when there are multiple CSRs. The average of the reported CDF values was lower by a factor of about five for multiple- than for single-CSR configurations. The maximum reported CDF contribution was lower by a factor of about ten for multiple- than for single-CSR configurations.

Plants with two (or more) CSRs usually reported divisional separation of equipment into the separate zones. Thus, no single fire should fail more than one division. Plants with one CSR typically rely on localized fire barriers and spatial separation to separate divisions and on fire detection and suppression systems to limit the impact of fires. Thus, some fraction of fires in these single CSR configurations have the potential to fail multiple divisions. This was generally assumed to be possible only if the fixed and manual suppression capabilities fail, and if the fire source is of sufficient intensity and in a proper location to cause fire spread. The amount of affected equipment in specific fire scenarios generally accounts for the variability in the CDFs.

Those submittals that ranked the cable spreading room as a significant CDF contributor commonly had only a single CSR that also housed electrical panels or other electrical equipment. The significant fire scenarios for these cases typically involved fires initiated in the electrical panels or equipment that damaged the cables overhead. Transient combustibles were also identified as significant fire CDF contributors for the CSR, but only in relatively few cases.

Some of the highest CDFs resulting from cable spreading room fires involved control room abandonment scenarios. Significant fires in cable spreading rooms can result in loss of control capability in the main control room. In such cases, plant procedures require the operators to transfer control to the remote shutdown panel(s). As with the control room fire scenarios, the plants that had CDF contributions for these scenarios tended to use high probabilities of fire non-suppression and high operator error probabilities to control the plant from the remote shutdown panel. In general, the same human error probability used for abandonment scenarios initiated by control room fires was used for abandonment scenarios initiated by cable spreading room fires.

In general, cable spreading rooms that did not contain electrical panels had low CDF contributions. Fires initiated by cables were generally not modeled due to the common assumption that cables qualified to Institute of Electrical and Electronic Engineers 383 (IEEE-383) [ANSI/IEEE, 1974] or equivalent standards have low frequencies of ignition. That left transient combustible fires, which were generally assumed to be of low intensity, had low frequencies due to combustible material controls, and were assigned partitioning factors to reflect the potential for such fires to occur only in a specific location that might lead to safe shutdown equipment damage. One licensee indicated that the generic transient-combustible fire frequency provided in the FIVE methodology was reduced by a factor of 10 to account for the fact that no transient-combustible fires in a cable spreading room had ever been recorded.

3.3.2.1.4 Cable Vaults/Tunnels/Chases

Results for cable vault and tunnel zones were somewhat similar to the results for cable spreading rooms. These zones often contain many of the same cables and functions that are routed through the cable spreading room, and have been identified in past fire PRAs as important contributors to fire CDF. In this case, variations in the zone naming schemes make it difficult to ensure that all such zones analyzed in the IPEEEs have been identified as a part of this review.

Approximately 55% of the plants either explicitly screened all of the identified cable vault and tunnel fire zones, or did not report a fire CDF contribution for any such zones implying that all such zones were screened. Approximately 15% of the plants reported ranked one or more such zones among the top five zone contributors to fire CDF. However, only eight plants reported zones with CDFs greater than 1E-6/ry and, of these, only two plants reported cable vaults that had CDF contributions greater than 1E-5/ry.

Commonly cited reasons for the low rankings were inaccessibility of the zones to plant personnel during normal operation, administrative controls that disallowed introduction of transient combustibles, raceway fire barriers, an automatic fire detection and suppression system, and a lack of fixed fire sources.

One of the plants with high cable vault contributions had two divisions of cables located in the zone, separated by some distance. Fire modeling indicated that an electrical panel fire, if not suppressed within 5 minutes, would result in sufficient heat to damage both divisions of cables. In this analysis, it was assumed that successful operation of the automatic suppression system would limit damage to a single division.

3.3.2.1.5 Turbine Rooms/Building

One somewhat surprising result was the ranking of the turbine building among the dominant fire zones in several submittals. Past fire PRAs have commonly concluded that the turbine building, while posing significant threat of severe fires, was not a significant contributor to CDF. These past PRAs had typically found little safety-related equipment in the turbine building. Hence, loss of the balance-of-plant (BOP) equipment in the turbine building was found to have little impact on nuclear safety.

A large number of the IPEEE submittals reported similar conclusions. Indeed, the majority of the submittals concluded that potential fires in various turbine building fire zones contributed less than 10% of the overall plant fire-induced CDF. However, a significant number of licensees did report the turbine building as a significant fire-induced CDF contributor. Specific observations relating to the CDF contribution of turbine building fire zones include the following.

- In 21 submittals (representing 30 units) the turbine building was explicitly screened or no contribution to fire-induced CDF was reported for turbine building areas. For an additional 10 submittals (representing 13 units) the contribution of the turbine building fire areas was reported as less than 1% of the total fire-induced CDF.

- Approximately 30% of the plants (counting by unit) reported at least one turbine building fire analysis zone that ranked among the top five contributors to fire-induced CDF.

- For five submittals (representing 10 units) the fire zone with the highest reported CDF contribution was identified as a turbine building fire zone.

- For one submittal (representing three units) the fire-induced CDF reported for the turbine building represented 97% of the total plant-wide fire-induced CDF. For a second submittal, representing one unit, the figure was 75%.

A subset of the IPEEE submittals was examined further to assess their treatment of and conclusions regarding turbine building fires. In particular, seven submittals (representing 12 units) were examined. These seven submittals include all those IPEEE submittals for which the turbine building fire zones accounted for 25%

or more of the fire-induced CDF and those for which the single most significant fire zone identified was a turbine building fire zone. The turbine building fire scenarios postulated in the corresponding IPEEE submittals are summarized as follows.

Case 1 - Millstone Unit 2: The original IPEEE analysis concluded that the turbine building represented about 26% of the overall plant fire-induced CDF. A range of fire scenarios was considered for various zones within the turbine building, including cable vaults, switchgear rooms, the load center room, pump pits, and the general turbine hall. Detailed quantitative analysis was performed for three scenarios, two involving general plant transients and one involving loss of instrument air. Ultimately, all the individual fire zones screened quantitatively (i.e., CDF below 1E-6/ry). A "special case study" of "large turbine building fires" including the potential for "collapse of the turbine building," yielded a bounding estimate of the turbine building CDF contribution (1.6E-6/year).

In response to a NRC RAI, the licensee identified two fire scenarios that had been improperly quantified in the original analysis. Each scenario involved turbine building fires that could cause cable damage leading to loss of the turbine-driven auxiliary feedwater system. The licensee's conservative estimates of the CDF for each of the as-found scenarios exceeded the original estimates of plant-wide fire-induced CDF by a factor of nearly 100. The licensee determined that these scenarios represented potential fire vulnerabilities (see Section 3.2.1.2). Plant changes were implemented to address these vulnerabilities. The final CDF estimates crediting the plant changes rendered the two scenarios minor contributors to fire-induced CDF (about 3% of the total fire CDF). In the final analysis, the turbine building still represents about 25% of the overall fire CDF based on the original "special case study." The licensee submittal states that "at (Millstone Unit 2) the turbine building is recognized as being very important to safe shutdown."

Case 2 - Quad Cities Units 1 and 2: The original Quad Cities fire analysis concluded that fire vulnerabilities did exist at the plant (see Section 3.2.1.2). The vulnerabilities were associated primarily with turbine building fires. The licensee implemented a number of plant improvements and re-quantified fire CDF using less conservative methods. The re-analysis showed that the vulnerabilities no longer existed. However, the turbine building still represents the single most significant contributor to the plant's fire-induced CDF. One significant factor in this assessment is the routing of numerous safety-related cables from the control building to the reactor building through the turbine building. Large oil fire scenarios postulated for the turbine building had the potential to compromise these cables. A second factor is that given some turbine building fires, safe shutdown may involve numerous remote operator actions. The complex nature of the required actions and, in a few scenarios, the location of the safe shutdown stations/equipment were factors in the human performance analysis results. A third factor is reliance on the availability of sister-unit equipment for safe shutdown that may not be available during outages of the sister-unit.

Case 3 - Oconee Units 1, 2, and 3: The Oconee IPEEE fire analysis concluded that "the dominant fire scenario .. is the large turbine building fire." In the fire analysis a fire that might spread throughout the turbine building is assumed. No credit is taken for fire barriers or fire dampers, although a fixed fire suppression system under the turbine is credited. A list of 124 separate turbine building fire sequences considered in the analysis is provided in the IPEEE submittal. The final CDF estimate for the plant is dominated by the turbine building fires (97% of the total fire CDF), and the turbine building analysis is dominated by four sequences (which account for nearly 60% of the total turbine building contribution); the next highest sequence accounts for less than 4% of the total contribution.

The licensee further states that the site's safe shutdown facility (SSF) was specifically designed to handle such fires. Hence, the random failure of SSF equipment was a key factor in CDF quantification. The four dominant sequences were associated with the SSF diesel generator failing to run or being in a maintenance outage, failure of the SSF auxiliary service water pump to start on demand, and failure of the "Train 2 Refrigeration Compressor" to start on demand. The analysis did include a human reliability analysis of the SSF operations, and many of the less significant scenarios do involve various human error/failure events.

Case 4 - Nine Mile Point Unit 1: The Nine Mile Point Unit 1 fire analysis included a detailed assessment of numerous turbine building fire scenarios. The submittal concluded that "the turbine building is an important area with regard to the likelihood of fires or other hazards causing core damage." It goes on to state that "the most important scenarios (only in localized areas) are those where a fire can cause loss of both emergency power boards and sometimes a loss of 115KV offsite power ..." Most of the contributing scenarios involved fires of various types that damage power cables for various systems that are routed through the turbine building. The CDF contribution arising from turbine building fires represents 75% of the total plant fire-induced CDF as reported in the IPEEE.

Case 5 - R. E. Ginna: CDF contributions are identified for two turbine building fire zones. In the turbine building basement, fires that damage offsite power cables feeding four 480V vital ac buses, combined with random failure of the diesel generators, may lead to a SBO. In the turbine building mezzanine, the two dominant scenarios involve fires that damage cables leading to either an SBO or loss of service water. Together, these zones represent about 25% of the total plant fire-induced CDF.

Case 6 - Arkansas Nuclear One Units 1 and 2: No detail was provided regarding the nature of the postulated turbine building fire scenarios. However, for each unit, the single most significant contributor to fire-induced CDF is a fire zone in the turbine building. For Unit 2 this zone represents about 40% of the total fire CDF. For Unit 1 the figure is about 20%.

Case 7 - Peach Bottom Units 2 and 3: The Peach Bottom IPEEE fire analysis did not carry through to a full CDF calculation. "Rather, an unavailability of selected systems was calculated using PSA modeling techniques and plant specific models." That is, not all potential accident mitigation strategies were credited. Nonetheless, the licensee study found that the most significant potential fire risk contributor was one zone in the turbine building. Two other turbine building fire zones were also identified as important fire contributors. The submittal provided little detail regarding the specific sequences associated with any given fire area. However, the submittal reached a general conclusion that "fires that impact offsite power and containment heat removal appear to have the largest effect when determining the screening potential of individual fire areas."

It appears that the most significant factor in the turbine building assessments was whether or not safety-related cables and/or equipment were located in the turbine building. These conditions were plant-specific. The cases where the turbine building was found to be an important contributor to fire CDF often involved offsite power and other power distribution equipment such as switchgear and motor control centers. Other systems, such as service water, were impacted on a case-specific basis. In at least one case, the routing of numerous safety-related cables through the turbine building and reliance on complex remote operator actions were also significant factors.

It was also apparent that the inherent potential for severe fires in the turbine building was a significant factor in the cited analyses. Most of the identified significant turbine building fire risk scenarios appear to be associated with large fires (often large oil fires) causing somewhat wide-spread fire damage up to and including total loss of the turbine building. Smaller fires did not appear to play a significant role in the final estimates of CDF contributions for these areas. In some cases fire scenarios involving more limited fires were explicitly found to have little CDF contribution.

3.3.2.1.6 Other Contributing Fire Zones

It was also of note that many other zones were ranked among the dominant fire CDF contributors by various submittals. These include some additional zones that can be easily identified as zones that are common to many plants, such as diesel generator, battery, electrical equipment/relay, intake structures, switchyards, and penetration rooms. They also include zones that are somewhat unique to each individual plant.

For example, in two cases involving four NPP units, many of the panels normally located in the main control room had been placed in a separate "Auxiliary Electric Equipment Room." This zone was found to be a dominant contributor to fire CDF. Other zones reported as significant fire CDF contributors included quite a wide range of zones depending on plant-specific factors. This included various zones of the reactor building or auxiliary building, shutdown board rooms, containment penetration zones, service water pump rooms, various electrical equipment zones, remote shutdown panel zones, and battery rooms.

In general, the most important factor contributing to the importance of these zones is the relationship of important cables to credible fire sources. In most cases, zones that contain cables for a significant number of important systems were important contributors to the CDF. For example, a fire in the CCW pump room at one plant was identified as causing loss of all CCW and subsequent unmitigated RCP seal failure. There were also many zones where the location of many important components may not translate to high fire-induced CDFs. Some fire zones were identified that have high conditional probabilities of core damage, but the resulting CDF is low due to a low frequency of fire due to lack of fixed sources (self-ignited cable fires generally being excluded from the analyses).

There were also many cases where the fire-induced failures were not substantial, but because of their nature, the additional random failures needed to result in core damage had high probabilities. For example, the dominant scenario at one plant was a fire in a diesel generator room that failed the diesel and caused a loss of offsite power. The additional failure of the redundant diesel generator to start resulted in an SBO that resulted in a LOCA from an RCP seal failure. No coolant injection systems were available to mitigate the LOCA.

3.3.2.1.7 Containment

One area that was consistently found to be an insignificant contributor to fire CDF was the containment building. All of the IPEEE fire analyses screened the containment as an insignificant CDF contributor. For BWR plants, this was often based on inerting of the containment structure during operation. For PWR plants, screening was typically based on a combination of low combustible fuel loads, spatial separation of critical cables, few fixed fire sources, essentially no possibility of transient combustibles, and the presence of automatic fire detection and suppression systems. (See further discussion in Section 3.4.9.2.2.)

3 - 26

3.3.2.2 Contribution of Multi-Zone Scenarios

Multi-zone fire scenarios consider fires that occur in one fire analysis zone that may spread to, or impact, an adjacent fire analysis zone. In this stage of the analysis, fire zones that were determined to be insignificant CDF contributors in and of themselves (e.g., due to the lack of safety equipment) may re-emerge as important CDF contributors if a potential exists for impact on an adjacent zone. Multi-zone sets typically involve pairs of adjacent fire zones, but may also involve three or more individual fire zones.

The vast majority of the IPEEE submittals included an initial screening analysis for multi-zone fire scenarios based on the approach outlined in FIVE. The FIVE approach is known as the Fire Compartment Interaction Analysis (FCIA). The FCIA considers a number of mitigating features, including the combustible fuel loading, fire detection and suppression capability, and the rating of the barrier between fire analysis zones, to determine whether or not a potential exists for fire spread from one fire analysis zone to another. When a multi-zone set displays various combinations of these mitigating features, the multi-zone fire propagation scenario is screened qualitatively (e.g., any pair of zones separated by a 2- or 3-hour rated fire barrier would automatically screen). Slightly less than half of the IPEEE submittals (32 of 70) screened all multi-zone scenarios using FCIA-based qualitative arguments.

In those cases where a multi-room scenario survived the FCIA screening process (i.e., was not eliminated), two approaches were possible. In many cases, licensees included quantitative screening, or analysis, of unscreened multi-zone scenarios (see further discussion of these cases below). In the other cases, licensees re-defined the fire analysis zone boundaries so as to combine the unscreened multi-zone set into a single larger fire analysis zone, an option specifically mentioned in FIVE. In such cases, the final results are typically presented as the CDF contribution for the larger combined analysis zone, rather than as a multi-zone scenario (see related discussion in Sections 3.4.2.1 and 3.4.6). That is, the CDF contribution arising from the original multi-zone scenarios may be masked within the overall CDF contribution for the newly defined larger fire analysis zone. Hence, there may be a pool of CDF contributors that actually derive from multi-zone scenarios as originally defined by the analysis, but that were not identified as multi-zone scenarios in the final reporting of CDF contributors. In such cases, any insights regarding multi-zone CDF would also be masked.

Just over half of the submittals (38) provided some quantitative assessment of the CDF contribution for one or more multi-compartment fire scenarios that did not screen qualitatively. These submittals generally fell into one of two categories. The first category includes those cases where the FCIA qualitative screening left unscreened scenarios, and those scenarios were analyzed quantitatively (as noted immediately above). The second category includes those submittals based on direct application of PRA-based methods (i.e., those that did not employ the FIVE methods). In both cases, it was commonly assumed that fire spread to an adjacent fire analysis zone would only occur given failure of fire-fighting efforts in the compartment of fire origin and failure of the intervening fire barrier. A failure probability of 0.01 per demand was often assumed to characterize fire barrier reliability.

Of these 38 submittals, 79% (30) concluded that all of the multi-compartment fire scenarios could be screened quantitatively. The remainder (i.e., 8 out of 38) provided CDFs for one or more unscreened multi-zone fire scenarios. It is interesting to note that two of these last eight submittals used the qualitative FCIA screening criteria and quantified the unscreened scenarios. The other six used a quantitative PRA-based methodology (e.g., a spatial interaction methodology) for the entire analysis (screening and quantification). As a very general observation, the FCIA screening method generally resulted in screening of the vast majority of multi-compartment scenarios. In contrast, the application of PRA-based methods generally led to the identification of numerous low-CDF multi-zone scenarios.

The results for the eight cases reporting quantitative multi-zone CDF estimates are summarized in Table 3.5. The total CDF contribution of the multi-zone scenarios ranges from 8E-8/ry to 6.7E-6/ry. As a fraction of the total plant-wide fire CDF, the multi-zone scenarios ranged from less than 1% to about 27%. Note that

Table 3.5: Summary of multi-compartment fire scenario quantification results for those plants that reported a CDF contribution for one or more multi-compartment fire scenarios

| Plant name: | Total fire CDF (/ry) | Multi-zone | | Comments: |
		CDF (/ry)	% of total	
Beaver Valley Unit 1	1.8E-5	5E-7	3%	Both units used spatial interaction method supplemented with qualitative screening criteria.
Beaver Valley Unit 2	1.1E-5	8E-7	7%	
Comanche Peak Unit 1	2.1E-5	7E-7	3%	PRA approach used. Fire suppression and barriers are credited. Screening criteria of 5E-7 applied to multi-zone versus 1E-7 for single-zone scenarios.
Fitzpatrick	2.6E-5	3.3E-6	12%	PRA approach used. Assumes multi-zone CCDP is unity. Credits fire frequency, non-suppression probability, barrier reliability, and a severity factor. No multi-zone set gives greater than 1E-6/ry CDF. 25 multi-zone sets contribute to final answer with five sets dominant.
Hatch Unit 1	7.8E-6	8E-8	1%	Spatial interaction method applied to screen multi-zone sets. Some multi-zone sets that did not screen were combined into larger zones for final analysis.
Indian Point Unit 2	2.5E-5	6.7E-6	27%	Multi-zone scenarios were not considered in the original analysis, but were analyzed in response to NRC review RAI. FCIA screening approach applied and unscreened scenarios were quantified.
Indian Point Unit 3	5.6E-5	5E-6	9%	Quantitative screening approach crediting fire frequency, fire suppression, and barrier reliability. Only one multi-zone set survived the screening at 1E-6/ry.
San Onofre Unit 2	1.6E-5	2E-6	12%	Initial screening using FCIA criteria. Four multi-zone sets survived qualitative screening. Zones were combined for final analysis, but are tracked explicitly. Only one of the four combined zones survived as a contributor in the final analysis.

Indian Point Unit 2 reported the highest CDF values for multi-compartment fire scenarios in terms of both the absolute and relative contribution. In this case, the licensee had not originally included multi-compartment scenarios in the IPEEE fire analysis. A revised analysis was provided in response to an RAI sent during the IPEEE review process, and it is this revised analysis that is the basis for the values reported here.

3.3.2.3 Dominant Accident Sequences

A review of the IPEEE results reveals that the dominant fire scenarios result in some sort of plant transient. Fire-induced LOCAs were considered for many plants. With few exceptions, these scenarios were not found to be important. The most significant exception was RCP seal LOCAs that were found to be important contributors for many Westinghouse PWR plants. It should be noted that there is a tentative basis for this insight since most licensees did not provide easily extractable information regarding the type of accident sequences that were contributing to the fire-induced CDF. The plant transients identified include loss of feedwater, main steam isolation valve (MSIV) closure, loss of offsite power (LOOP), and loss-of-support-system transients. The support system transients include loss of electrical buses (both ac and dc), loss of cooling water systems, loss of instrument air, and loss of heating, ventilation, and air conditioning (HVAC) systems.

The type of plant transient initiated by the fire is obviously a function of which system cables are located in the zone under analysis. Loss of electrical buses was a prevalent accident sequence for switchgear zone fires. Station blackout sequences were important in fire zones containing offsite power cables. Dual-unit LOOP sequences were identified as a potential outcome of switchyard fires at some plants.

Even less information was readily available concerning the types of plant accident sequences that were assumed, or determined by analysis, to occur as the result of fire damage. Although fire scenarios might cause failure of both coolant injection systems and decay heat removal systems (and their support systems), the specific type of plant accident sequence associated with any given fire scenario is not usually indicated in the submittals. The potential for spurious component actuation was generally not addressed in the scenario discussions. A small number of licensees did provide some indication of the type of accident sequence through their documentation of the plant damage states assigned to fire scenarios. None of the submittals discussed a CDF contribution associated with anticipated transient without scram (ATWS) sequences. It appears that none of the submittals evaluated the impact of fires on the reactor protection system.

LOCAs initiated by spurious opening of power operated relief valves (PORVs) or safety relief valves (SRVs) were generally not identified as significant contributors to the fire-induced CDF. However, some contribution from transient-induced LOCAs was noted. These sequences include transients with stuck open relief valves and RCP seal LOCAs. RCP seal LOCAs were identified as significant contributors at several Westinghouse PWRs. Westinghouse reactor coolant pumps have been perceived as more susceptible to seal failure than the pumps typically used in Babcock and Wilcox (B&W) and Combustion Engineering (CE) plants. The failures result from the loss of both seal injection from the charging pumps and loss of seal cooling, which is usually supplied by the component cooling water (CCW) system. The failure of the CCW system can also result in failure of the coolant injection systems need to mitigate the LOCA. For this reason, RCP seal failure logic has been incorporated into the IPE models used in the fire PRAs. This logic is variable as different plants have additional systems or actions in place to prevent and mitigate RCP seal LOCAs. The important RCP seal LOCA scenarios involve failures of component cooling water or service water systems (both fire-induced and random failures). Additionally, fire-initiated station blackout scenarios leading to RCP seal LOCAs were identified.

3.4 Models and Methods Perspectives

This section focuses on the overall methods of analysis applied in the IPEEE fire assessments. These discussions are not intended to establish the state-of-the-art in fire PRA or to expound on how a fire risk analysis "should" be done. Rather, the discussions consider how the chosen method impacts the results obtained and insights gained by licensees. Some discussion as to the efficacy and, in particular, the pitfalls of specific approaches as observed in the IPEEE is inevitable. However, the authors have attempted to avoid judgemental conclusions regarding a particular approach. Topics that became points of particular attention during the review process are also discussed. In many cases, the discussions compare the methods applied in the IPEEE to the methods discussed in NUREG/CR-2300, NUREG/CR-4840, NUREG/CR-2258, and other sources (e.g., Kazarians, 1985). Such discussions are intended to establish a basis for comparison of the IPEEE results and insights to those of past fire PRAs when such comparisons are appropriate.

This section opens with a general discussion of the overall methods chosen by licensees to support their IPEEE fire analyses (Section 3.4.1). The sub-sections which follow (Sections 3.4.2 through 3.4.9) are organized according to the steps commonly taken in the performance of a fire PRA. A typical fire PRA begins with a screening analysis to identify zones requiring some level of detailed analysis (Section 3.4.2). The detailed analysis then commonly follows a path involving the identification and characterization of fire sources (Section 3.4.3), fire growth and damage modeling (Section 3.4.4), fire detection and suppression analysis (Section 3.4.5), multi-zone fire analysis (Section 3.4.6), plant damage state and response assessment (Section 3.4.7), human reliability analysis (Section 3.4.8), and the assessment of containment performance (Section 3.4.9). The section then closes with a discussion of other related insights that do not fall explicitly into any one of the above categories (Section 3.4.10).

3.4.1 General Methods Perspectives

In this section the overall methodologies employed by licensees to identify and address fire vulnerabilities are discussed. This section focuses on the general methodologies employed, the extent of their application among licensees, and related observations. To begin, it is appropriate to discuss some aspects of the methods guidance set forth in Supplement 4 to Generic Letter (GL) 88-20 [U.S.NRC, 1991] and NUREG-1407.

GL 88-20, Supplement 4, and NUREG-1407 clearly imply that a probabilistic method was the preferred approach for the IPEEE process. While it is also stated that a licensee may use other methods, alternate methods were subject to review by U.S. NRC staff before application. In Supplement 4 to GL 88-20, the following statements address issues relevant to the selection of a methodology for the external events analysis:

> ... the Commission recognizes, based on U.S. NRC and industry experience with plant-specific probabilistic risk assessments (PRAs), that systematic examinations are beneficial in identifying plant-specific vulnerabilities to severe accidents which could be fixed with low-cost improvements.

The examination process for the IPEEE, in general, is similar to that for the internal events IPE ... Basically, the event/fault trees from the internal event IPE can be extended for external events PRAs, or used to identify important equipment for other acceptable evaluation methods . . .

The U.S. NRC recognizes that other methods (i.e., other than those presented in the Supplement 4 or NUREG 1407) capable of identifying plant-specific vulnerabilities to severe accidents due to external events may exist.

Fire-initiated events can be treated by performing a Level 1 fire PRA as described in NUREG/CR-2300 or a simplified fire PRA as described in NUREG/CR-4840.

The application of the above approaches involves considerable judgement with regards to the requested scope and depth of the study, level of analytical sophistication, and level of effort to be expended.

NUREG-1407 further clarifies the points made in Supplement 4 to GL 88-20, and provides some added detail about acceptable methodologies for performing the internal fire IPEEE. A Level 1 PRA is specifically noted as an acceptable methodology and NUREG-1407 cites background references documenting the fire PRA methods (NUREG/CR-2300, NUREG/CR-2815, NUREG/CR-4840, and NUREG/CR-5259). NUREG-1407 identifies the following steps as the major parts of a fire analysis:

- identify critical zones of vulnerability,
- calculate the frequency of fire initiation in each zone,
- analyze for disabling of critical functions,
- identify fire-induced initiating events/systems analysis, and
- perform containment analysis.

In the short explanations provided for these steps, NUREG-1407 discusses a number of specific topical areas of fire PRA interest, including the potential for cross-zone spread of fire, presence of transient fuels, location-specific evaluation of fire initiation frequencies, fire growth and spread and smoke effects, and detection/suppression effectiveness and reliability. The possibility of using other systematic examination methods (i.e., other than fire PRA) is also mentioned in NUREG-1407. Licensees were directed to request U.S. NRC review and acceptance of methods other than those specified in NUREG-1407.

After the publication of Supplement 4 to GL 88-20 and NUREG-1407, two methodologies, FIVE [EPRI, 1992] and the FPRAIG [EPRI, 1995], were developed by EPRI to provide licensees with tools to conduct the IPEEE fire examination. The objective underlying the development of FIVE, as quoted below from [EPRI, 1992], is:

... development of a more cost-effective and efficient examination methodology based on available information and knowledge obtained from Appendix R implementation as an alternative to the normal PRA process ...

In the introductory statements to FIVE it is further stated that:

> FIVE is oriented toward uncovering limiting plant design or operating characteristics (vulnerabilities) that make certain fire-initiated events more likely than others. It provides a combination of deterministic and probabilistic techniques for examining a power plant's fire probability and protection characteristics.

The guidance document for FIVE provides a description of the methodology and specifically addresses topics such as IPEEE documentation requirements and treatment of the issues raised in the Fire Risk Scoping Study (NUREG/CR-5088) [U.S.NRC, 1989] (issues that NUREG-1407 specifically requested that licensees address in their IPEEEs). FIVE was reviewed by the U.S. NRC staff and, after some modifications to the methodology and guidance document, was approved for use in the IPEEE process [U.S.NRC, 1991]. However, it should also be noted that FIVE in and of itself is largely equivalent to a fire area/zone screening analysis. It is not intended to produce a detailed quantification of fire CDF but, rather, to identify those plant areas/zones that might represent important fire CDF contributors. As will be noted below, most licensees who applied FIVE also applied quantitative fire PRA methods to refine and/or quantify the CDF contribution for unscreened areas/zones.

EPRI developed the FPRAIG with the objective of reducing conservatism in fire PRA methods. The NRC-supported review of the FPRAIG [Lambright, 1997] raised several methodological and data-related shortcomings. The FPRAIG review was completed in May 1999. At the time of publication of the review comments, many IPEEE submittals had already used the FPRAIG. Hence, a set of standardized or generic RAIs were developed to address the concerns raised in the review of the FPRAIG (see Appendix B for a discussion of the generic RAIs).

All current fire analysis methods are based on two fundamental premises: (1) the damage zone of a fire within a nuclear power plant is generally limited and nominally assumed to be bounded by rated fire barriers (with the exception of the multi-zone analysis), and (2) the significance of a fire scenario is dependent on the set of safe shutdown and core-cooling-related cables and equipment that may be damaged. In practice, the analysis of fire phenomena (i.e., fire ignition, growth, detection, and suppression) is separated from the analysis of loss of core cooling functions. All current fire analysis methods (i.e., FIVE, FPRAIG, and fire PRAs) follow this pattern.

Since a fire can occur virtually anywhere within a power plant, and may or may not affect safe shutdown and core cooling cables and equipment, the fire analysis must address a large number of fire scenarios. To minimize the overall level of effort, a screening of fire locations in the initial stages of analysis is desirable. For this reason, all current fire analysis methodologies include initial screening steps followed by detailed analysis of unscreened fire zones. It is generally in the detailed analysis that the fire phenomena, the impact on equipment and cables, and operator actions needed for safe shutdown and core cooling are considered.

In typical fire PRA approaches, the analyst tailors a loosely defined set of steps to best fit the application, zone, or scenario under analysis. In contrast, both FIVE and the FPRAIG provide a prescriptive approach to plant examination. Both methods include well-defined steps divided among several phases of analysis, graduated screening of plant zones, initial steps focusing on information gathering and screening, and use of probabilistic arguments to rank fire scenarios. Both methods also provide the input data needed to conduct a fire propagation analysis. FIVE includes a well-defined set of step-by-step worksheets with relevant input data for modeling fire ignition, growth, and damage. The FPRAIG allows more freedom to the analyst in terms of the probabilistic models applied. However, it also provides all needed input data. The approaches outlined in the FPRAIG are stated to be less conservative than FIVE.

All of the licensee IPEEE fire evaluations fell into one of the following fours categories of fire analysis approach:

- FIVE only,
- combination of FIVE and PRA methods from the FPRAIG,
- combination of FIVE and general fire PRA methods, or
- direct application of general fire PRA methods.

All of the submittals, as requested in NUREG-1407, included a discussion of the methodology adopted. From a review of those sections and the actual steps and data presented in other parts of each submittal, a methodology category was assigned to each submittal. Table 3.6 provides the number and percentage of submittals by the above-defined methodology categories.

Table 3.6: Methodologies employed in the IPEEE fire analyses

Method	Representation among all submittals	
	(# of submittals)	(% of total)
FIVE only	15	21%
FIVE, FPRAIG	23	33%
FIVE, PRA	19	27%
Fire PRA only	13	19%
Total:	70	100%

Those submittals that indicated little or no departure from the methodology and data provided in the reference [EPRI, 1992] were assigned to the "FIVE only" category.

Since the FPRAIG was specifically developed for use in the IPEEEs, to obtain some insights about this methodology, it was treated separately from more generalized approaches to fire PRA. "Combination of FIVE and PRA methods from the FPRAIG" was assigned to those submittals that began their analysis with a FIVE-based screening but went on to further quantify unscreened zones using PRA methods taken directly from the FPRAIG. In some of these cases, the FPRAIG was the primary methodology and FIVE fire propagation worksheets were used to analyze the possibility of fire damage to a specific set of equipment. Only one submittal could have been categorized as "FPRAIG only." Since the FPRAIG employs many of the methods and data from FIVE, that submittal was included in the "combination of FIVE and FPRAIG" category.

Two types of submittals were assigned to the "Combination of FIVE and general fire PRA" category. A group of submittals indicated that general fire PRA methods (not referenced to the FPRAIG) were used for the overall approach, and FIVE worksheets were used for fire propagation analysis. Another group used the initial steps of FIVE for the screening analysis, and COMPBRN [EPRI, 1991] was used for fire propagation analysis. The submittals in this group made no reference to the FPRAIG.

Those submittals that provided no mention of either FIVE or the FPRAIG in their methodology discussion were assigned to the "fire PRA only" category. This generally includes those submittals that went directly into a fire PRA approach from the outset without reliance on the FPRAIG. In two submittals, the fire hazard analysis methodology of NUREG/CR-0654 was employed. Those two submittals were also categorized as "fire PRA only" submittals.

Typically, each submittal provided a discussion of the methodology adopted, a list of fire compartments, areas, and zones, some discussion of how the analysis was conducted, intermediate analysis results, and the overall results of the analysis. None of the submittals concluded that there were plant features that could not be analyzed by the adopted methodology. From a review of the information provided, it can be inferred that all licensees were able to perform an assessment of fire risk and reach conclusions consistent with the objective of the IPEEE process using the available methodologies.

FIVE was used at some level by a significant majority of licensees. Table 3.6 shows that more than 80% of the submittals used FIVE to support their assessments. As noted above, from the perspective of the authors of FIVE, the main motivation underlying FIVE was implementation of a cost-effective approach to the IPEEE fire analysis. This was achieved, in general terms, through the use of conservative but simplified models and by utilizing information obtained from the plant's Appendix R compliance efforts. (All of the submittals, regardless of the methodology selected, did acknowledge that information related to Appendix R to 10 CFR Part 50 was used in the analysis.) However, a large majority of submittals utilizing FIVE indicated departure from the prescribed methods or data of FIVE. Of the 55 submittals that mentioned use of FIVE (either in its entirety or in part), all but five indicated that they deviated from the prescribed methodology or input data in some regard. In nine cases the deviations were minor, and the studies can still be considered to have been based almost entirely on FIVE. From the statements made in the submittals, and from a review of the results, it can be inferred that licensees chose to depart from FIVE when the results of the FIVE analysis were deemed to be unacceptably conservative or were perceived to present an unrealistic view of the fire CDF.

The following statement, quoted from one of the submittals, offers an interesting perspective into how some of the licensees viewed FIVE in relation to the FPRAIG and Appendix R:

> Although many compartments screened by applying the quantitative criterion in FIVE, it also became necessary to modify the FIVE process to evaluate [the plant]. The modifications to the FIVE process are described in detail in each section of this report. Briefly, the changes included more detailed analysis of affected circuits, improved fire initiation frequency quantification, inclusion of fire effects evaluations, and accrediting of fire prevention and suppression activities at the site. These modifications were primarily taken from the EPRI sponsored Fire PRA Implementation Guide (Ref. cited). This Guide draws on the FIVE methodology, adds data from NUREG/CR-4340 and NUREG/CR-2815, and includes insights from the SANDIA [Sandia National Laboratories] and EPRI fire research programs. This allows removal of some of the conservatism included in the original FIVE methodology, but ensures that the safe shutdown capability is maintained. The FIVE methodology is itself an extension of the 10 CFR 50 Appendix R Fire Hazards Analysis of the plant.

The majority of the submittals that used FIVE (about 70% of this group) elected to augment the methodology with data or methods from the FPRAIG or general fire PRA. As indicated in the above quotation, those submittals categorized as FIVE/FPRAIG or FIVE/PRA generally entailed the application of FIVE in the screening stages and introduction of other methods and data to quantify unscreened fire zones. That is, additional PRA-based methods were utilized primarily in the analysis of those zones that did not screen out in Step 3 of the FIVE methodology.

For example, the control room analysis methodology provided in the FPRAIG is a common addition to FIVE methodology. The use of revised heat loss factors and heat release rates, and the introduction of severity factor approaches (see Sections 4.3 and 4.4 below) were also common elements adopted from the FPRAIG. There were several cases where the main methodology and data were based on the FPRAIG, and FIVE worksheets were used for fire initiation frequency evaluation and fire propagation analysis.

For fire propagation analysis, three types of approaches were noted. Most FIVE-based submittals used the fire modeling worksheets in FIVE. Most PRA-based submittals used COMPBRN [EPRI, 1991]. In a small number of cases, while FIVE was the main methodology, COMPBRN was used for the fire propagation analysis either alone or in conjunction with FIVE worksheets. It is interesting to note that three submittals implied that the analysis was performed without any explicit modeling of fire propagation. Rather, judgement and conservative assumptions were used to assess the potential for fire growth and damage. In all three of these cases, the overall methodology was FIVE, and the total fire CDF ranged between 1.0E-05 to 5.0E-05 per reactor-year.

The perception that FIVE is generally a conservative approach in comparison to fire PRA methods appears to be confirmed when the total CDFs for various methodologies are compared. These results are illustrated in Figure 3.5. Those submittals based solely on FIVE, in general, reported larger fire-induced CDF results than the submittals that used other methods. It was also noted that the application of supplemental PRA-based methods beyond the FIVE analyses universally led to some reduction in the total CDF. Those submittals based solely on fire PRA, as a group, generally reported smaller CDFs than the submittals using other methods.

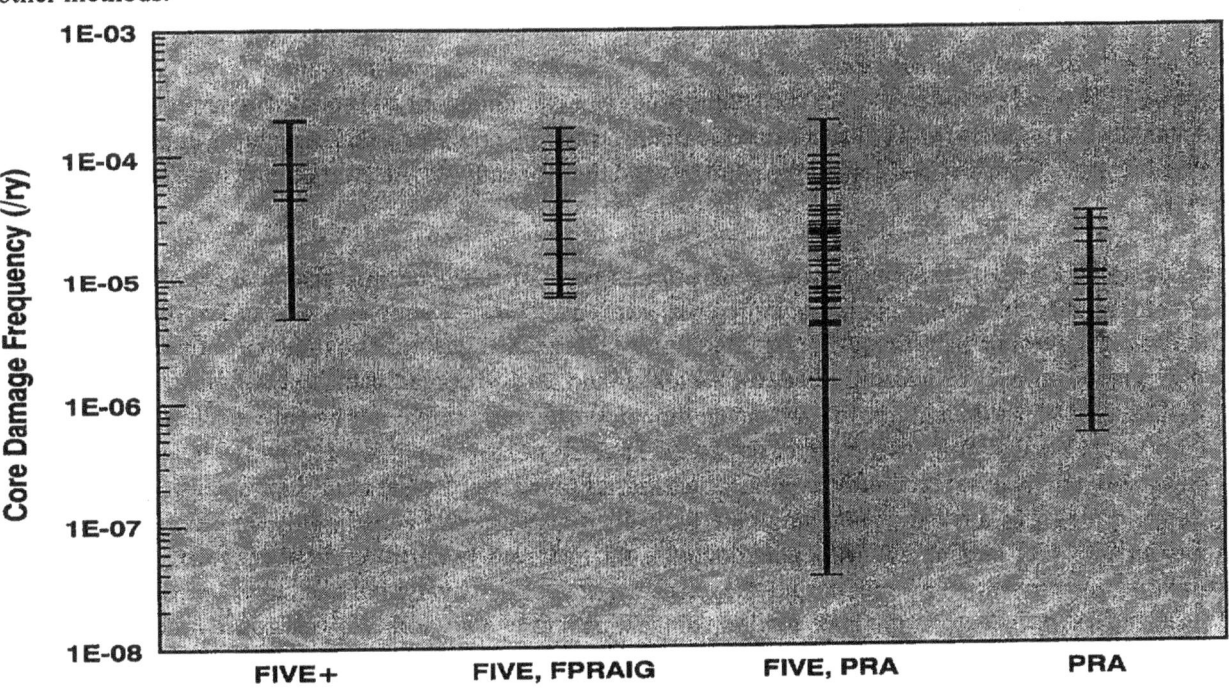

Figure 3.5 Reported total plant fire CDF versus the method of analysis employed

To summarize, all of the IPEEE fire analyses included the use of probabilistic approaches at some substantial level. A large majority of the submittals used FIVE in part or in whole. Of the submittals utilizing FIVE, most augmented FIVE with PRA methods taken either from the FPRAIG or from general fire PRA practice. The augmented analyses were typically pursued in order to reduce the conservatism perceived to exist in the FIVE screening results. The areas of augmentation varied among submittals. Typically, the screening steps were based on FIVE, and the most risk-significant contributors were analyzed further using methods from the FPRAIG or general fire PRA. None of the submittals indicated any zones where the selected methodology could not be used to address a specific plant feature.

3.4.2 Screening Analysis

3.4.2.1 Plant Partitioning

Fire is a highly spatial phenomena because any given fire will generally impact equipment within a limited spatial area of a plant. Hence, one of the first steps in a fire risk study is partitioning of the plant into physical regions commonly referred to as fire analysis zones or as fire compartments (per FIVE). All of the IPEEE fire analyses included plant partitioning, and the majority of the submittals provided a description of the partitioning basis and assumptions.

For the IPEEE studies, physical partitioning of the plant was universally completed as a part of the initial information gathering process and in conjunction with the first stages of qualitative screening. In defining fire analysis zones, all of the licensees applied a common conceptual definition of a fire zone (either explicitly or implicitly). A fire analysis zone was commonly defined as a physical region of the plant such that the effects of fires occurring within the region would, by and large, be confined to that region. However, in applying this general definition, licensees used a variety of partitioning assumptions and bases.

A majority of licensees based their fire analysis zones on the existence of substantial physical barriers to the spread of fire and fire effects. Two such approaches were predominant: (1) equate fire analysis zones to the Appendix R fire areas; and (2) subdivide the plant further by crediting other structures in partitioning. In practice, most licensees partitioned the plant beyond the Appendix R fire areas, at the least for selected fire areas.

In a smaller number of cases, licensees partitioned parts of the plant into fire analysis zones where no separating structures, or incomplete structures, existed. This last approach was generally based on the analyst's judgement that a fire and/or its damaging effects would not spread beyond the defined analysis zone (e.g., given limited fire sources, limited fuel loads, and no fire spread paths). Examples included zones partitioned off within a larger fire area even though those zones might not be fully enclosed (e.g., lacked doors), very large plant areas that were partitioned for analysis, zones separated by partial height fire barriers, and isolated hallways with limited combustibles that adjoined a larger fire area. One specific example is the reactor building in a BWR. These areas are typically quite large and contain only limited fire sources and combustible fuel loading. It was quite common for licensees to partition different levels of the reactor building into separate fire zones despite the existence of open hatchways between those levels. Even within a single level a licensee might have partitioned the area into two or more analysis zones based on extended spatial separation between PRA targets and limited fire ignition sources. Such practices were considered acceptable for the IPEEE process provided that there were no fire sources present that might threaten the larger area, and multi-zone fires were addressed appropriately.

The most significant potential impact of the partitioning process would be expected in the screening of fire areas. The initial screening of fire analysis zones was typically based on the assumption that any fire in the zone would damage all of the equipment housed within that zone (see Section 3.4.2.2 and Section 3.4.2.3). If the risk contribution given this conservative assumption is small, a fire analysis zone would be screened. Clearly, the partitioning assumptions can impact the early screening analysis because partitioning determines what equipment is assumed to be lost when a fire analysis zone is lost.

The most conservative partitioning approach observed in the IPEEE fire analyses, in general, was reliance on the Appendix R definition of fire areas. In comparison, if a more liberal partitioning approach is applied (i.e., partitioning the plant beyond the Appendix R fire areas), each fire analysis zone will, by comparison, contain less equipment, fewer fire sources, etc. Hence, a more limited fire analysis zone screens more easily, in general, than does a more extensive fire zone. This observation can be extended to both initial screening and to more detailed levels of quantitative screening as well.

Fire scenarios impacting an entire fire analysis zone were not widely postulated beyond the initial screening analysis steps. Rather, in virtually all of the submittals, the quantification of fire CDF was based on localized fire scenarios rather than on the assumption of wide spread damage to a fire analysis zone. That is, fire scenarios were developed to reflect specific fire sources leading to the loss of equipment in a limited portion of a given fire analysis zone, giving credit to detection and suppression of the fire before wide spread damage would be realized. In general, when considering such scenarios, the choices made in partitioning have little or no impact on each individual scenario because, as noted above, fire damage is generally predicted to remain localized to a region near the fire source. However, in the accumulation of the specific risk scenarios for a fire analysis zone, an impact might be observed. By subdividing the plant into more limited fire analysis zones, each zone is represented by a smaller number of specific fire scenarios. In turn, as scenarios are summed to estimate the total CDF for the zone, more limited zones would tend to have smaller CDF contributions than would corresponding but more extended fire analysis zones. Again, partitioning can impact fire analysis zone screening even at the level of detailed analysis.

In practice, it was not possible to clearly distinguish whether or not plant partitioning practices substantially impacted the results and insights gained from an IPEEE fire analysis. However, in cases where licensees were asked questions regarding partitioning assumptions, dominant fire scenarios that had previously been screened did not re-appear. The basis used for plant partitioning was questioned at some level in a significant number of the IPEEE reviews. These questions typically involved the following specific situations.

- Licensees who took credit for non-rated fire barriers were commonly asked questions to justify their partitioning assumptions. These questions were commonly resolved in one of two ways. In many cases, licensees demonstrated that the credited barrier was robust but simply lacked a specific fire rating. In other cases, verification was based on assurance that the implications of barrier failure had been considered.

- In a few cases, licensees who had relied upon the closure of large active fire barrier elements (in particular, doors) in plant partitioning were questioned. For example, in at least one case a normally open overhead roll-up door was credited as a fire barrier in partitioning. These cases were typically resolved through inclusion of fire barrier failure in the multi-zone fire analysis (see further discussion in Section 3.4.6).

- Licensees who credited partial height barriers in partitioning were also questioned. In these cases, the questions typically focused on the potential development of a damaging hot gas layer. These cases were typically resolved provided licensees considered hot gas layer scenarios in their fire analyses, and provided that the treatment of human actions considered the effects of smoke that could spread to the adjacent fire zones.

- Another partitioning practice commonly questioned was the partitioning of a fire analysis zone from a larger fire area when there were no physical barriers present. For example, in one case a hallway was partitioned and analyzed as a separate fire zone even though it was open at one end to a larger fire area. These cases were commonly resolved when licensees provided a more detailed explanation of, and justification for, the partitioning basis. In the example case, the licensee cited a low likelihood of significant fires or fire spread because the combustible load in the hallway was low, there were no significant fire sources (other than cables and potential transient fuel sources), and there were no combustible materials present in the area of the open hallway end that might contribute to fire spread to the larger fire area.

- In at least one case a licensee had treated cable raceways (trays and conduits) enclosed in a fire wrap as "virtual fire areas." That is, fire barrier clad raceways were treated as fire analysis zones independent of the larger fire area through which they passed. In this particular case, the licensee was questioned and did provide additional justification for this unique treatment. The basis for the rating of the fire barriers was established, and a qualitative discussion was provided outlining the impact on plant safety should the protected cables be lost to an exposure fire external to the fire barrier. The licensee also cited a lack of fire source threats sufficient to challenge the barriers. In this case, the practice was considered a weakness in the licensee's IPEEE analysis.

3.4.2.2 Qualitative Screening Criteria

All of the IPEEEs included at least one stage of fire analysis zone screening based on qualitative screening criteria. The overwhelming majority utilized the criteria set forth in the FIVE method [EPRI, 1992] explicitly, and the remainder of the submittals used an essentially equivalent criteria. In particular, fire analysis zones that "neither create a fire initiated event, nor cause the loss of safe shutdown functions will be screened from further consideration."[6]

In very few cases, generally involving early submittals, qualitative screening was based on a subtly different criterion deriving from an earlier draft version of FIVE. This draft version of FIVE stated that fire analysis zones could be screened *either* if equipment damage would not lead directly to a fire initiator *or* if no safe shutdown functions would be lost. Licensees who used this earlier version of the guidance were asked by the U.S. NRC to re-examine their screening results using the final FIVE guidance. Fire scenarios that were previously screened did not re-emerge as dominant contributors in any of these cases. In most cases, additional screening criteria were applied to screen the impacted zones (e.g., using quantitative criteria). In very few cases, licensees argued a low risk contribution for the impacted zones based on results for sister-unit sites with similar configurations where the more restrictive screening criteria were applied.

---

[6] See [EPRI, 1992], page 4-3.

3.4.2.3 Quantitative Screening Criteria

All of the IPEEE submittals applied at least one stage of quantitative screening for those areas that survived the qualitative screening. In a majority of cases, two or more stages of quantitative screening were applied. Indeed, the majority of the IPEEE fire analyses can be characterized as a continuing process of quantitative screening that incorporated progressive levels of detailed analysis. This is not inconsistent with past PRA practices.

In the majority of the submittals, the first stage of quantitative screening was based on the assumption that any fire in a fire analysis zone would damage all of the equipment in that zone. This is typical of fire PRA practice as described above, and only a small number of analyses bypassed this explicit step in screening altogether. However, in the vast majority of cases, as fire analysis zones were analyzed in increasing levels of complexity, any time a fire zone's CDF contribution fell below the screening criterion the zone was considered to have been screened. Such areas were typically not included in the final CDF estimates (i.e., there was no consideration of the screening truncation error). Given the IPEEE focus on identification of vulnerabilities, consideration of this potential truncation error was not deemed necessary in order to meet the IPEEE objectives.

The most commonly applied quantitative screening criterion was screening of fire analysis zones that fell below a CDF contribution of 1E-6/ry. This was the criterion recommended in both NUREG-1407 and FIVE. In relatively few cases, lower screening thresholds were applied. These typically involved three cases; licensees who concluded that the total plant fire CDF was below 1E-6/ry and chose to quantify fire CDF using a lower screening threshold; licensees who chose a screening criterion based on a fraction of the internal events CDF from the IPE (e.g., 1/100 of the IPE CDF); and licensees who went straight into a fire PRA analysis and applied a screening criterion typical of past fire PRAs (most commonly 1E-8/ry).

In general, a screening analysis was considered to have met the objectives of the IPEEE process provided that there was assurance that fire analysis zones were not screened prematurely. When cases of apparent premature screening were observed, the staff requested additional information from the licensee. These most commonly involved cases where credit was given to fire suppression (either manual or fixed systems) without consideration of the timing of fire damage versus detection/suppression (see Section 3.4.5) and/or without the application of severity factors during screening (see Section 3.4.10.2).

In very few cases, licensees performed quantitative screening on the basis of individual fire scenarios rather than based on fire zone contributions. This practice was also questioned in the review process. The perception of reviewers was that by dividing the fire threat in a given fire zone into small enough pieces (fire scenarios), one could ultimately screen out all fire scenarios as being below the screening threshold. This was found to be contrary to the IPEEE intent. Licensees in such cases were asked to revise their results based on screening of fire zones, not fire scenarios. In many of these cases, fire zones that were previously screened re-emerged as visible CDF contributors (i.e., above the screening criteria), or zone CDF contributions were increased when screened fire scenarios were re-introduced.

In very few cases, licensees screened fire scenarios by comparing the frequency of the fire initiating event to the corresponding initiating event frequency from the IPE study. That is, if the likelihood that a given fire might cause a particular initiating event was lower than the corresponding event frequency from internal events, then the fire scenario was screened. Licensees typically argued that the fire scenario was bounded by the internal events analysis. This approach was found to be inappropriate for the IPEEE process. It was intended that licensees would assess the actual plant fire risk regardless of its relative magnitude in comparison to internal events. Also, some recovery actions credited in the internal events analysis may not be possible or may have substantially lower likelihoods of success given a fire (see Section 3.4.8). Such cases were universally questioned, and licensees were asked to justify this screening criterion if the comparison was based solely on the initiating event frequencies without taking into account potential fire-induced failures of mitigating systems.

One final practice questioned by reviewers involved the application of CCDP values in screening that were derived directly from the internal events plant models. These models typically credit human recovery actions. In some cases, these human recovery actions might not be possible, or might be less reliable, given a fire. This practice would also generally exclude the consideration of spurious equipment actuations that might be postulated as a result of fire-induced cable failures and that might compromise the safe shutdown capability. Internal events models do not, in general, model spurious equipment actuations. Hence, without some review and modification of the plant models, these scenarios would not be captured. In such cases, licensees were asked to re-examine their screening results to ensure that the former situation, in particular inappropriate credit for adversely impacted operator recovery actions, was avoided (see Section 3.4.8). In the vast majority of cases, licensees concluded that the credited operator actions would not be impacted by the fire. Such scenarios did not re-emerge as dominant CDF contributors in any case.

Ultimately, licensees found that most fire zones at most plants could be screened in the IPEEE analyses (i.e., most plants were left with a relatively small number of unscreened zones). Indeed, a small number of licensees screened all of the individual plant fire zones as risk-insignificant. Fire PRAs commonly screen a majority of the fire analysis zones in a plant. Indeed, it is not uncommon for a fire PRA to consider detailed analysis in fewer that a dozen fire zones. With regard to the IPEEEs, the use of a 1E-6/ry CDF screening criterion meant that many fire zones that would nominally be expected to be visible contributors to fire CDF were screened by licensees (e.g., depending on the particular plant, cable spreading rooms, cable vault and tunnel areas, switchgear areas, and main control rooms for some plants). Here again, the IPEEE process focused on the identification of fire vulnerabilities. Hence, screening at this level was considered appropriate for the IPEEE process, whereas a more generalized PRA study would likely use a lower screening threshold.

3.4.3   Treatment of Fire Sources

One important step in a fire risk analysis is to identify and characterize the fire sources of concern. Characterization of a fire source includes establishing (1) which fire sources are to be included, (2) the location of the fire sources in the plant, (3) the frequency of occurrence of a given fire source or of fires in general in a given plant area, and (4) the characteristics of the source fire once ignited. The following subsections discuss these aspects of fire source characterization.

It is notable that all of the IPEEE analyses treated the task of identifying and characterizing fire sources using a combination of actual fire experience (fire databases), fire test results, and plant walkdowns. Most licensees relied on at least to some extent, if not entirely, the methods of analysis documented in FIVE [EPRI, 1992]. The EPRI "Fire Event Data Base" [EPRI, 1993] was also widely cited.

3.4.3.1 Identification and Characterization of Fire Sources

Fire sources are commonly divided into two broad classes; namely, in situ or fixed fire sources and transient fire sources. The treatment of each is somewhat unique. The fixed fire sources generally encompass all of the materials and equipment that are permanently located within the plant boundaries. This typically includes the full set of electrical equipment at the plant, and may include other items such as flammable gases. Self-ignited cable fires would also be categorized as in situ fire sources. Transient fire sources are those which are not permanently fixed in the plant, and typically include temporary storage items, accumulated refuse, packing materials, construction or maintenance support materials, and semi-permanent storage items (e.g., flammable liquid storage cabinets, protective clothing storage). These various fire sources are discussed in the subsections that follow.

One general observation can be made that spans the full range of fire sources considered by licensees in their IPEEE fire analyses. The vast majority of the IPEEE fire analyses were based on point estimates of the fire source intensity. That is, a given fire source would be assumed to have one particular heat release rate (HRR), and the fire damage scenarios were developed accordingly. In reality, fires in any particular source carry the potential for a range of fire intensities, depending on a number of factors that will influence fire growth behavior. Furthermore, the fire intensities that were assumed in the IPEEE process rarely bounded the range of fires that one might reasonably postulate involving any given fire source. While a few submittals did postulate large or bounding fires, the majority of fire IPEEE analyses did not consider the impact of larger fires on plant fire CDF.

Large severe fires that can cause wide spread damage to all equipment in a fire area are not commonly postulated in a fire PRA, except in screening assessments (although, again, some exceptions exist in the analysis of unscreened areas performed in the IPEEEs). Rather, in a fire PRA, fire models are used to assess the fire growth and damage potential of the fire sources postulated in the analysis of each scenario. These fire sources have commonly been represented by a range of fire intensities, even in the earliest fire PRA studies of the early 1980s. A typical fire PRA might, for example, postulate low, medium, and high heat release rate characteristics for any given fire source. Each "size bin" would be assigned a fraction of the total fire source frequency. This is where the concept of fire severity factors (see Section 3.4.10.2) was first introduced.

Fire models often predict fire growth and damage for the larger fires but not for the smaller fires. By considering only a single fire source intensity that may not represent the fire potential, the CDF contribution for some scenarios may be underestimated. In the review process, when such cases were identified, they were commonly questioned. In particular, cases associated with electrical panel and transformer fire sources were widely questioned. In response to these questions, licensees generally provided qualitative assessments of the potential impact (or lack thereof) of larger fires, re-analyzed the cases using a higher fire intensity, or assessed the margin between the intensity of fires postulated in the analysis and the fire intensity required to cause more wide spread damage.

Only a small number of submittals provided explicit treatment of the potential variation in fire size as a part of CDF quantification. For these licensees, it was common to find the greatest CDF contribution deriving from the larger fires, despite the fact that these fires were assumed to be less likely, in general, than smaller fires. This, too, is consistent with the findings of most past fire PRAs.

3.4.3.1.1 Electrical Panel Fires

Fires involving electrical panels were given considerable treatment in virtually all of the IPEEE submittals. Electrical panel fire scenarios were identified by most licensees as key contributors to fire CDF. This included scenarios in most of the commonly reported dominant fire zones such as the MCR, switchgear rooms, auxiliary electrical rooms, and relay rooms (see Section 3.3.2.1). The CSR was also commonly identified as an important fire CDF contributor and, in many cases, the risk contribution was dominated by fire scenarios involving electrical panels co-located in such zones (see Section 3.3.2.1.3). CSRs that lacked electrical panels (and/or other fire sources) were often found to have relatively small CDF contributions.

The treatment of electrical panel fires became a point of particular interest to IPEEE reviews following publication of the FPRAIG. One of two issues raised in this regard was that the FPRAIG recommended that panel fires could be modeled, in general, assuming an HRR of 69 kW (65 BTU/s). As discussed further in Appendix B, EPRI provided revised guidance regarding this topic that (1) described the conditions under which the 69 kW HRR value could be assumed to apply and (2) suggested use of a higher HRR value (200 kW or 180 BTU/s) for most other panel fires. Many licensees were asked to re-assess their electrical panel fire scenarios using this revised guidance. Responses to these questions generally fell into one of the following categories.

- In most cases, licensees concluded that raising the panel fire HRR did not introduce additional risk scenarios that had not been captured in the original quantification. That is, fire targets remained undamaged even given the higher HRR value.

- In a few cases, licensees cited that the increased HRR had no effect, specifically because the critical targets had already been assumed to be damaged given the 69 kW fire. Hence, again, no new scenarios were introduced.

- In a few cases, licensees did report that raising the fire heat release led to damage that had not been found possible before. As a result, some new fire scenarios were added to the quantification of fire CDF. Previously screened scenarios were not found to be dominant CDF contributors in any such cases.

- In many cases, licensees re-stated their bases for applicability of the originally assumed 69 kW (65 BTU/s) HRR using the revised EPRI guidance, and did not provide re-analysis results.

Overall, it is difficult to assess the impact that the assumptions regarding electrical panel fire intensity had on the results of the IPEEE fire analyses. It was clear that the impact was plant-specific as one might expect. For most plants no changes in CDF were reported; while for a minority, some previously screened fire scenarios re-emerged as visible (i.e., unscreened) CDF contributors. The differences in results appeared to be tied most directly to differences in the separation distance between panels and overhead cables and assumptions made regarding the "virtual height" of the fire (e.g., modeling the fire as being located on top of the panel, at the floor, or somewhere in between).

A second aspect of the FPRAIG that became a point of particular attention was the treatment of closed electrical panels. In particular, the FPRAIG recommended that electrical panels that lacked ventilation grills or other normally open penetrations could be screened a priori as exposure fire ignition sources (see Appendix B for a more detailed discussion). Revised EPRI guidance directed licensees to reconsider the screening of closed electrical panels, in particular, for electrical panels that might be subject to energetic (explosive) electrical faults. This included transformers and a range of 480V and higher electrical panels.

3 - 42

Licensee responses to this aspect of the question commonly followed the same pattern as those relating to panel HRR described immediately above. Relatively few licensees identified new fire scenarios of significance that had previously been screened.

Overall, electrical panels were found by licensees to be one of the most significant potential contributors to fire risk. At the same time, the methods of analysis applied to panel fires remain an area of quantification uncertainty and debate.

3.4.3.1.2 Self-Ignited Cable Fires

Nuclear plant experience includes fires that began as the result of a cable electrical overload and overheating of the cable (see, for example, [San Onofre, 1968]). Such fires are referred to as self-ignited cable fires. The treatment of self-ignited cable fires varied in the IPEEEs.

Most licensees followed the FIVE guidance which recommended that self-ignited cable fires occurring in a cable run would be limited to non-qualified cables.[7] As a result, most licensees dismissed self-ignited cable fires based on the use of qualified cables in the plant. Many plants that were built before 1975 (before the Institute of Electrical and Electronic Engineers (IEEE) cable qualification standard was adopted) also took this approach. In these cases, licensees cited that cables had been "back-qualified" as low flame spread during Appendix R implementation efforts and, again, dismissed self-ignited cable fires.

Relatively few licensees provided explicit treatment of self-ignited cable fires. Those licensees who treated such fires also stated that they had followed the FIVE guidance in this regard. In no case was a self-ignited cable fire scenario found to be a dominant CDF contributor. Indeed, self-ignited cable fires tended to screen based on the FIVE approach. Only in a very small number of cases were self-ignited cable fires found to be visible CDF contributors. These rare cases generally involved cable vault and tunnel areas or CSR areas that were devoid of other significant ignition sources. If risk-important cables converge within such a fire zone, forming a cable "pinch-point," then any significant fire might have the potential to challenge nuclear safety. In the final analysis, these scenarios were found to be visible but not dominant fire CDF contributors. This can be attributed to two likely factors. First, implementation of Appendix R has eliminated the most significant cable pinch-point problems. Second, while the consequences of a significant fire might be risk challenging, the likelihood that such a fire will arise from a self-ignited cable fire is considered very small.

In the United States, self-ignited fires are relatively rare even taking the nuclear industry experience as a whole. The frequency of such fires is further reduced when considering a fire scenario impacting a specific location within an individual plant. In FIVE,[8] the plant-wide self-ignited cable fire frequency was estimated

---

[7] Qualification in this context refers to qualification per the IEEE-383 flame spread test.

[8] To obtain the generic self-ignited cable fire frequency, FIVE divided the total number of fires reported by the number of reactor-years accumulated by the entire U.S. nuclear industry. However, such fires are argued to apply only to plants with un-qualified cable runs. These two statements are in conflict. The reactor-years of experience used in the fire frequency calculation should be limited to those plants subject to such fires rather than the entire industry. Based on the IPEEEs, only a small fraction of plants (not more than 1 in 10) contain cables that have not been qualified as low flame spread. As a result, FIVE may have understated the self-ignited cable fire frequency appropriate to those plants subject to

as 6.3E-3/ry as compared to a fire frequency for all fires generally assumed to be on the order of 0.1/ry. Under FIVE, the plant-wide fire frequency is partitioned to a specific fire zone using a weighting (or partitioning) factor based on the ratio of cable weight (or BTU content) in the area of interest to the total cable weight (or BTU content) for all Appendix R fire areas (excluding the rad-waste and containment areas). As a result, the fire frequency may be reduced by two orders of magnitude or more in the consideration of a specific fire scenario. Given a fire frequency of less than 1E-4 under the worst conditions, even a modest CCDP, on the order of 1E-2 or less, would lead to screening under the FIVE approach. The additional consideration of intervention by fire suppression would further reduce any potential contribution.

Given the low fire frequency cited in FIVE, for such fires to appear as significant CDF contributors required that the scenario be associated with a high CCDP value (on the order of 0.1 or greater) implying loss of multiple trains of safe shutdown equipment. Given implementation of Appendix R separation criteria, few such areas remain in U.S. plants. Furthermore, any area containing a cable pinch-point (i.e., a point where redundant safe shutdown cables are in close proximity and lack 3-hour barrier separation) would generally require fixed automatic detection and suppression (e.g., per Appendix R unless an exemption had been granted). Hence, substantial suppression credit could typically be taken in the quantification of such scenarios. This further reduces their potential CDF contribution.

Consistent with these observations, self-ignited cable fires were found to be of potential importance in only a very small number of cases. These cases generally involved areas devoid of other fixed ignition sources,[9] a convergence of risk-important cables, and some specific limitation to the fire suppression capability. The findings of the IPEEEs in this regard may not, however, be robust.

In the NRC review process attention regarding self-ignited cable fires focused on those areas devoid of other ignition sources. This commonly included cable tunnel areas and some cable spreading rooms (those that lacked any other electrical equipment or panels). The NRC generally questioned cases where a licensee had screened such fire zones based only on the fire ignition frequency. In most such cases, revised fire CDF estimates were provided (these often included transient fire sources as well, see Section 3.4.3.1.3), although, again, such scenarios did not appear as dominant CDF contributors.

3.4.3.1.3 Transient Fires

Transient fuel fires have one unique characteristic in comparison to other fire sources; namely, transient fuel fires are not fixed in place so that a fire involving these combustibles could nominally occur anywhere in the plant. This implies that transient fuel fires may threaten plant equipment, in particular cables, in locations where no other fire sources might be found.

---

such fires.

[9] Note that fire zones devoid of other fixed ignition sources are still potentially subject to both self-ignited cables fires (assuming cables are present) and transient fire sources. Hence, the treatment of transient fires and self-ignited cable fires is loosely linked in the sense that if such fire sources are found to be visible CDF contributors, it is likely that the same set of fire zones will be involved for both sources.

The treatment of transient fires varied substantially in the IPEEE studies. In a majority of cases, licensees provided explicit treatment of transient fire sources using the approach developed for fire PRA as outlined in FIVE. Under this approach one postulates that a transient fire may occur at any location in the plant. Fire frequency is based on partitioning the plant-wide transient fire frequency to the specific location of interest, typically based on floor area ratios (see Section 3.4.3.2.2 for additional discussion of fire frequency partitioning methods). The impact of a fire is then assessed in a manner similar to treatment of other fire sources.

In other cases, licensees provided a more limited examination of transient fires. For example, some studies considered transient fires only in areas where the fixed combustibles did not yield critical damage or where there were effectively no fixed fire sources present. For other areas, it was assumed that fires involving the fixed combustibles, being generally of higher frequency, would bound the contribution of transient fire sources. Licensees who took this approach were commonly asked to verify that there were no potential cable pinch-points that might be threatened by a transient source but were not threatened by fixed sources.

The treatment of transient fires was one area impacted by application of the FPRAIG. A statement was made in the FPRAIG to the effect that if the fixed fire sources in a fire zone screen, then it is likely the transient fire sources will also screen (see Appendix B for a more detailed discussion). A number of submittals interpreted this statement as implying that transients could be screened without further analysis if the fixed fire sources screened. Later guidance [EPRI, 1999] clarified that the intent of the passage was to reflect the likely outcome of the transient fire analysis, rather than allowing for direct screening of transient sources. A number of licensees who had misinterpreted the FPRAIG were asked to re-examine transient fire sources and did provide revised fire CDFs to reflect explicit treatment of transient fires.

Another assumption made by a large number of licensees related to crediting administrative controls/procedures in the analysis of transient fire sources. A number of licensees had dismissed transient fire sources, generally from specific fire zones, based on administrative controls that prohibited bringing significant quantities of transient fuels into the zone. These approaches were not generally accepted in the U.S. NRC review process. Rather, the reviewers commonly asked that the analysis be revised to reflect the potential that transient fires might occur at any location in the plant regardless of administrative controls. Reviewers typically cited that all plants have administrative controls and that transient fires have been recorded in administratively controlled zones. Hence, the reliance on administrative controls alone was not an adequate basis for screening transient fuel fires. As in other cases, a number of licensees did provide revised analyses to incorporate previously screened transient fires. Dominant fire scenarios did not arise from these revisions in any case, although new scenarios that were visible contributors to fire CDF were identified in a number of cases.

One specific class of transient fires is fires that result from welding or cutting operations. These fires often received unique treatment in the IPEEEs. Virtually all of the licensees cited that welding and cutting operations are subject to a specific fire safety notification and permit system. Furthermore, virtually all of the licensees who provided an explicit discussion of such fires cited that continuous fire watches are posted when such operations are active. Hence, most analyses assumed a substantial credit for prompt suppression of such fires. Often, a severity factor was applied to reflect an assumption that most such fires would be suppressed well before risk-important equipment might be threatened. Use of a severity factor of 0.1 was common (i.e., 10% of all fires might become threatening fires).

Overall, the IPEEE findings for transient fires were similar to those cited above for self-ignited cable fires. In one case (Millstone Unit 2) the licensee classified one scenario involving a relatively permanent fuel source classified (protective clothing storage bins and racks) as a transient fire exposing safety-related cables led to a fire vulnerability (see Section 3.2.1.2 for further discussion of this case). In a second case (Palo Verde) a transient fire scenario was found to hold the potential to cause a LOOP for all three units. For other licensees transient fires were rarely found to be significant contributors to fire CDF, although several licensees did identify transient fires as a visible (i.e., unscreened) contributor to fire CDF. Those areas where the contribution of transient fires was visible typically involved zones devoid of other ignition sources (such as cable vault and tunnel areas and some CSRs). However, fire analysis zones that lacked other fire sources often screened even given consideration of transient fires. Fire zones where transient fires were visible CDF contributors included areas with a convergence of safety-related cables and zones that lacked protection by automatic fire suppression systems.

The review also noted many cases where licensees proposed or implemented plant improvements as a result of the IPEEE analysis to enhance control of combustible materials. Combustible material control programs are in place at all plants. The cited IPEEE plant improvements typically focused on added administrative controls targeted to specific plant fire zones.

3.4.3.2 Estimating Fire Frequency

3.4.3.2.1 Generic Plant-Wide Fire Frequencies

All of the IPEEE fire analyses utilized generic fire data sources in establishing the plant-wide frequency of fires. The vast majority of submittals utilized the FIVE fire frequency values directly. FIVE called out fire frequency values for 11 generic "plant locations" and for 18 generic "plant-wide components."[10] Others used the FPRAIG values, which are quite similar to those cited in FIVE.

In very few cases, licensees applied their own analysis of existing databases, such as those published by the U.S. NRC (NUREG/CR-4586) [U.S.NRC, 1986] and EPRI [EPRI, 1993]. In such cases, it was more common for licensees to perform such assessments in the development of fire severity factors (see Section 3.4.10.2) rather than to estimate fire frequencies.

Based on these approaches, the applied fire frequencies were nominally quite consistent between submittals with a small number of specific exceptions. In a few cases, licensees had assumed fire frequency values for specific applications that were substantially lower than those cited in the above references. These cases were commonly questioned by the IPEEE reviewers, and most such cases led to revision of the CDF estimates for the impacted fire analysis zones. The revised CDFs would typically be documented in the licensees' RAI responses.

3.4.3.2.2 Fire Frequency Partitioning Practices

In the detailed analysis of plant fire scenarios, it is often necessary to assign a portion of a generic fire frequency to reflect the likelihood of fires in a specific fire analysis zone, a specific location within a zone, or involving a specific ignition source. This step of the analysis is referred to as fire frequency partitioning.

---

[10] See FIVE reference Table 1.2.

The fire frequency partitioning practices set forth in FIVE were utilized by the vast majority of licensees. However, in several cases, often specific cases associated with a particular fire source, licensees chose to apply conservative fire frequencies rather than going through the full partitioning practice. For example, partitioning of self-ignited cable fires according to FIVE requires the analyst to compare the mass of cables in the zone of interest to the total mass of cables in all Appendix R fire areas. Few plants attempted to estimate the mass of cables in a given zone, let alone the total mass of cables in the plant. Hence, it was more typical for licensees to simply apply a nominal partitioning factor (e.g., 0.1) as a conservative bound on any given fire area rather than attempting to quantify the required partitioning factors.

Relatively few questions arose during the review process regarding fire frequency partitioning practices. Questions that did arise typically involved the basis developed to support a unique partitioning factor, or the appearance that the FIVE guidelines had been misinterpreted or misapplied. These cases did not generally lead to substantial changes in fire CDF estimates.

In at least two cases, licensees were questioned as to their treatment of MCR fire frequency. In these cases, licensees stated that many of the components and panels that were located in the MCR at most plants were, for these plants, located in a separate fire area. Hence, the generic MCR fire frequency (nominally 1.9E-2/ry) was partitioned between these two fire areas. The partitioning was based on the relative number of panels in each area, and the bulk of the fire frequency was assigned to the alternate fire area rather than the MCR. Ultimately, this practice was accepted by reviewers in the context of the licensee's IPEEE process. However, it was not clear how unique this configuration actually was. Numerous licensees reported the existence of a relay room (or the apparent equivalent), and most treated such areas using fire frequency estimates for general control panels. Hence, some additional review of MCR/relay room fire frequency values may be beneficial. This topic was not pursued further under the IPEEE review process.

3.4.3.2.3 Plant-Specific Updates

It is common in fire PRA to update the generic fire frequency estimates derived from industry-wide experience to reflect the specific fire experience of the plant under analysis. In the IPEEE process, very few licensees specifically updated the generic fire frequencies. Those few who did update considered specific fire incidents that had occurred at the plant, and updated the fire frequencies either for those specific fire sources or for the impacted fire areas. All such cases utilized a Bayesian approach.

These updates had only a small impact on the assumed fire frequency. In general, the updates led to very slight increases in the assumed fire frequency values and the resulting CDF estimates. In no case did the updating of fire frequency play a key role in the IPEEE findings (e.g., no significant impact on fire zone screening, the overall fire CDF estimates, or identification of vulnerabilities and improvements).

3.4.4 Fire Modeling

For all IPEEE submittals reviewed, the fire analysis included an initial quantitative screening phase (see Section 3.4.2). In this phase the failure of all cables and equipment in a zone was typically assumed. This is a conservative approach that ignores the fact that some fires may be small and self-extinguishing, others may result in the failure of only a few pieces of equipment, and others may be extinguished by automatic or manual means before significant damage occurs. Based on this conservative assumption and using various screening protocols, those zones that would not pose a significant fire risk were screened out. In subsequent phases of fire analysis, the level of conservatism was reduced using various analytical methods.

The approaches and analytical models used by the licensees to assess the potential for fire growth and damage are discussed in this section. Section 3.4.4.1 provides a general overview of the fire growth modeling methods applied by licensees and the corresponding approaches used to assess fire damage. Section 3.4.4.2 discusses the assumptions made by licensees regarding equipment and cable damage thresholds. During the review of the IPEEE submittals, numerous issues were raised regarding the application of available models and input parameter values. Two issues surfaced for a number of submittals, the use of heat loss factors and the modeling of cable tray fires. These two issues are discussed in Sections 3.4.4.3 and 3.4.4.4 respectively. Additional issues were raised regarding the heat release rate from electrical cabinets and use of the modeling results to support the incorporation of severity factors. These two issues are also discussed separately in Sections 3.4.3.1 and 3.4.10.2, respectively.

3.4.4.1 Fire Growth and Damage Modeling

Licensees, with few exceptions, elected to model the progression of a fire event starting from a specific fire ignition source and progressing through damage to the targets of interest (cables and equipment). The ultimate purpose of the fire growth modeling was to assess the potential for a specific fire scenario to induce target damage. In general, the fire growth modeling and fire damage modeling were intimately linked. Hence, they are discussed together here. While a few licensees did not explicitly model the progression of a fire event, all performed some form of an assessment of the fire growth and damage potential.

As stated in NUREG-1407, the need to model fire growth and damage has been specifically recognized:

> Determine the likelihood of equipment being disabled by a fire. The areas to be addressed include:
>
> 1. Fire growth and spread, including the treatment of hot gases and smoke.
> 2. Detection/suppression effectiveness and reliability.
> 3. Component fragility to fire and combustion products.

These issues were addressed, in varying levels of detail, by all licensees in their detailed scenario analyses. In the initial quantitative screening phase, analysts typically assumed that any fire will cause widespread damage within the fire zone where the fire starts. The purpose of the detailed analysis is to establish the basis for reducing this conservative assumption and to find the appropriate probabilistic reduction factor for the occurrence frequency of a damaging fire. To achieve this, the fire growth and damage models were used to establish, for each specific fire source and set of targets, the following: (1) whether or not fire spread occurs, (2) whether or not damage is possible, (3) which targets (cables and equipment) may sustain damage, and (4) the length of time between fire ignition and damage. The damage time was typically used to establish whether or not fire detection and suppression before damage was possible (see Section 3.4.5).

Fire growth and damage are complex phenomena involving chemical reactions and both convective and radiative heat transfer. The processes typically modeled include the following:

- heat transfer from flames (radiative),
- heat transfer from the fire plume (convective),
- heat loss into walls and the ceiling,
- hot gas layer buildup under the ceiling and hot gas propagation,
- ignition of other materials, and

3 - 48

- heating and damage of target equipment and cables.

Most licensees used either COMPBRN[11] or the fire modeling spreadsheets provided in FIVE to model these processes. (Other tools and methods used by a few licensees will be discussed below.) COMPBRN is a computerized analytical tool that was developed for the purpose of modeling fire growth and propagation in a nuclear power plant compartment. COMPBRN allows users to specify fire sources, other combustibles, the location and characteristics of targets, and room characteristics. It then calculates the time to ignition of other combustibles and target damage (before the burning fuels are exhausted). COMPBRN can be exercised in either a point estimate mode or in an uncertainty mode. None of the licensees who applied COMPBRN appear to have exercised the code's uncertainty mode (all apparently used the point estimate mode).

As discussed in Section 3.4.1, FIVE is a fire analysis package that includes growth and damage analysis as an integral part of the methodology. It uses standardized lookup tables and worksheets to establish the fire parameters, the possibility of damage to the targets, and the associated time to damage. According to reference [EPRI, 1992], the formulations underlying the FIVE lookup tables were adopted mainly from COMPBRN. It is important to note here that FPRAIG also references the FIVE worksheets and lookup tables for fire growth and damage modeling. However, the FPRAIG recommends different parameter values in key areas than FIVE (see Section 3.4.4.3).

COMPBRN was used to support about 30% of the IPEEE submittals. All but two of the COMPBRN users chose to use a fire-PRA-based approach directly, or a combination of a fire PRA and the FIVE methodology (see Section 3.4.1). It is interesting to note that one submittal followed FIVE closely for all other elements of its analysis, but used COMPBRN to analyze one of the unscreened fire scenarios. Similarly, one submittal that used a combination of FIVE and the FPRAIG for its analysis opted to use COMPBRN in the fire modeling instead of the FIVE worksheets.

The COMPBRN results were, in some cases, used to justify a severity factor based on fire size. That is, the model was used to predict how large a fire was required to cause damage, and then a separate assessment of the likelihood that such a fire might occur was developed. Similarly, COMPBRN was used to demonstrate that some of the specific fire sources (fixed and transient) within a zone would not lead to damage to the targets of interest. In several cases, COMPBRN was also used to establish the characteristics of a hot gas layer in support of the multi-zone fire propagation analysis. More commonly, the model was used to establish the damage time for a given fire source.

In a few cases, COMPBRN results were used to justify a geometric partitioning factor as well. The geometric partitioning factor represented the fraction of the total zone floor area where the fire source can lead to damage to the target set. The model would be exercised moving the fire about the room to establish the areas leading to damage.

The FIVE worksheet approach was used for fire growth and damage analysis in approximately 60% of the submittals. More than half of the FIVE worksheet users used the parameter values provided in the FPRAIG. FIVE was used to model fire scenarios involving both fixed and transient combustibles. Typical scenarios modeled involved fires involving oil spills (or other liquid hydrocarbons), electrical panels, pumps, motors,

---

[11] In the vast majority of cases, the version COMPBRN IIIe was used. For simplicity, the model is referred to simply as COMPBRN.

cable insulation, or wood. The typical targets were cable trays above the fire source. In many cases, other thermal targets (such as electronic components) were also modeled. As with COMPBRN, the primary purpose of the FIVE-based modeling was to establish whether or not damage to the target set was possible for a given fire source in a given location. Similar to COMPBRN, FIVE was also used to establish the time to damage.

The FPRAIG recommends the use of the FIVE lookup tables and worksheets to conduct growth and damage analysis. As discussed in Section 3.4.4, the FPRAIG was developed to provide licensees with a less conservative approach to fire PRA. An important part of the FPRAIG is presentation of a set of suggested fire modeling input parameter values that are less conservative than those recommended in FIVE. Examples of those parameters include the heat release rate from various fire sources (e.g., electrical cabinets), severity factors, cable tray modeling, and heat loss factors. The validity of those values were challenged by the U.S. NRC reviewers of FPRAIG. Appendix B and Sections 3.4.3.1, 3.4.4.3, 3.4.4.4, and 3.4.10.2 contain additional information related to these topics.

A number of licensees did not use either the FIVE worksheets or COMPBRN to support the fire growth and damage analysis. Two such submittals (representing four NPP units) were based on the methods presented in NUREG/CR-0654. This approach predates the fire PRA methods development efforts of the early 1980s and is based instead on a node-based probabilistic model of fire propagation, detection, and suppression. Fires are generally considered at three levels of severity/damage. Phase 1 fires damage only the components involved in the fire initiation. Phase 2 fires damage equipment and cables in the immediate vicinity of the fire. Phase 3 fires cause widespread damage within the fire zone. Probabilistic split fractions are used to determine the likelihood that the fire progresses from one phase to another. Expert judgement is required to establish both the exact bounds of the damage assumed in each fire phase and the split fractions for progression of the fire from phase to phase. Because this approach is highly judgemental, and because its application in these cases resulted in very low probabilities of fire damaging scenarios in comparison to other licensees, the IPEEE reviewers found reliance on this approach to be a weakness of the submittal. (These concerns were resolved through performance of supplemental sensitivity studies by the licensee.)

Six of the submittals stated that the licensees did not perform any explicit fire propagation modeling. Typically, in these cases, the fire ignition frequency associated with the unscreened zone was reduced using partitioning factors that represented the fraction of fires that would occur in an area close to the targets (i.e., a geometric factor), and the fraction of those fires that would be severe enough to cause damage (i.e., a severity factor). Inherent in this approach is an assumption that the results of case-specific fire growth and damage modeling would be fully consistent with the broad fire experience statistics supporting the selected values for the two factors. This approach was commonly questioned in the IPEEE review process. Often, in response to the U.S. NRC RAIs, licensees provided qualitative arguments and some additional statistical analysis to support the bases for the original analysis. The application of severity factor approaches is discussed further in Section 3.4.10.2.

In summary, a large majority of the submittals included some analytical modeling of fire growth and damage processes for specific fire scenarios as part of the detailed analysis of the unscreened zones. They used either COMPBRN or the FIVE lookup tables and worksheets for this purpose. A number of these submittals used the parameter values provided in FPRAIG rather than those recommended in FIVE, and this became a point of considerable attention in the review process as discussed elsewhere in this report. In two specific cases, an older approach to fire hazards assessment that predates PRA methods was applied. This approach also became a point of focus during the review process. Finally, a number of licensees applied an approach that did not explicitly consider case-specific fire growth and damage behavior. Rather, the approach used past historical data to establish the likelihood of fire damage.

3.4.4.2 Equipment Damage Thresholds

The ultimate goal of the analytical methods used for fire growth and damage analysis is to estimate the time that target equipment and cables get damaged. Therefore, establishing the damage mechanisms and thresholds of these targets is an integral part of the analysis. The processes that take place inside a cable, a pump, or an electrical cabinet from exposure to fire are complex. Several parameters, such as intensity of the heat, presence of products of combustion, sensitivity of the component, and duration of exposure, influence the likelihood and timing of damage.

The vast majority of licensees considered only thermal damage to critical targets in the quantification of fire CDF. If other modes of damage were discussed (e.g., smoke damage, water sprays, flooding by fire suppression water), the discussion was strictly qualitative in nature. A small number of licensees argued that the screening analysis inherently encompassed all potential modes of fire damage because all equipment was assumed to be lost. However, in the detailed quantification, only thermal damage was considered.

For the IPEEEs, two general damage criteria were commonly considered, namely, the damage threshold temperature and the threshold heat flux. Threshold temperatures and heat flux values were widely taken from FIVE. It was generally observed that, consistent with past PRAs, the primary targets of interest were electrical cables. Cables were the focus of a large majority of fire growth and damage scenarios. FIVE recommended use of 700°F as the damage threshold temperature for those cables qualified per IEEE-383, and 425°F for the unqualified cables. The vast majority of licensees applied these values directly. A small number of licensees specifically discussed thermal damage to other components, such as pumps, motors, valves, and in particular electronic equipment. A range of threshold damage limits were applied to these cases, again almost universally derived from FIVE.

In several cases involving older plants (those built prior to 1975), licensees who had applied the damage thresholds associated with IEEE-383 qualified cables were asked to verify the qualification status of their cables or to re-analyze scenarios using the lower damage thresholds. In the majority of these cased, licensees were able to substantiate the qualification assumptions of the original analysis. A re-analysis was performed in only a small number of cases. Of the re-analysis cases, a very small number identified new fire scenarios.

3.4.4.3 Heat Loss Factor Modeling

One specific aspect of the fire modeling process that became a point of attention in the IPEEE review process relates to the application of fire modeling correlations utilizing a heat loss factor (HLF) approach. (This topic is discussed in greater detail in Appendix B.) In any zone fire some significant fraction of the heat released by the fire will be lost to the enclosure surfaces, and in particular, to the walls and ceiling of the enclosure. The HLF approach is a simplified method for treating this heat loss.

Under FIVE, a set of simplified engineering correlations is used to estimate the temperature rise in the fire plume, ceiling jet, and the hot gas layer. One factor in these calculations is the HLF. Under the FIVE approach, the HLF is assumed to be constant, and the value is selected by the analyst. Heat that is lost to the enclosure surfaces is not available to heat the air within the room. Hence, the higher the HLF, the lower the predicted fire-induced temperature rise.

FIVE had recommended that a value of 0.7 be assumed for the HLF. However, in the FPRAIG, HLF values ranging from 0.85 to 0.94 were recommended. An assessment of the impact of this change in the assumed HLF revealed that the higher HLF values resulted in underestimation of hot gas layer temperatures when the correlations were compared to test data.[12] Revised guidance from EPRI suggested, in general, a return to a 0.7 HLF. The one major exception involved cases where the fire was modeled as being located at or above 40% of the room height so that the hot gas layer volume was reduced to 60% or less of the total room volume.

Most of the licensees who had applied the FPRAIG were asked to re-assess potential hot gas layer exposures using the revised EPRI guidance. In the vast majority of these re-assessments, changes in the HLF had no impact on the predictions of hot gas layer damage (or the lack thereof) because while the predicted temperature rise did increase, the predicted hot gas layer temperature was still below the target damage threshold. In only a very few cases, generally involving smaller zones, did any changes result, and these changes did not lead to risk-dominant scenarios.

In general, NPP compartments are rather large, so it takes a substantial fire to create a damaging hot gas layer exposure. Hence, in many fire zones it is not reasonable to postulate hot-gas-layer-induced fire damage under any reasonable fire conditions. However, as was noted above (see Section 3.4.3.1), most licensees' assumptions regarding source fire intensity did not represent the full range of potential fire threats. As a result, while hot gas layer damage was rarely predicted in the IPEEE fire scenarios, this finding may not be robust for all such cases.

3.4.4.4 Modeling of Cable Tray Fires

One situation commonly encountered in the analysis of IPEEE fire scenarios is the spread of fire to and within an array of cable trays. Many of the dominant fire scenarios reported by licensees involved exposure fires (commonly from an electrical panel fire) that spread to or damaged overhead cable trays.

In past fire PRAs, this task was commonly handled by use of a compartment fire model, most commonly, the COMPBRN model [EPRI, 1991]. However, as discussed in Section 3.4.1, fire models such as COMPBRN were utilized by only a small number of licensees in their IPEEE analyses. Instead, simplified modeling approaches, primarily those documented in FIVE, were applied widely.

FIVE did include some guidance on the modeling of cable tray fires. In particular, FIVE provided a framework for assessing whether or not a cable tray exposed to an external fire source (an exposure fire) might ignite. For ignited trays, a simplified approach to estimating the heat output of a burning tray was also provided. IPEEE reviewers noted in early submittals that licensees found this approach to be somewhat challenging to implement. In particular, performing the assessment completely required an iterative approach. The initial source fire is modeled as exposing the first tray. If the first tray ignites, then a second calculation should be performed to model a combination of the original source plus the ignited tray to assess the potential ignition of additional trays. In theory, one could continue to iterate through tray-by-tray ignitions until all trays in a stack or room are ignited. This is the approach taken in COMPBRN. In practice, early submittals did not appear to be following up fully on the potential for ignition of secondary targets and the implication of growing cable tray fires.

---

[12] These validation studies were supported by the U.S. NRC Office of Nuclear Regulatory Research (RES) Fire Risk Methods research program, JCN Y6037 [Siu, 2000].

In the later FPRAIG a new approach to cable tray fire modeling was documented. This revised model provided a more concise approach to cable tray fire growth modeling (see Appendix B for additional detail). The FPRAIG model utilized tray-to-tray flame spread times observed during a single NRC-sponsored cable fire test [Klamerus, 1977] as described in NUREG/CR-5384. These flame spread times were to be applied directly to essentially all cable tray fire situations. This extrapolation of a single test to other fire scenarios was identified as a potentially optimistic practice by IPEEE reviewers. In particular, the cited test was designed to simulate a self-ignited cable fire rather than an external exposure fire, and yet the model was being applied to external exposure fire scenarios. Furthermore, licensees were interpreting the model to be both a fire growth model and a cable damage model. In effect, damage and ignition times were being equated, whereas in the test, cable damage was observed well before ignition.

Revised guidance from EPRI directed licensees to reconsider fire scenarios modeled using the original FPRAIG approach. In particular, licensees were directed to use the FPRAIG model only to estimate the fire spread behavior, and then only given that no substantive exposure fire source exists and the cables in question were of the low-flame-spread type (per IEEE-383). The fire spread model was then to be used in conjunction with the original FIVE model for cable HRR, and an independent assessment of fire damage for trays not (yet) involved in the fire was also to be made.

This particular fire modeling approach was only used in a small number of submittals. In response to the revised guidance, some re-assessments of fire growth and damage were made. In a very small number of cases, cable tray fire risk contributions increased modestly, generally due to the prediction of shorter damage times and corresponding reductions in credit for suppression before damage. In no case did new dominant fire scenarios emerge.

3.4.5 Detection and Suppression Modeling

An essential part of NPP fire protection strategy is the provision for detecting and suppressing a fire. Automatic detection of a fire in an NPP is generally done via fixed fire detection systems strategically placed in various plant locations. Most nuclear power plant zones with potential risk significance as identified in the IPEEEs are equipped with fixed fire detection systems. Typically, the detectors alarm both locally and at central locations, most often including the main control room and plant security offices.

Plant-wide fire suppression at all NPP sites is provided by a trained plant fire brigade, and virtually all of the IPEEEs provided some discussion of this capability. In addition, many compartments are provided with fixed fire suppression systems, some automatic and some manually actuated. It is important to note that not all plant areas are protected by fixed fire suppression systems. However, the majority of the zones that have been reported in the IPEEEs as significant CDF contributors were protected by a fixed system, and the vast majority of these were automatic suppression systems. The major exception to this observation is the MCR, which would not be protected by automatic suppression systems.

A range of fixed systems may be found in a nuclear power plant. The most common type cited in the IPEEE was water sprinkler systems. Gaseous (CO_2 or Halon) systems were also identified for many plants, especially in areas containing equipment that might be damaged by water sprays (e.g., electrical panel and relay rooms). All of the submittals cited the presence of portable extinguishers of various types even though fire extinguishers are not explicitly required for all plants. Fire water stand-pipes and manual hose stations located throughout the plant, which are required for all plants by the U.S. NRC fire protection regulations, were also universally cited in the IPEEEs.

In the context of fire risk analysis, the objective of the detection and suppression analysis is to assess the probability that any given fire is suppressed before it can damage the set of targets (equipment and cables) being threatened by that fire. Thus, when analyzing detection/suppression performance in a fire scenario, the time to suppress the fire (including detection time) is the main parameter of interest. By comparing the time to damage with the time to detect and suppress, current methodologies produce a non-suppression probability that is multiplied by the occurrence frequency of the fire scenario. This view of the fire detection suppression analysis was implemented by the vast majority of licensees.

Fire propagation models in some form (e.g., the FIVE worksheets and/or COMPBRN) are typically used to establish whether or not, for a specific fire source, damage to the target set is possible and, if possible, the time associated with that damage (see Section 3.4.4.1). To establish the corresponding non-suppression probability associated with a fire scenario, a number of approaches were taken in the IPEEE analyses.

One common approach was application of the methods established in FIVE. The FIVE methodology provides a set of system unavailabilities for various types of fixed automatic suppression systems. These unavailabilities typically range between 0.02 and 0.05 per demand. FIVE also provides a formula for calculating the failure probability of the fire brigade suppressing the fire within a specified time period for various types of fire sources (e.g., a cable fire, panel fire, MCR fire, and others). As part of that formula, FIVE specifies that the minimum fire brigade failure probability should be set at no less than 0.1. Thus, when using FIVE, if damage occurs before the time it takes for detection and suppression activities to be successful, the analysts used 1.0 for non-suppression probabilities. If damage occurs after the detection and suppression success time, the non-suppression probability was the product of automatic suppression system unavailability and fire brigade failure probability. This approach was applied widely in the IPEEE analyses, but many licensees deviated from the nominal approach as discussed further below.

One specific aspect of the FIVE formulae questioned in the IPEEE review process was that the estimates of fire suppression times and fire damage times were both unrealistically short under some analysis conditions. For example, in one case a submittal cited FIVE calculations that estimated a fire damage time of 4 seconds, and a fire suppression time of 3 seconds. Comparing the two values, the fire scenario was screened because suppression occurred before critical damage (by 1 second). When these results were questioned, the licensee provided a re-assessment of the scenario CDF contribution using alternative methods of analysis.

A second approach was taken from past fire PRA practice. Under this approach, COMPBRN is used to establish the time to fire damage (see Section 3.4.4.1). The failure probability of suppression within a given time is modeled as an exponential distribution. The damage time obtained from COMPBRN is used as the parameter of the suppression distribution. Only a small number of licensees used this approach, generally those who chose to go directly into fire PRA analysis without reference to either FIVE or the FPRAIG (see Section 3.4.1).

A third approach was that presented in the FPRAIG. This approach uses the same approach as COMPBRN, except that instead of the exponential distribution, it provides fire source-specific curves for the probability of suppression versus time to damage (i.e., cumulative fire suppression probability or fire duration curves). This approach treats manual fire-fighting activities using hoses and efforts using portable extinguishers separately. In particular, a severity factor approach can be applied to reflect prompt suppression by plant personnel using hand-held extinguishers.

3 - 54

The FPRAIG approach also includes crediting the recovery of a failed fire suppression system. That is, the general fixed suppression system unavailabilities from FIVE are cited, but for scenarios involving fixed system failure, the potential for system recovery (i.e., by personnel actions) is also credited. This approach became a topic of focus in the review process as discussed in Appendix B. As a part of the IPEEE reviews, the U.S. NRC staff sent RAIs to those licensees that took credit for such recovery actions to ensure that dependencies between recovery of the fixed system and subsequent fire suppression efforts were addressed. In general, the responses assessed the impact should the system recovery credit not be taken, and concluded that the impact on fire CDF was minimal.

The treatment of detection and suppression varied widely among the submittals. Many submittals gave little (or no) credit to the effectiveness of the fire brigade, nor did they include it in the fire modeling. That is, some analyses concluded that fire damage times were so short that the fire brigade would not have time to respond and prevent damage. More commonly, licensees simply assumed no credit for the manual fire brigade citing this as a conservatism of the analysis. One area where manual fire suppression was universally credited was the MCR. The manual non-suppression probability for the MCR varied widely, ranging in general between 0.0034 and 0.01, with a few cases of outliers at each end of this range.

Those submittals that included manual suppression in the analyses of fire scenarios outside the control room typically used 0.1 as the non-suppression probability consistent with the guidance in FIVE. In a few cases, licensees used non-suppression probabilities greater than those recommended in FIVE (i.e., they were more pessimistic).

In three specific cases, generally based on two separate but similar methods, an event tree was used to account for the different possibilities in terms of the severity of a fire, success or failure of automatic suppression systems, and success or failure of manual suppression efforts. Based on a combination of success and failure cases and fire severity level, categories of fire scenarios were defined. In these cases, the licensee initially obtained substantially reduced frequencies for damaging scenarios in comparison to other licensees. The primary factor in these assessments was that the analyst had credited three independent opportunities for fire detection and suppression (e.g., prompt intervention or self-extinguishment, intervention prior to fire spread beyond the fire source, and intervention before the entire room became involved in the fire). Each such opportunity was assigned a very low probability of failure. In two of these cases, the licensee responded to RAIs by providing a re-analysis that credited only one consolidated opportunity for detection and suppression of the fire. As a result, some previously screened fire scenarios re-emerged as dominant contributors to fire CDF.

Another approach taken by a large number of licensees, including many who applied the FIVE methodology, was to compare fire brigade response times obtained in fire drills to the predicted fire damage time. For example, in one case the licensee assumed 10 minutes for fire brigade response time to any plant fire area. If the fire damage times were longer than 10 minutes, the scenarios were screened. In effect, it was assumed that no fire damage would occur beyond that observed in the first 10 minutes of any fire. IPEEE reviewers cited that this approach was optimistic in that it did not consider the time needed to locate the fire (in perhaps a smoke-filled room), assemble the fire brigade in sufficient numbers to begin an attack on the fire, plan the strategy of attack, and apply the fire suppressant agent to control the fire. It also failed to address the potential that the fire brigade efforts might fail to promptly suppress the fire. Overall, the approach failed to address the potential for long-duration fires. Licensees who employed such assumptions in their analyses were commonly asked to re-assess the fire CDF, including consideration of longer duration fires. In a number of cases, this led to the identification of additional fire risk scenarios that had previously been screened.

Few of the submittals provided a discussion regarding the effectiveness of the detection and suppression system; that is, almost all licensees assumed that if a suppression system functioned, it would control the fire promptly. RAIs were sent to a number of licensees requesting information about the qualification of their systems, and in particular, the status of the systems in comparison to national fire codes and standards. Most licensees responded to these questions by stating that their systems either met, or met the intent of, the fire standards. However, a few acknowledged the existence of non-compliant fire protection systems. None of the licensees was asked to re-quantify any of their fire scenarios on this basis because no methods for such an assessment have yet been developed.

In summary, a small number of licensees took little or no credit for manual fire suppression in the quantification of fire risk. However, a large majority of licensees took some credit for both manual and fixed fire suppression capability. In the majority of cases, the simple probabilistic model recommended in FIVE was used. The vast majority of licensees did credit fixed fire suppression systems in areas equipped with them. In the majority of cases, the analysis of detection and suppression was based on a point estimate of fire damage time which was compared to a probabilistic assessment of fire suppression likelihood (or the non-suppression probability) in that same time period. In a small number of cases, licensees credited fire suppression systems without consideration of the damage time. In several submittals, the likelihood of fire suppression before damage was addressed through the application of severity factors (see Section 3.4.10.2).

3.4.6 Multi-Zone Fire Analysis

3.4.6.1 Multi-Zone Analysis Methodologies

One of the fundamental assumptions of most NPP fire analyses performed today is that fires will remain confined to one, or a small number, of adjacent zones. This assumption is supported by the fire experience in U.S. nuclear power plants. However, under special conditions, multi-zone fires may occur. This has been observed in a number of foreign NPP fire incidents [Kazarians, 2000]. While the foreign experience with regard to fire barrier performance is not directly applicable to U.S. plants, these incidents illustrate the potential impact that room-to-room fire spread might have on plant operations. The special conditions that might lead to inter-zone fire spread include features such as a normally open fire barrier element (e.g., a normally open door), an unsealed fire barrier penetration, high combustible loading concentrated in one location, combustibles near a fire barrier, and combustible pathways between zones.

The possibility of cross-zone fire spread is specifically mentioned in NUREG-1407 and was addressed in all of the IPEEE submittals reviewed. However, the methodologies employed varied significantly among the submittals. The applied methods can be grouped according to the following four categories:

- FIVE using the Fire Compartment Interaction Analysis (FCIA) criteria,
- FPRAIG-based methods,
- other qualitative methods, and
- other quantitative methods.

Both FIVE and the FPRAIG include methodologies for addressing fire scenarios that may affect multiple zones. Both guidance documents recognize that even if a zone is screened out as an insignificant individual fire CDF contributor, that zone might still be a fire threat to adjacent zones. Also, both documents recognize the possibility that the combination of two adjacent zones may be more significant to CDF than either zone taken alone. However, there is a significant difference between the two documents in the methodology proposed to address the multi-zone fire analysis issue.

FIVE uses a qualitative methodology, known as Fire Compartment Interaction Analysis (FCIA), to screen the barriers between zones. Six criteria are used in considering combustible loading, presence of detection and automatic suppression systems, and the lack of safe shutdown components within the zones. When the boundaries between two adjacent zones do not satisfy any of the established criteria, FIVE recommends additional analysis of fire spread potential between the two zones. If that possibility exists, FIVE recommends that the two zones be combined and treated, in effect, as one zone.

The FPRAIG includes a seven-step quantitative methodology for the analysis of multi-zone fire scenarios. The methodology is based on the premise that fire damage in the multi-zone fire scenarios requires that a hot gas layer initially formed in the exposing fire zone spreads to the adjacent fire zone. It also requires that the temperature of the combined zone hot gas layer be sufficient to cause damage in the adjacent zone. The possibility of a fire barrier failure is included in the analysis using probabilistic models. The final outcome of the analysis is the CDF associated with each multi-zone fire scenario.

Treatment of cross-zone fire impact is also a part of general fire PRA methodology. The references mentioned in NUREG-1407 (i.e., NUREG/CR-2300, NUREG/CR-2815, and NUREG/CR-4840) recommend the use of a fault tree approach, where the minimal cutsets for core damage are expressed in terms of the location of critical equipment and cables (e.g., fire zones or compartments). None of the submittals used this approach; hence, it is not included in the list of method categories provided above, and will not be considered further in this report.

Two types of approaches have been used in the IPEEEs that cannot be categorized as either FIVE or FPRAIG. In one such approach, qualitative arguments were used to screen out groups of adjacent zones, but they were different from the six criteria of FIVE. The other such approach was quantitative in nature. That is, in a few cases, probabilistic arguments were used (e.g., probability of barrier failure in conjunction with suppression system unavailability) to screen combinations of adjacent zones. A limited number of submittals used this approach in combination with a spatial interaction analysis to systematically examine the communication pathways between zones.

Tables 3.7 and 3.8 provide the number and percentages of submittals that used the above-defined analysis categories. It is evident from these tables that the most commonly used methodology is the FIVE-based FCIA. The majority of FIVE-based submittals (37 out of 57, or 65%) utilized this approach. The least commonly used approach is the one delineated in the FPRAIG. Five of the 13 "PRA only" submittals used spatial interaction analysis. Forty-seven of 70 submittals (67%) used a qualitative approach (including those who used the FIVE FCIA approach). In summary, most licensees utilized a qualitative approach rather than a quantitative one.

Table 3.7: Number of submittals in each general analysis approach category that used each of the four multi-zone analysis methods

Methodology	Total	FIVE, FCIA criteria	FPRAIG	Other (qualitative)	Other (quantitative)
FIVE only	15	14		1	
FIVE, FPRAIG	25	15	5		5
FIVE, PRA	17	8	2	5	2
Fire PRA only	13	1		3	9
Total:	70	38	7	9	16

Table 3.8: Percentage of submittals in each general analysis approach category that used each of the four multi-zone analysis methods

Methodology	FIVE, FCIA criteria	FPRAIG	Other (qualitative)	Other (quantitative)
FIVE only	93%		7%	
FIVE, FPRAIG	60%	20%		20%
FIVE, PRA	47%	12%	29%	12%
Fire PRA only	8%		23%	69%
Total:	54%	10%	13%	23%

Plant walkdowns were an integral part of multi-zone fire analysis. All submittals reported some level of plant inspection for the specific purpose of identifying the potential paths of propagation between zones to verify Appendix R analysis information (see Section 3.4.10.1).

3.4.6.2 Influence of Fire Zone Definition on Multi-Zone Analysis

Zone definition is a fundamental part of multi-zone fire propagation analysis. An Appendix R fire area is defined as a zone bounded on all sides by rated fire barriers sufficient to contain the fire threats within the zone. This commonly means the existence of fire barriers with at least a 2-hour fire endurance rating. Therefore, as reported in several submittals, the FIVE FCIA barrier screening criteria meant that Appendix R fire areas could for all practical intents be, a priori, screened out from further multi-zone analysis. Partitioning of the plant into fire areas, fire zones, and compartments is discussed in Section 3.4.2.1.

All IPEEE fire analyses used the information gathered by the licensees for compliance with the requirements in Appendix R to 10 CFR Part 50. An important part of that information includes fire areas, fire zones, and the contents of these locations in terms of equipment and cables. Thus, an important initial step of IPEEE fire analysis was to validate and redefine the information taken from the Appendix R analysis. Some of the submittals used the same set of fire zones and fire areas as used for Appendix R compliance without any need to alter them. However, some licensees found the Appendix R fire areas too strict and not conducive to a streamlined screening analysis.

From statements made in various submittals, it is inferred that, in many cases, the Appendix R fire areas contained a significant number of cables and equipment related to core cooling and safe shutdown. Hence, despite the presence of substantial, but perhaps un-rated, physical partitioning of the fire area, the fire areas had to be retained for detailed analysis. Therefore, these licensees elected to use other methods to define fire analysis zones. These licensees subdivided the Appendix R areas into fire zones, and used the qualitative screening criteria of FIVE (FCIA criteria) or, in some cases, fire propagation analysis (see Section 3.4.4) to support the assumption that all fires would be confined within a specific zone. Two observations are in order here. Many of the submittals reported that most of the fire analysis zones defined within an Appendix R fire area complied with the FCIA criteria. Those zones that did not meet the FCIA criteria were generally re-combined with a select few adjacent zones to form a "super-zone" that would comply with the FCIA screening criteria.

Hence, while some licensees did perform the IPEEE analysis based on the use of the Appendix R fire areas, most licensees further subdivided one or more fire areas into smaller fire analysis zones. Fire zones are convenient subdivisions of a fire area that may or may not be bounded by physical barriers. In those cases where barriers are present, they may not comply with either the Appendix R or the FCIA criteria. Therefore, a fire might propagate between adjacent fire zones. In most cases, licensees concluded that most fire zones as defined for the purposes of the IPEEE analysis did comply with FCIA screening criteria.

It must be noted that the FIVE and FPRAIG inter-zone fire analysis methods were developed with zones in mind. That is, the FIVE and FPRAIG criteria generally assume that fire zones will be bounded by physical barriers. In a few cases, licensees defined fire zones based on other criteria than physical barriers (e.g., no fire spread path, wide separation between combustible fuel or fire sources, subdivision of large open areas into multiple analysis zones). These licensees generally adopted an alternative approach to the analysis of inter-zone scenarios for these zones. The most common approach in such cases was the use of qualitative arguments to justify the initial zone definitions and establish that given only modest fire threats and substantial separation, wide spread fire damage was highly unlikely. This was common, for example, in the analysis of BWR reactor building fire areas. These areas tend to be very large and open areas. Several BWR submittals indicated that the FCIA criteria were not sufficient to screen fire zones in the reactor building. Fire propagation analysis of postulated fire scenarios or a probabilistic analysis of detection and suppression provided the additional basis to screen certain combinations of reactor building fire zones.

The following quote is taken from one of the submittals, and is considered typical of how the licensees viewed the issue of compartments, fire areas, and fire zones:

> The fire areas defined for the ... IPEEE-fire effort are not always consistent with those defined for the Appendix A and R efforts. ... Sub-areas were defined for those portions of the plant where the requirement for two- or three-hour fire-rated barriers could not be met. For some of these sub-areas, fire propagation evaluations were necessary to support partitioning of the plant.

> Table ... provides a cross-reference between the IPEEE-Fire definitions and that used in Appendix R. As can be seen from this table, a fire area (or sub-area) may contain several Appendix R fire zones. This was done to accomplish two goals; (1) streamline the screening task that is presented below and (2) minimize the number of fire propagation evaluations required to support sub-area definition.

3 - 59

Of the 70 submittals, 17 indicated that some of the fire analysis zones initially defined for the IPEEE analysis had to be regrouped to ensure that there is no possibility of cross-zone propagation. In one case, a licensee stated that while they began their IPEEE analysis using the Appendix R fire areas, they later concluded that this approach was impractical, and reconsidered their subdivision of the plant.

3.4.6.3 Qualitative Analyses

A majority of the submittals, as noted above, used FCIA screening criteria to investigate the possibility of fire propagation among fire areas, fire zones, and compartments. Fire areas as defined in the Appendix R analyses were widely found to comply with the FCIA criteria as noted above. Having verified this, licensees took one of the following two approaches to complete the analysis. Some licensees analyzed fire scenarios within each fire area using various detailed methods, and arrived at a total CDF for the fire area without further partitioning. Most submittals, however, subdivided the fire areas into smaller fire analysis zones, and repeated the FCIA analysis for compartments or fire zones within each fire area. If the latter approach was used, in some cases, the fire zones that did not meet the FCIA screening criteria were re-combined to define groupings of zones that would meet the criteria. Once a set of analysis zones, each meeting the FCIA screening criteria, were defined, the analysis of individual zone CDFs was completed. In either case, it was common that the CDF contribution for multi-zone fire scenarios was essentially rendered negligible.

It was also noted that when applying the FCIA criteria, licensees often found that only a subset of the six FCIA barrier screening criteria was applicable to their plant. That is, most licensees did not utilize all six criteria in screening their fire barriers. However, when all submittals are considered together, all six criteria were applied by the licensees.

3.4.6.4 Quantitative Analyses

3.4.6.4.1 Application of Quantitative Approaches

A number of submittals (33%) used quantitative methods to examine the possibility of fire effects propagating from one zone to another. Two types of quantitative methods were noted. A number of licensees chose to conduct fire propagation analysis to verify whether or not the postulated fires can have damaging effects in the adjacent zones. For example, the COMPBRN computer code was used to examine the formation and characteristics of the hot gas layer in the exposing area, and the FPRAIG formulae were used to examine the hot gas layer exposure in an adjacent zone. In several cases, for the postulated fire sources it was possible to show that none of the adjacent zones would be adversely affected (generally due to the limited size of the fire source and the large volume associated with the combined fire analysis zones). Such zones were then treated in a manner similar to those that meet the FCIA criteria (i.e., as individual fire analysis zones and CDF contributors).

A second probabilistic approach was to multiply the fire ignition frequency for the fire sources in a zone/location by an assumed fire barrier failure probability, suppression system unavailability and, in a few cases, by a severity factor. The product was assumed to represent the likelihood that a substantial unsuppressed fire would breach the fire barrier and threaten equipment in the adjacent area. The overall frequencies of occurrence obtained from this process, in most cases, were found to be less than the screening threshold (e.g., 1E-6/ry), and the associated zones were screened as insignificant CDF contributors. Typically, 0.1 has been used for barrier failure probabilities in such cases, consistent with the recommended values in the FPRAIG. (See Section 3.4.6.4.3 for further discussion on this topic.)

The method described in the FPRAIG was used for only a small number of submittals (seven). In each of these cases, the licensee concluded that the CDF associated with multi-zone fire scenarios is not significant. In these applications, the barrier failure probabilities and suppression system unavailability values recommended in the FPRAIG were used, and the zone sets were screened based on the associated CDF. It may be noted that the FPRAIG recommends that the adjacent zones be examined pair-wise. The submittals using this approach either specifically indicated that the analysis was based on pair-wise combinations of zones or did not provide any information in this regard.

Although a large number of submittals included a discussion of fire PRA, only four submittals followed the PRA approach, and did not augment it with either FIVE or the FPRAIG. Of these four submittals, three used spatial interaction analysis to identify potential risk-significant fire propagation scenarios among connected zones. The spatial interaction approach takes into account the probability of fire barrier failure. Of these four submittals, only one specifically indicated that the possibility of fire propagation beyond a pair of zones (i.e., scenarios involving three or more zones) had been addressed.

3.4.6.4.2 Multi-Zone CDFs

CDF was used in 39 submittals to screen zone-to-zone fire propagation scenarios. In addition to the fire PRA and FPRAIG-based submittals, some of those that used qualitative methods (e.g., FCIA) also estimated the CDF associated with inter-zone fire propagation scenarios. Of the submittals that reported a specific measure of inter-zone fire scenario risk significance, 80% (31 out of 39) concluded that none of the multi-zone fire scenarios were significant contributors to fire CDF. The remainder (i.e., 8 out of 39) provided CDFs for some unscreened multi-zone fire scenarios. It is interesting to note that two of these seven submittals reporting inter-zone CDFs used the FCIA screening criteria, and then quantified unscreened scenarios, while the other five used a direct quantitative methodology for the entire analysis.

It should also be noted that many submittals, especially those that used FCIA criteria, may have computed, but not reported, the CDF of fire scenarios that affect multiple zones as originally defined in the fire analysis. As noted above, in many such cases, the initially defined fire zones were recombined if the smaller zones did not pass the FCIA screening criteria. In such cases, the reported CDF results are typically based on the contributions for these recombined zones. This should be kept in mind when considering potential insights regarding inter-zone fire scenarios base on the IPEEEs.

The contribution of multi-zone CDFs to the overall fire risk ranges from less than 1% to about 30% (the latter case involving a PWR commissioned in the 1970s). Only one submittal, the original Quad Cities analysis, reported that fire propagation scenarios between zones may be a significant contributor to the fire CDF. However, this conclusion was changed after an updated version of the analysis was submitted to the U.S. NRC. In the original analysis, all of the unscreened inter-zone fire scenarios were found to have a CDF between E-5/ry and E-4/ry. In the revised analysis, none of the scenarios were found to be important. The changes implemented in the revised analysis include the use of a modified fire initiation frequency based on ignition sources (the original study used the fire initiation frequency of the entire zone), the treatment of hot gas layer effects, reduced fire barrier failure probability (in the original analysis, some of the barriers were assigned a 0.1 failure probability), and, in a few cases, reduced failure probability of the suppression system.

3.4.6.4.3 Barrier Failure Probabilities

The probability of fire barrier failure is addressed in several submittals, especially those that used a quantitative approach. In a few submittals that employed the FCIA criteria, barrier failure probabilities were also incorporated into the analysis. The recommended practice in the FPRAIG was used for the majority of these cases. In the screening steps, a failure probability of 0.1 was typically assigned to active barrier elements. If the scenario was found to be significant, other (lower) suggested failure probabilities were applied.

3.4.6.4.4 Summary of Multi-Zone Analysis

In conclusion, the possibility of cross-zone fires, as requested in NUREG-1407, was addressed in all of the IPEEE submittals. Most licensees used a qualitative approach, where the adequacy of fire barrier bounding a compartment, fire zone, or fire area is examined qualitatively. A smaller number of licensees used a quantitative approach that typically involved probabilistic modeling of fire barrier failure, suppression system failure, and fire severity, or a deterministic evaluation to demonstrate that fires would not threaten fire barriers or adjacent zones. A number of those submittals using quantitative analysis also used qualitative arguments to justify their conclusions about fire barrier adequacy. Most licensees concluded that multi-zone fire scenarios are not significant CDF contributors. A few reported CDFs that ranged from less than 1% to about 30% of total fire CDF.

3.4.7 Plant Response Models

This section provides a description of the plant PRA models used to evaluate the fire-induced CDFs at the plants.[13] The initiating events considered in the fire PRAs were generally identified in the submittals. Section 3.4.7.1 discusses the consideration given to transient, LOCA, and support system initiators in the fire PRAs. Just about all of the licensees used their IPE models or an updated version of the IPE models. The IPEEE submittals generally did not include the event trees utilized in the assessments, and no submittal presented the system fault trees. However, some modifications to these models necessary for the fire assessment are presented in Sections 3.4.7.2 through 3.4.7.4. Section 3.4.7.2 discusses some modifications made to the event trees and fault trees, and addresses how Appendix R and non-Appendix R components[14] were considered. The modeling of human error events is addressed in Section 3.4.7.2. Additional discussion on the fire impacts on human errors included in the IPE models and on human errors specifically added to the models for fire scenarios is presented in Section 3.4.8. Finally, most fire scenarios involve fire-induced damage to cables. Section 3.4.7.3 highlights the treatment of various cable failure modes in the fire assessments, including hot shorts that can lead to spurious component operation.

---

[13] The perspectives in this section are based on the review of a selected sample of 25% of the submittals.

[14] Appendix R components are those components credited in the Appendix R safe shutdown analysis.

3.4.7.1 Selection and Screening of Initiating Events

The licensees for the majority of the plants reviewed indicated that most fire events were modeled as general plant transients. Common variations of general plant transients that were assumed by some licensees to occur due to a fire include a main steam isolation valve (MSIV) closure event and a loss of main feedwater. In most cases, the licensees indicated it was not practical to trace cables for non-safety systems whose failure could lead to an actual MSIV closure or loss of feedwater event. Rather than attempt to analyze each cable in the plant to determine if it could cause or require a plant shutdown, it was assumed in some fire PRAs that every fire zone contained at least one such cable. However, some licensees did selective cable tracing in some fire areas to verify the absence of any cables that could cause a particular plant transient initiator, such as a loss of feedwater.

Even if there is no potential for an automatic scram due to a fire in a particular area, there is a potential for a manual scram. A manual scram may be required by abnormal operating procedures, including both fire procedures and procedures for abnormal conditions induced by a fire, or may be initiated by the operators based on their judgement. Some of the licensees who utilized an early version of FIVE methodology screened fire areas if no automatic scram mechanism was identified due to the fire (see Section 3.4.2.2). These licensees were requested to reevaluate such screened areas based on the arguments presented above. Some licensees indicated that a fire was assumed to always result in a manual reactor scram regardless of whether there was an identified automatic scram mechanism or not.

A fire-induced LOOP was considered in most studies. Some multi-unit sites evaluated dual-unit LOOP events. In the development of the safe shutdown paths required for meeting Appendix R requirements, offsite power was assumed not to be available; hence, cables associated with offsite power were not typically traced in the Appendix R compliance efforts. In order to credit offsite power in the fire IPEEEs, the licensees had to trace these cables to ensure that they would not be threatened in postulated fire scenarios. One licensee indicated that for fire scenarios which could affect offsite power, the conditional probability of core damage was calculated twice. In one calculation, offsite power was assumed to be lost due to the fire. In the other calculation, offsite power was not assumed to be damaged by the fire, but was allowed to randomly fail. This was done because the loss of offsite power has both positive and negative effects on the potential for core damage. If offsite power is lost, the diesel generators have to be relied upon to provide power to critical systems. However, a LOOP also would trip the reactor coolant pumps, which reduces the potential for an RCP seal LOCA. Because of this fact, the licensee recognized that assuming a LOOP would not necessarily have resulted in the highest CDF for a specific fire scenario and, thus, evaluated the conditional core damage probability for both situations. The higher of the two values was used by the licensee to calculate the CDF for the fire scenario. (The two values were not provided in the submittal.)

Fire-induced support system failures were accounted for in the fire assessments by failing support system components in the IPE models affected by each fire scenario. Thus, the potential for a fire-induced support system initiator was modeled in many submittals by using a general transient event tree. However, other licensees used event trees developed explicitly to model support system initiators. Those specific event trees were used to model fire scenarios that could damage the system. For example, a loss of component cooling water (CCW) event tree for a PWR would include the potential for an RCP seal LOCA.

A spurious opening of a pressurizer pressure operated relief valve (PORV) due to a fire was considered in many of the fire assessments. However, some were able to screen this initiator for certain fire areas because the cables for the block valves were not in the area. In addition, some dismissed this scenario on the basis that the probability of multiple hot shorts required to open both the PORV and its block valve is very small. One licensee (D.C. Cook) indicated that spurious PORV openings were not modeled because the failure of the PORV control cable due to a fire can be recovered in a relatively short time frame (30 minutes). The licensee indicates this assumption was supported by information in NUREG/CR-2258, which implies that an open PORV due to a hot short would subsequently close since the control cable would eventually short to ground, causing an open circuit. The licensee indicates that open circuits are the dominant failure mode for the PORV circuit since the conductors will eventually contact the grounded cable tray as insulation decomposes or melts away, opening protective fuses. Another licensee (Catawba) indicated spuriously open PORVs were not examined based on the argument that the PORV could be re-closed by removing power to the valve. For control room abandonment scenarios at Catawba, initiation of the safe shutdown facility (SSF) requires opening of disconnect switches that de-energize the PORVs.

Not all licensees indicated that the potential for fire-induced LOCAs was included in their assessments. One licensee indicated that even though explicit reviews of the potential for hot short-induced LOCAs were not included in their assessments, they were implicitly included due to the use of the IPE event trees in the assessment. The IPE event trees included branches for the occurrence of single and multiple stuck-open relief valves (SORVs). The licensee argued that while the probability of a hot short causing spurious safety relief valve (SRV) openings was not explicitly included in the model, the probabilities for random SORVs are similar in magnitude to the probabilities of single and multiple hot shorts. Therefore, explicit modeling of fire-induced SORVs would not result in significant changes in the CDF.

Another potential fire-induced LOCA scenario for BWRs involves hot shorts actuating the automatic depressurization system (ADS). Most BWR licensees addressed this scenario. A common fire location identified in the submittals where spurious ADS actuation could occur is the MCR. Recognizing this fact, one licensee (Cooper) indicated that the procedure for control room abandonment requires that operators set the two ADS inhibit switches to preclude a fire-induced ADS actuation. In addition, the occurrence of spurious ADS operation after setting the ADS inhibit switch is cited as a reason for evacuating the control room (such an event would indicate degradation of the MCR controls). In one control room scenario, a panel fire could result in a spurious ADS signal and simultaneously prevent initiation of the low pressure ECCS from the MCR. The condensate system would then have to provide coolant injection until the low pressure ECCS is initiated from the alternate shutdown panel.

Interfacing system LOCAs (ISLOCAs) were also considered in most of the fire assessments. In addition to being considered in the plant modeling, they were also considered in many of the containment performance assessments as potential containment bypass paths (see Section 3.4.9). The ISLOCA paths reviewed included ECCS lines, RHR suction lines, letdown lines, and sample lines off of the pressurizer that run to the quench tank and post-accident sample system. Lines containing a high/low pressure interface with a non-fire-susceptible closed valves (i.e., manual or check valves) were typically screened from the analysis. In addition, paths that had power removed from a susceptible valve were also screened. Other licensees argued that the occurrence of multiple independent hot shorts that would be required to result in spurious opening of redundant valves is unlikely and, thus, did not analyze the spurious opening (see Section 3.4.7.3).

3.4.7.2 Plant Models

The majority of the licensees indicated that the IPE models, or updated versions, were used in the fire IPEEEs. A few used a special safe shutdown fault tree. Most of the reported modifications and updates to the IPE models resulted from plant modifications that have been made since the original IPE models were constructed. Other modifications were made to enhance the model to account for some identified risk-beneficial action. For example, Byron 1 and 2 modified the IPE model to include cross-tying emergency buses between units, and D.C. Cook 1 and 2 credited cross-tying auxiliary feedwater trains. In addition, modifications were made to account for fire-specific impacts. For example, the Calvert Cliffs model explicitly included events related to control room fire scenarios, including abandonment scenarios. Most of the other licensees performed a separate control room abandonment evaluation that did not utilize the IPE model.

Although most of the licensees used their IPE models in the fire assessment, not all of them credited all of the mitigating systems included in the model. All licensees included Appendix R systems in the model since the location of the components and their associated cables had been determined in the plants safe shutdown analysis. However, there was some variability as to whether or not the non-Appendix R systems in the IPE models were credited. Most of the licensees credited all of the systems and components in their IPE models. Existing databases, drawings, cable routing information, and other resources were used to identify the locations of the non-Appendix R components and associated cables. Some licensees did not credit any non-Appendix R systems since obtaining the locations of those components represented a significant effort. However, other licensees only credited Appendix R systems in the fire area screening assessments but reviewed the unscreened fire areas in more detail to determine if some non-Appendix R equipment was located there. Finally, some licensees only credited selected non-Appendix R systems in both the screening and detailed analysis phases. In all cases, the offsite power cables were traced in order to credit offsite power in the analysis (Appendix R assessments do not credit offsite power). Other non-Appendix R systems credited in these selective models include a nonemergency startup feedwater train and the power conversion system.

When non-Appendix R equipment and associated cables were not located, the majority of the licensees assumed that the equipment would not be available (i.e., the basic events in the IPE models for the equipment was set to either TRUE or given a probability of 1.0). However, one licensee (Cooper) indicated that for some fire areas, non-Appendix R systems were credited even though it was not explicitly determined that cables for those systems were not in the area. The systems were credited for a few plant areas where the spatial arrangement of the plant buildings and discussions with plant design engineers were assessed as being sufficient to conclude that no damage to the systems would occur.

Not all components that were included in the IPE models were assumed to be susceptible to fire damage. In particular, all of the submittals assumed that passive components, such as pipes and tanks, were not vulnerable to fire damage. In addition, fire-induced failure of some active components, such as check valves, is not possible and, thus, was not considered. The main components evaluated for potential damage in fire scenarios were the control and power cables for active components, such as air-operated and motor-operated valves (AOVs and MOVs), pumps, air compressors, and heating, ventilation, and air conditioning (HVAC) fans. Fire-induced damage to the active components themselves was also considered in the majority of the fire PRAs. In addition, power distribution cables were also a major component of concern. Electrical and control cabinets were considered not only as fire ignition sources, but also were considered susceptible targets for damage from other ignition sources.

Some licensees indicated that some additional failures had to be added to the IPE models used in their fire PRAs. These included the following items.

- Components that were not modeled in the IPE because they are highly reliable compared to other components whose failure would have a similar impact on the system operation. In some cases, fire-induced failures of such components could be a significant contributor to the system failure, cables being the most common example.

- Spurious actuation of components was often ignored in the IPE models. Fire-induced spurious operation of components had to be included in some cases where spurious operation cannot be accounted for using the existing IPE model (see Section 3.4.7.3 for further discussion).

- Fire procedures can require the operators to open circuit breakers or pull fuses in order to prevent spurious operation of equipment. These operator actions need to be taken into account in a fire PRA.

All of the fire IPEEEs assumed that a fire-induced anticipated transient without scram (ATWS) is very unlikely. The reactor protection system (RPS) in both PWRs and BWRs is designed such that de-energization of trip circuits will result in control rod insertion. Although fires could conceivably cause hot shorts that could prevent a reactor trip for some time, one PWR licensee (Davis-Besse) indicated that the RPS circuits would not likely remain energized for a long enough time to result in damage to the core. All of the fire IPEEEs also neglected the potential for random RPS failures based on low probability of occurrence. As a result, fire-induced failure of ATWS mitigating systems, such as the standby liquid control system, was not included in the fire analyses.

3.4.7.3 Modeling of Hot Shorts and Spurious Operations

The topic of cable hot shorts and the potential spurious operation of plant equipment due to cable failures has been a topic of interest since the fire at Browns Ferry in 1975. In general, the IPE plant models do not include power, control, and instrumentation cables. Hence, for the purposes of the IPEEE analyses, licensees used a surrogate event approach when a fire scenario was identified that would fail a cable. The surrogate event postulated was failure of the component associated with the cable. Most of the licensees indicated that the fire-induced cable failure modes that were considered included open circuits and short circuits to ground. In addition, many specifically indicated that hot shorts (conductor-to-conductor shorts) were also considered.

Typically, the licensees indicated that the worst fire-induced cable failure mode was assumed to occur, and modified the plant model accordingly. For example, if a valve had to open for a system to operate, a fire-induced failure of the valve control or power cables was translated into failure of that valve to open. The valve was assumed to remain closed if the fire resulted in an open circuit or short to ground in either the power or control cables. If a hot short occurred involving either the control or power cable, the valve could spuriously close after opening. Therefore, any fire-induced cable failure mode could be translated to a valve failure to open. However, for normally closed (or open) valves that must remain in that position, spurious operation of the valve due to a hot short may not have been modeled. The modeling of this event appeared to be dependent upon whether or not spurious valve operation was included in the IPE models.

Another failure mode of concern regarding hot shorts in motor-operated valves (MOVs) was identified in NRC Information Notice 92-18. Hot shorts involving MOV control circuits can occur in locations within the circuit such that protective devices, such as limit switches and torque limiters, are bypassed. Such a hot short could cause an MOV motor to continue to drive the valve even after the valve has completely opened (or closed). The valve could be damaged to the point where manual opening of the valve would not be possible and could even cause valve rupture. Not all MOVs are susceptible to this failure mode (the valve motors are not large enough to damage the valve). Some licensees indicated their MOVs were modified to eliminate this concern. However, the majority of the licensees did not address this issue in their fire assessment. Thus, it is possible that recovery actions to manually open fire-damaged MOVs were optimistically applied in some fire assessments.

Although most licensees stated that all cable failure modes were considered in the fire assessment, it was not clear if the licensees actually traced the location of all conductors associated with a component. Conductors associated with the open and close logic of a valve or the start and stop logic of a pump can be in different cables which can be routed in different locations. Failure to trace all of the conductors can lead to erroneous results. For example, if a valve failure mode is failure to close, it is possible that only the locations of the cables containing conductors associated with the valve close circuit were traced. However, a hot short involving the conductor associated with the valve open logic can result in spurious valve opening, and failure to trace the cables containing these conductors could miss important component failures in specific fire scenarios. Erroneous results can also be obtained if the cables containing conductors associated with component indication or with actuation or protection signals are not located. Information with regard to this fact was limited in the submittals. In fact only one licensee (Davis Besse) stated that a detailed evaluation of circuit schematics was performed to identify which cables would not affect a circuit's function due to either hot shorts or open circuits.

There are also valves in systems whose failure can lead to a diversion of system flow that would be detrimental to the system operation. It is not clear that spurious operation of such valves was included in the IPE models. Thus, it is not clear whether fire-induced spurious operation of such valves was included in many of the fire assessments. It is noted that Appendix R assessments may include potential diversion path valves in the safe shutdown equipment list, but this may not be true if multiple simultaneous hot shorts are required to open the diversion path (e.g., two valves in series must open due to hot shorts). The cables associated with these valves are located as part of the Appendix R analysis. A few licensees indicated that a comparison of the Appendix R equipment list with the IPE model was performed and, in some limited cases, the IPE model was modified to include diversion paths. However, it was not generally indicated in the submittals if the potential for diversion paths was examined for non-Appendix R systems.

One licensee (D.C. Cook) indicated that spurious opening of both motor-operated and air-operated valves was not analyzed due to the use of a "double break" control circuit design (i.e., limit switch circuit breaks are installed at both the MCR and component ends of the circuit). Double-break control circuits have a control switch contact at the end of each control circuit leg. Opening or closing a valve requires closure of both contacts in the associated control circuit logic. Spurious operation of such a valve would require two hot shorts from the same power source, one bypassing each open contact.

Some licensees indicated that hot shorts in power cables were explicitly excluded from consideration in their fire PRAs. It appears that most, if not all, of the licensees ignored these types of hot shorts. The basis for this assumption was that three-phase hot shorts across the proper phases must occur for appropriate motor operation.

For those licensees that did include hot shorts in their assessments, the probability of a hot short used in the analysis was highly variable. Most of the licensees assumed that a hot short would occur, and used a probability of 1.0. In some cases, a lower probability was assigned in a specific fire scenario where the calculated core damage frequency was deemed to be exceedingly conservative. A value of 6.8E-2 suggested in NUREG/CR-2258 was used in many studies. Another common value assigned was a probability of 0.1

3 - 67

although a specific justification or basis for this value was not provided in any such case. When two or more hot shorts were required to provide an undesirable condition, it was common to treat the multiple hot shorts as independent events. Thus, the probability of two hot shorts was calculated by squaring the probability for one hot short.

In many instances, the U.S. NRC staff questioned licensees regarding their treatment of hot shorts and other control system interaction issues. However, the staff ultimately concluded that a full treatment of the potential circuit failure modes and effects concerns was a topic that was beyond the state-of-the-art in fire PRA at the time of the IPEEE analyses. Again, licensees were not expected to advance the state-of-the-art in their IPEEEs, and this is one area where state-of-the-art issues prevented licensees from providing more complete analyses. A range of activities are underway to address the circuit interaction issues, both within RES and NRR. The U.S. NRC staff concluded that the treatment of control systems interactions provided in the IPEEEs was acceptable, based on the information available at the time of the IPEEE's preparation. The staff has also concluded that those analyses did adequately address the objectives of the IPEEE program. In particular, the vast majority of licensees have provided an assessment of the capabilities and reliability of their safe shutdown provisions, and have assessed the CDF contribution should those efforts fail. The staff found such assessments adequate to meet the intent of the IPEEE process.

3.4.8 Human Reliability Analysis

It is clear that humans will have a significant role in recognizing and responding to events that occur during a fire in a nuclear power plant. In this context, it is important that appropriate human actions are modeled in the fire PRAs performed for the IPEEE program, and that appropriate human reliability analyses (HRAs) are conducted in analyzing and quantifying those human actions. The purpose of this section is to provide general descriptions of the approaches used by the licensees in modeling human actions in the fire IPEEEs, to discuss the nature of the HRAs performed to evaluate the likelihood of such actions, to identify the general results of these analyses, and to compare the IPEEE analyses to typical practice in general fire PRAs.

3.4.8.1 Modeling of Human Actions

As is discussed in Section 3.4.7.2, the majority of licensees utilized their IPE models as the basis for their fire models, and generally retained the human actions included in those models. Pre-accident human errors, such as failure to restore components following test or maintenance and miscalibration of instrumentation, were retained since they occur prior to the occurrence of a fire. The human error probabilities (HEPs) for the pre-accident human error events used in the IPEs were also used in the fire assessments.

The inclusion of post-accident human actions was more variable. While the vast majority of the licensees retained the post-accident human errors modeled in the IPEs, including recovery actions, many also added recovery actions specific to the fire sequences. Frequently added recoveries included the following actions:

- manually opening motor-operated valves when fire-induced cable damage occurs,
- pulling fuses or opening breakers to prevent spurious component operation,
- starting diesel generators,
- manually starting auxiliary feedwater (AFW) pumps,
- opening doors and starting fans after loss of normal ventilation in critical areas,
- recovering/providing component cooling water or standby service water,
- placing control room HVAC in recirculation mode,

- cross-tying various systems (including between dual units), and
- restoring loads after inducing an SBO per procedure (SISBO plants).

The most common fire-induced (or fire-specific) human action modeled in the fire assessments involved safe shutdown from outside the control room. This action becomes necessary when operators must evacuate the MCR as a result of habitability or controllability problems, whether caused by a fire in the MCR or by a fire in another area such as the cable spreading room. Most licensees considered MCR evacuation scenarios arising from fires within the MCR. However, few considered such scenarios arising from fires outside the MCR. Such scenarios could arise if smoke or combustion products from adjacent areas enters the MCR in sufficient quantities to compromise habitability, or if the fire damaged cables supporting MCR circuits.

There is variability in the remote shutdown capabilities at the plants. Some plants have all (or at least most) of the required controls and instrumentation at one location, while others have the controls in multiple panels, which requires significant coordination of actions. Even the plants that appear to have most of the required controls and instrumentation at one location (i.e., a centralized remote shutdown panel (RSP)) generally required that some local actions be taken in order to achieve safe shutdown. Some licensees rely entirely on actions at the individual component location, and others argue that shutdown can be reasonably achieved completely through local actions if for some reason their RSP is unavailable. However, plants that model shutdown from the RSP did not generally attempt to also take credit for completely shutting down the plant with local actions.

The capabilities to isolate the RSP(s) from the control room are variable. Some plants have transfer switches that isolate circuits in the remote shutdown panel from those in the MCR. Some utilize different power sources for the two sets of controls, while others use different fuses off of the same power source to provide for circuit independence in the event the control room circuit has failed prior to transfer. It appeared that many plants considered the transfer process in their representation of successful shutdown from outside the MCR, but for many it was difficult to tell whether they did so or not.

It is interesting to note that quite a few submittals did not explicitly include the action(s) needed to shut down the plant from outside the control room in their initial analyses. Some argued that the necessity of MCR abandonment was so unlikely that such scenarios would not make a significant contribution to CDF. Others did not provide a basis for not modeling the action. These cases were questioned by the NRC staff during the review process, and licensees were requested to provide an assessment of remote shutdown reliability. For those licensees that did model the control room abandonment actions, including those who did so in an RAI response, there was significant variability in how they represented and quantified the relevant steps (see Section 3.4.8.2).

It was also a common practice in the fire assessment not to credit operator actions that must be performed at the location of the fire. However, some submittals indicated that actions, such as manually opening valves, were credited in the analysis if the time available to perform such actions extended until after the time when the fire would be expected to be suppressed. For example, one licensee (Crystal River) took credit for all human actions in their IPE for which 3 or more hours would be available and also used the existing HEP for each such action from the IPE. Another licensee (Quad Cities) did the same as long as 30 minutes were available for the action, the action would take place in a building other than where the fire was located, and the fire was not in the pathway from the MCR to the location of the fire. It was common practice not to credit ex-control-room operator actions when the fire was located in a zone that was in the path required to get to the component. However, when alternate paths were available, the action was credited. In most of these cases, it was not clear if the HEPs were adjusted to account for the fact that alternate paths to the component would have to be identified.

Overall, licensees have either provided specific assessments of the reliability of credited human actions, or have, at the least, assessed the impact of failure to achieve credited human actions in their IPEEE fire studies. While these analyses may not be as complete as those documented in past fire PRAs, they were found by the NRC staff to meet the intent of the IPEEE process. In particular, licensees, by and large, have assessed the potential risk implications of failure to successfully implement their credited operator recovery actions, including in particular, remote shutdown actions. It is also noteworthy that a large number of the cited IPEEE plant improvements are related to improvements and enhancements to operator procedures and training (see Section 3.2.1).

3.4.8.2 Quantification of Human Actions

As discussed above, it appears that most of the licensees included in their IPEEE fire analysis the pre-accident human error events that were modeled in the IPEs and (appropriately) used the existing HEPs for those events. However, the approaches for quantification of the post-accident human actions retained from the IPEs were more variable. At least a few licensees used the existing HEPs without making any adjustments to reflect the potential impact of fire conditions. This was done for both MCR and ex-control-room actions. One argument presented for not changing these HEPs was that the values from the IPE were already conservative. The most common argument (especially for MCR actions) was that the operators would not be significantly affected by what was going on outside of the control room. The licensees did not generally address the impact from some potential fire-induced stressors on the HEPs. These stressors include the potential that at least one operator may not be available due to fire brigade responsibilities, that the fire may result in spurious signals and alarms that would provide confusing information to the operator, and that the fire and the presence of even small amounts of smoke might have negative psychological effects on some operators and other plant staff needed to respond to the event. Few submittals considered these factors in determining MCR-related HEPs, regardless of their approach.

With respect to other treatments of HEPs modeled from the IPEs, some licensees simply applied a performance shaping factor (PSF) of, for example, 5 or 10 as a multiplier on all the existing HEPs to reflect additional influences such as the increased stress that a fire might create for the operators. Some licensees examined each human action and used expert judgement to decide whether a multiplier (or a simple increase in the value) to reflect fire conditions should be applied. Others assigned screening values (generally around 0.1, but ranging to 1.0 for events that might be directly influenced by the fire) with the idea of doing a more detailed fire-based evaluation if needed. Finally, some licensees re-evaluated all of the existing HEPs and re-quantified them to more precisely model the potential effects of the fire on human performance.

The HRA methods used, and the consideration of fire impacts, varied significantly. There are many important factors that could influence the modeling of human performance in fire scenarios. Examples of such factors include the following items:

- stress,
- manning level in the MCR,
- time available,
- fire location,
- accessability,

- available paths to the fire,
- smoke levels,
- use of breathing apparatuses,
- barriers to communication,
- relevant training and experience,
- adequacy of indications in the MCR and at local sites,
- effects of spurious signals and alarms, and
- number of concurrent actions.

Of these factors, it appeared that most of the IPEEE fire analyses only considered time, stress, and the availability of open paths to the location of the task. Initial estimates (based on a sampling of about half the submittals) suggest that about 60% of the licensees did some basic HRA other than assigning screening values, but about 80% of those only modified the quantification to reflect very simple aspects of the fire-related context.

Again, while the licensee analyses may not be as complete as those typically performed in support of a full-scope fire PRA, they were found by the U.S. NRC staff to meet the intent of the IPEEE process. In particular, the licensees' submittals have included the consideration of human action failure events. In many cases, licensees have identified the human actions that were most important to fire CDF (or CDF reduction), and have considered the potential impact of fire on those reliability estimates. Many licensees also implemented IPEEE-based plant improvements aimed at increasing the reliability of their operators (improved procedures, enhancements to training to reflect IPEEE insights, etc.).

3.4.8.2.1 Fire-Induced Recovery Actions and MCR Evacuation

In addition to the human actions modeled from the IPEs, many licensees also modeled recovery actions specific to the fire scenarios. Examples of the types of actions modeled were noted above. In general, licensees tended to explicitly quantify such actions and to consider at least some fire-related conditions, such as available paths to the location of the action, in determining the HEPs. However, many simply assigned screening values to these events. In most instances the screening values appeared to be reasonably conservative (typically 0.1), but this was not always the case. Interestingly, no situations were identified in which any of the screening values used for any of the modeled events were ever revisited and given a more detailed analysis.

As discussed above, the most common human recovery action added to the fire models involved achieving safe shutdown from outside the MCR. This action could become critical when habitability or controllability problems arise in the MCR. In determining the HEPs for deciding to evacuate the MCR and successfully controlling the plant from an RSP, there are a number of factors that could be considered. Examples include the following items:

- the procedures available,
- how often the relevant actions are practiced,
- the potential impact of crew reluctance to abandon the MCR,
- the impact of potential confusion about the need to evacuate the MCR (e.g., because of spurious signals and confusing indications),
- the number and complexity of the actions required,
- the number of different locations that must be visited,

- the extent to which multiple actions must be coordinated,
- the ability to communicate between different sites,
- the need to wear breathing apparatus while performing the actions, and
- the adequacy of the human-machine interface at the RSP.

There was little information in the IPEEE submittals to indicate the licensees had considered many of these factors in quantifying this general action to take control of the plant from outside the MCR. In general, the licensees that quantified this action seemed optimistic that operators could and would take the appropriate actions if necessary. This is not to say that the licensees necessarily assigned optimistic values for the action, but rather that they did not in general identify a need to explicitly consider factors that could influence performance. For example, it seems clear that the number and complexity of the actions required could have a significant impact on success (see discussion of SISBO plants below), yet few licensees provided evidence that they explicitly modeled these factors in determining the HEPs. As with the quantification of other actions in the models, some licensees assigned screening values to evacuating the MCR, while others attempted a more detailed analysis. Detailed HEPs associated with safe shutdown from outside the MCR included values ranging from 0.1 to 1.3E-3 and, interestingly, screening values also ranged from 0.1 to 1.0E-3.

3.4.8.2.2 Self-Induced Station Blackout (SISBO)

Factors such as the number and complexity of the actions required for safe shutdown outside the MCR are particularly relevant to plants which functionally induce an SBO (a self-induced station blackout or SISBO) when shutting down the plant in the response to a fire (in some cases, whether the MCR is abandoned or not). Several plants have developed specific procedures to be followed in case of fire in which plant equipment is purposely de-energized, and only a limited set of equipment is re-powered and used to bring the plant safely under control. Such a strategy severely limits the potential for adverse effects from hot shorts, including spurious operations of equipment, and misleading or conflicting instrument and indication signals. Implementation of the SISBO strategy has typically led to complicated procedures. It is unclear from the submittals the level of detail applied in the analysis of the risk and human performance effects. Some other plants, even though they do not strictly use the SISBO concept, also often have complicated fire procedures for de-energizing and re-energizing plant equipment. There are potential disadvantages to putting the plant into a loss of power condition. These include the use of complicated procedures requiring multiple actions in many different locations, and the potential that once stopped, equipment may not restart when required. As noted above, the primary advantage of such a response scheme is to avoid hot shorts and other similar fire-induced equipment effects and interactions that might be detrimental to achieving plant shutdown during a significant fire. No risk tradeoff studies have been documented, either in the IPEEEs or elsewhere, to assess whether or not risk has actually been lowered by adoption of these SISBO procedures.

It does not appear that the unique characteristics of the SISBO and similar strategies have been fully addressed by most licensees in determining the likelihood of operators successfully achieving all of the relevant actions needed to shut down the plant. However, at least one plant (Kewaunee) did model the many steps involved in achieving plant control using the SISBO approach, and at least considered the likely impact of related stress on operator performance. In their approach, specific actions involved in controlling the plant from the RSP, such as isolating nonessential equipment and restoring power to electrical busses, starting and loading the diesels, and establishing AFW flow from the RSP, were quantified separately, thus modeling and quantifying critical aspects of the shutdown process. Interestingly, Kewaunee (one of the few licensees to present importance measures) noted that due to the manual actions necessary to respond to a fire, human error was an important contributor to fire CDF, contributing 56% to the fire CDF (based on Fussell-Vesely importance). In general, past fire PRAs have not considered SISBO scenario modeling in detail either. Hence, this area would require advancement of the state-of-the-art and, therefore, lies outside the scope of the IPEEE process.

3.4.9 Containment Performance Perspectives for Fire

The requirements for assessing containment performance during internal fire events were outlined in Generic Letter 88-20, Supplement 4, Appendix 2.

> The evaluation of the containment performance for external events should be directed toward a systematic examination of whether there are sequences that involve containment failure modes distinctly different from those found in the IPE internal events evaluation or contribute significantly to the likelihood of functional failure of the containment (i.e., loss of containment barrier independent of core melt). It should recognize the role of mitigating systems, and should ultimately result in the development of accident management procedures that could both prevent and mitigate the consequences of the severe accidents. The most efficient way to accomplish this is to use the information developed for the IPEEE to:
>
> - identify mechanisms that could lead to containment bypass,
> - identify mechanisms that could cause failure of the containment to isolate, and
> - determine the availability and performance of the containment systems under the external hazard to see if they are different from those evaluated under the internal event evaluation.
>
> Additional guidance on the containment performance associated with external events can be found in NUREG-1407.

Specifically, NUREG-1407 includes the following additional guidance on performing the containment analysis.

- Perform containment analysis if containment failure modes differ significantly from those found in the IPE internal events evaluations.
- Perform in a fashion similar to an internal-initiator PRA.

The methods used in the IPEEEs for assessing containment performance during internal fire events are discussed in this section. The results of those assessments are presented.

3.4.9.1 Methods Used for Assessing Containment Performance

No licensees identified new containment failure modes that resulted from fires. Thus, the majority of the licensees did not perform Level 2 fire PRAs. Instead, the licensees met the guidance in GL 88-20 by assessing the potential for containment bypass or isolation failure initiated by a fire and determining the availability of the containment heat removal systems during postulated fires. The emphasis on containment bypass or isolation failure directly correlates with the potential for large early radionuclide releases which provide the highest consequences from severe core damage accidents.

A large number of licensees performed a limited containment performance assessment that consisted of determining whether a fire can lead to containment bypass, isolation failure, or failure of containment heat removal. In most cases, this assessment was performed according to the guidance provided in FIVE and in the FPRAIG. The FIVE methodology requires a containment performance assessment for all fire zones that have CDFs greater than 1E-6/yr. In particular, fires scenarios resulting in CDFs greater than this limit and in plant damage states not included in the IPE were to be subjected to a containment performance evaluation. The containment performance assessment is to include the following items:

- An assessment of the potential for a fire in the area of concern to damage equipment or prohibit manual operator actions used to accomplish the containment function, and
- Identification of a minimum set of equipment and manual actions necessary to achieve the containment function.

The FPRAIG provides similar guidance to that provided in FIVE in that containment performance (heat removal and isolation functions) only has to be evaluated for fire scenarios that do not screen. Additional guidance is provided for evaluating containment bypass scenarios. The guidance consists of a review of the ISLOCA paths identified in the IPE. Each of these paths can be screened according to the FPRAIG if the following criteria are satisfied.

- The pathway does not contain any fire-susceptible valves. ISLOCA paths that contain only manual valves, check valves, or motor-operated valves where the power is removed can be screened from further consideration.
- The pathway requires random faults with probabilities of less than 1E-5. The product of this probability and an average frequency of a fire in a zone (1E-2/yr) ensures that the frequency of a bypass scenario is less than 1E-7/yr.

For unscreened paths, the FPRAIG indicates that the CDF must be calculated. If the path only includes fire-susceptible valves, then the locations of the cables for those valves should be identified and included in the fire modeling in the same fashion as for the cables for other mitigating equipment. If the path contains one closed non-fire-susceptible valve, then the FPRAIG suggests that the probability of containment bypass can be bounded by the probability of the random failure of that valve (i.e., the fire-induced failure of the susceptible valve is assumed to be 1.0).

3.4.9.2 Containment Performance Results and Findings

The quantitative results for those plants that performed a Level 2 fire PRA are provided in Section 3.4.9.2.1. The results for fire initiators are compared against those for other internal events reported in the IPEs. Because only a few Level 2 fire PRAs were performed, the results should be used cautiously. The results of the qualitative containment performance assessments performed by the majority of the licensees are summarized in Section 3.4.9.2.2.

3.4.9.2.1 Results from Level 2 Fire PRAs

The integrated conditional containment failure probabilities (CCFPs) from the IPEEEs that performed a Level 2 assessment are summarized in Table 3.9. These results are compared against the Level 2 results from the IPEs for the same plants. As indicated, the CCFPs calculated for fire scenarios are generally similar to those obtained for other internal events. In addition, the reported conditional probabilities of containment bypass and early failure for fire scenarios are generally small for most of the plants. The reasons for the major differences in the fire and external event CCFPs are discussed below.

There are two multi-unit sites that performed Level 2 PRAs. No substantial differences in the containment performance were identified for the two Hatch units. However, there was some variation at the Beaver Valley units that paralleled the differences in the internal events CCFPs. The small bypass CCFPs for Beaver Valley 1 and 2 involve a failure of containment isolation. It is noted that the dominant core damage scenarios are more likely to result in fire-induced containment isolation failure at Beaver Valley 1 than at Beaver Valley 2. However, the large bypass CCFPs which include early structural failure are similar for both plants.

The fire-induced CCFPs for the single-unit plants that performed Level 2 PRAs were similar to those from the internal event analysis except for Fort Calhoun. This plant had a higher containment bypass contribution that is attributable to fire-induced containment isolation failures.

Table 3.9: Conditional containment failure probabilities during fire accidents

Plant IPEEE	Percent							
	Bypass		Early Failure		Late Failure	No Failure	Over pressure Failure[2]	Vented[2]
	Small	Large	Small	Large				
General Electric - Mark I								
Hatch 1								
Fire	0%				44%[1]	11%	44%	1%[3]
Other internal events	1%				19%[1]	49%	25%	5%[3]
Hatch 2								
Fire	1%				54%[1]	14%	31%	1%[3]
Other internal events	1%				20%[1]	53%	21%	5%[3]
Oyster Creek								
Fire	6%	13%			60%	21%		
Other internal events	7%	16%			26%	51%		
General Electric - Mark II								
LaSalle 1 & 2	No results provided in submittal							
General Electric - Mark III								
No plants in this category performed Level 2 PRAs								
PWR - Ice Condenser								
Catawba 1 & 2	No results provided in submittal							

Table 3.9: Conditional containment failure probabilities during fire accidents - (Continued)

Plant IPEEE	Bypass		Early Failure		Late Failure	No Failure	Over pressure Failure[2]	Vented[3]
	Small	Large	Small	Large				
PWR - Subatmospheric								
Beaver Valley 1								
Fire	41.3% (5.4% large, 35.9% small)				39%	20%		
Other internal events	27.3% (5.0% large, 22.3% small)				43%	29%		
Beaver Valley 2								
Fire	3.9% (2.9% large and 1% small)				76%	20%		
Other internal events	7.6% (1.6% large, 6.1% small)				52%	40%		
Millstone 3								
Fire	<0.1%		<0.1%		41%	59%		
Other internal events	<1%		<0.1%		20%	80%		
PWR - Large Dry								
Calvert Cliffs 1								
Fire	0%		2%	7%	56%	37%		
Other internal events	3%		9%		40%	48%		
Calvert Cliffs 2	No results provided in submittal							
Fort Calhoun 1								
Fire	21%		2%		41%	36%		
Other internal events	11%		2%		28%	60%		
San Onofre 2 & 3								
Fire	2%		1%		15%	82%		
Other internal events	7%		<0.1%		9%	84%		
Vogtle 1 & 2								
Fire	1%					99%		
Other internal events	3%		<0.1%		0%	96%		

[1] Listed in the submittal as containment over temperature failures.
[2] Containment over pressure failures could be either early or late failures.
[3] These contributions are from wetwell venting.

Overall, those licensees that performed a Level 2 fire PRA indicated that their assessments did not identify any unique containment failure modes or vulnerabilities to early containment failure. However, Calvert Cliffs Unit 1 identified a new plant damage state (PDS) related to fire-induced core damage. This PDS represents a high-pressure core melt that results in a large early containment failure with no containment cooling. This PDS resulted from fire scenarios which could result in spurious opening of containment isolation valves. Many of these fire scenarios were in the control room and required control room evacuation. The Calvert Cliffs IPEEE submittal notes that the contribution from early small containment failures was larger in the IPE assessment primarily due to a steam generator tube rupture which was not a concern in the fire PRA.

3.4.9.2.2 Containment: Bypass, Isolation, and Heat Removal

As indicated previously, the majority of the containment performance assessments documented in the IPEEE submittals were limited to the review of the potential for any fire to result in containment bypass, loss of containment isolation, or loss of containment heat removal. The summary of qualitative insights discussed in this section is based on the review of a selected sample of approximately 25% of the submittals. The results of this limited review indicate that a single fire can neither completely destroy the ability to isolate the containment nor fail all of the containment heat removal systems.

Many of the licensees indicated that the potential for fire-induced containment bypass and isolation failure was only analyzed for areas that were not screened in the core damage assessment. Most of the licensees used 1E-6/yr as the CDF screening criterion. Thus, the potential for containment bypass in some plants due to fires in areas with CDFs less than 1E-6/yr was not evaluated. Although this practice meets the intent of GL 88-20, it should be realized that not all areas where fires could result in a large early release were systematically identified and evaluated by some of the licensees.

In most of the IPEEEs reviewed for this assessment, the containment itself was screened as a significant fire area. In fact, the FPRAIG methodology specifically excluded the need to analyze containment fires. The licensees' basis for screening the containment generally included one or more of the following arguments which are provided in the FIVE and FPRAIG methodologies.

- Historically, there have been few fires inside the containment.
- Most containment fires occurred during plant shutdown, rather than during power operation.
- Previous fire PRAs have found that such fires are not risk-significant.
- There is a low likelihood that a fire in containment could affect redundant trains.
- A hot gas layer is unlikely to form that could damage cables.

Most of the historical containment fires have involved problems in the reactor coolant pump oil collection systems. These problems have been addressed by design improvements mandated by Appendix R. Also, it should be noted that fires inside Mark I and II containments during power operation are precluded because these containment types are inerted. If a fire were to occur, many of the licensees argue that spatial separation of equipment would limit the impact of a containment fire. In addition, the licensees state that the fire impact on the containment structure itself (including penetrations) would be minimal.

Several licensees addressed the potential impact of a fire on penetration seals. The penetrations included hatches, pipes, and electrical penetrations assemblies. Equipment and personnel hatches were identified as using mechanical closure mechanisms: i.e., inflatable seals, which need pneumatic or electrical power to function and which would be susceptible to fire damage, were not used. These hatch seals and piping and electrical penetration seals were listed as unlikely to degrade because the penetrations are qualified as fire barriers, and direct fire damage is unlikely due to the absence of fire sources near the penetrations (including transient sources). It was recognized that the most likely fire scenario that would damage the penetration seals would require generation of a hot gas layer. However, one licensee states this type of fire scenario would be unlikely since it would require failure of fire suppression.

The review of the containment bypass function generally involved a review of the high-pressure/low-pressure ISLOCA paths identified in the IPE. Most relied on their Appendix R assessments which required a review of containment bypass. The ISLOCA paths reviewed included ECCS lines, RHR suction lines, letdown lines, and sample lines off the pressurizer that run to the quench tank and post-accident sampling system. In one PWR submittal (Davis Besse), the licensee only addressed the potential for an ISLOCA occurring from fires inside the containment. The majority of the licensees addressed the potential for ISLOCAs due to fires outside the containment.

Lines containing a high/low pressure interface with two or more non-fire-susceptible closed valves were typically screened per the guidance in the FPRAIG. The screening criteria identified in the submittals include the following:

- the path contains two or more non-fire-susceptible valves (closed manual valve, check valves, or motor-operated valves with the power removed),
- the interfacing line is less than 2" in diameter (within the normal makeup capacity), and
- heat exchanger tube or cooling coils (including RCP seal cooling coils) designed to operate under differential pressure conditions were excluded.

In many of the IPEEEs, the RHR suction lines (i.e., the pipe connecting the primary coolant system to the RHR pump suction) were not screened based on these criteria. A fire in at least one fire area could potentially cause spurious opening of both valves. This potential was identified in the plant Appendix R evaluations and was alleviated by the removal of power to one of the valves during normal operation. To meet Appendix R requirements, one licensee indicated in their submittal that containment isolation is provided through the use of alternate isolation valves or by alternate isolation circuits for a fire-damaged valve.

For some lines with high/low pressure interfaces, multiple hot shorts would be required to result in spurious opening of redundant valves. The general argument provided in the submittals for such paths is that the occurrence of multiple independent hot shorts is unlikely and, thus, the risk from such scenarios is negligible.

Licensee reviews of the containment isolation paths generally consisted of an examination of the fluid lines that penetrate the containment. Licensees identified paths that connect the containment atmosphere or water spaces (the sump in PWRs and the suppression pool in BWRs) with closed systems (e.g., the RHR system in BWRs), paths connecting the reactor vessel to closed systems outside the containment (e.g., shutdown cooling systems), and paths connecting the reactor vessel to the environment (e.g., the main steam lines in BWRs where the MSIVs must close). In addition, paths connecting the containment atmosphere to the environment (e.g., containment venting paths) were also explicitly identified in some submittals. One licensee indicated that the list of valves reviewed was equivalent to those on the Appendix J containment isolation valve list.

The review of the containment isolation paths generally utilized screening criteria to eliminate many of these lines. Examples of the screening criteria include the following items:

- the line is small in diameter (typically less than 2"),
- the line is closed to the reactor coolant system and the containment atmosphere,
- the line is closed to the environment outside the containment, and

- the line contains non-fire-susceptible isolation valves (e.g., check valves, de-energized closed MOVs or normally closed manual valves).

In most submittals, the licensees indicated that the potential for hot shorts leading to spurious valve operation was considered in the assessment of the containment isolation function. However, one licensee indicated that the conditions required to obtain hot shorts are difficult to achieve. In this case the licensee concluded that any containment isolation path with a normally closed motor-operated valve or an air-operated valve that fails closed on loss of power does not represent a vulnerable containment bypass path.

Typically, only a few bypass paths were unscreened. Unscreened paths identified in the reviewed submittals included containment sump pump paths and containment purge paths. As a result of fire, the containment isolation valves in these lines may open or remain open. Alternatively, a fire may result in closure of the containment isolation valves. A typical procedural requirement is to verify that containment isolation has occurred given generation of an isolation signal, and to manually close any path that is found not to have closed automatically. One licensee indicated that operator action, as provided in procedures, could isolate any valve remotely as long as the route to the valve did not proceed through the fire area. Typical fire areas identified in the reviewed submittals where containment isolation valve operation may be prevented include the control room, cable spreading rooms, and switchgear rooms. Other locations include the remote shutdown panel room and battery charger rooms.

One licensee indicated that the location of the cables for the containment isolation valves had not been identified as part of the study. Thus, the automatic isolation of the valves given a fire could not be ensured. However, the licensee indicated that manual closure of the valves is likely since procedures are in place directing the operators to verify and ensure containment isolation. Based on credit for manual closure, the only threat to containment isolation would be a fire that prevents access to an open containment isolation valve. However, since fires are typically suppressed within an hour, the licensee argued that manual closure of any containment isolation valve located in the area could be performed before core damage could occur as a result of the fire.

One licensee addressed fire-induced containment isolation failures by comparing the total flow area from the failed isolation paths against the bypass area modeled in the IPE Level 2 analysis (an assumed 4" diameter hole). In every case but one, the total area of the isolation paths that could fail open due to fires in the unscreened fire areas was within the bypass area that was assumed in the IPE Level 2 analysis. However, for all penetration paths reviewed, additional features that provide some assurance against the release of radioactive material were identified. These included either normally closed manual valves or check valves to isolate the flow path; the flow path would direct any release to a waste storage tank, or the flow path is closed and, thus, would route any release back to the containment.

Licensees generally reviewed the containment cooling function by identifying if a single fire can result in failure of all trains of containment cooling systems. For PWRs, containment cooling systems include the containment fan coolers and/or containment sprays. Most of the PWR submittals that were examined in this study indicated only one or the other system was reviewed. Since there are generally redundant trains that are divisionally separated, the majority of the licensees indicated that a single fire would not result in loss of all containment heat removal.

Some licensees indicated that the containment heat removal capability during fires would not be any worse than during a random event. For example, the Comanche Peak submittal indicated that the dominant fire scenarios may result in loss of the containment sprays (the fan coolers are not credited for containment heat removal). The containment sprays were also not available for the dominant scenarios reported in the Comanche Peak IPE. However, the licensee indicates that since Comanche Peak is housed in a large dry containment, a large early release is not caused by a failure of containment heat removal.

Other licensees did not specifically examine the effects of fire on containment heat removal. One licensee (D.C. Cook) indicated that since containment failure due to over pressurization would not occur for 30 hours, there is sufficient time to recover one of the containment spray trains even if it had been damaged by fire. The licensee assigned a 0.1 probability for failing to perform this recovery action leading to containment failure.

Based on the limited reviews of the containment isolation and containment heat removal functions, the majority of the licensees for the plants reviewed for this report concluded that the impact of fire on the containment is within accepted limits.

For BWRs, containment heat removal is accomplished using some of the same systems that remove heat from the vessel (i.e, the RHR system). In addition, containment venting is also credited in many BWR IPEs. Because of the feedback of the containment cooling systems on the operability of coolant injection systems in BWRs, use of the BWR IPE models in a fire PRA ensures that the containment heat removal function was accounted for in the IPEEEs. However, for those licensees that did not trace cables related to these systems, separate evaluations would be required to assess the potential for loss of these systems in any given fire scenario.

At least one licensee with two plants housed in ice condenser containments (D.C. Cook) addressed the effect of fire on the hydrogen igniters as part of their containment performance assessment. The assessment addressed the potential identified in the IPE for hydrogen damage as a result of a station blackout. The licensee indicated that the fire damage scenarios were dominated by loss of component cooling water scenarios (seal LOCAs) and not SBO sequences. The licensee also indicated that the cables for the hydrogen igniters were not traced and, thus, the igniters may not be available for fire-induced core damage accidents. However, the licensee indicated that hydrogen was not considered to be a significant concern for fire scenarios because of the low core damage frequency contribution that could be impacted by the lack of hydrogen igniters, the significant chance that hydrogen igniters would not be impacted in many of the fire scenarios, the large amount of time available to recover the igniters before critical conditions are reached (8 to 16 hours), and the relatively low probability that the containment would fail if the igniters did not function.

Although the containment performance reviews performed according to the FIVE methodology by the licensees were generally qualitative in nature, some quantitative information was provided. For example, the licensee for Cooper reported that 96% of the fire-induced CDF involved loss of decay heat removal or delayed station blackout sequences. These sequences do not lead to large early releases.

3.4.10 Other Fire Perspectives

3.4.10.1 Utilization of Walkdowns

One common aspect of IPEEE fire analyses was the performance of plant walkdowns in support of the analysis. All of the licensees conducted one or more walkdowns in their fire IPEEE. Indeed, it was apparent that the vast majority of studies included multiple plant walkdowns.

Typical objectives of the walkdowns included identification and mapping of in situ (or fixed) fire sources, data gathering in preparation for fire modeling, identification and mapping of risk-important cables and equipment (damage targets), transient fuel reviews, fire detection and suppression system examination, and fire barrier examination in support of the multi-zone analysis. Licensees commonly reported that valuable insights were gained through the plant walkdowns, although very few cited specific examples of the insights gained.

The majority of licensees also included at least one focused walkdown conducted in coordination with seismic specialists to address the seismic-fire interaction issues. (See Chapter 2 of this report for further discussion of the seismic-fire interaction assessments.)

In many cases, plant walkdowns were also used to screen fire ignition sources and/or ignition source/target combinations. That is, after completion of preliminary fire modeling calculations, fire areas that survived the initial screening process would be walked down to assess thermal damage potential for specific combinations of fire source and thermal targets (equipment and cables). The most common approach was to use the target damage worksheets provided in FIVE.

These calculations predict the damage height/distance for equipment and cables located in the plume or ceiling jet. The calculations also estimate damage distances for direct radiant heating based on the intensity of the fire source. These damage distances define a critical damage zone for a given fire source (e.g., a pump or electrical panel). Components within this damage zone might be damaged given a fire involving that particular fire source.

Information on the critical damage zone would often be used during plant walkdowns. Fire source/target sets would be examined to determine if risk-important targets were within the critical damage zone of the source. If not, then the fire source would typically be screened from further consideration (assuming that hot layer effects and propagation of the fire to secondary fuels could also be dismissed).

Overall, it was clear from the submittals that plant walkdowns played an important role in virtually all of the IPEEE fire analyses. This was a desirable and anticipated insight. The U.S. NRC guidance relating to the IPEEE process (NUREG-1407 and GL 88-20, Supplement 4) specifically encouraged the use of plant walkdowns in the IPEEE process. Past experience has commonly shown that spending time in the plant examining the areas under analysis is a critical need in a fire PRA. This perception appears to have been borne out by the IPEEEs.

3.4.10.2 Utilization of Severity Factors

The application of severity factor approaches in the IPEEE fire analyses became a point of U.S. NRC review attention for a large number of licensee submittals. In very general terms, a severity factor is a fractional value (between 0 and 1) that is used to adjust fire frequency estimates to reflect some specific mitigating pattern of behavior illustrated by the fire events. In some past PRAs, severity factors were used to partition the total fire frequency to reflect a range of fire sizes experienced in real events. For example, an analyst may choose to model "small," "medium," and "large" fires by assigning a fraction of the total fire frequency to each fire size (e.g., 60% of fires might be assumed to be small, 30% medium, and 10% large — illustrative values only). Indeed, approximately half[15] of the IPEEEs did utilize severity factors in this manner (often in addition to other severity factors).

In the IPEEE fire analyses the concept of fire severity factors was used extensively and in more generalized ways. This was particularly true for the later IPEEE submittals including, in particular, those performed after publication of the FPRAIG. One of the most common approaches applied by licensees was based on or is similar to, a severity factor approach outlined in the FPRAIG. This approach assumes that some significant fraction of fires will remain nonthreatening, and need not be considered in fire CDF estimation (the complement representing those fires that might be risk important).

It has been widely observed that most actual fires do not lead to any significant equipment or plant damage. Many licensees chose the severity factor approach to capture and quantify this behavior. In a typical case, the fire frequency for a given fire scenario would be multiplied by a severity factor. The result is an estimate of the frequency of potentially risk-important (threatening) fires. The values applied generally ranged from about 0.05 to 0.7, with some outliers observed at both ends of this range.

The basis for generating severity factors varied from submittal to submittal and often within a submittal, depending on the fire source under consideration. That is, in most submittals using severity factors, different severity factor approaches were applied to different fire sources. For example, in a given submittal some fire sources might have been treated using split fractions for large and small fires, while others were treated using a severity factor for threatening fires. Still other fire sources might not have been adjusted at all.

Common bases for definition of severity factors included the following (in descending order of frequency of use).

- Severity factors cited in the FPRAIG were applied directly by licensees. These factors were based on an examination of events in the EPRI fire event database [EPRI, 1993]. In the FPRAIG, engineering judgement and other unspecified criteria were applied to assess whether or not each fire was severe. The criteria vary somewhat depending on the fire source being considered. The severity factors then reflected the ratio of severe (and indeterminate) fires to the total number of fires in each of seven fire source groups (panels, transformers, pumps, etc). The FPRAIG severity factors ranged from 0.08 to 0.2.

- Fire severity factors were applied to reflect a split in large versus small fires for specific classes of fires (the classical fire severity factor approach as discussed above). Most commonly, 10–30% of fires were assumed to be large and 70–90% small. This was most commonly applied to transient fires. Other common applications included oil spills, transformer fires, and pump/motor fires.

- Licensees assumed that only fires that required intervention by the fire brigade, manual hose streams, and/or fixed fire suppression systems would be potentially risk important. This approach typically led to fire severity factors of 0.1 or less.

---

[15] Of the 103 reactors represented in the 70 IPEEE submittals, it could not be determined whether severity factors were or were not used for 22 reactors. The result cited is based on a reactor count rather than a count of submittals (i.e., reactors analyzed with versus without severity factors, indeterminate cases omitted).

- Licensees eliminated fires from the fire frequency calculation if the fire self-extinguished without any specific intervention by plant personnel or fixed suppression systems.

- Fire severity factors were applied to electrical panel fires to reflect the potential for a fire to damage equipment outside the panel. Typical values in this case ranged from 0.1 to 0.25.

- Fire severity factors were applied based on the radial distance between critical targets and the fire source. Curves for four types of equipment fires are cited in these cases; namely, control panels, high voltage components, low voltage components, and mechanical equipment. This method was typical of one particular analysis approach and, when questioned by the NRC staff, licensees were unable to document a basis for the cited severity factor versus distance curves. Hence, most such questions led to a re-quantification by licensees who originally employed this approach.

- Fire severity factors were applied only in the analysis of multi-room fire scenarios. This factor typically reflected the likelihood of a fire sufficiently large so as to threaten fire barriers and/or create a threatening hot gas layer in both rooms. Values of 0.1 were typical for this approach (see Section 3.4.6).

- Only fires that lasted beyond a specific time period (most commonly 5 minutes) were considered potentially risk important.

- Only fires that led to full room involvement were considered risk important.

Of these approaches, only the first was traceable to a published work (in this case the FPRAIG). In the remaining cases, the severity factors were typically developed based on a reexamination of the fire event database by the analysts themselves.

In many IPEEE analyses, multiple severity factors were applied to each individual fire scenario. For example, in the quantification of electrical panel fire scenarios, a severity factor from the FPRAIG might be applied in combination with a severity factor for panel fires damaging equipment outside the panel. At least three licensees took independent credit for fires that self-extinguished, prompt intervention by plant personnel, and prompt intervention by fixed fire suppression systems. In all of these cases, the severity factors were assessed as fully independent parameters. As a result, the frequencies of threatening fires were commonly reduced by one to two orders of magnitude (or more) in comparison to the frequency of all fires.

In many submittals, analysts also treated fixed fire suppression systems in virtually the same manner as a severity factor. In effect, the reliability of the fixed suppression system, typically ranging from 0.02 to 0.05 conditional probability of failure on demand, was treated as a severity factor. That is, if the suppression system went off, then no risk-significant damage was assumed. (See Section 3.4.5 for further discussion of detection and suppression modeling.)

A number of potential concerns were raised by IPEEE reviewers regarding severity factors as used in the IPEEE fire assessments. In particular, reviewers cited the following as potential points of concern.

- The severity factor approach addresses fire mitigation features based on generic industry-wide data. As such, it does not fully consider plant-specific and scenario-specific features that may significantly influence the development of a given fire scenario. As a result, scenario quantification based on severity factor approaches tends to produce generic CDF results that may not fully reflect the actual plant-specific conditions of the fire scenario under analysis.

- Using a severity factor and taking credit for subsequent detection and suppression efforts may be "double counting." The severity factors typically credit behaviors that impact the general duration of fires. These same statistics and behaviors are widely used to estimate fire durations and the likelihood that fire suppression efforts will be successful.

- The severity factor approach may neglect the dependencies associated with subsequent suppression efforts. If, for example, the application of a severity factor means that only challenging fires are modeled, then subsequent fire-fighting efforts should reflect the fact that the fire brigade (or the fixed systems in some cases) would be faced with a "challenging" fire rather than a "typical" fire.

- There was typically no clear assurance provided in the submittals that the data used to develop the severity factors was consistent with the data used to develop the corresponding fire ignition frequencies. Each of the generic fire frequency values used in the IPEEE process was developed using only a subset of the total fire events. The available fire frequencies reflect fires occurring in specific plant locations, involving specific fire sources, and/or occurring during specific modes of plant operation (typically at-power only). As noted in Section 3.4.3.2, most IPEEEs used the fire frequency values presented in FIVE. However, FIVE does not identify the fires that actually went into the various fire frequency values or those that were screened from any given frequency calculation. Without this information, when an independent analyst develops a fire severity factor to complement any given fire frequency value, there is no clear assurance that the exact same set of fire events has been considered as would be appropriate.

- One feature that makes many fires nonthreatening is their location in the plant. That is, most fires do not occur in critical locations and, hence, have no real potential to spread and/or cause risk-significant damage. Fire location is explicitly treated in the partitioning of fire event frequencies to specific fire areas, specific locations within a fire area, and/or specific fire sources (see Section 3.4.3.2.2). Hence, use of a severity factor in addition to fire source partitioning factors may also represent "double counting."

- The use of multiple severity factors in the quantification of a single fire scenario carries a significant potential for double-counting mitigating features. This particular practice was the one questioned most frequently by the NRC.

The use of severity factors had a notable impact on the fire-induced CDF estimates for the scenarios where they were applied. In most cases where severity factors were applied, fire CDF values were reduced by at least a factor of five, and commonly by one order of magnitude or more. Whether or not this credit was fully warranted in all cases remains a point of uncertainty. As noted in the first bullet item above, the approach tends toward production of generic rather than case-specific CDF results.

There is also a potential for optimism in the severity factor approach depending on the how the severity factors were implemented and on case-specific details of the quantified scenarios. Severity factor approaches are, in effect, "shortcuts" to the analysis of phenomena that may mitigate or prevent fire damage. Hence, a more detailed analysis may well reach the same conclusion or result as the analysis that takes the severity factor "shortcut." For example, in many cases, no additional detection/suppression credit was taken beyond the severity factor. For these cases, an argument can be made that application of more traditional methods of detection and suppression analysis might well have yielded similar, or perhaps lower, CDF results. However, without the full details of the fire scenario under analysis (e.g., details that were generally relegated to second-tier IPEEE documentation), it is not possible to state definitively that a particular application of the severity factor approach was, or was not, fully reflective of the actual scenario conditions.

Severity factor approaches were widely questioned by the U.S. NRC during the review process. In most cases, licensees responded by restating the basis for the applied approach, and by providing more detailed information on the specific severity factors applied in the analysis. Relatively few licensees requantified their CDF estimates based on the RAIs. In the context of the IPEEE process, analyses utilizing severity factor approaches were generally found acceptable provided that (1) the values applied in the analysis were clearly stated such that reviewers could ascertain the impact that the severity factors had on CDF quantification, and (2) re-quantification of the impacted scenarios without crediting the severity factors would not lead to a potential fire vulnerability. However, the application of severity factor approaches is a potential weakness of those IPEEEs utilizing such approaches.

3.5 Summary and Conclusions

The fire portions of the IPEEE submittals were reviewed in this chapter with the objective of providing perspectives in the following areas:

- fire-related vulnerabilities and plant improvements identified by the licensees as a result of the IPEEE process,
- fire-induced CDFs, the important fire areas at each plant, and important design and operational features that affect the fire-induced CDF,
- the impact of fires on containment performance,
- methods used in the fire assessments, including their strengths and weaknesses and the impact of key assumptions made in the analyses, and
- the extent to which the licensees have met the intent of Supplement 4 to GL 88-20 as it pertains to fire analysis.

The perspectives for each of these areas are summarized below.

3.5.1 Summary of Vulnerabilities and Plant Improvements

Out of all the IPEEE submittals, only two licensees, representing three nuclear power plant units, identified fire vulnerabilities. In one case (Quad Cities), the vulnerabilities were identified in the licensee's original IPEEE submittal and a detailed re-analysis by the licensee showed that fire vulnerabilities did not exist. However, the licensee did make plant improvements as a result of the insights gained in the original IPEEE analysis and credited some of those improvements in the re-analysis. In the second case (Millstone 2), two fire vulnerabilities were identified, and the licensee implemented plant improvements involving rerouting of control cables in the turbine building to address these vulnerabilities.

It was interesting to note that for each of the two plants where vulnerabilities were identified, the vulnerabilities included fire safety issues in the turbine building. It is often observed that the turbine building primarily services the secondary (power generation) side of the plant. Hence, for many plants the turbine building was not found to be a significant fire risk contributor. However, in these two cases, the turbine building housed important safety-related cables and equipment which did play a substantial role in safe shutdown. The turbine building also presents substantial fire hazards. In both of these cases, postulated large fires in the turbine building led to identification of fire vulnerabilities. Turbine building areas were also identified by many other licensees as important CDF contributors.

Despite the fact that the vast majority of licensees identified no fire-related vulnerabilities, the majority of licensees, over 60%, did identify and/or implement plant improvements to reduce fire risk. A total of approximately 242 fire-related plant improvements were identified by licensees. (This total number excludes the many seismic-fire interaction improvements that are discussed in Chapter 2 of this report.) Improvements were identified for 44 plant sites.

The majority of the cited plant improvements (about 57%) were associated with various plant procedures, including operating procedures, maintenance procedures, combustible controls, enhancements to operator training, and enhanced fire brigade training. The remaining improvements (about 43%) were related to physical plant/hardware changes. These included general plant system design changes, enhancements to fire protection features, relocation of critical cables, and upgrading of fire barriers.

3.5.2 Quantitative Findings and Insights

The fire-induced CDFs reported by the licensees range from approximately 4E-8 to 2E-4 per reactor-year. The IPEEE fire analyses have broadly found fire CDF to be roughly on a par with, and in some cases greater than, internal events CDF. The vast majority of licensees reported fire CDF values that equal at least 10% (or greater) of the internal events CDF. About 25% of the submittals reported fire-induced CDF values that exceeded the corresponding plant internal events CDF (as reported in the IPE).

The IPEEE results appear to confirm the general perception that fire risk is more a function of spatial phenomena than it is a function of plant systems design. There were no clear patterns relating to fire-induced CDF that could be attributed to differences in the plant system design features. In the vast majority of cases, licensees concluded that the dominant fire CDF contributors were those areas that held both significant fire sources and important equipment and cables. Hence, it appears that spatial factors, the convergence of fire source and targets, were more significant in determining fire risk than were plant systems design features. Areas devoid of either fire sources or important equipment and cables generally were screened.

In the specific case of the main control room (MCR), fire CDF was dominated by the abandonment scenarios, that is, unsuppressed fires leading to MCR abandonment. In this case, fire CDF estimates were driven largely by two factors, namely, the assumed conditional probability of MCR abandonment and the reliability of human actions associated with plant shutdown using the remote shutdown capability.

Overall, the two types of fire analysis zones found most often to be the single highest fire CDF contributors were switchgear areas and MCRs. These results are broadly consistent with the findings of past fire PRAs. The next most commonly identified areas were areas of the turbine building and cable spreading rooms for plants with only a single cable spreading room. Other commonly reported areas include electrical equipment rooms, diesel generator rooms, cable vault and tunnel areas, and battery/charger rooms. A range of other areas are identified as important on a plant-specific basis.

Fire sources considered in the fire assessments included both fixed sources (e.g., electrical panels, pumps, transformers, and electrical cables) and transient combustibles. Electrical panel fires were the most significant fire CDF contributors in most submittals. In a minority of submittals, transient-combustible fires were also found to be significant.

Fire-induced transients were found to be the most important accident sequences. These included loss of feedwater and MSIV closure transients, LOOP events, and loss of support system initiators. LOCAs induced by spurious opening of PORVs or SRVs were generally not identified as significant contributors to the fire-related CDF. However, fire scenarios resulting in RCP seal LOCAs were important for many Westinghouse PWRs.

The majority of the licensees screened all scenarios involving propagation of a fire from one zone to another. Of the submittals that provided some quantitative assessment of the CDF contribution from multi-zone fire scenarios, 80% concluded that these scenarios were not significant (i.e., the scenarios were screened). The rest reported CDF contributions ranging from 1% to 30% of the overall fire-induced CDF.

There were also some limited insights gained regarding plant types and overall fire risk. For example, BWRs as a group tended to report lower fire-induced CDFs than did PWRs. Two factors appeared to contribute to this result. First, BWRs tend to have a greater diversity and redundancy of plant systems. This appears to have reduced the fire-induced CDF for BWRs in general. Second, at PWRs scenarios involving seal LOCAs were found to be important CDF contributors. This raised the general fire-induced CDF results for PWRs as a group.

The fire-induced CDF reported by the newer plants (i.e., those licensed to operate after January 1, 1979) and older plants (those for whom the Appendix R backfit requirements applied) all show considerable variability but displayed no clear trend with respect to plant vintage. One possible interpretation of this result is that fire protection backfit programs for older plants have successfully brought their fire-induced CDFs in line with those of the newer plants. The level of review afforded the IPEEEs cannot, however, support a definitive explanation for this observation.

In terms of containment performance, all licensees concluded that fires did not lead to any new or unique containment failure modes compared to the internal event IPE results. Relatively few licensees included Level 2 PRA quantification of fire-induced containment failure scenarios. Those few who did perform such analyses concluded that fire-induced early containment bypass scenarios were of low likelihood in comparison to such scenarios as analyzed in the IPEs.

3.5.3   Fire Methodology Perspectives

For the purposes of the IPEEE fire assessments, all licensees utilized probabilistic analysis methods in one form or another. By far the most commonly cited analysis approach was the EPRI FIVE methodology [EPRI, 1992]. The FIVE methodology was cited as being used to support about 81% of the licensees' IPEEE submittals. However, most of these submittals also went beyond the FIVE approach and applied PRA methods as a supplement to the FIVE method. Of the licensees who utilized FIVE, 74% went on to quantify unscreened fire scenarios using supplemental PRA methods. About 19% of licensees chose to directly implement fire PRAs without reference to FIVE.

The selected methodology did have some impact on the final estimates of fire CDF, but ultimately appeared to have little impact on the overall findings of the IPEEE studies (e.g., identification of dominant areas contributing to fire CDF). FIVE is fundamentally a prescriptive fire PRA-based screening approach. Hence, licensees who applied FIVE obtained quite consistent screening results compared to those licensees who implemented more general fire PRA methods directly. Some differences were noted in the final reported CDF estimates. As expected, since FIVE is primarily a screening method, those licensees who stopped with FIVE screening generally obtained higher total CDF estimates than those who continued with more detailed fire PRA-based quantification of unscreened zones.

Plant walkdowns were important sources of information for the licensees' fire evaluation. Virtually all of the submittals cited at least one, and often several, plant walkdowns focused on fire safety. Typically, at least one walkdown was performed to address seismic-fire interactions. Most licensees cited that plant walkdowns were used to support a range of IPEEE analysis needs including defining IPEEE fire analysis zones, identifying fire sources, mapping the location of important cables and equipment, developing input parameters for fire modeling, reviewing fire protection systems, and screening fire source/target combinations based on the results of fire modeling.

There was significant variation among the submittals in the methods and assumptions applied to support particular aspects of the fire assessments. The impacts of individual modeling choices on the fire CDFs cannot, in general, be isolated from the other modeling factors and from plant design differences. Areas of methodological variability observed included the following.

- Only a small number of licensees provided explicit treatment of the potential variation in fire size in their evaluation of the CDF for each fire area. The majority of submittals are based on the analysis of those fire intensities considered representative of the most likely fires. When fire size was explicitly treated, the greatest CDF contribution generally derived from larger fires, despite the fact that these fires were assumed to be less likely.

- Electrical panel fires were identified as key contributors to the fire-induced CDF at most plants. However, the methods of analysis varied substantially with regard to the assumed fire intensity, the potential for spread and/or damage outside a panel, the fire duration, effectiveness of suppression, application of severity factors, and the physical extent of damage that might be observed.

- Self-ignited cable fires were generally assumed possible only for plants that did not use IEEE-383 or equivalent low-flame-spread cables (consistent with the FIVE approach). The majority of licensees either cited use of IEEE-383 qualified cables in construction or back-qualification of the cables used at the plant to the IEEE-383 flame spread test or an equivalent test after construction had been completed. In these cases, self-ignited cable fires were not considered. In the other cases, cable-initiated fires were only found to be important in a few cases. These generally involved areas devoid of other fixed ignition sources, an area where risk-important cables converged, and had some specific limitation to the fire suppression capability.

- Many of the submittals included the application of severity factor approaches for CDF quantification. These approaches utilize industry wide experience-based statistics in lieu of scenario-specific analyses. A wide variety of such approaches were used in the IPEEE fire analyses.

3.5.4 Comparison with Past PRA Studies

Several plant-specific fire PRAs had been prepared before the issuance of Supplement 4 to GL 88-20 [U.S. NRC, 1992]. Reference [Siu, 1997] provides a list of these studies. Of the 19 studies reported in [Siu, 1997], two were sponsored by the U.S. Department of Energy, five by the U.S. NRC and the rest (i.e., 12 studies) by the licensees. Table 3.6 in Volume 2 summarizes key results of the 12 past fire PRAs and provides similar information from the corresponding IPEEE submittals.

Only five of the earlier fire PRA studies were used by the licensee when preparing their IPEEE submittals. New studies were conducted to prepare IPEEE submittals for the rest of the plants. Four of the five studies were sponsored by the licensee. All four were modified to reflect new data, changes to plant configuration, or changes to model recovery actions. In the case of the La Salle submittal, the licensee elected to use the fire PRA that was conducted by Sandia National Laboratories for the NRC as the basis for its IPEEE submittal. In this case, the licensee considered the Sandia study as sufficiently detailed to warrant its use in meeting the intent of Supplement 4 to GL 88-20.

Table 3.6 in Volume 2 shows that the fire CDFs reported in past fire PRAs are comparable to the CDFs reported in the IPEEE submittals. This table also shows that for all cases for which a corresponding past fire PRA exists, the CDF reported in the IPEEE submittal is smaller or equal to that presented in the corresponding fire PRA. The difference between the two CDFs, in the majority of the cases, is small (less than a factor of two). In two cases the difference is noticeable: a factor of about 10 (Indian Point 2) and a factor of four (Three Mile Island 1). In the case of Indian Point 2 the difference is mainly due to plant modifications that were implemented since the original study. In the case of Three Mile Island 1 detailed modeling of recovery actions is one of the differences cited in the submittal.

When each past PRA is compared with its corresponding submittal, Table 3.6 in Volume 2 shows that the list of important contributors (in terms of plant areas or rooms) is practically the same for most of the cases. However, it should be noted that the relative ranking of important contributors is rarely the same. This may be a result of small differences in methodology and data employed. Without a close examination of the studies, the differences between relative ranking of contributors cannot be properly explained. It should also be noted that in the case of the past fire PRAs, only one of the 19 reported turbine building fires as being an important fire risk contributor. On the other hand, in the case of the IPEEE submittals, close to half included this plant area in their list of important contributors to fire risk.

3.5.5 Meeting the Intent of the IPEEE Program

Based on the review of the fire portions of the IPEEE, it has been concluded that all licensees met the intent of the IPEEE process with regard to their fire analyses. Specifically, the fire portions of the IPEEE have resulted in the following.

- The licensees have obtained an increased appreciation of severe accident behavior at their plants resulting from fire initiators. This appreciation was enhanced by the participation of plant personnel in performing these fire assessments (including participation in plant walkdowns).

- Licensees have gained an understanding of the most likely severe accident sequences that could occur at their plants from fires during full power operation. The screening and detailed assessment of fire scenarios have resulted in an understanding of the type of fires that can occur at their plants and the impact of those fires on available mitigating systems.

- The licensees have obtained both a qualitative and quantitative understanding of the overall likelihood of core damage resulting from fire events. In addition, a qualitative understanding of the impact of fires on containment performance has also been achieved (a quantitative understanding was also achieved for the few licensees who performed a Level 2 fire PRA).

- The majority of the licensees have utilized the results of the fire assessments to identify plant improvements to reduce the likelihood of core damage and fission product releases. Thus, the implementation of these improvements has or will improve safety at the plants.

4. HIGH WINDS, FLOODS, AND OTHER EXTERNAL EVENTS

4.1 Introduction

This section summarizes the key results from 70 IPEEE submittals with regard to high winds, floods, and other (HFO) external events, including transportation and nearby facility accidents, and plant-unique hazards. External flooding events were evaluated in the IPEEE program, while internal flooding was addressed in the IPE program. Table 4.1 gives a list of the HFO-related external event topics discussed in NUREG-1407.

Table 4.1: Potential natural and man-induced events to be considered for HFO external events (from NUREG-1407)

Man-Induced Events	
Aircraft impact	
Industrial or military facility accident (offsite toxic or combustible/explosive gas/chemicals)	
Pipeline accident (onsite toxic or combustible/explosive gas)	
Release of chemicals from onsite storage	
Turbine-generated missiles	
Natural Events	
Avalanche	Internal flooding
Coastal erosion	Landslide
Drought	Lightning
Dust storms	Low lake or river water level
External flooding (e.g., high tide, lake, or river water level)	Meteorite
Extreme winds and tornadoes	Sandstorm
Fog	Seiche (oscillatory waves)
Forest fire	Severe temperature transients (hot or cold)
Frost	Snow
Hail	Storm surge
Hurricane	Volcanic activity (including volcanic ash)
Ice (blockage of intakes, etc.)	Waves
Intense precipitation	

4.1.1 Objectives

The objectives of this chapter are to discuss the HFO review findings reported in the licensees' submittals, and to identify insights gleaned from the staff's reviews of the submittals.

4.1.2 Organization

This chapter specifically addresses the HFO areas of the IPEEE, and is organized in the following seven major subsections.

- Section 4.1 provides an introduction including the objectives and organization of this chapter. This section also gives background information including some historical perspectives for HFO events, guidance for conducting the HFO reviews, and an overview of the results.

- Section 4.2 discusses the perspectives gleaned from the IPEEE evaluations of high winds, including tornadoes, tornado missiles, and hurricanes. Potential vulnerabilities associated with severe high wind conditions are discussed, including plant improvements that licensees have considered or implemented to reduce the plant risk associated with these events.

- Section 4.3 discusses the perspectives gleaned from the IPEEE evaluations of external floods, including intense rainfall resulting in site flooding and roof ponding; flooding from nearby bodies of water, including wave runup from rivers, lakes, and the ocean; potential flooding from postulated dam failures; and flooding as the result of snow melt. Potential vulnerabilities resulting from external floods are discussed with plant improvements that licensees have considered or implemented to reduce the plant risk associated with such flooding.

- Section 4.4 discusses perspectives gleaned from the IPEEE evaluations of accidents related to transportation or nearby industrial facilities. Potential vulnerabilities from such accidents are discussed with plant improvements that licensees have considered or implemented to reduce the plant risk associated with these types of events.

- Section 4.5 discusses other types of external events that can occur. This category includes events such as onsite hazardous material spills; hydrogen line breaks; effects from low-temperature conditions, such as icing and blockage of cooling water intake lines; blockage of drains and intakes from debris; other weather conditions, such as wind-blown sand and dust; and any other plant-unique hazard events.

- Section 4.6 discusses some general observations regarding HFO events. Topics included in this section are containment performance, unresolved safety issues (USIs) and generic safety issues (GSIs), human actions, HFO-related information gained from plant walkdowns, a summary of related plant improvements, general perspectives, and some perspectives regarding the impact of the HFO event analyses on plant safety.

- Section 4.7 provides a summary and conclusions gleaned from the HFO reviews.

4.1.3   Background

This section provides background information including a historical perspective for the HFO external events and a discussion of the guidance used in conducting reviews of these events.

4.1.3.1   Historical Perspectives on High Winds, Floods, and Other External Events

The primary regulatory basis governing the HFO-related design aspects of nuclear power reactors is contained in Appendix A to 10 CFR Part 50, "General Design Criteria for Nuclear Power Plants." General Design Criterion (GDC) 2 defines design bases requirements for protection against natural phenomena. GDC 2 identifies the following performance criterion:

> Structures, systems, and components important to safety shall be designed to withstand the effects of natural phenomena, such as earthquakes, tornadoes, hurricanes, floods, tsunami, and seiches without loss of capability to perform their safety functions. The design bases for these structures, systems, and components shall reflect (1) appropriate consideration of the most severe of the natural phenomena that have been historically reported for the site and surrounding area, (2) appropriate combinations of the effects of normal and accident conditions with the effects of the natural phenomena, and (3) the importance of the safety functions to be performed.

In 1975, the NRC published the Standard Review Plan (SRP), which provides standardized review criteria to assist the staff in evaluating safety analysis reports submitted by license applicants. Since its first publication, the SRP has undergone several revisions (the latest being 1981) to incorporate new developments in design and analysis technology. The SRP sections that address plant safety issues relevant to the IPEEE HFO events include SRP Section 2.2.1, "Site Location and Description," and Section 2.2.2, "Identification of Potential Hazards in Site Vicinity." The review criteria in these SRP sections include the locations of transportation routes (water, rail, car) in the vicinity of the plant; pipelines that may contain hazardous materials; and fixed manufacturing, processing, and storage facilities. The review of these areas focuses on the potential for a release of hazardous material that could cause a fire, an explosion, or a threat to the habitability of the plant's control room. These two sections and other SRP sections that are relevant to the IPEEE HFO events are listed in Table 4.2.

There are also a number of regulatory guides that address the technical issues related to the IPEEE HFO events, as follows:

- Regulatory Guide 1.59, "Design Basis Floods for Nuclear Power Plants,"
- Regulatory Guide 1.76, "Design Basis Tornado for Nuclear Power Plants,"
- Regulatory Guide 1.102, "Flood Protection for Nuclear Power Plants,"
- Regulatory Guide 1.115, "Protection from Low-Trajectory Turbine Missiles," and
- Regulatory Guide 1.117, "Tornado Classification."

Table 4.2: Standard review plan sections relevant to HFO events

SRP section	Title
2.2.3	Evaluation of Potential Accidents
2.3.1	Regional Climatology
2.3.2	Local Meteorology
2.4.1	Hydrologic Description
2.4.2	Floods
2.4.3	Probable Maximum Flood (PMF) on Streams and Rivers
2.4.4	Potential Dam Failures
2.4.5	Probable Maximum Surge and Seiche Flooding
2.4.6	Probable Maximum Tsunami Flooding
2.4.7	Ice Effects
2.4.10	Flooding Protection Requirements
2.4.11	Cooling Water Supply*
3.3.1	Wind Loading
3.3.2	Tornado Loadings
3.4.1	Flood Protection
3.4.2	Analysis Procedures
3.5.1.4	Missiles Generated by Nature Phenomena
3.5.1.5	Site Proximity Missiles (Except Aircraft)
3.5.1.6	Aircraft Hazards
3.5.2	Structures, Systems, and Components to Be Protected from Externally Generated Missiles
* SRP Section 2.4.11 refers to potential interference with the ultimate heat sink, such as ice blockage, debris, droughts, etc.	

The acceptance criteria for each HFO area given in the SRP are specifically tied to the corresponding GDCs for that topic and the regulatory guides that address that area. Hence, there is a close connection between the review of HFO events and the other related NRC regulatory guidance.

There are two other NRC programs that are directly related to the IPEEE HFO events. These programs are the Generic Safety Issues (GSIs) Program and the Systematic Evaluation Program (SEP). GSI-103, "Design for Probable Maximum Precipitation" (PMP), involved an evaluation of a plant's capability to withstand severe rainfall using updated site-dependent PMP values developed by the National Oceanic and Atmospheric Administration. GSI-172, "Multiple System Responses Program (MSRP)," addressed a number of generic plant safety concerns. One of the MSRP issues that directly relate to HFO events is the effects of flooding and/or moisture intrusion on non safety-related and safety-related equipment. An aspect of the HFO reviews was to determine if the GSIs discussed above could be verified on a plant-specific basis as part of the IPEEE program.

The SEP was initiated in the mid-1970s. This program recognized that many safety criteria, including those associated with HFO events, had evolved since the initial licensing of the earliest nuclear power plants. The purpose of the SEP was to develop a systematic and documented basis for the safety of the older plants by comparing them to the current licensing criteria.

Among the many technical issues that were included as a part of the SEP were six issues related to the HFO events. These issues were (1) dam integrity and site flooding, (2) site hydrology and ability to withstand floods, (3) industrial hazards, (4) tornado missiles, (5) severe weather effects on structures, and (6) design codes, criteria, and load combinations. The IPEEE-related SEP issues are described in more detail in Section 5.4.7 of this report.

The following section of this report provides guidance for conducting IPEEE HFO reviews. As discussed in NUREG-1407, one of the approaches that a licensee could use in analyzing of the HFO events was to determine if the plant conforms to the guidance in the NRC's 1975 Standard Review Plan coupled with a plant walkdown. This approach was widely used by licensees in performing their evaluations of the HFO events.

4.1.3.2 Guidance for Conducting IPEEE HFO Analyses

Guidance for conducting HFO analyses for the IPEEEs is provided in Section 5 of NUREG-1407, "Procedural and Submittal Guidance for the Individual Plant Examination of External Events (IPEEE) for Severe Accident Vulnerabilities" (NUREG-1407). In particular, NUREG-1407 recommends a progressive screening approach to identify potential HFO-related vulnerabilities at U.S. nuclear power plants. This progressive screening approach, summarized below, represents a series of steps or analyses in increasing level of detail and effort.

- Review the plant-specific hazard data and licensing basis and determine if any significant changes that could impact the IPEEE have occurred since the issuance of the operating license.

- Determine whether the plant conforms to the guidance in the NRC's 1975 Standard Review Plan (SRP) (NUREG-0800), and perform a plant walkdown.

- If the plant does not conform to the 1975 SRP guidance, one or more of the following optional steps may be taken:

    – Determine if the hazard frequency of the original design is acceptably low, by demonstrating that the hazard frequency is less than 1E-5 per year.

    – If the event cannot be screened out on the basis of hazard frequency, perform a bounding analysis. Such an analysis should be performed using conservative parameters, and is intended to show that the hazard would not result in a bounding CDF contribution above the screening criterion of 1E-6 per reactor-year (ry).

    —   Perform a PRA.

- High winds, floods, transportation, and nearby facility accidents are to be explicitly addressed in each licensee's IPEEE submittal, while "other" additional external events are to be addressed if they are applicable to a specific site.

- An analysis of containment performance for HFO events is not needed unless the licensee predicts or identifies plant-unique accident sequences that are different from those determined by the internal events IPE.

- As an alternative to the above options, a licensee may request that the staff review any other systematic examination method to determine its acceptability for IPEEE purposes.

These various options are graphically shown in Figure 4.1, which is taken from NUREG-1407.

4.1.4 Overview of Results

A summary of the HFO-related IPEEE results for the 70 plants reviewed is given in Table 4.1 of Volume 2 of this report. This table includes the method used by each licensee to evaluate HFO events, the estimated CDF, if reported, and HFO-related improvements that licensees have implemented or planned. As indicated in this table, all licensees have addressed a range of HFO events at their plants.

In the majority of the HFO event analyses, licensees have screened out these events on the basis of qualitative assessments, consistent with one of the accepted approaches given in NUREG-1407. A qualitative assessment typically involved demonstrating conformance with the 1975 SRP criteria (or for several plants the criteria in the updated 1981 SRP) coupled with a plant walkdown. The purpose of the walkdown is to identify any changes in the plant configuration from the original design basis that may impact the IPEEE evaluation and also to identify any specific plant areas that may not necessarily have been part of the design basis but could significantly impact the IPEEE evaluation (e.g., a roof design that could potentially be overloaded during heavy rainstorms because the drains are susceptible to being blocked with debris). There are three forms of quantitative analyses that licensees have used in the HFO-related IPEEEs, each involving a different level of detail and resulting in a different type and amount of information. These three evaluation methods (analysis of hazard frequency, bounding analysis of estimated CDF contributors, and PRA) are described in Section 4.1.3.2 and Figure 4.1. As in other applications, licensees that performed PRAs for HFO-related studies have used varying degrees of conservatism, some with best-estimate parameters and others with more conservative values.

Table 4.3 shows the relative distribution of the evaluation methods used by the licensees in performing their HFO reviews. This table summarizes the methods chosen by the licensees for analyzing the topical event categories of: high winds in general, tornadoes, tornado-generated missiles, floods, other external events in general, chemical releases, hydrogen explosions, and aircraft crashes. Table 4.3 also indicates that most of the HFO-related IPEEE studies (approximately 80%) were performed using the qualitative screening method,

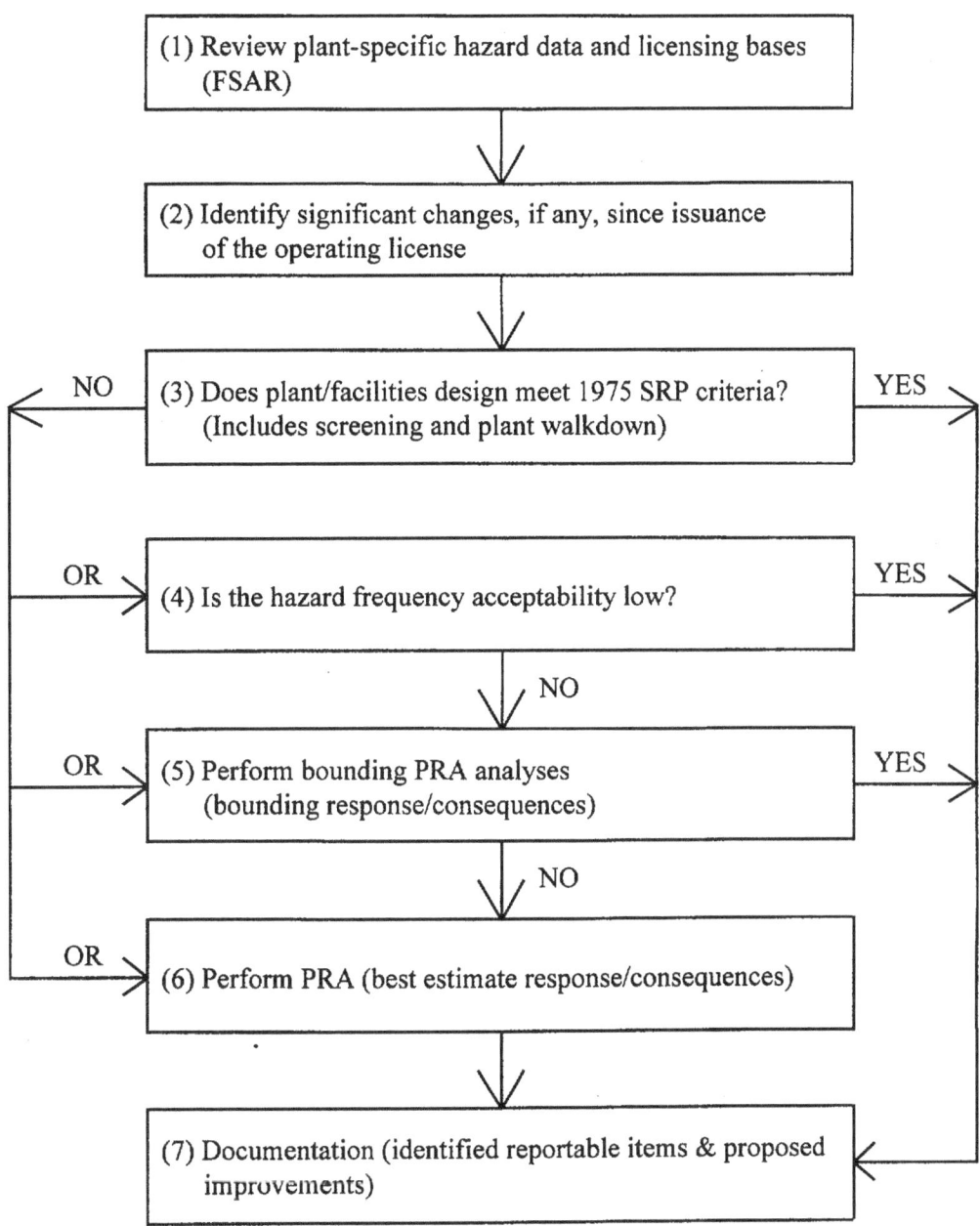

Figure 4.1 Recommended IPEEE approach for high winds, floods, and other external events

as allowed in NUREG-1407. The PRA applications, including both full and partial bounding PRAs, accounted for roughly 15% and, lastly, the initiating event hazard frequency method was used least frequently (less than 5%).

None of the 70 IPEEE submittals identified any HFO-related vulnerabilities; however, 34 submittals reported that they had either made, or were considering, a total of 64 HFO-related plant improvements; 36 submittals reported that they had not identified any needed improvements. Tables provided in this chapter show the number of improvements for each event category, and the number of plants making improvements for each category of events.

Section 4.6 summarizes the general observations and insights pertaining to the HFO IPEEE submittals.

Table 4.3: Licensees' methods of analysis for HFO external events
(by topic)

| Event category | Number of applications by analysis type | | |
	Qualitative screening[1]	PRA[2]	Hazard frequency[3]
High winds (general)	55	13	2
Tornadoes	51	17	2
Tornado-generated missiles	56	12	2
Floods	58	12	0
Other events (general)	60	7	3
Chemical releases	57	10	3
Hydrogen explosions	59	8	3
Aircraft crashes	58	8	4

Notes:
1. As allowed by NUREG-1407, this approach involves confirming that the plant is in conformance with the 1975 SRP criteria coupled with a walkdown to confirm that changes have not occurred at the plant that would impact on the IPEEE or that there are important plant-unique situations that should be considered.
2. Some of the applications of PRA used best-estimate input parameters, and others used some bounding parameters to simplify the analysis.
3. In this approach, an event is screened out if the calculation of the initiating frequency (e.g., the likelihood of a damaging tornado event) has an estimated frequency below some screening value (a typical value used is 1E-5 events/year).

4.2 High Winds

4.2.1 Introduction

The external events category of high winds comprises tornadoes, hurricanes, and straight winds.

4.2.2 High Winds Quantitative Results

Among the 17 plant submittals that reported a CDF from high winds, the results have ranged from less than 2E-7/ry to 6E-5/ry.

Typically, the dominant CDF sequence associated with high winds involved a loss of offsite power (LOOP) in combination with random failure of emergency ac power. Other random failures that licensees reported as being significant contributors to CDF for high wind events include the loss of service water, auxiliary feedwater, feed-and-bleed cooling, and high-pressure injection. In addition, one plant postulated that wind-generated missiles could fail the diesel generators, service water system condensate storage tank, or ventilation system, thereby leading to core damage. Another plant identified the diesel fuel oil transfer pumps and lines as being exposed to tornado-induced missiles.

The review process revealed that some licensees had employed optimistic assumptions in their analysis of high winds. In response to related RAIs, the licensees either revised their analyses or provided information to show that their assumptions were appropriate. For example, in one submittal, the licensee's treatment of direct winds initially screened out wind speeds from 108 to 125 miles per hour. However, upon subsequent analysis, the licensee found that such wind speeds could lead to station blackout, and increased the plant's CDF contribution from 2E-6/ry to 8E-6/ry.

4.2.3 High Winds Qualitative Results

As seen in Table 4.3, qualitative analysis involving the demonstration of conformance with the 1975 SRP was used much more frequently than either PRA (full and bounding assessment) or hazard frequency screening for high winds (i.e., 55 cases versus 13 and 2 cases, respectively).

4.2.4 Plant Improvements for High Winds

The plant improvements that the licensees reported to increase protection against the effects of high winds included 7 procedural improvements and 10 plant hardware improvements. Table 4.5 of this volume lists the individual improvements for high winds which are also identified in the plant-specific summaries in Table 4.1 of Volume 2.

4.2.5 General Insights for High Winds

As would be expected, the incidence of a specific type of high wind that is of significant magnitude to cause power plant damage is very region-specific in the United States. Hurricanes are the dominant potentially damaging high wind source in the coastal areas, while tornadoes dominate inland, particularly in the Midwest and South. One of the more damaging ways in which high wind effects contribute to plant CDF is through impact of wind-generated missiles, particularly tornado-generated missiles. Seventeen plant improvements related to high winds were cited by the licensees as a result of their IPEEEs. This accounted for approximately 27% of all of the HFO-related improvements. See Table 4.4 for a summary of the relative distribution of the HFO-related improvements.

Table 4.4: Total number of plant improvements for high winds, floods, and other external events*

External event	Number of improvements	Percentage
High winds	17	27%
External flooding	32	50%
Transportation or nearby facility accidents	5	8%
Other external events including plant-unique hazards	10	15%
Total	64	100%

* This table gives the total number of improvements cited in the submittals for all 70 IPEEE plants. These improvements include both procedural and hardware improvements. Some of the improvements cited by the licensees in their submittals were still under consideration at the time the licensees sent their IPEEEs to the NRC. Therefore, the number of actual improvements that have been implemented is not known, but is likely to be somewhat less than 64. A small number (less than five) of the improvements had been implemented before the IPEEE, but were IPEEE-related.

Table 4.5: Plant improvements to protect against high winds

Procedural improvements
Special plant procedures
Arrangement for the timely delivery of additional diesel generator fuel oil during storms
Emergency procedures to inspect diesel generator fuel oil transfer pumps and to isolate oil leakage and provide for makeup after a high wind event
Special training sessions for plant personnel, including training in the use of redundant instrumentation locations
Additional sheltering plans for plant personnel
Revised emergency procedures based on lessons learned from Hurricane Andrew
Emergency procedures to prevent ventilation failures during hurricanes

Hardware improvements
Tornado protection of the diesel generator exhaust system
Protection for the diesel generator room air supply
Addition of an air-cooled diesel generator (added before the IPEEE)
Addition of a tornado missile shield in the door of a technical support center
Addition of a tornado missile shield for an opening of an auxiliary building
Protection of cooling ducts and dampers in the control and diesel generator rooms during high wind conditions
Modifications to strengthen the diesel generator exhaust stacks
Improved mechanical hold downs for hydrogen tanks
Modifications to exterior doors to withstand pressure differentials during high winds
Strengthening of exhaust stacks of nearby fossil plant to prevent collateral damage from high winds

4.3 External Floods

4.3.1 Introduction

Sources of external floods are intense rainfall (including hurricanes); dam failures; wind-driven waves from lakes, rivers, or the ocean; abnormally high water levels from the same; and melting snow. Potential damage modes are site flooding resulting in water ingress into areas housing vulnerable safety-related equipment and water ponding on roofs that could potentially fail from the increased roof loading.

4.3.2 External Floods Quantitative Results

Of the licensees' submittals, 12 reported CDF contributions for external flooding ranging from about 2E-8/ry to about 7E-6/ry. Typically, floods induced by dam breaks, hurricanes, or intense precipitation have been treated as leading to a LOOP, which the licensees usually assumed to be irrecoverable, and additional random failures could then lead to core damage. Other submittals listed additional flood-related damage, including the loss of function of the intake structure; failures of diesel fuel oil transfer pumps; and potential failures of safety-related equipment in the diesel generator, auxiliary, and turbine buildings.

4.3.3 External Floods Qualitative Results

Just as for high winds, licensees used the qualitative screening approach more often than PRA or hazard frequency screening (58 cases versus 12 and 0 cases, respectively). In few instances where flood hazards were screened out, the IPEEE review process revealed that a relatively small increase in the critical flood level (perhaps just a few inches) could result in a significant change in the predicted annual rate of flood occurrence, such that these events could no longer be screened out, and additional analysis would then be needed to assess the consequences. On the other hand, many of the flooding assessments were conservative in that the licensees assumed that the effects from a number of possible conditions were cumulative (e.g., assuming a concurrent combination of peak wind-driven wave heights and peak high-water levels). Given the substantial uncertainties involved in developing site-specific flood hazard curves, a consideration of possible combinations of multiple effects causing a range of flood levels would have enhanced the robustness of some of the licensee's analyses and lent greater confidence to their findings.

Where applicable, most submittals considered and screened out potential failures of upstream dams that could lead to flooding at the plant site.

A few licensees proposed flood-related countermeasures that may be optimistic. For example, one licensee took credit for sandbagging up to a level of 9 feet. In several other submittals, flood barriers made of various construction materials, such as logs or concrete beams, were credited with being effective for preventing flooding, but the submittals did not discuss whether the licensees performed confirmatory testing to verify the effectiveness of certain of these mitigating actions.

4.3.4 Plant Improvements for External Floods

Plant improvements that were cited to provide further protection against flooding included 15 procedural improvements and 17 plant hardware improvements. Table 4.6 of this volume lists the individual flood-related improvements, which are also identified in the plant-specific summaries in Table 4.1 of Volume 2.

4.3.5 General Insights About External Floods

As for high winds, the effects of flooding are seen to be very region-specific and are more common in certain areas of the United States than in others. Plant sites 1n coastal locations are most susceptible to hurricane-induced flooding, as well as high precipitation levels. Certain rivers and lakes are more prone to have combinations of high winds and associated waves combined with high water levels, and other areas in the Northern and Western United States are subject to heavy snows with subsequent melting and flooding. As indicated, this category of the HFO-related events accounted for more of the cited plant improvements (approximately 50%) than any other HFO-related area.

Table 4.6: Plant improvements to protect against external floods

Procedural improvements
Improved emergency procedures for flooding conditions
Increased maintenance of drainage structures
Improved plant flood mitigation procedures
Increased inspection of roof drains
Procedures and inspections associated with the expeditious installation of special flood doors when needed
Special procedures for removal of snow and ice
Surveillance of a drain flapper valve for drainage from a control building
Evaluation of closure times for flood gates to aid in emergency planning
Revised procedures based on lessons learned regarding flooding from Hurricane Andrew
Procedures regarding water drainage from the turbine building during heavy rainfall
Procedures to prevent water flow from the turbine building into the main control room
Improved procedures to protect against local river flooding
Improved emergency operating procedures in the event of a dam failure

Hardware improvements
Scuppers in parapet walls to promote drainage and reduce roof ponding loads during heavy rainfall
Provisions for portable pumps
Upgrading flood-resistant doors
Provision for sandbags
Sealing of conduits
Addition of weather stripping to doors in buildings housing safety-related equipment
Addition of screens on equipment hub drains in a 480V switchgear room to preclude foreign material intrusion
Flood protection of a service water pump motor
Alteration of local site topography to reduce potential site flooding
Addition of a seiche (oscillatory wave action) protection barrier to protect the fuel oil transfer pumps for the diesel generators from flooding
Improved penetration seals to protect against potential flooding between service and auxiliary buildings
Modifications to the service water pump house roof to allow existing scuppers to drain excess rainwater more effectively
Refurbishment of existing flood walls and stop logs
Raised elevation of diesel generator fuel oil transfer pumps to protect against hurricane surge
Sealing of underground conduits to the switchgear rooms against water intrusion
Sealing penetrations in the diesel fuel oil transfer pump house to protect transfer pumps
Addition of a pump in the cooling tower area to remove excess water during heavy rainfall

4.4 Accidents Involving Transportation or Nearby Facilities

4.4.1 Introduction

Examples of events in this category include accidents involving hazardous chemical spills; fires or explosions from railway shipping or truck transport in the area of the plant (typically within a 5-mile distance); hazardous chemical spills, fires, or explosions from commercial facilities in the vicinity of the plant (e.g., chemical processing or storage plants, hydrogen storage tanks, etc.); and aircraft crashes.

4.4.2 Results of Analyses

Although only a few submittals document PRA results or CDF bounding assessments for these specific types of accidents (e.g., aircraft crashes), none of the submittals identified a CDF from accidents involving transportation or nearby facilities above the NUREG-1407 screening criterion of 1E-6/ry.

The large majority of the licensees performed qualitative as opposed to PRA or hazard frequency screening for their IPEEE transportation analyses. As observed for the treatment of the other HFO events, most submittals did not report walkdown procedures, walkdown team composition, or detailed walkdown findings. Many of the submittals primarily relied on existing analyses and documents as the basis for screening out transportation and nearby facility accidents.

4.4.3 Plant Improvements for Transportation or Nearby Facility Accidents

Plant improvements that were cited to protect against these types of events included just three procedural improvements and two plant hardware improvements. As indicated in Table 4.4, this category accounted for the fewest number of HFO-related plant improvements (8%). Table 4.7 of this volume lists the individual improvements related to transportation and nearby facility accidents, which are also identified in the plant-specific summaries in Table 4.1 of Volume 2.

Table 4.7: Plant improvements to protect against transportation and nearby facility accidents

Procedural improvements
Addition of plant guidelines to exclude flights over the plant by company pilots
Addition of restrictions to exclude all flights over the plant
Coordination with the U.S. Coast Guard to prevent further shipping of explosive materials on a nearby shipping channel
Hardware improvements
Addition of a backup cooling water intake structure for added protection against barge accidents (added before the IPEEE)
Addition of concrete barriers placed around a propane tank near the diesel generator rooms to protect against possible vehicle impact and subsequent explosions and fires

4.4.4 General Insights for Transportation or Nearby Facility Accidents

Transportation and nearby facility accidents do not vary regionally as much as weather-related external events, such as high winds and flooding. All areas of the United States where plants are located may have nearby roadways, rail traffic, water traffic, air traffic, and industrial facilities. While these types of events were not found to account for a significant risk contribution in any of the IPEEE submittals, and the relative number of plant improvements was much smaller than for the other HFO-related topics, these classes of accidents have rather unique aspects. That is, the plant-specific situation could change rather quickly. Fore example, a company could begin to transport hazardous materials by a route (by water, rail, or roadway) sufficiently close to the plant to pose a hazard, or a nearby industrial facility could establish a new storage facility for hazardous materials on its property but close enough to the plant to pose a potential risk. These changes could conceivably be made without the knowledge of the plant safety personnel, and those making the changes may not be particularly sensitive to the potential impact on the plant's safety. Although these types of accidents have not been found to represent a significant risk in the IPEEEs, this emphasizes the need for communication between licensees and nearby facilities to ensure the use of up-to-date information.

4.5   Other External Events Including Plant-Unique Hazards

4.5.1   Introduction

Besides high winds, floods, and transportation and nearby facility accidents, a wide variety of less likely other external events could possibly affect the plant risk, and these required consideration in the IPEEE evaluations. Table 4.1 gives a list of other types of events. Although most of these other events could easily be screened out, a few were found to have an impact on a site-specific basis as discussed below.

4.5.2   Other External Events Quantitative and Qualitative Results

As seen in Table 4.3, only a few (seven) licensees reported quantitative CDF estimates for this category of external events. One submittal (Haddam Neck) reported a CDF contribution of 8E-6/ry from lightning and 7E-6/ry from snow and ice. Lightning was assumed to cause a LOOP, with a number of other random failures being required to result in core damage. In the ice and snow analysis, the licensee found that the screen house, service building, and primary auxiliary building did not have roof load capacities much more than the snow load for a 100-year return interval. However, critical equipment failures attributable to roof collapse, combined with a number of other random failures, were required to lead to core damage.

NUREG-1407 did not require an explicit evaluation of HFO events other than high winds, external flooding, and accidents involving transportation or nearby facilities. Consequently, some submittals did not report an analysis of "other" HFO events. For those that did, most screened these events using qualitative screening techniques (e.g., showing conformance with the 1975 SRP criteria). For these other events, the number of qualitative screening applications compared with PRA and hazard frequency screening was 60, 7, and 3, respectively. In submittals that reported risk results for some "other" HFO event, most were found to have CDF contributions less than the NUREG-1407 screening criterion of 1E-6/ry.

Two submittals reported the existence of a plant-unique hazard related to failure of downstream dams and related loss of a cooling source. In one case, the hazard was screened out since it is covered as a design basis accident. In the other case, the hazard is also a design basis event, but the licensee estimated an initiating event frequency and performed a bounding CDF analysis on the basis of the applicable conditional core damage probability (CCDP) in order to screen out the hazard.

4.5.3   Plant Improvements for Other External Events

The improvements for this category included six procedural and four plant hardware improvements. As indicated in Table 4.4, the 10 improvements in the "other" category accounted for approximately 15% of all of the HFO-related improvements. Table 4.8 of this volume lists the individual improvements for this category, which are also identified in the plant-specific summaries in Table 4.1 of Volume 2.

Table 4.8: Plant improvements to protect against other external events

Procedural Improvements
Special report regarding onsite hazards from potentially dangerous materials
Notice regarding the onsite storage and transportation of hazardous materials
Evaluation of control room habitability regarding plans for storing hazardous materials onsite
Increasing the distance from a recently enlarged hydrogen storage system to the nearest safety-related equipment
Guidance to prevent the buildup of hydrogen gas in letdown storage tank rooms
Procedures to prevent stacking of containers in close proximity to safety-related equipment
Hardware improvements
Modifications to prevent ice formation on service water pumps serving the diesel generators
Addition of screens on drains to prevent foreign material intrusion into safety-related equipment spaces
Modifications to ventilation system exhausts systems to protect against potential combustible gas explosions
Modifications to a plant intake structure to prevent blockage from detritus (debris)

4.5.4   General Insights About Other External Events

While most plants did not report a significant hazard contribution attributable to these types of events, and most completely screened out this HFO category, there was one notable exception. Lightning and hazards associated with snow and ice were reported to have a relatively high CDF contribution at Haddam Neck (i.e., greater than the NUREG-1407 screening criterion of 1E-6/ry). While the CDF contributions for these events were estimated to be above the screening criterion at Haddam Neck, they still represent a small fraction of the overall plant CDF and are not large enough to be considered vulnerabilities. As indicated, this category of potential plant hazards is often unique to the plant and, in some cases, is regional in that the hazards are weather related.

4.6 General Observations and Insights about HFO External Events

4.6.1 Containment Performance Perspectives

None of the 70 IPEEE submittals identified any plant-unique accident sequences associated with containment performance that are different from those determined by the internal events IPE. Consistent with the guidance in Section 5.2 of NUREG-1407, no additional containment performance is needed for HFO events.

4.6.2 Unresolved Safety Issues and Generic Safety Issues

Unresolved safety issues (USIs) and generic safety issues (GSIs) are discussed in depth in Chapter 5 of this report. Those issues pertaining particularly to the HFO part of the IPEEE review are discussed briefly below.

All submittals provided some discussion concerning GSI-103, "Probable Maximum Precipitation." For this issue, some of the licensees stated that they had taken measures to protect roofs of safety-related buildings from the effects of roof ponding predicted as a result of intense local precipitation (e.g., the addition of scuppers to aid in draining the water). As noted in Table 5.2 and Section 5.4 of this report, three plants have not completely verified GSI-103.

The HFO IPEEE submittals did not explicitly discuss other GSIs or USIs. Nonetheless, certain information provided in the submittals is considered relevant for addressing issues associated with GSI-156, "Systematic Evaluation Program (SEP)," and GSI-172, "Multiple System Responses Program (MSRP)," as discussed below.

4.6.2.1 GSI-156, Systematic Evaluation Program

This generic issue has five sub-issues related to HFO events that are discussed below.

- *Dam Integrity and Site Flooding.* When applicable to the plant, HFO IPEEE submittals generally discussed the potential for, and effects of, site flooding as a result of independent or combined failures of upstream and downstream dams. Two submittals also considered the potential for loss of cooling water caused by failure of an onsite dam.

- *Site Hydrology and Ability to Withstand Floods.* HFO IPEEE submittals generally provided discussions that are directly relevant to this issue in their assessments of floods.

- *Industrial Hazards.* HFO IPEEE submittals generally provided discussions that are directly relevant to this issue in their assessment of accidents involving transportation and nearby industrial facilities.

- *Tornado Missiles.* HFO IPEEE submittals generally provided discussions that are directly relevant to this issue in their assessment of high winds and tornadoes.

- *Severe Weather Effects on Structures.* In general, HFO IPEEEs screened out the effects of direct winds and flooding on plant structures. Nonetheless, where applicable, the submittals generally provided relevant information concerning the effects of wind-induced missiles on those structures.

4.6.2.2 GSI-172, Multiple System Responses Program

With regard to GSI-172, the only HFO-related issue regarding GSI-172 is the effects of flooding and/or moisture intrusion on non safety-related and safety-related equipment. With respect to safety-related equipment, HFO IPEEE submittals generally provided discussions that are directly relevant to this issue in their assessment of floods. However, the submittals generally did not discuss flooding or moisture intrusion effects on non-safety-related equipment. This omission is not important from an IPEEE perspective since these effects do not contribute significantly to the plants' external event CDFs.

4.6.3 Human Actions

Where applicable, the HFO submittals documented operator recovery actions to mitigate the effects of HFO-induced plant transients. In those instances, the important operator recovery actions included recovery of offsite power or diesel generators given a tornado- or high-wind-induced LOOP, and use of sandbagging or installation of stop logs to mitigate an external flood. In some cases, the licensees' assessments of recovery actions may have been somewhat optimistic. The submittals did not discuss whether licensees performed confirmatory testing to verify the effectiveness of certain of these mitigating actions. However, as indicated in Section 4.3.3, flooding analyses tended to include conservative assumptions and, in addition, flooding levels do not generally change rapidly for topological configurations around plants. Plant operators should have time to initiate emergency actions (e.g., including plant shutdown) if conditions require such actions.

4.6.4 Walkdown Perspectives

Most of the HFO submittals provided some general description regarding walkdown findings. One licensee reported that they believed that the updated FSAR data constituted a more reliable information source than a plant walkdown. Most of the submittals reviewed did not provide specific detailed information regarding either walkdown findings or walkdown team composition. Licensees employed walkdowns to confirm that no significant changes have occurred since the plant operating license was issued. Specifically, walkdown findings noted in regard to flooding events included the identification of two conduits for flood entry into critical structures, the discovery that loads on the roof of a spent fuel cooling pool from roof ponding could potentially exceed the roof's design load, and identification of flood pathways (including non-water-tight doors). Walkdown findings pertaining to high winds consisted primarily identifying exposed components and nearby objects for wind-induced missiles.

4.6.5 Summary of Plant Improvements

Procedural enhancements related to HFO events have included provisions for sandbagging, closing or welding doors, hooking up pumps, providing new electrical circuits to reduce the risk from flooding, and provision for routine inspection and maintenance of drains. Two submittals reported that the licensees were considering the development of severe accident management guidance to reduce the risk of high winds. One submittal indicated development of guidance to ensure that a flood door can be installed in 8 hours, for the purpose of reducing flooding risk.

Hardware improvements include (among others) refurbishing a flood wall, strengthening non-safety stacks to prevent collapse onto safety structures in high-wind events, installing weather stripping and other modifications to enhance flood protection at entry pathways, replacing drain screens, and providing equipment (such as portable water pumps) to enhance flood protection. At least one HFO submittal noted that hardware changes that had been implemented as a result of their IPE analyses (i.e., the addition of diesel generators) have also reduced the risk associated with HFO events.

Overall, for most licensees, the HFO IPEEE program has resulted in a greater level of appreciation of the potential risk impact of high winds and tornadoes, external flooding, and other external initiators.

4.6.6 General Perspectives

As shown in Table 4.1 of Volume 2, the CDF estimates for high winds (including tornadoes) and external flooding have been found to range from 2E-8/ry to 6E-5/ry. Conservative bounding analysis estimates of CDF for high winds and external floods have been reported and, while the associated risks were not categorized as "vulnerabilities," they have resulted in a number of plant improvements (see Table 4.1 of Volume 2; Tables 4.4, 4.5, 4.6, 4.7, and 4.8 of this volume; and Sections 4.2.4, 4.3.4, 4.4.4, and 4.5.4 of this volume). All IPEEE submittals screened out accidents involving transportation and nearby facilities.

Additional general review observations pertaining to HFO submittals include the following.

- Licensees' application of PRA techniques in HFO IPEEEs has varied considerably in scope, detail, and rigor. Simplified PRA approaches have generally been implemented, whereas to a lesser extent, detailed state-of-the-art PRA studies have been performed for some or all of the HFO initiators at a plant.

- Where the HFO IPEEE submittals have adopted the use of PRA methods or applicable PRA bounding analyses, licensees have commonly used the IPE conditional core damage probabilities (CCDPs) for events such as the loss of offsite power or loss of service water. However, the accident conditions associated with the IPEEE HFO events can be significantly different than the IPE conditions for these events. In certain cases, the accident sequences and associated CCDPs used to assess the HFO events may not have reflected the potential for the degradation of equipment performance as a result of conditions such as high winds or floods (particularly on exposed components). Consequently, in some of these cases, the resulting quantitative CDFs may have been underestimated, but not enough to mask a vulnerability.

- The HFO events are, by nature, somewhat different than the seismic and fire external events in the following respects. Certain HFO events can involve changes in the external environment that take place over time. An example of this is one case where a licensee reported that they discovered that explosive materials were being shipped on a nearby waterway. The licensee reported that when this was discovered, arrangements were made with the U.S. Coast Guard to prevent a recurrence. As discussed earlier, these types of events have not been found to be a significant risk contributor in the IPEEEs, but they emphasize the need for communication between licensees and other transportation and nearby facilities to ensure the use of up-to-date information.

4.6.7 Impact of the IPEEE HFO External Events Program on Plant Safety

Although no IPEEE submittal reported any HFO-related vulnerabilities, the HFO IPEEEs have resulted in numerous improvements in the form of procedural enhancements, severe accident management guidelines, and hardware improvements. Table 4.4 of this volume gives the number of improvements that licensees identified for the major IPEEE event categories; Tables 4.5, 4.6, 4.7, and 4.8 list the individual improvements by HFO topic; and Table 4.1 of Volume 2 lists the improvements on a plant-specific basis.

Given that many licensees reported improvements associated with HFO events, the HFO IPEEE program has had a significant impact on improving plant safety. Of the 70 plant submittals, 34 cited a total of 64 individual HFO-related improvements. Except for one case (Salem), the submittal did not provide information to quantify the reduction in CDF that resulted from these improvements. In the case of Salem, the licensee improved door seals to prevent flooding into a building that houses safety-related equipment. The IPEEE submittal reported that the CDF contribution was reduced from approximately 1E-4/ry to 1E-7/ry as a result of this improvement. Perhaps most important, it is clear from the documentation provided in the submittals that licensees' efforts to assess the potential hazards from HFO-related events have enhanced the knowledge of plant personnel regarding these types of events specifically for their plants.

4.7   Summary and Conclusions

For those cases where licensees performed PRAs or CDF bounding analyses, the estimated CDF results varied from plant to plant as demonstrated by the following information.

- For high winds and tornadoes, the plant-specific CDF results vary from less than 2E-7/ry to 6E-5/ry.

- For external flood events, the plant-specific CDF results for 12 plants vary from about 2E-8/ry to about 7E-6/ry.

- For transportation and nearby facility accidents, 8 plants reported that the plant-specific CDF results from PRA studies or bounding analyses are below the NUREG-1407 screening criterion of 1E-6/ry.

- One submittal (Haddam Neck) reported bounding analysis CDF results of 8E-6/ry for lightning events and 7E-6/ry for snow and ice.

- One submittal (South Texas) reported CDF results of 8E-6/ry for a chemical release from a nearby chemical facility.

- One submittal (Salem) reported a plant improvement that reduced the external events CDF by three orders of magnitude from approximately 1E-4/ry to approximately 1E-7/ry. The plant modification cited was the improvement of door penetration seals between the service and auxiliary buildings to protect against external flooding.

Regarding HFO-related plant improvements, 34 of the 70 plant submittals cited a total of 64 individual improvements. Sixteen plants cited more than one HFO-related improvement with one plant (Turkey Point) indicating that they were considering as many as five improvements. These improvements are summarized in Tables 4.4 through 4.8 in this volume and on a plant-by-plant basis in Table 4.1 of Volume 2. Thirty-six plants reported no HFO-related improvements.

All HFO evaluations reviewed screened out accidents involving transportation and nearby facilities, as well as other plant-unique hazards when encountered.

Of the 70 IPEEE submittals, most indicated that some type of walkdown was performed for HFO events during the IPEEE. However, one submittal stated that the licensee believed that a review of the updated FSAR data constituted a more reliable information source than a plant walkdown. The submittals usually did not provide detailed descriptions of the walkdown procedures and results.

As discussed in Section 4.6.7, the licensees' evaluations of HFO events have not identified any vulnerabilities to these type of events. However, the extent of the documentation submitted by the licensees regarding their evaluations, and the list of HFO-related plant improvements, suggest that the IPEEEs have significantly contributed to the licensees' understanding of, and preparation for, potential HFO events.

5. UNRESOLVED SAFETY ISSUES AND GENERIC SAFETY ISSUES

5.1 Introduction

This chapter discusses the unresolved safety issues (USIs) and generic safety issues (GSIs) that were addressed under the IPEEE program. Specifically, in accordance with Supplement 4 to Generic Letter (GL) 88-20 and the associated guidance in NUREG-1407, "Procedural and Submittal Guidance for the Individual Plant Examination of External Events (IPEEE) for Severe Accident Vulnerabilities," the NRC requested that licensees provide information to address the following issues:

- USI A-45, "Shutdown Decay Heat Removal Requirements,"
- GSI-103, "Design for Probable Maximum Precipitation,"
- GSI-131, "Potential Seismic Interaction Involving Movable In-Core Flux Mapping System Used in Westinghouse Plants,"
- GSI-57, "Effects of Fire Protection System Actuation on Safety-Related Equipment," and
- Sandia Fire Risk Scoping Study (FRSS) issues.

In addition, the four other GSIs listed below have external event aspects, but were not specifically identified as issues to be verified under the IPEEE program and, therefore, were not explicitly discussed in Supplement 4 to GL 88-20 or NUREG-1407. After issuing the generic letter, the NRC evaluated the scope and the specific information requested in the generic letter and the associated IPEEE guidance. The NRC concluded that the plant-specific analyses requested in the IPEEE program could also be used, through a satisfactory IPEEE submittal review, to evaluate and verify the external event aspects of the following safety issues:

- GSI-147, "Fire-Induced Alternate Shutdown/Control Room Panel Interactions,"
- GSI-148, "Smoke Control and Manual Fire-Fighting Effectiveness,"
- GSI-156, "Systematic Evaluation Program (SEP)," and
- GSI-172, "Multiple System Responses Program" (MSRP).

It should be noted that there is some overlap among the issues discussed in this chapter and, although the majority of these issues are covered within the IPEEE scope, a number of issues (or sub-issues) have aspects related to internal events (which were covered in the IPE program), as well as aspects related to external events. Only external events aspects are covered in this chapter. Some of these issues relate to seismic events, fires, and HFO events and, therefore, are also discussed in Chapters 2, 3, and 4, respectively. Table 5.1 summarizes this information for the issues (and sub-issues) that are covered within the IPEEE scope.

As shown in Table 5.1, a number of these issues are very closely related. Some issues or sub-issues are identical in scope, but may have different or similar titles. For example, GSI-147, "Fire-Induced Alternate Shutdown/Control Room Panel Interactions" (discussed in Section 5.4.5), is identical to the FRSS issue with the same title[1] (discussed in Section 5.4.9.1.5).

---

[1] This issue, which NUREG/CR-5088 originally identified as one of the Sandia Fire Risk Scoping Study issues, was later designated as a generic issue and was tracked in the NRC's generic issue program (NUREG-0933).

Table 5.1: Generic safety issues addressed in the IPEEE program

Generic Safety Issue (GSI)	Area[1]	USI/GSI	FRSS	GSI-156	GSI-172	Remark[2]
Shutdown Decay Heat Removal Requirements	S,F	USI A-45				EX
Potential Seismic Interaction Involving the Movable In-Core Mapping System	S	GSI-131				C
Effects of Fire Protection System Actuation on Safety-Related Equipment	S,F	GSI-57	X		X	P
Fire-Induced Alternate Shutdown/Control Room Panel Interaction	F	GSI-147	X			C
Smoke Control and Manual Fire-Fighting Effectiveness	F	GSI-148	X			P
Seismic-fire Interactions	F		X		X	C
Adequacy of Fire Barriers	F		X			C
Effects of Hydrogen Line Ruptures	S,F				X	C
Settlement of Foundations and Buried Equipment	S			X		P
Dam Integrity and Site Flooding	S,HFO			X		C
Seismic Design of Structures, Systems, and Components	S			X		C
Common Cause Failures Related to Human Errors	S,F				X	EX
Non-Safety-Related Control System/Safety-Related Protection System Dependencies	S,F				X	EX
Effects of Flooding and/or Moisture Intrusion on Non-Safety-Related and Safety-Related Equipment	F,HFO				X	EX
Seismically Induced Spatial and Functional Interaction	S				X	C
Seismically Induced Flooding	S				X	C
Seismically Induced Relay Chatter	S				X	C
Evaluation of Earthquake Magnitudes Greater than Safe Shutdown Earthquake	S				X	C
Design for Probable Maximum Precipitation	HFO	GSI-103				C
Site Hydrology and Ability to Withstand Floods	HFO			X		P
Industrial Hazards	HFO			X		C
Tornado Missiles	HFO			X		C
Severe Weather Effects on Structures	HFO			X		C
Design Codes, Criteria, and Load Combinations	S,HFO			X		C
Shutdown Systems and Electrical Instrumentation and Control Features	F			X		EX

[1]S=seismic, F=internal fires, HFO=high winds, floods, and other external events

[2]C=issue covered by IPEEE; EX=only external event-related aspects of issue covered; P=partially covered (refer to specific section of the text for details)

The scope of most of these generic issues is covered in its entirety by the IPEEE program. These issues are noted in the remarks column of Table 5.1 by the letter "C" (i.e., the issue is covered by the IPEEE). As noted above, the scope of some issues includes aspects of both internal and external events. For example, USI A-45, "Shutdown Decay Heat Removal Requirements," includes potential plant vulnerabilities associated with internal event initiators as well as external event initiators. The IPEEE program covers only the external event-related aspects of this issue. (The internal event aspects were covered in the IPE program.) Issues such as this are noted by "EX" (i.e., only the external event-related aspects of the issue are covered) in the remarks column of Table 5.1. The other designator in the remarks column is "P" (i.e., is partially covered in the IPEEE program). The scope of these issues, as defined in NUREG-0933, includes some aspects that go beyond those that are covered by the IPEEE program. For example, GSI-148, "Smoke Control and Manual Fire-Fighting Effectiveness" (discussed in Section 5.4.6), does not cover the effects of potentially damaging mechanisms, such as smoke, on equipment. Data on smoke-induced damage to equipment are sparse and, hence, it was not anticipated that the IPEEE analyses would assess this potentially damaging mechanism. Other parts of GSI-148 are covered by the IPEEE program (see Section 5.4.6). Each of these issues and sub-issues is discussed in more detail in Section 5.4.

As discussed in previous chapters, there were 70 IPEEE submittals; however, the staff prepared only 69 staff evaluation reports because one plant (Haddam Neck) was permanently shut down after providing its IPEEE submittal. Therefore, the discussions and tables in this chapter related to USIs and GSIs (which are addressed in the staff evaluation reports) address only 69 submittals.

Sections 5.2 and 5.3 discuss the process used by licensees and the staff, respectively, in evaluating the USIs and GSIs. This is followed by Section 5.4, which describes each individual issue and sub-issue and presents an overview of their treatment in the IPEEE submittals. Section 5.5 presents a summary and the staff's conclusions.

5.2   Overview of Licensees' Assessment Processes

This section describes the processes that the licensees used to arrive at their conclusions regarding the verification of the USIs and GSIs that they were asked to address within the context of the IPEEE program. In general, the licensees' processes included performing seismic, fire, and HFO walkdowns, which involved USI/GSI aspects related to the individual plant. In the case of seismic walkdowns, the licensees used a seismic review team (SRT) to review documentation of the walkdowns that were conducted and, in some cases, performed additional verification walkdowns.

The licensees also used probabilistic risk assessment (PRA) techniques to examine the dominant accident sequences and their associated initiating events. When these examinations revealed no vulnerability or no particular plant feature with a potentially significant risk contribution, the licensees concluded that the external event aspects of the considered USIs and GSIs were verified. Usually, the licensees also subjected their assessments and conclusions to an independent peer review before submitting the IPEEE study to the NRC.

5.3 USI/GSI Staff Review Evaluation Process

This section discusses the process that the staff used to assess the acceptability of the licensees' conclusions regarding the USIs and GSIs in the IPEEE submittals. The staff's judgement regarding for USI and GSI verification was based on the following criteria.

- The licensee's IPEEE is complete with regard to USI and GSI coverage.

- The licensee's assessment demonstrated an in-depth knowledge of the external event aspects and plant characteristics that are relevant to the issues discussed.

- The licensee's assessment results are reasonable given the design, location, features, and operating history of the plant.

An issue is thus considered verified if the submittal did not identify any potential vulnerabilities associated with its related concerns, or the licensee implemented plant-specific improvements to eliminate or reduce the significance of the identified potential vulnerabilities at the plant. For example, during plant walkdowns, some licensees identified improvements to strengthen equipment anchorages to reduce seismically induced spatial interactions (one of the MSRP sub-issues discussed in Section 5.4.8.2.7). In a few cases, licensees identified improvements related to a generic issue that were planned, but had not been implemented at the time of the IPEEE submittal. Confirmation that "planned" improvements have been made with regard to a generic issue is recommended.

The staff assessed the acceptability of the licensees' conclusions on the basis of information in the IPEEE submittals, which was sometimes supplemented by the licensees' responses to the staff's requests for additional information (RAIs) seeking clarification or supplemental assessments of certain aspects of the submittal.

Furthermore, the staff established an IPEEE Senior Review Board (SRB), which held meetings on a regular basis. The SRB comprised NRC staff and consultants with specialized expertise in the various aspects of external events and PRA. In these meetings, the SRB members provided their perspectives on the IPEEE review findings, and recommended actions on the basis of their technical specialities. In this manner, the SRB provided additional assurance that each review met the IPEEE program objectives.

The IPEEE reviews showed that most of the submittals contain information that addresses most of the GSIs. However, if a submittal did not discuss the issue or sub-issues, and the reviewers determined whether the missing information could cause the licensee to overlook a potential vulnerability at their plant. On the basis of the SRB members' expert judgement and information on similar issues from other IPEEE submittals, RAIs were sent to licensees if a potential vulnerability could have been missed or if information in response to the RAI would be likely to uncover a significant problem with the IPEEE results. However if a licensee's submittal did not address an issue or sub-issue, but did not miss a potential vulnerability, the NRC's staff evaluation report (SER) identified the omission as a "weakness" in the submittal. In such cases, the submittals still meet the intent of Supplement 4 to Generic Letter 88-20, but the GSI may not be "verified" for that plant.

Table 5.2 shows the status of each of the IPEEE-related USI and GSI issues for all of the plants. A "yes" indicates that the particular issue was verified for that plant. A "no" indicates that the staff did not have sufficient information from either the submittal or the responsea to RAIs to determine whether the issue was adequately addressed. An "N/A" means that the issue was not applicable to the given plant. For example, GSI-131, "Potential Seismic Interactions Involving the Movable In-Core Flux Mapping System Used in Westinghouse Plants," only applies to Westinghouse plants. Several issues (e.g., GSI-156, GSI-172, and the FRSS issues) comprise a number of sub-issues. Issues in Table 5.2 that are shown to be "partially" verified indicate that one or more of the sub-issues may not be verified, but the remaining sub-issues are verified.

Table 5.2: IPEEE USI/GSI verification

Plant name	USI A-45	GSI-57	GSI-103	GSI-131	FRSS	GSI-147	GSI-148	GSI-156	GSI-172
Arkansas 1 & 2	Yes	Yes	Yes	N/A	Yes	Yes	Yes	Yes	Yes
Beaver Valley 1	Yes	Yes	Yes	Yes	Yes	Yes	Yes	N/A	Yes
Beaver Valley 2	Yes	Yes	Yes	Yes	Yes	Yes	Yes	N/A	Yes
Braidwood 1 & 2	Yes	Yes	Yes	Yes	Yes	Yes	Yes	N/A	Yes
Browns Ferry 2 & 3	Yes	Yes	Yes	N/A	Partial	Yes	Partial	Yes	Partial
Brunswick 1 & 2	Yes	Yes	Yes	N/A	Yes	Yes	Yes	Yes	Yes
Byron 1 & 2	Yes	Yes	Yes	Yes	Yes	Yes	Yes	N/A	Yes
Callaway	Yes	Yes	Yes	Yes	Yes	Yes	Yes	N/A	Yes
Calvert Cliffs 1 & 2	Yes	Yes	Yes	N/A	Yes	Yes	Yes	Yes	Yes
Catawba 1 & 2	Yes	Yes	Yes	Yes	Yes	Yes	Yes	N/A	Yes
Clinton	Yes	Yes	Yes	N/A	Yes	Yes	Yes	N/A	Yes
Columbia Generating[1]	Yes	Yes	Yes	N/A	Yes	Yes	Yes	N/A	Yes
Comanche Peak 1 & 2	Yes	Yes	Yes	Yes	Yes	Yes	Yes	N/A	Yes
Cooper	Yes	Yes	Yes	N/A	Yes	Yes	Yes	Yes	Yes
Crystal River 3	Yes	Yes	Yes	N/A	Yes	Yes	Yes	N/A	Partial
D.C. Cook 1 & 2	Yes	Yes	Yes	Yes	Yes	Yes	Yes	Yes	Yes
Davis Besse	Yes	Yes	Yes	N/A	Yes	Yes	Yes	Yes	Yes
Diablo Canyon 1 & 2	Yes	Yes	Yes	Yes	Yes	Yes	Yes	N/A	Yes
Dresden 2 & 3	Yes	Yes	Yes	N/A	Yes	Yes	Yes	Yes	Yes
Duane Arnold	Yes	Yes	Yes	N/A	Partial	Yes	Partial	Yes	Yes
Farley 1	Yes	Yes	Yes	Yes	Yes	Yes	Yes	N/A	Partial

---

[1] Formerly known as Washington Nuclear Project No. 2 (WNP-2).

Plant name	USI A-45	GSI-57	GSI-103	GSI-131	FRSS	GSI-147	GSI-148	GSI-156	GSI-172
Fermi 2	Yes	Yes	Yes	N/A	Partial	Yes	Partial	N/A	Yes
Fitzpatrick	Yes	Yes	Yes	N/A	Yes	Yes	Yes	Yes	Yes
Fort Calhoun	Yes	Yes	Yes	N/A	Yes	Yes	Yes	Yes	Yes
Ginna	Yes	Yes	Yes	Yes	Yes	Yes	Yes	Yes	Yes
Grand Gulf	Yes	Yes	Yes	N/A	Yes	Yes	Yes	N/A	Yes
Hatch 1 & 2	Yes	Yes	Yes	N/A	Partial	Partial	Partial	Yes	Partial
Hope Creek	Yes	Yes	Yes	N/A	Yes	Yes	Yes	N/A	Yes
Indian Point 2	Yes	Yes	Yes	Yes	Partial	Yes	Partial	Yes	Yes
Indian Point 3	Yes	Yes	Yes	Yes	Partial	Yes	Partial	Yes	Yes
Kewaunee	Yes	Yes	Yes	Yes	Partial	Yes	No	Yes	Partial
LaSalle[2]	Yes	No	Partial	N/A	Partial	Yes	No	N/A	Partial
Limerick 1 & 2	Yes	Yes	Yes	N/A	Yes	Yes	Partial	N/A	Partial
Millstone 2	Yes	Yes	Yes	N/A	Yes	Yes	Yes	Yes	Yes
Millstone 3	Yes	Yes	Yes	Yes	Yes	Yes	Yes	N/A	Yes
Monticello	Yes	Yes	Yes	N/A	Yes	Yes	Yes	Yes	Yes
McGuire 1 & 2	Yes	Yes	Yes	Yes	Yes	Yes	Yes	N/A	Yes
Nine Mile Point 1	Yes	Yes	Yes	N/A	Partial	Yes	Partial	Yes	Yes
Nine Mile Point 2	Yes	Yes	Yes	N/A	Yes	Yes	Yes	N/A	Yes
North Anna 1 & 2	Yes	Yes	Yes	Yes	Yes	Partial	Partial	N/A	Partial
Oconee 1, 2, & 3	Yes	Yes	Yes	N/A	Partial	Yes	Partial	Yes	Yes
Oyster Creek	Yes	Yes	Yes	N/A	Partial	Yes	Partial	Yes	Yes
Palisades	Yes	Yes	Yes	N/A	Yes	Partial	Yes	Yes	Yes
Palo Verde 1, 2, & 3	Yes	Yes	Yes	N/A	Yes	Yes	Yes	N/A	Yes

---

[2] The licensee relied exclusively upon previously published NRC PRA reports (NUREG/CR-4832, "Analysis of the LaSalle Unit 2 Nuclear Power Plant: Risk Methods Integration and Evaluation Program (RMIEP)," and NUREG/CR-5305, "Integrated Risk Assessment for the LaSalle Unit 2 Nuclear Power Plant: Phenomenology and Risk Uncertainty Evaluation Program (PRUEP)") and provided no additional information related to generic issues. This is evidenced by the lack of verification for any issue outside of those that could be deduced from the RMIEP study.

Plant name	USI A-45	GSI-57	GSI-103	GSI-131	FRSS	GSI-147	GSI-148	GSI-156	GSI-172
Peach Bottom 2 & 3	Yes	Yes	Yes	N/A	Yes	Yes	Yes	Yes	Yes
Perry	Yes	Yes	Yes	N/A	Yes	Yes	Yes	N/A	Yes
Pilgrim	Yes	Yes	Yes	N/A	Yes	Yes	Yes	Yes	Yes
Point Beach 1 & 2	Yes	Yes	Yes	Yes	Yes	Yes	Yes	Yes	Yes
Prairie Island 1 & 2	Yes	Yes	Yes	Yes	Yes	Yes	Yes	Yes	Yes
Quad Cities 1 & 2	Yes	Yes	Partial	N/A	Yes	Yes	Partial	Yes	Yes
River Bend	Yes	Yes	Yes	N/A	Yes	Yes	Yes	N/A	Yes
Robinson 2	Yes	Yes	Yes	Yes	Yes	Yes	Yes	Yes	Yes
Salem 1 & 2	Yes	Yes	Yes	Yes	Yes	Yes	Yes	N/A	Yes
San Onofre 2 & 3	Yes	Yes	Yes	N/A	Yes	Yes	Yes	N/A	Yes
Seabrook	Yes	Yes	Yes	Yes	Partial	No	No	N/A	Partial
Sequoyah 1 & 2	Yes	Yes	Partial	Yes	Yes	Yes	Yes	N/A	Yes
Shearon Harris	Yes	Yes	Yes	Yes	Partial	Yes	Partial	N/A	Yes
South Texas 1 & 2	Yes	Yes	N.A.[3]	Yes	Yes	Yes	Yes	N/A	Yes
St. Lucie 1 & 2	Yes	Partial	Yes	N/A	Partial	Yes	Partial	N/A	Partial
Summer	Yes	Yes	Yes	Yes	Yes	Yes	Yes	N/A	Yes
Surry 1 & 2	Yes	Yes	Yes	Yes	Yes	Yes	Yes	Yes	Yes
Susquehanna 1 & 2	Yes	Yes	Yes	N/A	Yes	Yes	Yes	N/A	Yes
Three Mile Island 1	Yes	Yes	Yes	N/A	Yes	Yes	Yes	Yes	Yes
Turkey Point 3 & 4	Yes	Partial	Yes	Yes	Partial	Yes	No	Yes	Partial
Vermont Yankee	Yes	Yes	Yes	N/A	Yes	Yes	Yes	Yes	Yes
Vogtle 1 & 2	Yes	Yes	Yes	Yes	Partial	Yes	Partial	N/A	Partial
Waterford 3	Yes	Yes	Yes	N/A	Yes	Yes	Partial	N/A	Partial
Watts Bar 1	Yes	Yes	Yes	Yes	Yes	Yes	Yes	N/A	Partial
Wolf Creek	Yes	Yes	Yes	Yes	Yes	Yes	Yes	N/A	Yes

[3] A new PMP evaluation was not required for South Texas because the impact of the new PMP criteria had previously been evaluated as part of the operating license process in 1989, in accordance with GL 89-22, "Potential for Increased Roof Loads and Plant Area Flood Runoff Depth at Licensed Nuclear Power Plants Due to Recent Change in Probable Maximum Precipitation Criteria Developed by the National Weather Service."

(The plant-specific tables in Volume 2 of this report provide additional information showing which sub-issues are or are not verified for each plant.) For those issues that have not been completely verified, the NRC staff will determine if any additional actions or assessments are needed to verify these GSIs. This follow-up will be done separately from the IPEEE program.

The following sections discuss the unverified USIs and GSIs or portions thereof for each plant listed above.

5.4 IPEEE-Related USIs and GSIs

This section discusses the USIs and GSIs that are addressed in the IPEEE submittals. Each specific issue includes the following:

- a description of the issue,
- a discussion of findings and plant modifications that impact this particular issue, and
- additional observations regarding the issue.

5.4.1 USI A-45, "Shutdown Decay Heat Removal (DHR) Requirements"

5.4.1.1 Issue Description

The objective of USI A-45 is to determine whether the decay heat removal function at operating plants is adequate and whether cost-beneficial improvement(s) could be identified. The internal event aspects of USI A-45 were subsumed in the IPE (Generic Letter 88-20); therefore, the external event aspects, including fire-related issues and seismic adequacy of the decay heat removal systems, are included in the IPEEE. Thus, the purpose of the IPEEE related to USI A-45 is to identify any significant and unique seismic and fire vulnerabilities in the decay heat removal function.

5.4.1.2 Findings and Related Plant Modifications

Most licensees explicitly addressed USI A-45 in their IPEEE submittals. Those submittals that did not explicitly mention this issue implicitly addressed USI A-45 by providing adequate information on the potential loss of decay heat removal capability through the evaluation of seismic and fire events, which would ensure adequate decay heat removal under these conditions.

The seismic evaluation of all plants included decay heat removal equipment. Plants that performed a seismic PRA provided a quantitative evaluation of the contribution of potential loss of decay heat removal to the estimated CDF.

The plants that performed seismic margin analyses (SMA) included the equipment that would be used for decay heat removal on their IPEEE safe shutdown equipment list (SSEL). The licensees then performed a fragility analysis of all of the equipment on the SSEL. For licensees that performed an SMA, this analysis resulted in identification of each component's high confidence of low probability of failure (HCLPF) value. Usually, the licensees would state that most or all of the components' HCLPF values were greater than the review-level earthquake (RLE) value (usually 0.3 g except for six plants that had 0.5 g — see Section 2.1.3.2) and would only identify those components that had HCLPF values close to or below the RLE. Those licensees that had HCLPF values below the RLE usually either performed a more detailed evaluation that resulted in removing the components from the SSEL, the revised HCLPF value being higher than the RLE, or citing some plant change that would result in a higher HCLPF value. In some cases, the licensees determined that there was no cost-beneficial modification that would significantly improve the HCLPF value. All plants had HCLPF values for the equipment on the SSEL in excess of the safe shutdown earthquake (SSE).

NUREG-1407 identified 10 plants as "reduced-scope" plants. These plants are located in areas where the seismic challenge is deemed to be significantly reduced, such that the design basis earthquake is an adequate representation of the perceived seismic challenge. For these plants, the RLE was the same as the SSE. Therefore, for reduced-scope plants, demonstrating that the equipment on the SSEL would remain functional at the SSE level and there were no vulnerabilities was sufficient for addressing USI A-45.

Some licensees addressed potential loss of decay heat removal capability in the event of a fire through a fire PRA, a few of which included Level 2. Some plants used the decay heat removal model from their IPE to model postulated fire events as part of their IPEEE. Other plants developed alternative success paths. Typically, these drew on previous work, such as the fire hazard analyses conducted in accordance with Appendix A to 10 CFR Part 50, or compliance with Appendix R to 10 CFR Part 50.

5.4.1.3 Observations

Whether a licensee used an SPRA or an SMA for the seismic IPEEE, the capability of decay heat removal functions is directly included by definition. Thus, any findings encountered in the IPEEE with respect to seismic capability of DHR functions also apply to USI A-45. In other words, for seismic events, USI A-45 perspectives are a subset of the IPEEE perspectives. Consequently, the IPEEE submittals generally reiterated those seismic IPEEE findings pertaining to DHR capability as the basis for the verification of USI A-45.

The NRC concludes that all plants have adequately addressed USI A-45. All plants have identified at least one method of removing decay heat for postulated fire events. While not all plants have an identified margin in excess of the needs for safe shutdown during an SSE (e.g., the reduced-scope plants) the NRC has determined that the IPEEEs have performed an adequate assessment to identify potential vulnerabilities in the decay heat removal systems consistent with the guidance in NUREG-1407, and no vulnerabilities were found.

5.4.2 GSI-57, "Effects of Fire Protection System Actuation on Safety-Related Equipment"

5.4.2.1 Issue Description

GSI-57 addresses the potential that the activation of fire suppression systems, either as part of actual fire-fighting or spuriously, might result in damage to plant systems and components. The analytical results obtained for prioritization of this issue by the NRC identified the following dominant risk contributors as:

- seismically induced fire plus seismically induced suppression diversion, and
- seismically induced actuation of the fire protection system (FPS).

The NRC anticipated that licensees would conduct seismic and fire walkdowns, as described in Section 7.0 of EPRI's Fire-Induced Vulnerability Evaluation (FIVE) methodology. These walkdowns were expected to assess whether (1) an actuated FPS would spray safety-related equipment, and (2) some protective measures, if needed, could be implemented to prevent the safety-related equipment from being sprayed by fire suppressants.

Other potential damage mechanisms, such as smoke and fire suppressant damage (either from fixed systems or manual actions), have not been considered. In general, this is an area where the database on equipment vulnerability is rather sparse. Similarly, analytical methods and tools (such as computer codes) have not generally been evaluated in the context of fire risk assessment. Hence, it is not anticipated that the IPEEE analysis would provide a detailed assessment of smoke- and suppressant-induced damage.

5.4.2.2 Findings and Related Plant Modifications

Some licensees noted that their fire protection system was designed in accordance with the guidelines of Category II/I in safety-related structures and areas (Regulatory Guide 1.29, "Seismic Design Criteria," Revision 3, September 1978, Regulatory Position C.2). This guideline states that wherever a Category II component (e.g., the non-safety-related fire protection system) is installed above a Category I component (i.e., safety-related), no failure mode of the Category II system or component is to adversely impact the Category I system or component. This includes seismic events. Thus, seismically induced failure of the fire protection system could fail the piping, but the failed piping would not adversely impact the performance of the safety-related structures, systems, or components. This includes the potential falling of the failed pipe and the potential release of water from the failed pipe.

Many licensees noted that some, or all, of their water-based fire protection systems required two diverse actions for initiation (pre-action type). One action would be for a smoke detector to open a supply valve in the fire protection system, while the second action is heat from the fire to melt the fusible link in the sprinkler head. For this type of system, the licensees concluded that inadvertent activation of the fire protection system by a seismic event or associated dust was not a problem.

Most licensees performed walkdowns as part of the verification of this generic issue. Typically, these walkdowns reviewed the spatial relationship between the fire protection system and safety-related components. This was particularly applicable to those licensees that had deluge fire protection systems. The safety-related components were reviewed to ensure that postulated failure of the fire protection system under seismic conditions would not adversely affect safety-related equipment from a falling component or from the water released from the fire protection system. The walkdowns also identified the presence of seals in the top of safety-related cabinets to prevent water intrusion and of area drains to remove excess water to prevent flooding. Most floor drainage systems were sized for flooding induced by pipe breaks. Generally, fire protection systems have lower flow rates and would be less likely to flood a compartment. However, some licensees have identified potential drain plugging issues and have revised or developed procedures to periodically inspect the drainage system to reduce the probability of plugging.

The impact of CO_2 or Halon protective system actuation was also reviewed as it relates to potential effects on personnel (e.g., control room operators) and equipment (e.g., operation of the diesel generators) in the area. Usually potential problems from these systems were dismissed as having an insignificant impact on plant safety or were beyond the scope of this generic issue. Data on the effects of smoke and fire suppressants on equipment are limited, and such effects were considered to be beyond the scope of the IPEEE program.

A few licensees discussed the potential effects of corrosion, buildup of soot, or other combustion products on equipment operability. Those that discussed this aspect stated that potential damage would occur over a much longer period of time than required to establish cold shutdown. Corrective maintenance would resolve any long-term problem that might be caused by these mechanisms. The majority of the submittals did not discuss the impact of combustion products on equipment operability or stated that there was insufficient information to address the issue.

A number of licensees stated that operators in their plants receive training on the use of the abnormal operating procedures for fire situations. Some of the licensees stated that training included live fire or live smoke conditions. Frequently, the licensees stated that timing records are kept for the fire brigade training exercises. Some licensees used this information to demonstrate that the manual fire-fighting times used in the IPEEE are conservative.

The licensees concluded that the impact of seismically induced activation of fire suppression systems, suppressant diversion, and adverse effects on safety-related components was negligibly small.

5.4.2.3 Observations

The information provided in the submittals is usually qualitative and provides little detail. Table 5.1 of Volume 2 of this report lists the plants and whether they addressed the two items in the generic issue. All but four of the plants have provided adequate information to verify this generic issue. One plant (LaSalle) provided no information, and three provided only partial information. Review of the submittals indicates that the licensees generally have an appreciation for the potential impacts of fire systems on safety-related components and systems.

5.4.3   GSI-103, "Design for Probable Maximum Precipitation"

5.4.3.1 Issue Description

The latest probable maximum precipitation (PMP) criteria published by the National Weather Service (NWS) of the National Oceanic and Atmospheric Administration (NOAA) may identify higher rainfall intensities over shorter time intervals and smaller areas than have previously been considered. This could result in higher site flooding levels and greater roof ponding loads than have been used in previous design bases. The IPEEE program includes an assessment of the effects of applying these new PMP criteria to each plant in terms of potential severe accident vulnerabilities associated with onsite flooding and roof ponding. To provide the revised PMP estimates, licensees typically used the information in the NOAA Hydrometeorological Report (HMR) 51, "Probable Maximum Precipitation Estimate, United States East of 105th Meridian," HMR 52, "Application of Probable Maximum Precipitation Estimates – United States East of the 105th Meridian," and HMR 53, "Seasonal Variation of 10-Square-Mile Probable Maximum Precipitation Estimates, United States East of the 105th Meridian."

5.4.3.2 Findings and Related Plant Modifications

Typically, licensees determinee the revised PMP rate and evaluated the ability of the roofs to withstand the new accumulation of water. Table 5.2 of Volume 2 of this report shows the PMP information provided in the submittals. Usually, the roofs can withstand the additional loads because the excess rainfall overflows the roof parapets. In some cases, licenses installed scuppers in the parapets to accommodate additional precipitation. In many situations, licensees credited roof drains for water removal. Such licensees frequently identified a new or existing procedure to periodically inspect the roof drainage system for potential blockage. In the unusual case that a structure was found to be unable to withstand the new loadings, the licensee evaluated the impact of roof failure and water intrusion into the building. No plant vulnerabilities related to this issue were identified in the IPEEE submittals.

Another PMP-related consideration involves its effect on nearby rivers and streams, and the resulting potential for failures of dams and levies. The submittals provided different levels of detail. Some submittals provided a short qualitative narrative. Other submittals provided significant detail. The latter showed that the licensee considered the entire drainage area into a river (or other body of water), and evaluated the impact of this increased water flow on site water levels and on dams and levies. Frequently, licensees consulted with other organizations (e.g., the U.S. Army Corps of Engineers). In some cases, licensees identified static water levels. However, in most cases where detailed information was provided, the licensees also considered wave runup and wind effects to determine the maximum water level at the site. The licensees then compared this water level to the flood protection elevation provided to safety-related structures, systems, and components. Table 5.2 of Volume 2 of this report shows the external flooding elevations and flood-protected elevations provided in the submittals. When licensees identified the potential for flooding of a structure, the licensee reviewed the potential effects of the flooding and either determined that the potential flooding would not adversely affect the plant, or made plant changes including installation of seals, procedures for timely plant shutdown, or procedures to prevent flooding (e.g., installation of sand bags around doorways). Table 5.3 of Volume 2 of this report lists the improvements identified in the submittal for each plant. In one case, the service water systems and a train of the fire protection system could be lost. In this case, the licensee identified actions that could be taken in a timely manner to prevent the total loss of service water.

The last PMP consideration relates to local intense PMP. This issue addresses the potential that site drainage might not adequately remove very intense local precipitation at the site. The licensee usually addressed this by reviewing site elevations and drainage capabilities. Either the resulting water level at the safety-related structures was bounded by the flood water elevation (most frequent finding) or the licensee evaluated the potential in-leakage. The licensee found that (1) this potential in-leakage would result in insignificant water accumulation; (2) it would result in significant water accumulation, but the water level would remain below the elevation of safety-related components; or (3) the potentially affected components would perform their intended function in a submerged condition (least frequent finding). Thus, all licensees concluded that local intense PMP was not a problem.

Most licensees included a confirmatory plant outdoor walkdown to identify building doors and penetrations that might be vulnerable to moisture intrusion. These walkdowns also involved examining of the roof drain systems and plant site drainage. Occasionally, these walkdowns identified weaknesses, and the licensee made some plant change. For example, recognizing the need for the roof drainage system to perform its intended function, one licensee instituted a surveillance procedure to periodically inspect the drains for obstructions.

5.4.3.3 Observations

All but three plants verified all aspects of GSI-103. As shown in Table 5.3, these three plants verified some, but not all, parts of this issue. Two plants neglected to address the issues of roof ponding and external flooding from the revised PMP-induced flooding, and one plant did not address site drainage.

Table 5.3: Unverified areas related to GSI-103

Plant	Revised PMP data	Roof ponding	Site drainage	External flooding*
LaSalle	Not Verified	Verified	Not Verified	Illinois River
Quad Cities 1 & 2	Not Verified	Verified	Not Verified	PMP
Sequoyah 1 & 2	Verified	Not Verified	Verified	Verified
* Source of external flooding that was not verified (i.e., from dam or pond failures) or river flooding as the result of the revised PMP				

One plant (Salem) installed new penetration seals between the service and auxiliary buildings. These new penetration seals significantly reduced the core damage frequency from external floods from approximately 1E-4/ry to 1E-7/ry.

For a few plants, the revised PMP is less than the design basis PMP; nonetheless, the overall conclusion is that the original design and construction of the plants included sufficient margin to allow variations of up to two to three times the original design basis PMP without adversely impacting safe operation of the plant.

5.4.4 GSI-131, "Potential Seismic Interaction Involving the Movable In-Core Flux Mapping System Used in Westinghouse Plants"

5.4.4.1 Issue Description

This issued was identified because portions of the in-core flux mapping (ICFM) system in Westinghouse plants are located directly above the seal table, and may not have been seismically analyzed. Failure of this equipment during a seismic event could potentially result in multiple failures at the seal table and could produce a small-break LOCA (SBLOCA) as a result of instrument tube failure(s). The potential interaction between the seal table and non-seismic Category I systems associated with the movable ICFM system can be identified during the seismic IPEEE walkdown. This issue may be dealt with in the following ways:

- demonstrate that the issue is not applicable to the site, or
- demonstrate that the restraints provide adequate capacity to withstand seismic forces, or
- document and implement administrative controls that preclude unrestrained mobile cart motion.

5.4.4.2 Findings and Related Plant Improvements

Licensees performed walkdowns to verify that previous modifications to their ICFM system were adequate, or to identify potential interactions between the seal table and the ICFM.

Table 2.13 of Volume 2 of this report summarizes the characteristics of the ICFM system for Westinghouse plants. It identifies previous upgrades for each plant and summarizes IPEEE findings and related plant improvements. The improvements ranged from procedures to restrain a chain from falling to installation of angle irons welded to the seal table to bolt the transfer table in place when not in use.

5.4.4.3 Observations

GSI-131 applies only to Westinghouse plants that have a movable ICFM system (see Table 2.13 of Volume 2). For 39 of the 69 plants, GSI-131 is not relevant. For 3 of the 30 Westinghouse plants (Kewaunee, Point Beach 1 and 2), the issue is only partially relevant due to an immobile configuration of the flux mapping cart. Of the 30 plants affected by this generic issue, 19 (~63%) had already verified the issue and completed the modifications that were needed to ensure the that Category II ICFM equipment would not adversely impact the Category I seal table. This was verified by walkdowns and reviewed by a seismic review team. Six plants did not identify any evaluation of this issue before the IPEEE. As part of the IPEEE review, these six plants determined that the as-found condition of the ICFM and seal table was adequate. Many of the plants made some modification to their procedures to provide increased assurance that the ICFM would be left in the appropriate configuration when it is not in use. Table 2.13 of Volume 2 of this report lists this information by individual plant.

In some cases, the licensees undertook a walkdown to verify the installation of a previous improvement as part of the seismic IPEEE. Some plants implemented hardware improvements related to GSI-131 by either replacing the flux mapping system cart hold down bolts or installing stiffener and anchor assemblies for the mapping carts. A few submittals (at least 13 of 30) indicated that the licensees evaluated the capability of the ICFM system for RLE loads. In one case (Kewaunee), the licensee implemented an administrative procedure to help eliminate the potential for an interaction hazard involving an overhead chain hoist. In another submittal (North Anna), the existing configuration of the moveable flux mapping system was found to be adequate, provided that operators reinstalled bolts connecting the cart frame to its supporting beams whenever the cart was moved into position above the seal table. Overall, all 30 plants for which this issue is applicable verified this generic issue.

5.4.5 GSI-147, "Fire-Induced Alternate Shutdown and Control Room Panel Interactions"

5.4.5.1 Issue Description

The issue of control systems interactions is primarily associated with the potential that a fire in the plant (e.g., in the main control room (MCR)) might lead to potential control system vulnerabilities. Given a fire in the plant, the likely control systems interactions are between the control room, the remote shutdown panel, and shutdown systems. The guidance for performing such an assessment is provided in NUREG/CR-5088, "Fire Risk Scoping Study." The following specific areas should be addressed in the IPEEE fire analysis.

- *Electrical independence of the remote shutdown control systems.* The primary concern for control systems interactions occurs at plants that do not provide independent, remote shutdown control systems. The licensees' processes to (a) verify electrical independence and (b) evaluate the level of indication and control of remote shutdown control and monitoring circuits should be reviewed.

- *Loss of control equipment or power before transfer.* The licensees' processes for evaluating the loss of control power for certain control circuits as a result of hot shorts or blown fuses before transferring control to remote shutdown locations should be assessed.

- *Spurious actuation of components leading to component damage, a loss-of-coolant accident (LOCA), or an interfacing systems LOCA.* The licensees' processes for evaluating the spurious actuation of one or more safety-related or safe shutdown-related components as a result of fire-induced cable faults, hot shorts, or component failures leading to component damage, LOCA, or interfacing system LOCAs before taking control from the remote shutdown panel should be assessed. This should also include assessment of the spurious starting and running of pumps, as well as the spurious repositioning of valves.

- *Total loss of system function.* The licensees' processes for evaluating total loss of system function as the result of fire-induced redundant component failure or electrical distribution system (power source) failure should be assessed.

5.4.5.2 Findings and Related Plant Modifications

All but four[4] of the licensees provided adequate information in their IPEEE submittals to verify GSI-147. Table 5.4 of Volume 2 of this report identifies the unique features at specific plants and the areas where adequate information was not provided to verify appropriate implementation of GSI-147.

Many plants relied, in part, on compliance with the requirements of Appendix R to 10 CFR Part 50, or the counterpart guidelines in NUREG-0800, "Standard Review Plan," Section 9.5.1, "Fire Protection Program," and related Branch Technical Positions. As part of the IPEEE review related to fire events and as part of the Sandia Fire Risk Scoping Study, the licensee verified that the plants have the ability to transfer adequate control from the control room to alternate locations to achieve plant safe shutdown conditions (i.e., the alternate location is electrically independent of the control room). The IPEEE submittals indicated that control of any errant equipment would be regained once control was transferred from the control room to the alternate shutdown locations. The licensees stated that no unrecoverable effects from errant equipment would be sustained until control was regained. Once the transfer is accomplished from the control room, the area with the fire is independent from the systems that would be used to control the plant, thereby precluding the total loss of system function for those systems. The Appendix R reviews considered spurious actuation of components, one at a time. As part of the fire IPEEE review, some licensees considered multiple hot shorts, including, in one case (Cooper), the concurrent, independent, spontaneous, and spurious hot short powering of each of the six automatic depressurization system valves. Spurious actuation reviews generally included power cables and signal (or instrumentation) cables. Generally, the potential loss of power to equipment was addressed by feeding the alternate shutdown equipment through a separate, independent breaker or fuse. This alternate feed line was engaged as the control was transferred from the control room.

---

[4] The four plants that did not provide sufficient information to verify GSI-147 are Hatch, North Anna, Palisades, and Seabrook. The first three plants provided adequate information for three of the four aspects of this issue described in Section 5.4.5.2. The fourth plant, Seabrook, only mentioned in the submittal that control systems interactions were treated in the fire area screening and detailed plant response evaluation. However, the submittal did not address any of the four specific areas. Although the staff could not conclude that this issue was verified for Seabrook, the licensee did perform a quality fire analysis and analyzed control room fire scenarios in detail. Overall, the staff felt that the licensee's IPEEE process was capable of identifying the most likely severe accidents and severe accident vulnerabilities and, therefore, the Seabrook IPEEE met the intent of the IPEEE program. However, the staff's SER noted a weakness in the IPEEE in that GSI-147 was not considered verified for that plant.

Only one plant (Surry) identified any plant modifications specifically related to this issue. In this case, Surry modified some circuits to ensure that the diesel generators and the alternate shutdown panel could be isolated from the control room and to reduce the likelihood of spurious power operated relief valve actuations.

5.4.5.3 Observations

The information in the IPEEE submittals provided a wide range of information on this topic. Some submittals provided sparse information (e.g., "generally immune to the effects of control system interactions" and using the FIVE guidance), while other submittals provided very specific information (e.g., being necessary to perform one or more actions at 14 alternate shutdown panels). The plants' capabilities also varied from having a black-start combustion turbine generator set with dedicated components to plants that use one electrical division of the normal plant equipment with power and control isolation from the control room. Most plants with safe shutdown facilities[5] also require or preferentially desire some operator action(s) or equipment operation outside of the safe shutdown facility in the event of control room abandonment. The effectiveness of the previous work associated with Appendix R (and its counterpart in the Standard Review Plan) is evidenced by only one plant finding the need to make a plant modification related to its alternate shutdown capability. Overall, the staff found that 94% of all plants provided adequate information to verify this generic issue.

It should be noted that the IPEEE program was not intended to enhance or go beyond the current state-of-the-art. This includes potential electric circuit interactions as the result of postulated fires. For the most part, licensees satisfactorily performed the review of their plants in accordance with the guidance in the generic issue and the state of circuit interaction knowledge at the time of the IPEEE submittals. Recently, the NRC and industry initiated further investigations to determine the likelihood of the different potential fire-induced cable failure modes (circuit interactions). This ongoing investigation is aimed at providing an improved basis for the treatment of circuit interactions and indicates that there is a potential for additional cable interactions that may need to be considered that are beyond those evaluated as part of this generic issue and the IPEEE program. However, this investigation is not complete at this time. Therefore, with the possible exception of the four plants mentioned above, the staff considers GSI-147 to be verified, while recognizing that, at some future date, some related further consideration may be necessary.

5.4.6   GSI 148, "Smoke Control and Manual Fire-Fighting Effectiveness"

5.4.6.1 Issue Description

Smoke control and manual fire-fighting effectiveness are associated with the concern that a potential exists for the buildup of smoke to hamper the efforts of the fire brigade to extinguish fires in a timely manner before damage can occur to plant systems and components important to safety. (It should be recognized that the brigade response time is not equal to the extinguishment time.) Any risk-significant fire will generate significant amounts of smoke. Smoke can impact plant risk in several ways.

---

[5] A safe shutdown facility is an independent, dedicated method of providing safe shutdown. Typically, safe shutdown facilities include an independent, dedicated, black-start power source, pump(s), water supply, and instrumentation and controls that are located outside of the normal plant facility buildings. Generally, only piping, isolation valves, and level instrumentation are located within normal plant facility buildings and are used by the safe shutdown facility.

- Smoke can reduce manual fire-fighting effectiveness (e.g., by causing access problems to the affected fire zone or by causing difficulties in actually locating the fire within the zone), cause misdirected suppression efforts, and subsequently damage equipment that is not directly involved in the fire.

- Smoke can damage or degrade electronic equipment thereby resulting in functional loss or spurious response. However, very little experimental data is available with regard to equipment response in smoke environments and the methodology for including smoke in PRAs has not been adequately developed. Hence, the IPEEE analysis was not expected to provide an assessment of the effect of smoke on equipment.

- Smoke can hamper an operator's ability to safely shutdown the plant by causing evacuation of control centers and subsequent reliance on alternate shutdown capability.

- Smoke can initiate automatic fire protection systems in areas away from the fire, thereby potentially damaging safety-related systems or components. This aspect is separately addressed in GSI-57, "Effects of Fire Protection System Actuation on Safety-Related Equipment" (see Section 5.4.2).

5.4.6.2 Findings and Related Plant Modifications

Of the IPEEE submittals, only 19 credited manual fire-fighting actions. In addition, 25 submittals identified manual fire-fighting for only select areas (e.g., the control room) or select accident scenarios. Normally, not crediting manual fire-fighting is a conservative approach to the assessment of fire growth and direct fire damage timing issues because this assumes that all equipment within a fire zone is destroyed. Usually, those submittals that credited manual fire-fighting also considered the following:

- delays in manual actuation of suppression systems (e.g., while verifying the existence of a fire),
- delays in locating the fire, once the fire brigade has arrived,
- time required to extinguish or substantially control a fire, once fire-fighting has begun, and
- fire brigade training.

Two of the submittals that credited manual fire-fighting actions did not discuss fire brigade training, fire-fighting equipment, or timing.

Although not taking credit for manual fire-fighting actions in the licensee's analysis is conservative from a PRA standpoint, submittals that did not credit manual fire-fighting actions may not have considered the following potential effects of manual suppression:

- potential damaging effects of misdirected fire suppressants (e.g., to adjacent safety-related equipment), and
- barriers breeched by fire-fighting personnel (e.g., leading to the spread of smoke, fire, or both to adjacent fire areas).

Not considering the potential effects of misdirected suppression was deemed to be a shortcoming in the IPEEE submittals that took some credit for manual fire-fighting. Not considering the potential adverse effects of breaching fire barriers was also deemed to be a weakness. However, even in cases for which the licensees took no credit in the IPEEEs for manual fire-fighting the submittals provides information related to fire

5 - 17

brigade training, drills, record keeping, and timing, consistent with the guidance in EPRI's FIVE methodology. In some cases, the information was very detailed. Several submittals identified that training exercises were carried out under live fire or live smoke conditions. In one case (Grand Gulf), the licensee simulated the actual plant configuration for the fire exercise with live fire and changed the configuration for each drill. Another submittal (Salem) identified that there is a dedicated fire department for the plant.

Some licensees discussed the potential for the effects of fire to adversely affect equipment that is not directly involved with the fire. This includes potential effects (corrosion or buildup of soot and/or other combustion products) that occur over a much longer period of time than that required to establish cold shutdown. In such cases, the submittal identified that corrective maintenance would resolve any induced equipment problem. The remaining submittals did not discuss the impact of combustion products on equipment operability. Some submittals (e.g., Browns Ferry and Farley) limited their discussion of mitigating the effects of smoke to the use of self-contained breathing apparatus and portable ventilation equipment. Two submittals (Grand Gulf and Waterford 3) specifically identified that fire brigade members were educated on the toxic and corrosive characteristics of combustion products. It should be noted, however, that there is little information about this topic in the currently available literature.

The IPEEE submittals did not identify any plant modifications or procedural changes associated with this generic issue. Table 5.5 of Volume 2 of this report provides plant-specific information found in the SERs and TERs related to this generic safety issue.

5.4.6.3 Observations

Manual fire-fighting activities were credited in 19 submittals, were credited for only select fire areas or fire scenarios in 25 submittals, and were explicitly not credited in 13 submittals. This generic issue was verified for 49 plants (71%), partially verified for 17 plants (25%), and not verified for 3 plants (4%).

5.4.7   GSI-156, "Systematic Evaluation Program"

5.4.7.1 Issue Description

The Systematic Evaluation Program (SEP) was developed to review plants that were licensed before the 1975 edition of the Standard Review Plan (SRP) was issued (i.e., were licensed without explicitly addressing the information in the 1975 SRP). Of the 70 submittals, 31 are for plants that are in the SEP program. (The remaining 29 submittals are for plants that are not in the SEP program.) Nine SEP issues were reviewed as part of the IPEEE program. Each of these issues is discussed in the following sections.

5.4.7.1.1 Site Hydrology and Ability to Withstand Floods

The objective of this issue is to identify the site hydrologic characteristics to ensure the capability of safety-related structures to withstand flooding, to ensure adequate cooling water supply, and in-service inspection of water-control structures. This issue involves assessing the following:

- hydrologic conditions - to ensure that plant design reflects appropriate hydrologic conditions,
- flooding potential and protection - to ensure that the plant is adequately protected against floods, and
- ultimate heat sink - to ensure an appropriate supply of cooling water during normal and emergency shutdown conditions.

Issues related to in-service inspection of water-control structures constitue compliance issues that are not part of the IPEEE program.

5.4.7.1.2 Industrial Hazards

The objective of this issue is to ensure that the integrity of safety-related structures, systems, and components would not be jeopardized as a result of accident hazards from nearby facilities. Such hazards include shock waves from nearby explosions, releases of hazardous gases, or chemicals that result in fires or explosions, aircraft impacts, and missiles resulting from nearby explosions.

5.4.7.1.3 Tornado Missiles

The objective of this issue is to ensure that plants that were constructed before 1972 (SEP plants) are adequately protected against tornadoes. Safety-related structures, systems, and components need to be able to withstand the impact of an appropriate spectrum of postulated tornado-generated missiles.

5.4.7.1.4 Severe Weather Effects on Structures

The objective of this issue is to ensure that safety-related structures, systems, and components are designed to function under all severe weather conditions to which they may be exposed. Meteorological phenomena to be considered include straight wind loads, tornadoes, snow and ice loads, and other phenomena that are deemed to be significant for a particular site.

5.4.7.1.5 Design Codes, Criteria, and Load Combinations

The objective of this issue is to ensure that structures that are important to safety should be designed, fabricated, erected, and tested to quality standards that are commensurate with their safety function. All structures that are classified as Seismic Category I are required to withstand the appropriate design conditions without impairment of structural integrity or reduction in the performance of the required safety functions. Due to the evolutionary nature of design codes and standards, operating plants may have been designed to codes and criteria that differ from those that are currently used in evaluating new plants. Therefore, the review is to ensure that Category I structures will withstand the appropriate design conditions (i.e., against seismic events, high winds, and floods) without impairment of structural integrity or reduction in the performance of required safety functions.

5.4.7.1.6 Dam Integrity and Site Flooding

The objective of this issue is to ensure the ability of a dam to prevent site flooding and ensure a cooling water supply. The safety functions normally include remaining stable under all conditions of reservoir operation, controlling seepage to prevent excessive uplifting water pressures or erosion of soil materials, and providing sufficient freeboard and outlet capacity to prevent overtopping. Therefore, the review is to ensure that adequate safety margins are available under all loading conditions, and uncontrolled releases of retained water are prevented.

The seismic portion of the IPEEE address the concern regarding site flooding resulting from seismic failure of an upstream dam and loss of the ultimate heat sink caused by the seismically induced failure of a downstream dam.

5.4.7.1.7 Settlement of Foundations and Buried Equipment

The objective of this SEP issue is to ensure that safety-related structures, systems, and components are adequately protected against excessive settlement. The scope of this issue includes reviewing subsurface materials and foundations in order to assess the potential static and seismically induced settlement of all safety-related structures and buried equipment. Excessive settlement or collapse of foundations could result in failures of structures, interconnecting piping, or control systems, such that the capability to safely shut down the plant or mitigate the consequences of an accident could be compromised. This issue, which primarily applies to soil sites, involves two specific concerns, namely the (1) potential impact of static settlements of foundations and buried equipment where the soil might not have been properly prepared, and (2) potential seismically induced settlement and soil liquefaction following a postulated seismic event. The potential impact of static settlements of foundations and buried equipment is not believed to pose any significant safety concern and is not included in the IPEEE program.

5.4.7.1.8 Seismic Design of the Structures, Systems, and Components

The objective of this SEP issue is to review and evaluate the original seismic design of safety-related structures, systems, and components, to ensure the capability of the plant to withstand the effects of a safe shutdown earthquake (SSE).

5.4.7.1.9 Shutdown Systems and Electrical Instrumentation and Control Features

With regard to shutdown systems, this issue addresses the capacity of plants to ensure reliable shutdown using safety-grade equipment. The electrical instrumentation and control issue addresses the functional capabilities of electrical instrumentation and control features of systems that are required for safe shutdown, including support systems. These systems should be designed, fabricated, installed, and tested to quality standards and remain functional following external events.

In the IPEEE, licensees were requested to address USI A-45, "Shutdown Decay Heat Removal (DHR) Requirements" (refer to Section 5.4.1 of this report), and to identify potential vulnerabilities associated with DHR systems following the occurrence of external events. The verification of USI A-45 addresses this SEP issue.

5.4.7.2 Findings and Related Plant Improvements

As shown in Table 5.6 of Volume 2 of this report, all of the SEP plants have provided sufficient information in their IPEEE submittals to verify all of the GSI-156 issues. The IPEEE submittals did not explicitly identify any plant modifications or improvements related to this generic safety issue. However, some plants made modifications related to HFO external events (e.g., for protection from tornado-generated missiles and floods) that overlap some of the SEP areas.

By virtue of the licensees having an acceptable IPEEE with regard to external flooding, the site-specific sub-issues related to site hydrology and ability to withstand floods, severe weather effects on structures (water related), and dam integrity and site flooding have been satisfactorily verified. By virtue of the licensees having an acceptable IPEEE with regard to seismic events, the sub-issues related to design codes, criteria, and load combinations; settlement of foundations and buried equipment; and seismic design of structures, systems, and components have been satisfactorily verified. By virtue of the licensee having an acceptable IPEEE with regard to HFO events, the site-specific sub-issues related to industrial hazards, tornado-generated missiles, and severe weather effects on structures (wind related) have been satisfactorily verified. By virtue of the licensee having an acceptable IPEEE with regard to USI A-45, "Shutdown Decay Heat Removal Requirements," the sub-issue related to shutdown systems and electrical instrumentation and control functions has been satisfactorily verified.

5.4.7.3 Observations

Even though the SEP issues were not explicitly identified in Generic Letter 88-20 or NUREG-1407, the NRC has determined that licensees for all of the 31 SEP plants performed an adequate assessment to identify vulnerabilities related to the 9 SEP issues discussed above, and these issues are considered verified.

5.4.8 GSI-172, "Multiple System Response Program"

5.4.8.1 Issue Description

GSI-172, "Multiple System Response Program" (MSRP), addresses concerns raised by the Advisory Committee on Reactor Safeguards (ACRS) regarding safety issues that might exist and might not be addressed by the NRC's existing generic safety issues. Each of the 11 MSRP issues reviewed as part of the IPEEE program are discussed in the following sections.

5.4.8.1.1 Effects of Fire Suppression System Actuation on Non-Safety-Related and Safety-Related Equipment

Fire suppression system actuation can have an adverse effect on safety-related components either through direct contact with suppression agents or through indirect interaction with non-safety-related components. This issue is addressed by the verification of GSI-57, which is discussed in Section 5.4.2 of this report.

5.4.8.1.2 Seismically Induced Fire Suppression System Actuation

Seismic events can potentially cause multiple fire suppression system actuations which, in turn, may cause failures of redundant trains of safety-related systems. Analyses currently required by fire protection regulations generally only examine inadvertent actuations of fire suppression systems as a single, independent event, whereas a seismic event could cause multiple actuations of fire suppression systems in various areas of the plant. This issue is addressed by the verification of GSI-57, which is discussed in Section 5.4.2 of this report.

5.4.8.1.3 Seismically Induced Fires

Seismically induced fires have the potential to cause multiple failures of safety-related systems. The occurrence of a seismic event could create fires in multiple locations, thereby simultaneously degrading fire suppression capability and, therefore, preventing mitigation of fire damage to multiple safety-related systems. This issue is addressed by the verification of the Fire Risk Scoping Study (FRSS) issue entitled "Seismic-Fire Interactions," discussed in Section 5.4.9.1.1 of this report.

5.4.8.1.4 Effects of Hydrogen Line Ruptures

Nuclear power plans use hydrogen in electrical generators to reduce windage losses and as a heat transfer agent. Hydrogen is also used as a cover gas in some tanks (e.g., volume control tanks). Leaks or breaks in hydrogen supply piping could result in the accumulation of a combustible mixture of air and hydrogen in vital areas, resulting in a fire and/or explosion that could damage vital safety-related systems in the plants.

5.4.8.1.5 Non-Safety-Related Control System/Safety-Related Protection System Dependencies

Multiple failures in non-safety-related control systems may adversely impact safety-related protection systems as a result of potential unrecognized dependencies between control and protection systems. The concern is that plant-specific implementation of the regulations regarding separation and independence of control and protection systems may be inadequate. The licensees' IPE process should provide a framework for systematic evaluation of interdependencies between safety-related and non-safety-related systems and identify potential sources of vulnerabilities. The dependencies between safety-related and non-safety-related systems resulting from external events (i.e., concerns related to spatial/functional interactions) are addressed in GSI-147 (Section 5.4.5), the fire risk scoping study (Section 5.4.9.1.5), and the MSRP issue on seismically induced spatial and functional interactions (Section 5.4.8.1.7 of this report).

5.4.8.1.6 Effects of Flooding and/or Moisture Intrusion on Non-Safety-Related and Safety-Related Equipment

Flooding and water intrusion events can affect safety-related equipment either directly or indirectly through flooding or moisture intrusion of multiple trains of non-safety-related equipment. This type of event can result from external flooding events, tank and pipe ruptures, actuation of fire suppression systems, or backflow through part of the plant drainage system. The IPE process addressed the concerns of moisture intrusion and internal flooding (i.e., tank and pipe ruptures or backflow through part of the plant drainage system). The IPEEE program addressed the external flooding-related aspects of this issue (discussed in Section 4.3 of this report) and the potential effects of actuation of the fire suppression system on safety-related equipment (see Section 5.4.2).

5.4.8.1.7 Seismically Induced Spatial/Functional Interactions

Seismic events have the potential to cause multiple failures of safety-related systems through spatial and functional interactions. Some particular sources of concern include ruptures in small piping that may disable essential plant shutdown systems; direct impact of non-seismically qualified structures, systems, and components that may cause small piping failures; seismic functional interactions of control and safety-related protection systems via multiple non-safety-related control system failures; and indirect impacts, such as dust generation, that disable essential plant shutdown systems.

5.4.8.1.8 Seismically Induced Flooding

Seismically induced flooding events can potentially cause multiple failures of safety-related systems. The rupture of small piping could provide flood sources that could potentially affect multiple safety-related components simultaneously. Similarly, non-seismically qualified tanks are a potential flood source of concern.

5.4.8.1.9 Seismically Induced Relay Chatter

Essential relays must operate during and after an earthquake, and must meet one of the following conditions:

- remain functional (i.e., without occurrence of contact chattering),
- be seismically qualified, or
- be chatter acceptable.

It is possible that contact chatter of relays not required to operate during seismic events may produce some unanalyzed faulting mode that may affect the operability of equipment required to mitigate the event. These would be defined as "low-ruggedness" or "bad actor" relays.

5.4.8.1.10 IPEEE-Related Aspects of Common Cause Failures Related to Human Errors

Common cause failures resulting from human errors include operator acts of commission or omission that could be initiating events or could affect redundant safety-related trains needed to mitigate the events. Other human errors that could initiate common cause failures include manufacturing errors in components that affect redundant trains, and installation, maintenance, or testing errors that are repeated on redundant trains. In the IPEEE, licensees were requested to address only the human errors involving operator recovery actions following the occurrence of external events.

5.4.8.1.11 Evaluation of Earthquake Magnitudes Greater Than Safe Shutdown Earthquake

This issue was identified to address concerns that adequate margin may not have been included in the design of some safety-related equipment. As part of the IPEEE, all licensees were expected to identify potential seismic vulnerabilities or assess the seismic capacities of their plants by performing either a seismic PRA or a seismic margins assessment (SMA). The licensees' evaluation for potential vulnerabilities (or unusually low plant seismic capacity) to seismic events addresses this issue.

5.4.8.2 Findings and Related Plant Improvements

Of the 69 submittals, 56 provided sufficient information to adequately verify all 11 MSRP sub-issues. The remaining 13 IPEEE submittals did not provide adequate information to verify one or more of these MSRP issues. Of those 13 submittals, 5 contained information to only partially verify one or more of these issues. Table 5.4 identifies which portion(s) remain(s) unverified for these five plants. Figure 5.1 shows the distribution of unverified or partially unverified sub-issues by plant. As this figure shows, most plants (56) have verified all of the GSI-172 issues. This figure also shows that only one plant (LaSalle) did not provide adequate information to verify 7 of the 11 issues, and one plant (St. Lucie) had 5 issues that remain unverified. Figure 5.2 shows the distribution of unverified or partially unverified sub-issues by sub-issue. As this figure shows, the most frequent unverified issue deals with human error-induced common cause failures related to external event initiators (approximately 10% of the plants). The next two most frequent unverified issues relate to evaluation of seismically induced flooding and potential hydrogen line ruptures (each approximately 7% of the plants).

None of the submittals explicitly identified that any plant modifications or improvements were directly related to the MSRP issues. However, improvements made in conjunction with other external events (e.g., flooding) would also produce a benefit relative to the MSRP issues.

Table 5.4: Partially verified GSI-172 sub-issues by plant

Plant	Aspect verified	Aspect not verified
Hatch 1 & 2	Seismically induced fires for SSEL electrical cabinets	Seismically induced fires for non-SSEL electrical cabinets
	Hydrogen tank ruptures	Hydrogen line ruptures
	Safety/non-safety system interactions	Hot shorts
LaSalle	Effects of flooding on equipment	Effects of moisture intrusion on equipment
Limerick 1 & 2	Flooding from all external sources	Seismically induced internal flooding
	Common cause human factors related to fire events	Common cause human factors related to seismic events
North Anna	Common cause human factors related to fire events	Common cause human factors related to seismic events
Seabrook	Seismically induced fires from equipment interactions	Seismically induced fires from electrical cabinet interactions
	Hydrogen tank ruptures	Hydrogen line ruptures

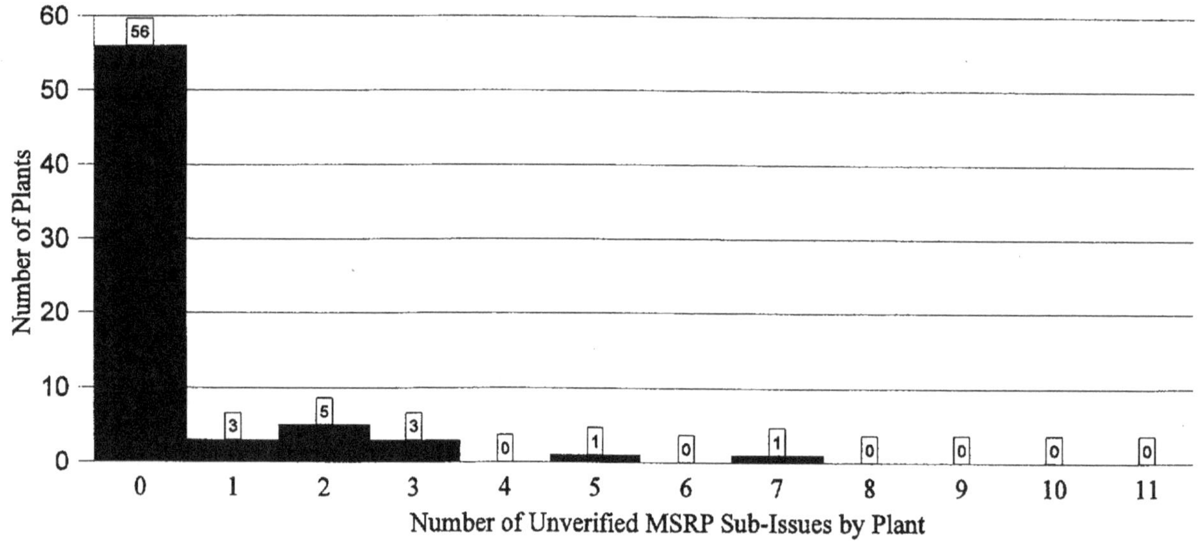

Figure 5.1 Number of unverified GSI-172 issues by plant

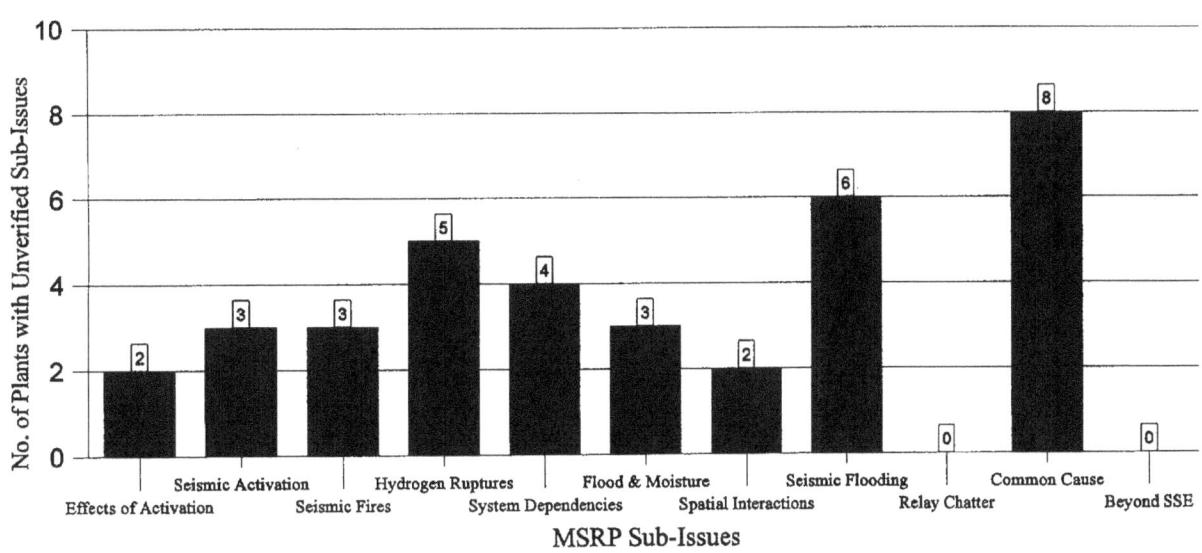

Figure 5.2 Number of unverified GSI-172 issues by issue

5.4.8.2.1 Effects of Fire Suppression System Actuation on Non-Safety-Related and Safety-Related Equipment

All of the IPEEE submittals reported that the licensee had qualitatively examined issues related to inadvertent fire suppression system actuation. To varying degrees, such examinations included the potential for, and effects of, inadvertent fire suppression systems actuation.

In most of the submittals, licensees included considerations related to inadvertent fire suppression system actuation within the scope of their overall seismic walkdown. The most consistent strong points of these evaluations appear to be the treatment of inadvertent fire suppression systems actuation and the identification of concerns regarding potential interaction with safety equipment. However, the level of effort, scope, and detail varied significantly among the IPEEE submittals. Two submittals (LaSalle and St. Lucie) did not include any evaluation. In most other cases, licensees limited their evaluations exclusively to assessing direct impacts on safe shutdown equipment or safety-related equipment.

Many of the submittals did not consider the potential effects of inadvertent fire suppression system actuation on non-safety-related equipment. Most considered non-safety-related equipment to be unnecessary for safe shutdown, or stated that the equipment and floor drains would be adequate to prevent unacceptable internal flooding. See Section 5.4.2 on GSI-57, "Effects of Fire Protection System Actuation on Safety-Related Equipment," for additional discussion related to this issue.

5.4.8.2.2 Seismically Induced Fire Suppression System Actuation

All of the IPEEE submittals reported that the licensees qualitatively examined issues related to seismically induced fire suppression system actuation. To varying degrees, such examinations included the potential and effects of seismically initiated actuation and degradation of fire suppression systems.

In most of the submittals, licensees included considerations related to seismically induced fire suppression system actuation within the scope of their overall seismic walkdown. The most consistent strong point of these evaluations appears to be the treatment of inadvertent actuation of the fire suppression system. However, the level of effort, scope, and detail directed toward addressing issues related to seismically induced fire suppression system actuation varied significantly among the IPEEE submittals. Three submittals (North Anna, St. Lucie, and Turkey Point) did not include any evaluation. In most other cases, licensees limited their evaluations exclusively to assessing direct impacts on safe shutdown equipment.

Many of the submittals did not include a consideration of the potential for seismically induced loss of fire suppression systems. In the remaining cases, some licensees sought to include all relevant plant areas and equipment in their evaluations. Such relevant items include, for instance, fire suppression system components and non-safety-related piping and tanks, which may not be part of the seismic plant model or safe-shutdown equipment list, but may nonetheless be important or may have indirect effects on safety-related equipment.

In a number of the IPEEE submittals, the evaluation of seismically induced fire suppression system actuation resulted in plant improvements. Some of the relevant improvements included strengthening component anchorages, replacing vulnerable (e.g., mercury) relays and switches, and implementing procedures to properly secure transient fire-protection equipment.

For additional information, refer to the discussion on GSI-57, "Effects of Fire Protection System Actuation on Safety-Related Equipment," in Section 5.4.2.

5.4.8.2.3 Seismically Induced Fires

All of the IPEEE submittals reported that the licensees qualitatively examined seismically induced fire interaction issues as part of the treatment of Sandia fire risk scoping study issues. A few licensees performed a PRA study for seismically induced fire-initiating events; albeit the level of detail varied from a simplistic probabilistic analysis to inclusion in their plant's seismic or fire PRA.

In most of the submittals, licensees included seismically induced fire considerations within the scope of their overall seismic walkdown. The level of effort, scope, and detail directed toward addressing seismically induced fire issues varied significantly among the IPEEE submittals. One licensee (LaSalle) did not discuss seismically induced fire evaluations in their IPEEE submittal. In most other cases, licensees limited their seismically induced fire evaluations exclusively to assessing direct impacts on safe shutdown equipment.

Some licensees sought to include all relevant plant areas and equipment in their evaluations of the potential and effects of seismically induced fire events. Such relevant items include, for example, non-safety-related piping and tanks containing flammable materials, which may not be part of the seismic plant model or safe shutdown equipment list, but may have indirect effects on safety-related equipment.

In some of the IPEEE submittals, the evaluations of the seismically induced fire interaction resulted in plant improvements. An example of the relevant improvements is the installation of restraints for gas cylinders.

5.4.8.2.4 Effects of Hydrogen Line Ruptures

All but 5 of the 69 submittals provided sufficient information to verify this MSRP issue. Of these five submittals, two (Hatch and Seabrook) addressed the potential effects of hydrogen tank ruptures, but did not discuss the potential for hydrogen line ruptures. The other three submittals did not specifically discuss the potential failure of hydrogen lines or tanks. The other licensees considered the potential effects of ruptures of hydrogen lines and tanks. These licensees found that the potential rupture of either hydrogen lines or tanks did not significantly contribute to the core damage frequency and, thus, this aspect was considered verified. Licensees typically addressed this issue by performing plant walkdowns following EPRI's FIVE methodology. FIVE calls for licensees to "identify any flammable liquid or gas storage vessel or piping (e.g., hydrogen) and whether these vessels are subject to leakage under seismic conditions."

5.4.8.2.5 Non-Safety-Related Control System/Safety-Related Protection System Dependencies

The dependencies between non-safety-related control systems and safety-related protection systems resulting from external events are related to GSI-147, "Fire-Induced Alternate Shutdown/Control Room Panel Interactions," and the MSRP issue on seismically induced spatial and functional interactions. Generally, licensees took the position that since safe shutdown could be achieved either from the main control room or the alternate shutdown panel(s) using only safety-related equipment, any failure or failures of non-safety-related equipment would not inhibit achieving safe shutdown conditions. All but four submittals provided sufficient information to verify this issue. Licensees provided different levels of detail. Of the four submittals that did not provide adequate information to verify this issue, three did not provide any discussion related to this issue, and one did not address the hot short aspect of this issue. See Sections 5.4.5 and 5.4.8.2.7 for additional discussion related to this issue.

5.4.8.2.6 Effects of Flooding and/or Moisture Intrusion on Non-Safety-Related and Safety-Related Equipment

Frequently, the discussion of this issue in the IPEEE submittals related to the ability to adequately protect safety-related equipment from external flooding. External flooding is covered by the licensees' HFO analyses (see Section 4.3). A satisfactory HFO evaluation verifies the flooding aspect of this issue.

The other aspect of this issue relates to moisture intrusion into equipment. All but three submittals provided adequate information for the staff to conclude that this aspect of this issue was verified. Generally, this information related to the licensees having adequately addressed the potential effects of seismically induced failure or actuation of the fire protection system and the potential effects of misdirected spray from manual fire-fighting activities, since these are the two main sources of water for potential moisture intrusion into equipment. See Section 5.4.2 for additional discussion.

5.4.8.2.7 Seismically Induced Spatial-Functional Interactions

All but two of the IPEEE submittals provided sufficient information on the licensees' examinations related to seismic spatial-functional interaction issues. In most of the submittals, licensees considered seismic spatial-functional interaction within the scope of their overall seismic walkdown (see Chapter 2). However, the level of effort, scope, and detail directed toward addressing seismic spatial-functional interaction issues varied significantly among the IPEEE submittals. In most cases, licensees limited their evaluations of seismic spatial-functional interactions exclusively to assessing the direct impacts on safe shutdown equipment.

In some of the IPEEE submittals, the evaluations of seismic spatial-functional evaluations resulted in plant improvements. Some of the relevant improvements included strengthening component anchorages, anchoring cabinets together, and implementing procedures to properly secure transient fire-protection equipment. In one instance, the licensee evaluated the potential for seismically induced toxic chemical release as part of its seismic interactions walkdown. As a result, the licensee identified a plant-specific improvement related to strengthening the anchorage of an ammonia storage tank.

5.4.8.2.8 Seismically Induced Flooding

Some licensees undertook quantitative assessments of components' seismic capacities related to seismically induced flooding interactions. A few licensees performed a PRA study for seismically induced flooding events, albeit the level of detail varied from simplistic probabilistic analysis to inclusion in their plant's seismic PRA.

In most of the submittals, licensees included seismically induced flooding considerations within the scope of their overall seismic walkdown. However, the level of effort, scope, and detail directed toward addressing seismically induced flooding issues varied significantly among the IPEEE submittals. All but six of the licensees provided adequate information to verify this issue. Of the remaining six submittals, five did not provide any discussion of evaluations related to seismically induced flooding in their IPEEE submittal, and one licensee did not provide adequate information to completely verify this issue. In most other cases, licensees limited their seismically induced flooding evaluations exclusively to assessing direct impacts on safe shutdown equipment.

Some licensees sought to include all relevant plant areas and equipment in their evaluations of the potential for and effects of seismically induced flooding events. Such relevant items include, for example, non-safety-related piping and tanks that may not be part of the seismic plant model or safe-shutdown equipment list, but may nonetheless be important or may have indirect effects on safety equipment.

In some of the IPEEE submittals, the evaluations of seismically induced flood interaction resulted in plant improvements. Some of the relevant improvements include adding seals to waterproof electrical cabinets and implementing enhanced drain inspection procedures. Evaluations of external flooding (see Chapter 4) also addressed this sub-issue.

5.4.8.2.9 Seismically Induced Relay Chatter

All of the submittals provided adequate information to verify this issue. In a few plants, low-ruggedness relays have been encountered in the circuits involving only IPEEE success paths (i.e., IPEEE equipment that was not redundant to USI A-46). Of the 27 licensees that performed a seismic PRA (SPRA) as part of their IPEEE, 14 included relays in the PRA models. Others performed separate evaluations to determine the ruggedness of relays. When relays are explicitly modeled in the PRA, the effect of low-ruggedness relay chatter on accident sequences is clearly identified and quantified. Most of SPRAs did not credit recovery actions in their logic model.

When licensees encountered low-ruggedness relays, they often existed only in alarm circuitry, were assessed as having negligible consequences, or the licensees assumed that operator actions would provide for effective reset. In only limited instances, licensees actually proposed replacing relays specifically on the basis of the analysis for the IPEEE. For additional information, see Section 2.3.1.4.

5.4.8.2.10 IPEEE-Related Aspects of Common Cause Failures Related to Human Errors

All of the 69 IPEEE submittals (which excludes Haddam Neck) provided some treatment or discussion of non-seismic failures and human actions. Of the 69 submittals, 61 provided adequate information to verify this issue, 2 provided adequate information to partially verify this issue, and 6 did not provide adequate information to verify this issue.

For seismic PRAs, operator actions were introduced in seismic event-tree and fault-tree models, which generally reflect the logic used in the plant's internal events PRA. However, the seismic impacts on operator error rates were modeled in a highly variable fashion. In some instances, licensees developed simplified operator error fragilities. In other instances, licensees applied judgemental scaling factors (in relation to the importance of the human action) on internal event error rates, or other means to account for seismically related performance shaping factors.

With regard to the treatment of human actions in IPEEEs that used a seismic margin assessment (SMA), the staff's reviews found that the submittals typically provided only limited discussion of the impact of seismic events on operator error rates. Generally, the SMA IPEEE submittals took the approach of relying on those success paths that are most familiar to plant operators and that use the most reliable equipment. In one SMA, the licensee applied quantitative screening criteria with respect to random failure rates and human error rates. Licensees have generally reported the timing and locations of required human actions, and have commented qualitatively on their reliability.

The approaches varied for quantification of the post-accident human actions retained from the IPEs. A few licensees used the existing IPE HEPs without making any adjustments to reflect the potential impact of fire conditions. These submittals did not address the potential that at least one operator may not be available as the result of fire brigade responsibilities, the fire may result in spurious signals and alarms that would provide confusing information to the operator, or the fire and the presence of even small amounts of smoke might have negative psychological effects on some operators and other plant staff who are needed to respond to the event. Regardless of their approach, few submittals considered these factors in determining HEPs.

Some licensees simply applied a performance shaping factor (PSF) of, for example 5 or 10, as a multiplier on all the existing IPE HEPs to reflect potential influences (e.g., increased stress) that a fire might create for the operators. Some licensees examined each human action and used expert judgement to decide whether a multiplier (or a simple increase in the value) should be applied to reflect fire conditions. Others assigned "conservative" screening values (generally around 0.1, but ranging to 1.0 for events that might be directly influenced by the fire) with the idea of doing a more detailed evaluation, if needed. Finally, some licensees re-evaluated all of the existing HEPs and re-quantified them to more precisely model the potential effects of the fire on human performance.

The licensees' submittals considered human action failure events. In many cases, licensees identified the human actions that were most important to CDF (or CDF reduction), and considered the potential impact of fire effects on those reliability estimates. For more discussion, see Section 3.4.8.

5.4.8.2.11 Evaluation of Earthquake Magnitudes Greater than Safe Shutdown Earthquake

This issue is verified by licensees providing an acceptable seismic IPEEE. The specific seismic review-level earthquake varies, depending on the plants' location and the IPEEE review level identified in NUREG-1407 (see Chapter 2 for details of the seismic submittals). All submittals provided adequate information to verify this issue.

5.4.8.3 Observations

Even though these MSRP issues were not explicitly identified in either Generic Letter 88-20 or NUREG-1407, a large majority of the licensees (approximately 80%) provided sufficient information in their IPEEE submittals to verify all 11 MSRP sub-issues. Only one plant (LaSalle) had seven unverified MSRP issues. Table 5.7 of Volume 2 of this report identifies the verification of each FRSS issue by plant.

5.4.9 Sandia Fire Risk Scoping Study Issues

5.4.9.1 Issue Description

Section 4.2 of NUREG-1407 includes the following statement:

> The use of an existing fire PRA for the internal fires IPEEE is acceptable, provided the PRA reflects the current as-built and as-operated status of the plant and the licensee addresses the deficiencies of past PRAs that are identified in the Fire Risk Scoping Study (NUREG/CR-5088).

EPRI's FIVE methodology, which the NRC staff concluded was acceptable for use in the fire IPEEE, provides guidance for licensees to use in addressing the Sandia FRSS issues. The following sections discuss each of the five FRSS issues that were to be addressed as part of the IPEEE. As noted below, several of these FRSS issues are closely related, or identical, to other generic issues discussed in this chapter.

5.4.9.1.1 Seismic-Fire Interactions

The issue of seismic-fire interactions primarily involves three concerns. First is the potential that seismic events might result in fires internal to the plant. Such threats might be realized as a result of inadequately secured liquid fuel or oil tanks, breakage of fuel lines, or rocking of unanchored electrical panels (either safety- or non-safety-grade). The second concern is the potential that seismic events might render fixed fire suppression systems inoperable. This could include detection systems, fixed suppression systems, and fixed manual fire-fighting support elements, such as the plant's fire protection system's water distribution system. The third concern is that a seismic event might spuriously activate fixed fire detection and suppression systems. The spurious operation of detectors might both complicate operator response to the seismic event or cause the actuation of automatic fire suppression systems. Actuation of a suppression system may lead to flooding problems, habitability concerns (in the case of CO_2 systems), diversion of suppressants to non-fire areas (rendering them unavailable in the event of a fire elsewhere in the plant), the potential for over-dumping of gaseous suppressants (resulting in over pressurization of a compartment), and spraying of important plant components.

5.4.9.1.2 Adequacy of Fire Barriers

The common reliance on fire barriers to separate redundant components needed to achieve safe shutdown has elevated the risk sensitivity of fire barrier performance. Degraded fire barrier penetration seals and unsealed penetrations in some barriers can contribute to this source of fire risk. Barrier reliability and inter-compartment fire effects relate to the potential that fires in one area might impact other adjacent or connected areas through the spread of heat and smoke. In general, a licensee's fire IPEEE analysis should address this concern by considering the following factors:

- manual fire-fighting activities might allow the spread of smoke and heat through the opening of access doors, and
- failure of active fire barrier elements, such as normally open doors, water curtains, and ventilation dampers, would compromise barrier integrity.

5.4.9.1.3 Smoke Control and Manual Fire-Fighting Effectiveness

Sensitivity studies have shown that prolonged fire-fighting times can lead to a noticeable increase in fire risk. Smoke, identified as one of the major contributors to prolonged response times, can also cause misdirected suppression efforts and hamper the operator's ability to safely shut down the plant. This issue evolved as GSI-148, which is discussed in Section 5.4.6 of this report.

5.4.9.1.4 Equipment Survival in a Fire-Induced Environment

The FRSS investigated the potential susceptibility of equipment damage to indirect or secondary fire involvement through the environment created by fires, fire suppression, and the spurious operation of fire suppression systems. The FRSS found that past spurious actuation of suppression systems had a range of effects, including induced plant scrams. Several events were identified in which significant degradation of plant operability resulted. This issue is assessed as part of GSI-57, "Effects of Fire Protection System Actuation on Safety Related Equipment," which is discussed in Section 5.4.2 of this report.

5.4.9.1.5 Fire-Induced Alternate Shutdown/Control Room Panel Interactions

Control system interactions involving a combination of fire-induced failures and spurious actuation, and high-probability random equipment failures, were identified as potential contributions to fire risk. Sensitivity studies were performed which indicated that these interactions could have a significant impact on the fire core damage frequency. This issue was later classified as GSI-147, which is discussed in Section 5.4.5 of this report.

5.4.9.2 Findings and Related Plant Modifications

Of the 69 submittals, 16 did not provide adequate information to verify one or more of the sub-issues in the FRSS. Twenty-seven licensees used the FIVE methodology in addressing the FRSS issues. Figure 5.3 shows the distribution of unverified or partially unverified FRSS issues by issue, while Figure 5.4 shows the distribution of unverified or partially unverified issues by plant. Figure 5.3 shows that the most common unverified FRSS issue (14 plants) is related to smoke control and manual fire-fighting effectiveness. This is not surprising, for as with GSI-148, if a licensee did not take credit for manual fire-fighting actions in their

IPEEE fire analysis, there might not be sufficient information to verify this FRSS issue. For additional discussion directly related to this issue, see Section 5.4.6.

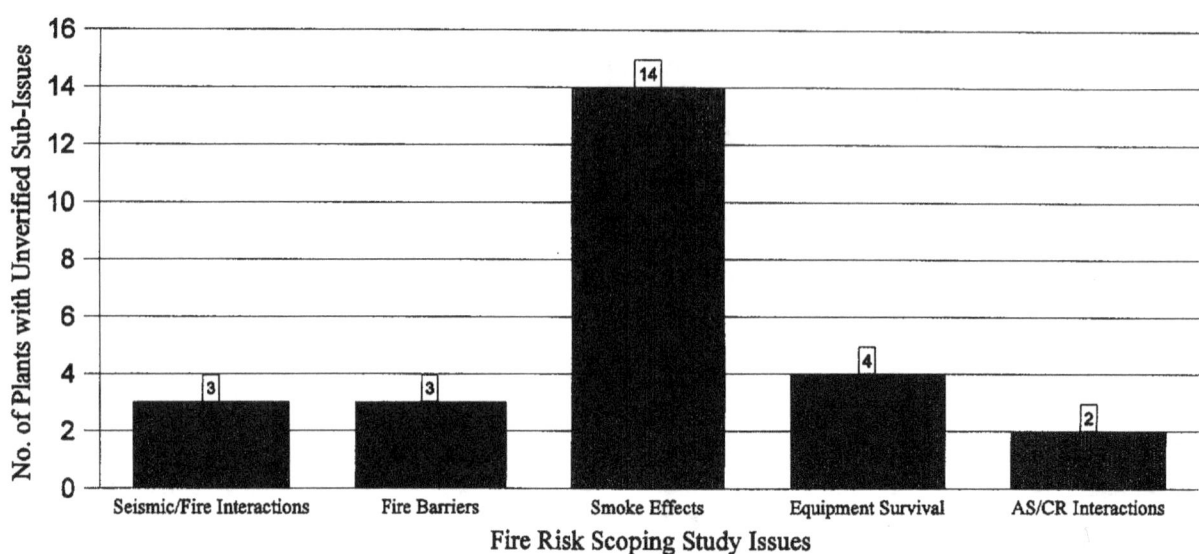

Figure 5.3 Number of unverified FRSS issues by issue

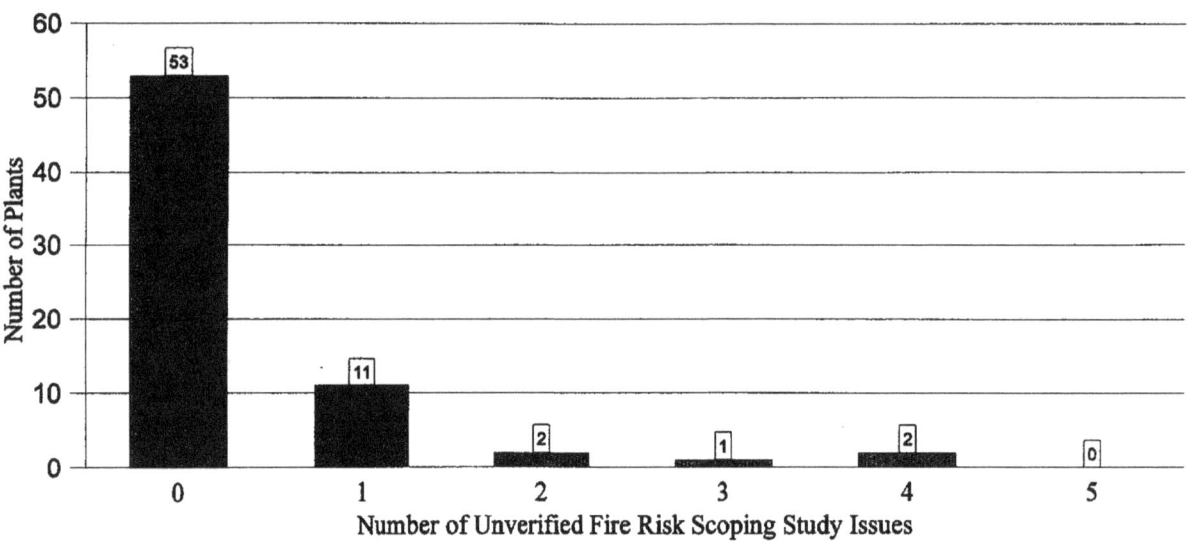

Figure 5.4 Number of unverified FRSS issues by plant

Figure 5.4 shows that two licensees each had four unverified FRSS issues. Table 5.8 of Volume 2 of this report shows that one of these two plants (LaSalle) did not provide information to explicitly address these four issues, and the other plant (Hatch) provided information to partially verify each of the four issues. Except for these two licensees, almost all of the FRSS issues (excluding smoke effects) were verified for most of the plants.

Table 5.8 of Volume 2 of this report identifies the verification of each FRSS issue by plant. This table also provides comments on plant-unique or interesting characteristics related to these issues and why these issues were partially or not fully verified.

Only one plant (Surry) explicitly identified any plant modifications that directly related to the FRSS issues. In this case, the licensee modified some electric circuits to ensure that the diesel generators and the alternate shutdown panel could be isolated from the control room and to reduce the likelihood of spurious power operated relief valve actuations. Although other plants did not explicitly identify plant enhancements related to the FRSS issues, plant modifications identified for other issues could also be an improvement for one or more of the FRSS issues (e.g., securing bottle gas tanks related to seismic-fire interactions).

5.4.9.2.1 Seismic-Fire Interactions

All but 3 of the 69 submittals provided adequate information to verify this FRSS issue. Licensees frequently assessed the potential seismic-fire interactions as part of their seismic and fire walkdowns. The potential for seismic events to initiate a fire related to the potential for an earthquake to result in a rupture of combustible gas lines, cylinders, or tanks. The most frequent plant enhancement related to this issue was to ensure that the existing procedures for securing the cylinders were followed. Combustible fluids are generally not stored or used near safety-related equipment. Generally, the tanks are outside, and the primary use of hydrogen is in the turbine building for generator cooling. Acetylene is stored in areas with no safety-related equipment.

The licensees also considered the potential for seismically induced failure of the fire protection system. This included evaluating potential failures that could adversely affect safety-related structures, systems, or components. Generally, the licensees identified the fire protection system piping to be designed to the seismic Category II/I criteria, or identified similar standards if they did not explicitly refer to the II/I criteria. The II/I criteria states that any seismic Category II (i.e., non-seismic Category I) structure, system, or component that is installed over a seismic Category I structure, system, or component will not fail in such a manner as to adversely affect the seismic Category I structure, system, or component; however, the seismic Category II structure, system, or component may no longer be functional. Some licensees identified that although the fire protection system was not designed as seismic Category I, a review of the system indicated that it would likely remain functional after an earthquake (e.g., some hangers might fail, but the piping would remain essentially intact).

Licensees generally used one of three methods to address the potential for seismic activity to actuate the fire protection system. First, most water systems are of the dry pipe design (i.e., a valve needs to open to flood the spray lines, and the fusible link in the sprinkler heat needs to melt before water is discharged from the system). Having both of these events occur solely as a result of a seismic event was deemed to be unlikely. A second type is the wet pipe fire protection system design. This design is similar to the dry pipe design except that water is maintained at the sprinkler head. In this case, the fusible link prevents discharge. This fusible link is not susceptible to failure from dust that might be stirred up as a result of a seismic event. Finally, there are gas suppression systems that use Halon or CO_2 as the fire suppressant. Inadvertent activation of these systems would not aversely affect the equipment in an area that was not already damaged by a fire (e.g., in the cable spreading or switchgear rooms). These gas suppressant systems are for limited areas and are independent of the water suppressant systems used elsewhere in the plant.

5.4.9.2.2 Adequacy of Fire Barriers

All but 3 of the 69 submittals provided adequate information to verify this FRSS issue. Licensees typically addressed barrier integrity in their submittals by discussing the plant's inspection, surveillance, and maintenance program that was used to verify the integrity of penetration seals (including door and hatch seals) and doors. The percentage of the seals that were inspected, as well as the interval of inspection, varied considerably from plant to plant. The inspections ranged from a small percentage of the accessible seals per calendar quarter to a larger percentage every 18 months (refueling outage). Licensees also cited inspection procedures ensure that fire doors remain closed. Welding activities could necessitate having doors open or partially open for hoses or cables to pass through, thereby breaching a fire barrier. Therefore, fire watches were commonly identified as the means to prevent welding activities from starting fires and to quickly suppress fires that might occur.

Given the licensees' programs for barrier integrity, the submittals typically assumed that the fire barriers would perform their intended function, as designed. A few licensees considered the potential consequences if a fire were to breach a fire barrier and adversely affect equipment in the adjacent fire area. Licensees usually addressed these consequences by considering the fire barrier to be ineffective with some small probability. Generally, the licensees found that, in these cases, the multi-zone fire scenarios were not a significant contributor to the plant's fire CDF.

Those licensees that took credit for or provided information related to manual fire-fighting activities usually included some discussion of the effects of smoke. Generally, the submittals indicated that the large volume of the adjacent fire area would dilute any smoke and heat that entered through a door opened for manual fire-fighting purposes. The licensees concluded that the results of such a fire barrier breach would not inhibit fire-fighting activities.

5.4.9.2.3 Smoke Control and Manual Fire-Fighting Effectiveness

Of the 69 submittals, 14 did not provide sufficient information to verify this FRSS issue. Most submittals included some discussion of the fire brigade training. Some train under live smoke conditions, while one licensee (Grand Gulf) also simulates the actual plant configuration and changes the configuration for each fire drill. Since this FRSS issue is the same as GSI-148, "Smoke Control and Manual Fire-Fighting Effectiveness," see Section 5.4.6 of this report for more discussion concerning this issue.

5.4.9.2.4 Equipment Survival in a Fire-Induced Environment

All but 4 of the 69 submittals provided adequate information to verify this FRSS issue. Many licensees identified that some, or all, of their water-based fire protection systems to require two diverse actions for initiation (pre-action type). One action would be for a smoke detector to open a supply valve in the fire protection system, while the second action is the fire's heat to melt the fusible link in the sprinkler head. For this type of system, the licensees concluded that inadvertent activation of the fire protection system by a seismic event or dust was not a problem.

Licensees also reviewed the impact of CO_2 or Halon protective system actuation as it relates to the potential effects on personnel (e.g., control room operators) and equipment (e.g., operation of the diesel generators) in the area. Licensees usually dismissed potential problems from these systems as insignificant to safety or beyond the scope of this generic issue. Data on the effects of smoke and fire suppressants on equipment is limited and beyond the scope of the IPEEE program.

Some licensees discussed the potential for the effects of fire to adversely affect equipment that is not directly involved with the fire. This includes potential effects of corrosion, buildup of soot, or other combustion products. Those that did discuss this aspect stated that potential damage would occur over a much longer period than required to establish cold shutdown. Corrective maintenance would resolve any long-term problem that might be caused by these mechanisms. The remaining submittals did not discuss the impact of combustion products on equipment operability.

5.4.9.2.5 Fire-Induced Alternate Shutdown/Control Room Panel Interactions

All but 2 of the 69 submittals provided adequate information to verify this FRSS issue. Generally, the submittals identified that the plants have the ability to transfer adequate control from the control room to alternate locations to achieve plant safe shutdown conditions (i.e., the alternate location is electrically independent of the control room); control would be regained after being transferred from the control room to the alternate shutdown locations; the review considered spurious actuation of components; and the potential loss of power to equipment was addressed by feeding the alternate shutdown equipment through a separate, independent breaker or fuse. Since this FRSS issue is the same as GSI-147, "Fire-Induced Alternate Shutdown/Control Room Panel Interactions," see Section 5.4.5 of this report for more discussion concerning this issue.

5.5   Summary and Conclusions

This chapter discusses a total of 31 IPEEE-related unresolved safety issues and generic safety issues, including USI A-45, GSI-57, GSI-103, GSI-131, GSI-147, GSI-148, GSI-156 (9 SEP issues), GSI-172 (11 MSRP issues), and five FRSS issues. Nine of these issues were explicitly discussed in Supplement 4 to Generic Letter 88-20 and NUREG-1407 (USI A-45, GSI-57, GSI-103, GSI-131, and the five FRSS issues). The other 22 issues were not explicitly discussed in the Generic Letter 88-20 or NUREG-1407. However, the NRC believes that the plant-specific analyses that were requested in the scope of the IPEEE program could also be used, through a satisfactory IPEEE submittal review, to evaluate and verify the external event aspects of these generic issues. Section 5.4 of this report discusses each of these issues, the related findings, and plant modifications. Detailed plant-specific tables concerning these USIs and GSIs are provided in Section 5 of Volume 2 of this report.

One of the major achievements of the IPEEE program was the verification of a large majority of these generic issues. As shown in Table 5.2, most of the plants verified a large majority of these issues. Figure 5.5 graphically illustrates these results. Of the 69 submittals, 44 provided sufficient information to verify all 31 USIs and GSIs. The remaining 25 submittals had one or more generic issue(s) unverified or only partially verified[6]. USI A-45, GSI-131, and GSI-156 (9 SEP issues) were fully verified for all plants. Of the other

---

[6] If a licensee's submittal did not address a generic issue, but did not overlook a potential vulnerability, the NRC's Staff Evaluation Report for that plant identified te omission as a weakness in the submittal. In such cases, the submittal still meets the intent of the IPEEE program, but the GSI may not be "verified" for that plant. For those issues that have not been completely verified, the NRC staff will determine if any additional actions or assessments are needed to verify these GSIs. This follow-up will

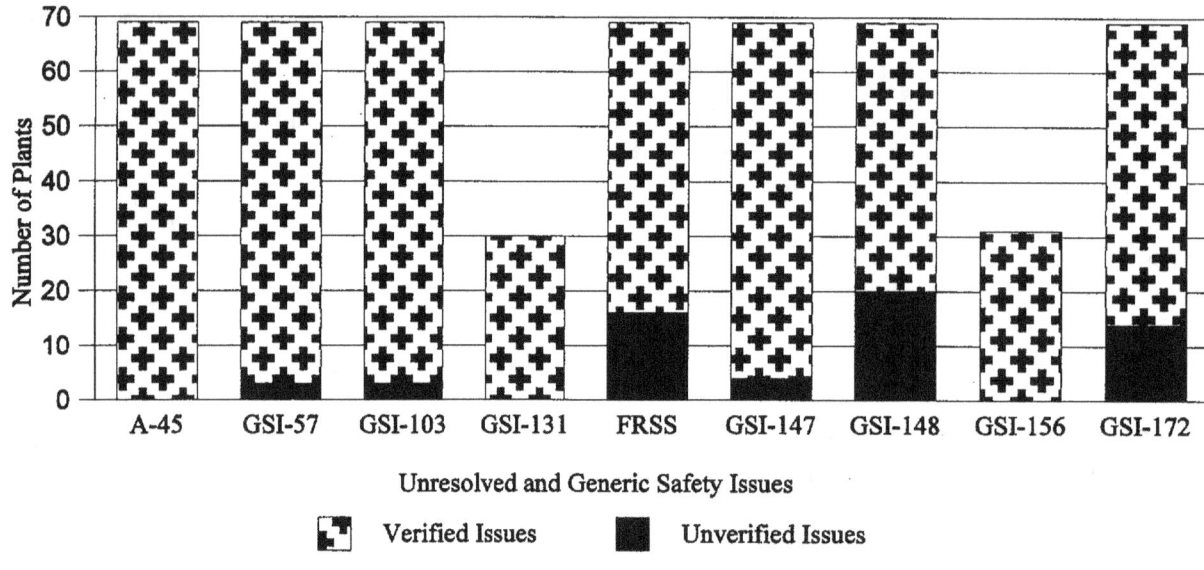

Figure 5.5 Number of unverified or partially verified generic issues by plant

generic issues, GSI-57, GSI-103, and GSI-147 were verified for approximately 95% of the plants. GSI-172 and the FRSS issues were verified for almost 80% of the plants.[7] Even the issue that was most commonly unverified, GSI-148, was still verified for 70% of the plants. Not surprisingly, those issues that were explicitly identified in Supplement 4 to Generic Letter 88-20 or NUREG-1407 had a higher percentage of verification than those that were not explicitly identified. Nevertheless, even those issues that were not identified were verified for most of the plants. One submittal (LaSalle) did not provide any information to verify generic issues. Those sub-issues that could be verified relied on information that could be deduced from an old PRA.

With regard to GSI-148, a number of licensees did not take credit for manual fire-fighting actions in their IPEEE fire analyses. Although this assumption is conservative from a PRA standpoint (i.e., could lead to a higher estimated fire CDF), the submittals for these cases did not consider the potential damaging effects of misdirected suppression on adjacent safety-related equipment. Therefore, this generic issue was not considered verified for those plants. One of the FRSS issues, "Smoke Control and Manual Fire-Fighting Effectiveness," is essentially the same as GSI-148. As shown in Figure 5.3, the most commonly unverified FRSS issue by far was the issue of smoke effects. Therefore, if a submittal did not provide adequate information to verify GSI-148, that submittal also lacked adequate information to verify one of the FRSS issues. This contributed to the FRSS issues being only partially verified for a number of plants.

---

be done separately from the IPEEE program.

[7] GSI-172 (MSRP) and the FRSS issues actually comprised 11 and 5 separate issues, respectively. All plants verified at least some of these MSRP and FRSS issues. If one or more individual MSRP or FRSS issue(s) were not verified for a plant, Table 5.2 identifies the issue as "partially verified" for that plant. Figure 5.5 graphically reflects the same information as Table 5.2.

6. REFERENCES

ANSI/IEEE, "IEEE Standard for Type Test of Class 1E Electrical Cables, Field Splices, and Connections for Nuclear Power Generating Station," ANSI/IEEE Std. 383-1974.

EPRI, "A Methodology for Assessment of Nuclear Power Plant Seismic Margin," NP-6041, October 1988.

EPRI, "A Methodology for Assessment of Nuclear Power Plant Seismic Margin," NP-6041-SL, Revision 1, August 1991.

EPRI, "Probabilistic Seismic Hazard Evaluation at Nuclear Plant Sites in the Central and Eastern United States: Resolution of the Charleston Earthquake Issue," EPRI NP-6395-D, April 1989.

EPRI, "COMPBRN IIIE: An Interactive Computer Code for Fire Risk Analysis," EPRI NP-7282, May 1991.

EPRI, "Fire-Induced Vulnerability Evaluation (FIVE)," TR-100370, April 1992.

EPRI, "Fire Events Database for U.S. Nuclear Power Plants," NSAC-178L, January 1993.

EPRI, "Methodology for Developing Seismic Fragilities," TR-103959, June 1994.

EPRI, "Fire PRA Implementation Guide," TR-105928, December 1995.

EPRI, "Guidance for Development of Response to Generic Request for Additional Information on Fire Individual Plant Examination of External Events (IPEEE)," EPRI Project No. 689, Final Report, May 1999 (provided to the U.S. NRC under cover from D.J. Modeen, May 24, 1999).

Kazarians, M., N.O. Siu, and G. Apostolakis, "Risk Analysis for Nuclear Power Plants: Methodological Developments and Applications," *Risk Analysis*, Vol. 5, No. 1, March 1985.

Kazarians, M., S.P. Nowlen, and F. Wyant, "Risk Insights Gained from Fire Incidents," Draft Report, U.S. NRC, September 2000 (available through the U.S. NRC Public Document Room).

Klamerus, L.J., "A Preliminary Report on Fire Protection Research Program (July 6, 1977)," SAND77-1424, SNL, October 1977.

Lysmer, J., et al., "FLUSH – A Computer Program for Approximate 3-D Analysis of Soil Structure Interaction Problems," EERC 75-30, Earthquake Engineering Research Center, UCB, November 1975.

Lysmer, J., et al., "SASSI – A System for Analysis of Soil Structure Interaction," UCB/GT181-0, Geotechnical Engineering, UCB, April 1981.

NFPA, "Performance-Based Standard for Fire Protection for Light Water Reactor Electric Generating Plants," NFPA-805, (draft issued for public proposals), November 11, 1998.

NEI, "Severe Accident Issue Closure Guidelines," Revision 1, NEI 91-04, December 1994.

NUMARC, "Severe Accident Issue Closure Guidelines," NUMARC 91-04, January 1991.

San Onofre Nuclear Generation Station Unit 1, "Report on Cable Failures — 1968," Southern California Edison Co., May 1968.

SQUG, "Generic Implementation Procedure for Seismic Verification of Nuclear Power Plant Equipment," Revision 2 (Corrected), February 14, 1992.

U.S. NRC, "Potential for Loss of Remote Shutdown Capability During a Control Room Fire," Information Notice 92-18, February 28, 1992.

U.S. NRC, "Policy Statement on Severe Accidents Regarding Future Designs and Existing Plants," *Federal Register*, Vol. 50, p. 32138, August 8, 1985.

U.S. NRC, "Nuclear Plant Fire Protection Functional Responsibilities, Administrative Controls, and Quality Assurance," Generic Letter 77-02, 1977.

U.S. NRC, "Fire Protection Rule (45 FR 76602, November 19, 1980)," Generic Letter 81-12, February 20, 1981, and Clarification Letter, March 1982.

U.S. NRC, "NRC Positions on Certain Requirements of Appendix R to 10 CFR, Part 50," Generic Letter 83-33, October 19, 1983.

U.S. NRC, "Fire Protection Policy Steering Committee Report," Generic Letter 85-01, January 9, 1985.

U.S. NRC, "Implementation of Fire Protection Requirements," Generic Letter 86-10, April 24, 1986.

U.S. NRC, "Fire Endurance Test Acceptance Criteria for Fire Barrier Systems Used To Separate Redundant Safe Shutdown Trains Within the Same Fire Area," Generic Letter 86-10, Supplement 1, March 25, 1994.

U.S. NRC, "Removal of Fire Protection Requirements from Technical Specifications," Generic Letter 88-12, August 2, 1988.

U.S. NRC, "Individual Plant Examination for Severe Accident Vulnerabilities, 10 CFR 50.54(f)," Generic Letter 88-20, November 23, 1988.

U.S. NRC, "Initiation of the Individual Plant Examination for Severe Accident Vulnerabilities, 10 CFR 50.54(f)," Generic Letter 88-20, Supplement 1, August 29, 1989.

U.S. NRC, "Individual Plant Examination of External Events (IPEEE) for Severe Accident Vulnerabilities, 10 CFR 50.54(f)," Generic Letter 88-20, Supplement 4, June 28, 1991.

U.S. NRC, "Individual Plant Examination of External Events (IPEEE) for Severe Accident Vulnerabilities," Generic Letter 88-20, Supplement 5, September 8, 1995.

U.S. NRC, "Seismic Design Criteria," Regulatory Guide 1.29, Revision 3, September 1978.

U.S. NRC, "Standard Review Plan for the Review of Safety Analysis Reports for Nuclear Power Plants — LWR Edition," NUREG-0800, June 1987.

U.S. NRC, "Procedural and Submittal Guidance for the Individual Plant Examination of External Events (IPEEE) for Severe Accident Vulnerabilities," NUREG-1407, June 1991.

U.S. NRC, "Individual Plant Examination Program: Perspectives on Reactor Safety and Plant Performance," NUREG-1560, December 1997.

U.S. NRC, "Research Needs in Fire Risk Assessment," *Proceedings of 25th U.S. Nuclear Regulatory Commission Water Reactor Safety Information Meeting*, Bethesda, Maryland, NUREG/CP-0162, Vol. 2, pages 93-116, N. Siu, J.T. Chen, and E. Chelliah, October 20-22, 1997.

U.S. NRC, "Development of Criteria for Seismic Review of Selected Nuclear Power Plants," NUREG/CR-0098, BNL, May 1978.

U.S. NRC, "Nuclear Power Plant Fire Protection-Fire Hazards Analysis (Subsystems Study Task 4)," NUREG/CR-0654, SNL, September 1979.

U.S. NRC, "Revised Livermore Seismic Hazard Estimates of 69 Nuclear Plant Sites East of the Rocky Mountains," NUREG/CR-1488, LLNL, April 1994.

U.S. NRC, "Fire Risk Analysis for Nuclear Power Plants," NUREG/CR-2258, UCSB, Los Angeles, Calif., September 1981.

U.S. NRC/ANS/IEEE, "PRA Procedures Guide," NUREG/CR-2300, January 1983.

U.S. NRC, "Probabilistic Safety Analysis Procedures Guide," NUREG/CR-2815, Bari, R.A., et. al., August 1985.

U.S. NRC, "An Approach to the Quantification of Seismic Margins in Nuclear Power Plants," NUREG/CR-4334, August 1985.

U.S. NRC, "An Experimental Investigation of Internally Ignited Fires in Nuclear Power Plant Control Cabinets, Part I – Cabinet Effects Tests," NUREG/CR-4527, Volume 1, SAND86-0336, SNL, April 1987.

U.S. NRC, "An Experimental Investigation of Internally Ignited Fires in Nuclear Power Plant Cabinets, Part II – Room Effects Tests," NUREG/CR-4527, Volume 2, SAND86-0336, SNL, October 1988.

U.S. NRC, "Users Guide for a Personal-Computer-Based Nuclear Power Plant Fire Data Base," NUREG/CR-4586, SAND86-0300, SNL, August 1986.

U.S. NRC, "Accident Sequence Evaluation Program – Human Reliability Analysis Procedure," NUREG/CR-4771, SAND 86-1996, SNL, February 1987.

U.S. NRC, "Analysis of the LaSalle Unit 2 Nuclear Power Plant: Risk Methods Integration and Evaluation Program (RMIEP)," NUREG/CR-4832, Vols. 1-10, SNL, March 1993.

U.S. NRC, "Procedures for the External Event Core Damage Frequency Analyses for NUREG-1150," NUREG/CR-4840, SAND88-3102, SNL, November 1990.

U.S. NRC, "Fire Risk Scoping Study: Investigation of Nuclear Power Plant Fire Risk, Including Previously Unaddressed Issues," NUREG/CR-5088, SAND88-0177, SNL, January 1989.

U.S. NRC, "Seismic Hazard Characterization of 69 Nuclear Power Plant Sites East of the Rocky Mountains," NUREG/CR-5250, LLNL, January 1989.

U.S. NRC, "Individual Plant Examination of External Events: Guidance and Procedures," draft NUREG/CR-5259, March 1989.

U.S. NRC, "Integrated Risk Assessment for the LaSalle Unit 2 Nuclear Power Plant: Phenomenology and Risk Uncertainty Evaluation Program (PRUEP)," NUREG/CR-5305, Vols. 1-3, SNL, 1992.

U.S. NRC,"A Summary of the U.S. NRC Fire Protection Research Program at Sandia National Laboratories: 1975-1987," NUREG/CR-5384, SNL, December 1989.

U.S. NRC, Letter, from A.C. Thadani, NRC/NRR/DST, to W.H. Rasin, NUMARC, Subject: "NRC's Staff Evaluation Report on Revised NUMARC/EPRI Fire Vulnerability Evaluation (FIVE) Methodology," August 21, 1991.

U.S. NRC, "Assessment of the Impact of Appendix R Fire Protection Exemptions on Fire Risk," SECY-99-182, July 9, 1999.

U.S. NRC, "Fire Protection for Operating Nuclear Power Plants," Draft Regulatory Guide DG-1097, Revision 1, June 2000.

Wong, H., and Luco, J., "Soil Structure Interaction: A Linear Continuum Mechanics Approach (CLASSI)," Report CE, Department of Civil Engineering, USC, Los Angeles, Calif., 1980.

GLOSSARY

Active fire barrier — a fire barrier element that must be physically repositioned from its normal configuration to an alternative configuration in order to provide its protective function. Examples include ventilation system fire dampers and normally open fire doors.

Anomaly — an observed plant condition that deviates from a normal configuration or otherwise apparently fails to satisfy expected criteria.

Anticipated transient without scram (ATWS) — a perturbation in the state of some system or component at full reactor power that initiates a deviation from the full-power, steady-state operating conditions that has been previously considered and analyzed which would normally result in a reactor scram. However, in this case, the reactor does not scram, either automatically or manually.

Appendix R fire area — an area, as defined in the analysis pursuant to Appendix R to Title 10, Part 50, of the *Code of Federal Regulations* (10 CFR Part 50), "Fire Protection Program for Nuclear Power Facilities Operating Prior to January 1, 1979," that is sufficiently bounded by fire barriers such that it will withstand the fire hazards within the fire area and, as necessary, will protect important equipment within a fire area from a fire outside the area. A fire area must be made up of rated fire barriers with openings in the barriers provided with fire doors, fire dampers, and fire penetration seal assemblies having a fire resistance rating at least equivalent to the barrier in which it is installed.

Appendix R fire zones — subdivisions of a fire area, as specified in Appendix R to 10 CFR Part 50.

Appendix R requirements — fire protection requirements specified in Appendix R to 10 CFR Part 50. (It should be noted that while some Appendix R requirements apply to all plants operating before January 1, 1979, plants licensed after January 1, 1979, are not subject to Appendix R requirements. Instead, these plants must meet the fire protection condition(s) of their licenses, which are based upon the guidelines of NUREG-0800, "Standard Review Plan for the Review of Safety Analysis Reports of Nuclear Power Reactors — LWR Edition," June 1987, specifically Branch Technical Position CMEB 9.5-1, which mirrors Appendix R with additional information.)

"Bad actor" relay — a low-ruggedness relay, as defined in guidance and procedures pertaining to USI A-46 and the Seismic Quantification Utilities Group (SQUG).

Barrier failure — the breach of a fire barrier, by a fire or other cause, which could permit propagation of a fire or its combustion products across the barrier.

Bounding analysis — an analysis that intentionally makes use of methods and assumptions (e.g., those pertaining to parameters describing a hazard, a resulting initiating event, and a plant's resistance to the initiator) designed to result in an upper-bound or demonstrably conservative estimate of risk.

Charleston Earthquake Issue — an issue initiated by a 1982 U.S. Geological Survey letter that pointed out the possibility that large, damaging earthquakes have some likelihood of occurring at locations where such events may not previously have been considered in developing past licensing decisions. (As a result of work carried out by the NRC and EPRI to resolve this issue, eight plants at five Eastern U.S. sites were identified as having a sufficient likelihood of being affected by large, damaging earthquakes beyond the licensing bases, such that further assessment was deemed to be warranted.)

Common cause failure (also referred to as "common mode failure") — a single event, action (e.g., improper maintenance activity), or condition (e.g., stress corrosion cracking) that adversely affects two or more similar or identical components at the same time. (Since this report deals with external events, the common cause failure can also be an external event that affects multiple (similar or dissimilar) components in the same area.)

COMPBRN — a computer code described in EPRI NP-7282, "COMPBRN IIIE: An Interactive Computer Code for Fire Risk Analyses," May 1991.

Component — an item of plant equipment (e.g., a pump, valve, pipe, etc.) or a structural feature (e.g., a building, masonry wall, stack, etc.) that is designed to perform a particular function. (For purposes of system modeling, a component is the lowest level of detail used in representing a piece of plant hardware and defining its associated failure as a basic event.)

Conditional core damage probability (CCDP) — a probability of reaching core damage given an event (initiator), in combination with a specific (degraded or normal) plant condition. (For example, the initiator might be a wind-induced loss of offsite power, and an associated degraded plant condition might be crimping of an exposed diesel generator exhaust stack resulting from a wind-induced missile. In this case, the CCDP would be determined by evaluating the plant model for a loss of offsite power initiator where either an increased failure probability or guaranteed failure of at least one diesel generator is assumed.)

Conservative deterministic failure margin (CDFM) — an estimate of the high-confidence of low-probability of failure (HCLPF) capacity of a component, determined in accordance with the procedure recommended in EPRI NP-6041.

Containment failure modes — a mutually exclusive set of descriptive states used to categorize the characteristics of containment failure. (For example, such descriptive states might consist of "early isolation failure," "late isolation failure," "early containment bypass failure," "early over-pressure failure," etc.)

Containment performance — the ability of a nuclear plant containment to fulfill its intended function in the event of challenges presented by a severe accident. (Such ability can be assessed through qualitative and/or quantitative evaluation. A quantitative measure of containment performance would be the conditional probability of containment failure given core damage.)

Control systems interaction — the potential of fire to adversely affect the ability of plant operators to achieve safe shutdown from either the control room or the remote shutdown panel as a result of fire-induced circuit failures. (For example, a fire may damage common circuits or cables in a way interferes with the ability to achieve safe shutdown conditions. Control systems interaction is identified as Generic Safety Issue (GSI) 147.)

Core damage — a state of clad oxidation and fuel damage caused by a prolonged uncovering and heating of the reactor core, as a result of an imbalance in heat generation and heat removal.

Core damage frequency (CDF) — the frequency, per reactor-year, of the occurrence of severe accidents that lead to core damage.

Cross-zone analysis — the analysis of a potential fire scenario involving fire propagation between adjacent fire zones.

Cut set — any combination of a set of events (e.g., occurrence of an initiating event and component failures) that, if they occur, would result in an undesirable condition (e.g., onset of core damage or containment failure).

Dependency — requirement external to a structure, system, or component (SSC), and upon which the SSC's function depends.

Design basis event — any of the events specified in a nuclear power plant's licensing basis that are used to establish acceptable performance for safety-related functions. (Such events include anticipated transients, design basis accidents, external events, and natural phenomena.)

Dominant contributor — an accident class that has a major impact on the total core damage frequency, or a containment failure mechanism that has a major impact on the total radionuclide release frequency.

Eastern U.S. seismicity issue — formerly the Charleston Earthquake Issue. (See "Charleston Earthquake Issue.")

EPRI seismic margin assessment (SMA) methodology — a methodology, described in EPRI NP-6041, for seismic assessment of a plant and determination of component and plant HCLPF capacities, which uses success paths as the approach for systems modeling.

Event tree — a quantifiable logical network that begins with an accident initiator or condition; progresses through a series of branches that represent possible system performances, human actions, or phenomenological behaviors; and ultimately leads to either a safe, stable state or an undesirable one, such as core damage or containment failure.

External event — an accident initiator that originates outside a nuclear power plant's internal systems, and in combination with safety system failures and/or operator errors, may induce core damage accident sequences. (Examples of external events include earthquakes, tornadoes, external floods, and fires.)

External flood — a flood initiated outside the plant that can affect the operability of internal plant systems.

Fault tree — a graphical representation that shows the logical relationships among possible basic failure events, and provides a concise and orderly description of the various combinations of such events that may occur within a system and could result in some predefined, undesirable event for that system.

Feed-and-bleed — a method to provide core cooling in a pressurized water reactor (PWR) (without the use of feedwater or steam generators) by providing (feeding) primary coolant makeup to the core, while removing decay hear by opening the pressurizer power-operated relief valves (PORVs) or safety valves to remove (bleed) primary fluid having elevated temperature.

Fire area — a physical area bounded on all sides by rated fire barriers. (See also "Appendix R fire area.")

Fire barrier — elements of construction (walls, floors, and their supports), which may incorporate beams, joists, columns, penetration seals or closures, fire doors, and fire dampers that are rated by approving laboratories (usually in terms of hours of resistance to fire), and are used to prevent the propagation of fire.

Fire compartment — in fire analysis, an enclosure or space bounded by non-combustible barriers, where heat and products of combustion generated from a fire will be substantially confined within the enclosure.

Fire compartment interaction analysis (FCIA) — a procedural step in the EPRI fire-induced vulnerability evaluation (FIVE) methodology, in which qualitative consideration is given to the potential for interacting fire spread between compartments and the consequences of such fire spread on plant shutdown.

Fire damage modeling — modeling of all pertinent and necessary fire damage sequences (including fire scenarios and fire-induced sequences).

Fire-induced vulnerability evaluation (FIVE) — a quantitative screening technique sponsored by the EPRI under the guidance of the Severe Accident Working Group of the Nuclear Management and Resources Council (NUMARC) and the industry's experts, for the purpose of addressing the fire portion of licensees' IPEEE studies.

Fire PRA methodology — the set of procedures, based on probabilistic risk analysis, for estimating the core damage frequency attributable to fire events.

Fire zones — subdivisions of a fire area. (See also "Appendix R fire zones.")

Focused-scope — a term used in NUREG-1407 to designate a somewhat narrowed set of aspects, relative to the broader full-scope aspects, to be included in the seismic IPEEE assessment for a specified group of nuclear power plants. The plants in this category are to perform a detailed walkdown of the safe shutdown equipment list (SSEL), an evaluation of low-ruggedness relays, a screening assessment of structures and SSEL items for a 0.3g peak ground acceleration (PGA) review-level earthquake (RLE), calculation and reporting of HCLPF capacities for the weaker elements, and determination and reporting of the plant's HCLPF capacity.

Fragility — the conditional probability that a component, system, or plant will fail, given the occurrence of a specified value of a load parameter (e.g., in the case of seismic fragility, the load parameter is typically a measure of ground acceleration). A component fragility curve, which is equivalent to the probability distribution function of the component's capacity, is used in a PRA to determine the component's failure probabilities under various load levels.

Free field — a location at which the ground motion from a seismic event can be recorded without experiencing a measurable influence of ground-motion effects caused by the dynamic response of constructed features.

Free-field peak ground acceleration (PGA) — peak acceleration of the ground motion experienced in a seismic event for free-field conditions.

Full-scope — a term used in NUREG-1407 to designate the broader set of aspects, relative to the focused-scope aspects, to be included in the seismic IPEEE assessment of a specified group of plants. The plants in this category are to perform a seismic IPEEE that goes beyond the focused-scope assessment, particularly in regard to the breadth of relay chatter evaluation, the effort expended in investigating potential soil failures, and the list of components for which HCLPF calculations are performed.

Functional interaction — the potential effects of one component or system upon another as a result of their functional interdependencies.

Generic implementation procedure (GIP) — the screening guidance given in the "Generic Implementation Procedure for Seismic Verification of Nuclear Power Plant Equipment," which was developed under the sponsorship of the Seismic Qualification Utility Group (SQUG).

Generic issue (GI) — A concern that may affect the design, construction, or operation of all, several, or a class of nuclear power plants, which either does not affect safe operation of the plant or the safety significance of the issue has not yet been determined.

Generic Letter 88-20 — a letter issued by the NRC to all licensees on November 23, 1988, which requested that U.S. nuclear power reactor licensees submit an individual plant examination (IPE) for severe accident vulnerabilities for each licensed nuclear power plant.

Generic Letter 88-20, Supplement 4 — a letter issued by the NRC to all licensees on June 28, 1991, which requested that U.S. nuclear power reactor licensees submit an individual plant examination of external events (IPEEE) for severe accident vulnerabilities to external events for each licensed nuclear power plant.

Generic Letter 88-20, Supplement 5 — a letter issued by the NRC to all licensees on September 8, 1995, which notified all U.S. nuclear power reactor licensees about modifications to the seismic reviews that are to be performed as part of the IPEEE program for focused-scope and full-scope plants.

Generic safety issue (GSI) — according to NUREG-0933, "A Prioritization of Generic Safety Issues," a GSI is a safety concern that may affect the design, construction, or operation of all, several, or a class of nuclear power plants, and may have the potential for safety improvements and promulgation of new or revised requirements or guidance.

Ground motion — the strength of shaking experienced at a specified location within the ground or on the ground surface, which is usually described for engineering purposes by either a time history of ground acceleration or a response spectrum that conveys the strength of response accelerations of simple harmonic oscillators versus their vibration periods or frequencies.

Hazard — a potential source of risk (e.g., combustible materials, high-pressure piping, chemical solutions, storms, earthquake sources, landslides, meteors, etc.).

Hazard curve — A curve conveying the annual rate of occurrence of a hazardous event versus the value of a parameter that characterizes the severity of the hazard. (Hazard curves are most often used to quantify the threat of various earthquake ground motions, extreme wind speeds, and extreme flood levels.)

High-confidence of low-probability of failure (HCLPF) capacity — an earthquake acceleration level for which a given component, system, or plant is evaluated as having a 95% confidence that the chance of its failure is 5%.

High wind, flood, and other (HFO) external events — the external events examined in an IPEEE, excluding seismic and fire events. HFO events include high winds and tornadoes, external floods, transportation and near facility accidents, and other unscreened or plant-unique hazards.

Hot short — an electric cable failure mode, resulting from a fire, which involves making an electrical connection between a conductor with power and a conductor that does not currently have power, without a simultaneous short-to-ground or open-circuit condition. Such a fault might, for example, simulate the closing of a control switch, cause errors in an instrument reading, or result in the application of power to an unpowered circuit.

Human error probability (HEP) — (See "Human error rate.")

Human error rate — a measure of the likelihood that an operator will fail to initiate the correct, required, or specified action or response needed to allow the continuous or correct functioning of an item of equipment. (Human error rate and human error probability are used interchangeably.)

In-core flux mapping (ICFM) system — a system used in a PWR to measure the strength and distribution of neutron flux in the reactor core.

Individual plant examination (IPE) — an evaluation to identify any plant-specific vulnerabilities to severe accidents initiated by internal events, including internal flooding, during full-power operation. (Generic Letter 88-20 requested that each licensee of a United States nuclear power plant perform such an evaluation for its plant(s).)

Individual plant examination of external events (IPEEE) — an evaluation to identify any plant-specific vulnerabilities to severe accidents initiated by external events during full-power operation. (Generic Letter 88-20, Supplement 4, requested that each licensee of a United States nuclear power plant perform such an evaluation for its plant(s).)

Interfacing system loss-of-coolant accident (ISLOCA) — an accident in which reactor coolant is released at high pressure into a low-pressure system, resulting in a loss of reactor coolant that cannot be isolated.

Internal events — accident initiators (including internal flooding) that originate within a nuclear power plant and, in combination with safety system failures and/or operator errors, may induce core damage accident sequences.

Internal fire — a fire initiated anywhere within the plant boundaries, including areas within plant structures and buildings, as well as contiguous outdoor areas such as the electrical switchyard and transformer areas.

Internal flood — a flood initiated within the plant that can affect the operability of internal plant systems.

Level 1 analysis — an identification and quantification of the sequences of events leading to the onset of core damage.

Level 2 analysis — an evaluation of containment response to severe accident challenges, including quantification of the mechanisms, quantities, and likelihoods of radioactive material releases from the containment given core damage accident sequences.

Loss-of-coolant accident (LOCA) — an accident caused by a break in the reactor coolant system pressure boundary.

Low-ruggedness relay — a relay or relay-type device (switch/contact) that has the potential to change state, or to oscillate between states (i.e., chatter), under a relatively low-intensity seismic event.

Minimal cut set — a necessary and sufficient combination of events (e.g., occurrence of an initiating event and component failures) that would result in some undesirable condition (e.g., onset of core damage or containment failure). (See also "Cut set.")

Mission time — the time period that a system or component is required to be operable in order to carry out its intended mission. (For example, a containment spray mission time of 24 hours implies that containment sprays are required to be operable for 24 hours following their demand, in order to prevent containment failure from occurring within that time period.)

Modified focused-scope — a focused-scope seismic evaluation that makes use of the relaxations and other provisions described in GL 88-20, Supplement 5.

Modified full-scope — a full-scope seismic evaluation that makes use of the relaxations and other provisions described in GL 88-20, Supplement 5.

Multiple system responses program (MSRP) — the program described in NUREG/CR-5420, "Multiple System Responses Program — Identification of Concerns Related to a Number of Specific Regulatory Issues."

National Fire Protection Association (NFPA) codes and standards — consensus codes and standards intended to minimize the possibility and adverse consequences of fires.

NEI 91-04, "Severe Accident Closure Guidelines" — guidelines proposed by the Nuclear Management and Resources Council (NUMARC) (now, the Nuclear Energy Institute (NEI)) that are intended to identify vulnerabilities that may lead to a severe accident, and that have been proposed as a basis for resolving severe accident issues.

NRC seismic margin assessment (SMA) methodology — a methodology for seismic assessment of a plant and determination of component and plant HCLPF capacities, which uses event tree and fault tree modeling instead of the success path approach that has been adopted in the EPRI SMA methodology.

NUREG-1407 — a report issued by the NRC in June 1991, entitled "Procedural and Submittal Guidance for the Individual Plant Examination of External Events (IPEEE) for Severe Accident Vulnerabilities." This report provides guidance for performing and reporting the results of the IPEEE analyses.

Outlier — a component that cannot be screened out because a condition that violates one or more key criteria of standard screening tables is encountered in a seismic walkdown or documentation review.

Passive component — a component, or part of a component, that performs its intended function without any moving parts or changes in state. (Examples of passive components include tanks, piping runs, valve bodies, and ductwork.)

Passive fire barrier — a fire barrier that provides its protective function while in its normal orientation, without any need to be repositioned. (Examples of passive fire barriers include walls and normally closed fire doors.)

Peak ground acceleration (PGA) — for purposes of IPEEEs, the PGA is the same as the "free-field peak ground acceleration."

Performance shaping factor (PSF) — an influence on the performance of an operator. (PSFs are a key underlying aspect of the concept that human error rates for a set of specified actions can be derived by investigating how a small set of influences affect the likelihood of success or failure of the operator(s). PSFs include such items as training, experience, availability and quality of a procedure, stress, interdependence among operators, environment, and timing.)

Plant — a general term used to refer to a nuclear power facility, including one having a single reactor unit or multiple units.

Plant-level capacity — the quantification of a plant's ability to resist the effects of a given hazard. (Plant-level seismic capacity is typically conveyed by a fragility curve or an HCLPF value. In the EPRI SMA methodology, the plant-level seismic capacity can be conveniently approximated as the lowest HCLPF capacity among those components (including structures) that are relied upon to achieve safe shutdown conditions in the most rugged success path. In the NRC SMA methodology, the plant-level seismic capacity can also be approximated if the Boolean expression for core damage and the HCLPF capacities for components included in this expression are known.)

Plant logic model — a mathematical representation that simulates the behavior of a plant in response to an initiating event. The mathematical representation is used to (a) delineate sequences of events that could result in a state of core damage or a state of safe shutdown, and (b) to quantify the frequencies of such event/accident sequences. A plant logic model typically involves the development of event trees and associated fault trees that describe the combinations of basic events leading to the event-tree top events.

Probabilistic risk assessment (PRA) — an analytical process that quantifies the likelihood of possible adverse consequences. For a nuclear power plant, this process focuses on evaluating the design, operation, and maintenance of a plant in regard to potential severe accidents and adverse effects on the health and safety of the public. The risk evaluation process involves three sequential parts or "levels" (Level-1 addresses potential accident sequences leading to core damage; Level-2 addresses potential releases of radiological materials outside of the containment in the event of core damage; and Level-3 addresses potential adverse health, safety, and environmental consequences resulting from transport of the radiological elements in the event of radiological releases.)

Probable maximum precipitation (PMP) — the probable maximum rainfall, as stated in Generic Letter 89-22. (The PMP pertains to phenomena associated with spatially and temporally localized intense precipitation. Such phenomena are usually distinct from phenomena associated with the probable maximum flood (PMF), which generally results from a longer-term collection of rainfall distributed within a drainage basin and subsequent transport of water (i.e., flood routing) to the site location of interest.)

Qualified cable — a cable that is certified to meet all of the requirements of the IEEE standard No. 383 (including both the flame spread and the LOCA exposure test protocols).

Random failure — an independent, unrelated failure of which an occurrence can be represented by a probability distribution. (In IPEEEs, this term typically refers to failure events that are not caused by, or related to, the external event being analyzed.)

Rated fire barrier — a fire barrier with a fire endurance rating established in accordance with the test procedures of NFPA 251, "Standard Methods of Fire Test of Building Construction and Materials."

Reactor coolant pump (RCP) seal LOCA — a loss-of-coolant accident resulting from a failure of a reactor coolant pump seal.

Reactor-year — 365 full days (8,760 hours) of operation of a single reactor unit at full or partial power. (A reactor-year does not include the shutdown and restart intervals or the downtime of the reactor.)

Recovery action — an operator action intended to restore equipment that has failed or been rendered unavailable (e.g., as a result of testing and maintenance) back to an operable status.

Reduced-scope — a term used in NUREG-1407 to designate a limited implementation of the seismic margin method, which emphasizes a seismic walkdown and evaluation of outliers with respect to the design basis level, and which is to serve as the seismic IPEEE assessment approach for a specified group of nuclear power plants. (NUREG-1407 assigned plants to this category on the basis that they are located in areas that have a low seismic hazard.) The plants in this category do not need to perform HCLPF calculations, an assessment of soil failures, or a relay evaluation (beyond the requirements of USI A-46, if applicable).

Relay chatter — the oscillation of relay contacts between open and closed positions during a seismic event.

Remote shutdown panel (RSP) — the capability to achieve safe shutdown from outside the control room. While the term "remote shutdown panel" is commonly used both in this report and elsewhere, the term is inaccurate if not somewhat misleading. Plants are required to have a capability to achieve a safe, cold shutdown from outside the control room. In many cases, this is accomplished at one location, thus explaining the common usage of remote shutdown "panel." However, there is no actual requirement for any new or special panel to be used in the event of a fire in the control room. Thus, any mention in this report of RSP should be understood to be a general reference to the capability of achieving safe shutdown from outside the control room, rather than the existence of a specific panel (or panels).

Request for additional information (RAI) — an inquiry sent to a licensee from the NRC for the purpose of obtaining additional information that clarifies the IPEEE submittal.

Review-level earthquake (RLE) — the specific earthquake level recommended in NUREG-1407 for which a seismic evaluation is conducted. This earthquake level governs the criteria that are applied in screening components. In addition, for seismic margin assessments, this earthquake level defines the spectral acceleration values (based on the spectral shape defined by NUREG/CR-0098) from which the seismic demands are derived for use in calculating HCLPF capacities of components. (For seismic PRAs, NUREG-1407 indicates use of the site-specific 10,000-year median uniform hazard spectral shape for developing seismic demands.)

Roof ponding — the accumulation of rain water on the roof of a structure. The term "roof ponding" also pertains to the specific phenomenon in which roof ponding loads lead to sagging (vertical deformations associated with flexure) of the roof that, in turn, leads to additional collection/ponding of water and correspondingly increased loads, potentially resulting in roof instability or failure.

Safe shutdown earthquake (SSE) — the design basis earthquake defined for a nuclear power plant, in accordance with Appendix A to 10 CFR Part 100.

Safe shutdown earthquake (SSE) spectrum — the ground response spectrum associated with a safe shutdown earthquake.

Safe shutdown equipment list (SSEL) — the list of components required for safe shutdown in the event of a specific initiator.

Safe shutdown model — a mathematical representation of the behavior of plant systems, components, and actions that are needed to bring a plant to safe shutdown.

Safety-related structures, systems, and components — those structures, systems, and components that are relied upon to remain functional during and following design basis events to ensure the integrity of the reactor coolant pressure boundary, the capability to shut down the reactor and maintain it in a safe shutdown condition, or the capability to prevent or mitigate the consequences of accidents that could results in potential offsite exposure comparable to the guidelines in 10 CFR 50.34(a)(1) or 10 CFR 100.11.

Scaling factor — a number used to adjust (multiply) the seismic demands determined from some previously performed (e.g., design or reevaluation) building response analysis, in order to estimate the demands associated with a seismic margin earthquake (SME).

Screening analysis — a quantitative or qualitative evaluation used to narrow the list of items that require more detailed assessment. (In a seismic assessment, a screening analysis based on a walkdown and/or documentation review, supplemented by anchorage calculations, is typically performed in order to identify components that require further treatment (e.g., HCLPF or fragility calculations). In a fire assessment, a screening analysis is performed to eliminate fire areas and/or zones that have a negligible CDF contribution. In an HFO assessment, an initial overall screening analysis is performed to exclude hazard categories that have negligible CDF contributions.)

Seismic capacity — the highest seismic demand level (e.g., peak ground acceleration) that a structure, system, or component can withstand and still continue to perform its intended function.

Seismic Category 1 structure — a structure designed to withstand a safe shutdown earthquake (also simply referred to as a Category 1 structure).

Seismic demand — the influences (e.g., stresses and strains, or accelerations/forces and deformations) experienced within (or by) a structure and/or imposed on equipment, as a result of an applied earthquake loading/input. (Seismic demands on equipment are typically characterized by means of in-structure response spectra, or for ground-mounted equipment, the input ground response spectrum. Seismic demands on structures can also be characterized by the input ground response spectrum, although the forces or deformations that are experienced at a particular critical location in the structure (e.g., shear forces on a roof diaphragm) usually provide a more meaningful and precise description of the seismic demand.)

Seismic-fire interaction evaluation — an assessment of seismically induced fires, including the inadvertent actuation of fire protection systems.

Seismic-flood interaction evaluation — an assessment of the effects of a seismic event on the potential occurrence of a flood and plant response to flooding.

Seismic hazard — any feature capable of causing ground motion, and any phenomenon related to, or caused by, ground shaking (e.g., ground movement, liquefaction, landsliding, seiche), which has the potential to produce adverse effects.

Seismic margin — the ability of a plant, system, component, or structure to safely withstand seismic demands or input ground-motion levels beyond those imposed by the design basis earthquake.

Seismic margin assessment (SMA) — a methodology for assessing the seismic capacities and seismic margin of a nuclear power plant. (As described in NUREG-1407, two NRC and EPRI have independently developed two alternative approaches for performing SMA.)

Seismic margin earthquake (SME) — the specific earthquake ground motion spectrum used as input for a seismic margin assessment.

Seismic margin methodology (SMM) — (See "Seismic margin assessment (SMA).")

Seismic PRA (SPRA) methodology — an analytical process used to estimate a plant's frequency of core damage as the result of seismic events. (See also "Probabilistic risk assessment (PRA) methodology.")

Seismic Qualification Utilities Group (SQUG) — a group of nuclear power plant owners who have worked together to pool their experience data on component behavior in past earthquakes, and have sponsored the development of the "Generic Implementation Procedure for Seismic Verification of Nuclear Power Plant Equipment." (See also "Generic implementation procedure (GIP).")

Senior review board (SRB) — a panel of independent experts, consisting of NRC staff and consultants from national laboratories, that performed peer reviews of each IPEEE review in order to ensure the consistency and completeness of the review process.

Sensitivity analysis — an assessment in which one or more input parameters are varied in order to observe their effects on results.

Settlement — downward movement of the ground surface (or of a building or other facility that is founded on, or within, the ground) as the result of the compaction or consolidation of the underlying soil.

Severe accident — an accident that goes beyond the design basis of the plant and results in core damage.

Severe accident management—the implementation of strategies and guidance developed for incorporation into a plant's emergency response procedures to arrest the progression of an accident sequence, or to prevent or reduce the release of radioactivity into the environment.

Soil liquefaction — a phenomenon in which submerged ground materials (particularly, loose cohesionless soils, and some types of sensitive clays) develop high pore pressures under repeated load cycles (that cause rearrangement of soil structure and diminished resistance between soil grains), with a resulting significant loss of shear strength and development of large shear strains.

Soil-structure interaction (SSI) — the dependent relationship between ground motion and building response, where ground motion affects a building's vibratory behavior, and the building's vibratory response (in turn) alters the characteristics of the ground motion. Soil-structure interaction can have an important influence on the demands experienced by a structure and the equipment housed in or near that structure, particularly for the case of a massive structure having a large foundation. (See also "Free field" and "Ground motion.")

Spatial interaction — a potential adverse influence between plant components as a result of their spatial proximity. (Examples of spatial interactions include pounding of adjacent cabinets, water or chemicals spraying on equipment as a result of activation or breach of overhead fire-suppression lines, and overhead fluorescent light tubes falling and shattering inside open cabinets/panels, among many others.)

Spectral shape — the shape (i.e., plotted pattern that does not change with uniform scaling) of a response spectrum associated with a given ground motion. (See also "Ground motion.")

Spurious actuation — an undesirable actuation of a component or system as a result of an uncontrolled or unintended signal.

Standard Review Plan (SRP) — review guidance for nuclear power plant license applications, as issued by the NRC in NUREG-0800, "Standard Review Plan for the Review of Safety Analysis Reports for Nuclear Power Plants," June 1975.

Station blackout (SBO) — the complete loss of alternating current (ac) electric power to the essential and nonessential switchgear buses in a nuclear power plant (i.e., loss of the offsite electric power system concurrent with a turbine trip and unavailability of the onsite emergency ac power system).

Steam generator tube rupture (SGTR) — a PWR severe accident sequence initiated by the breach of at least one steam generator tube.

Step 1 review — a review of a licensee's IPEEE submittal and associated documentation by the NRC and NRC contractor(s). If needed, the Step 1 review may include one or more RAIs.

Step 2 review — a review of the Tier 2 IPEEE documentation retained for audit (as specified in Section 8.2 of NUREG-1407) and maintained by the licensee at its plant or company offices. If needed, the Step 2 review may include a walkdown to confirm specific features of the plant's configuration or screening basis, as encountered in the licensee's IPEEE submittal or Tier 2 documentation.

Submittal-only review — a review of an IPEEE on the basis of the information in the IPEEE submittal and additional information obtained from the licensee's responses to RAIs.

Success path — a specific combination of safety-system trains that accomplish the four principal functions of reactivity control, reactor pressure control, reactor coolant inventory control, and decay heat removal, and that together are capable of bringing a plant to a stable condition (either hot or cold shutdown) and maintaining that condition for at least 72 hours.

Success path equipment list (SPEL) — the list of components needed to achieve chosen success paths.

Supplemental technical evaluation report — a report prepared by NRC staff or NRC contractors that describes additional technical review findings resulting from consideration of a licensee's responses to a final round of RAIs.

Surrogate element — a representative element used in an SPRA to account for the effects of the components that are screened out during the walkdown and screening phase of the SPRA. The failure of a single surrogate element represents the failures of several screened components.

Systematic Evaluation Program (SEP) — an NRC program for examining plants that were licensed before the agency issued the 1975 SRP guidance on regulatory issues.

Technical evaluation report (TER) — a report that describes the technical findings of the review of a licensee's IPEEE submittal and associated documentation.

Tier 2 documentation — information retained for audit by a licensee, as specified in Section 8.2 of NUREG-1407. In general, Tier 2 documentation consists of information and materials that the licensee used in preparing its IPEEE but did not include in its submittal to the NRC (for example, notebooks and detailed calculations), and that by the licensee keeps at the plant site or the corporate office.

Tornado-generated missile — an object that is lofted and transported by a tornado.

Transient — a perturbation in the state of some system or component at full reactor power that initiates a deviation from the full-power, steady-state operating conditions. Transients that are of interest consist of those where the plant systems cannot respond to the deviation in time to restore the plant to its full-power, steady-state conditions before one or more monitored parameters deviates outside of the acceptable operating bounds. Such parameters that exceed operating bounds will trigger events that lead to a reactor scram, which would then call upon operation of the safety-related core heat removal systems.

Transient combustibles — Combustible materials that can easily be moved or stored either temporarily or on a long-term basis. Transient combustibles are typically associated with maintenance, plant modifications, poor housekeeping, or the temporary accumulation of waste materials or storage within the plant.

Transportation and nearby facility accidents — potentially adverse events that are associated with manmade hazards that may occur sufficiently close to the plant to cause an initiating event. Transportation accidents involve moving vehicles (i.e., planes, ships, barges, trucks, and railroad cars) that pass near the plant and may potentially cause an explosion that results in significant over pressure loads and missiles; impact with plant structures or components; or a release of hazardous material and formation of a traveling vapor cloud with the potential for ignition, explosion, or toxic conditions. Nearby facility accidents involve incidents at industrial facilities located within a local proximity to the plant, with possible release of hazardous materials, rupture of a pipeline carrying a hazardous gas or liquid under pressure, and other undesirable events.

Uncertainty analysis — an evaluation process to quantify the epistemic variability in a PRA estimate which derives from incomplete knowledge in formulating PRA models and incomplete knowledge of input variables.

Uniform hazard spectrum (UHS) — a response spectrum for which there is a constant annual frequency of exceedance of spectral values across all vibration periods. A uniform hazard spectrum is constructed as a plot of independently predicted spectral values — each having a given hazard (i.e., annual exceedance frequency or return period), a given confidence level (e.g., 50th percentile for a median spectrum), and a given damping value (typically 5%) — versus the vibration frequencies (or vibration periods) associated with the spectral values.

Unit — a single nuclear power reactor with its associated structures, systems, and components. (Nuclear power plant sites may have one or more units. At sites having multiple units, some support systems may be shared between units.)

Unresolved safety issue (USI) — according to NUREG-0933, "A Prioritization of Generic Safety Issues," a USI is a matter affecting a number of nuclear power plants that poses important questions concerning the adequacy of existing safety requirements for which a final verification has not yet been developed and which involves conditions that are not likely to be acceptable over the lifetime of the affected plants.

USI A-17 — Unresolved Safety Issue (USI) A-17, "Systems Interaction in Nuclear Power Plants."

USI A-45 — Unresolved Safety Issue (USI) A-45, "Shutdown Decay Heat Removal Requirements."

USI A-46 — Unresolved Safety Issue (USI) A-46, "Verification of Seismic Adequacy of Equipment in Operating Plants," which is intended to assess the seismic ruggedness of safety-related equipment to withstand a safe shutdown earthquake in those plants with construction permit applications docketed before about 1972.

Walkdown — an inspection of local areas within and around a nuclear power plant during which systems, components, structures, hazard sources, etc., are physically located and examined, in order to collect relevant plant information; verify plant configuration; evaluate the potential significance of hazards and adverse configurations; verify the location of important equipment; assess the adequacy of installation/construction, condition, and operating status of equipment; ascertain any environmental effects or system interaction effects on equipment, which could occur during accident conditions. (It should be recognized that the seismic walkdown, fire walkdown, and HFO walkdown each have distinct objectives and procedures, although the walkdown treatment of interactions among these events (e.g., seismic-fire interactions or seismic-flood interactions) usually involves a joint set of objectives and procedures.)

APPENDIX A - GUIDANCE ON IPEEE-RELATED REQUESTS FOR ADDITIONAL INFORMATION

The staff developed and used the following guidelines to determine when to send requests for additional information (RAIs) to licensees in order for the staff to complete its IPEEE reviews.

- It is not possible to conclude that the licensee met the intent of the IPEEE generic letter in one or more particular area(s).

- The response to the RAI is necessary to complete the final assessment of the submittal.

- The methodology and/or data used in the submittal is unacceptable, which could result in incorrect ranking or screening, masking, underestimating, or incorrect evaluation. See Table A.1 below.

- Information in response to the RAI would be likely to uncover a significant problem with the results, such as incorrect ranking or screening, masking, underestimating, or incorrect evaluation. See Table A.1 below.

- A plant has a significant assumption or result that is different from other plants in the same group (and the basis or justification is not provided), which could result in incorrect ranking or screening, masking, underestimating, or incorrect evaluation. See Table A.1 below.

Table A.1: Guidance for issuing RAIs

incorrect ranking or screening; or masking	significant risk contributor
	significant plant vulnerability
	important fire areas
	significant fire scenarios
underestimating	plant fire or seismic CDF
incorrect evaluation	core damage frequency
	containment response
	high-confidence of low-probability of failure (seismic)

In general, the staff did not send RAIs under the following circumstances.

- There could be a potential weakness, but the response to the RAI would not add to the review or would not provide any significant additional insights.

- Information provided in response to the RAI would not contribute to the review or would not impact the assessment of the submittal conclusions or vulnerabilities.

- The response to the RAI would not alter the scenario rankings.

- Issuing an RAI to many licensees does not constitute sufficient reason to issue it to another licensee.

- Documentation is weak but, in general, the results are "typical" of what would be expected.

In issuing RAIs, the staff considered the following guidelines.

- The question(s) should be specific. Ask focused questions aimed at a particular issue. For example, do not ask open-ended questions, such as "provide more information about your treatment of human error probabilities (HEPs)." Instead, ask questions, such as "identify the scenarios screened from further analysis based on quantification of HEPs, and discuss how the effects of postulated fires were considered in determining HEPs."

- Ask the question(s) in a way that is clear to the licensee and requests specific information. Avoid asking questions that can be answered "yes" or "no" without providing additional necessary information.

- The RAI should not ask for additional analyses or sensitivity studies, unless such analyses were called for in the IPEEE submittal guidance (i.e., NUREG-1407) and one or more of the guidelines on the previous page apply. Instead, if an assumption or parameter in the submittal appears to be optimistic, provide background related to the issue being addressed, and ask the licensee to either provide a basis for using the parameter in question or repeat the analysis using a value that can be justified.

- Each question should be reviewed by someone other than the author to ensure that it is clear and not subject to alternative interpretations. The reviewer should check each question against the guidelines listed above.

APPENDIX B - GENERIC RAIs RELATED TO THE FIRE PRA IMPLEMENTATION GUIDE

B.1   Background

In preparing their IPEEE, a number of licensees have applied the Fire PRA Implementation Guide (FPRAIG or simply "the Guide"), which the EPRI published in December 1995 [EPRI, 1995]. The FPRAIG provides both general and specific guidelines for performing a fire PRA. The NRC sponsored a review of the FPRAIG from the perspective of the IPEEE program needs [Lambright, 1997]. This review found that (1) the overall fire PRA approach suggested by the FPRAIG is consistent with the current fire PRA state-of-the-art, (2) some of the detailed discussions on fire PRA methods and issues "are an improvement over what can be found in the open literature," and (3) the Guide also provides useful, practical tips, notations, and cautionary statements. However, the review also found that the Guide contains a number of shortcomings "that could potentially lead to either optimistic results or masking of information needed for identifying potential vulnerabilities." The review recommended a set of 15 generic RAI questions that the staff could ask of licensees that employ the FPRAIG.[1] Subsequent IPEEE reviews identified one additional shortcoming that led the staff to add a 16th generic RAI to the list.

Following the FPRAIG review, the NRC and EPRI jointly agreed to an approach for resolving the generic RAIs in a manner that is suitable for the IPEEE program. Consistent with the IPEEE intent, the objective of the resolution approach was not to define nor advance the state-of-the-art but, rather, to ensure that IPEEEs that relied on methods documented in the Guide were capable of identifying plant fire vulnerabilities. This approach led to specific suggestions concerning how licensees should respond to each of the 16 generic RAIs. The following discussions address these generic RAIs, the concerns raised, and the resolution strategies that EPRI ultimately recommended to licensees. Note that the discussion of how the resolution of these issues might have impacted the results or insights of an IPEEE fire analysis is deferred to the body of this report.

B.2   Human Error Probabilities for the Fire Screening Analysis

A licensee's PRA typically credits a variety of human actions, which typically relate to manual actions that are used to recover or bypass a failed system, or to remotely operate a system or component. The internal event models typically include credit for human recovery actions and include an associated human error probability (HEP) for each credited action. These same internal event models are commonly adapted for use in a fire analysis. However, during a fire, some of the recovery actions credited in the internal event analysis might not be possible or might be associated with higher HEP values.

For example, recovery actions that require passage through, or entry into, an area that is impacted by a postulated fire (e.g., the area where the fire occurs or an adjacent area that might be impacted by smoke and heat from a fire) would not typically be credited in the analysis of that fire scenario. Similarly, if the normal path to the location of a credited recovery action is blocked, but an alternate path to the location is available, a higher HEP might be assigned.

---

[1] The review also identified a number of concerns that were not reflected in the generic RAIs, either because their verification was deemed not to be essential to the IPEEE process, or because they were deemed not to affect a large number of studies.

In the original guidance provided in the FPRAIG, direct use of the internal event models was allowed for a number of situations. This inherently included credit for all modeled human recovery actions using the internal events HEP values. This neglected the potential impact of fire on the credited operator actions. The primary concern of IPEEE reviewers was that crediting such human actions without review during the fire area/zone screening analysis might lead to premature screening of potentially important fire areas/zones.

The generic RAI asked licensees to explain how fire effects were treated in assessing the reliability of credited human actions and to assess the impact on fire area screening if such actions were not credited. The revised EPRI guidance ultimately recommended that licensees (1) re-examine the human recovery actions credited in the fire analysis to ensure that the actions were possible given the fires being postulated, and (2) assess any potential fire effects on the reliability of the credited actions. One specific issue in fire PRA involves the treatment of operator actions taken within the main control room. For the purposes of the IPEEE process, EPRI recommended that such actions could be assumed to be unaffected by fires outside the main control room.

B.3   Heat Loss Factors and Simplified Hot Gas Layer Modeling

The FIVE method implemented a simplified approach to enclosure fire response modeling, which was also adopted under the FPRAIG. That is, rather than exercising a fire model for each fire scenario, engineering correlations (in the form of tabular worksheets) were adopted to estimate fire plume, ceiling jet, and hot gas layer exposure conditions for a given fire in a given fire zone.

One important aspect of enclosure fire modeling is heat transfer to the enclosure surfaces. Testing has shown that enclosure surfaces absorb a significant amount of heat during a fire, and this moderates the resulting air temperatures within the enclosure. Most enclosure fire models address this behavior through direct modeling of surface heat transfer. The correlations used are generally both complex and time-dependent. One of the significant simplifications invoked in the FIVE/FPRAIG correlations is that heat losses to enclosure surfaces are addressed through a heat loss factor (HLF). The HLF was defined as the fraction of the heat generated by the fire that is assumed to be lost to the enclosure surfaces. Heat lost to the surfaces is not available to heat the air within the room. Under the FIVE/FPRAIG approach, the HLF is assumed to be constant for a given fire scenario, and its value is selected by the analyst.

FIVE recommended using an HLF of 0.7; that is, 70% of the fire's heat is lost to the enclosure surfaces. In the NRC reviews of FIVE,[2] this value appeared to yield reasonable estimates of hot gas layer response. The FPRAIG endorsed the use of these same engineering correlations, but recommended that HLF values ranging from 0.85 to 0.94 were more appropriate. These values were derived from "An Experimental Study of Upper Hot Layer Stratification in Full-Scale Multi-room Fire Scenarios" [Cooper, 1982].

The NRC recommendation for using substantially higher HLF values as a point of potential concern because the HLF directly impacts the assumed plume, hot gas layer, and ceiling jet temperatures obtained from the correlations. For example, with an HLF of 0.94, just 6% of the total fire heat release is assumed to be available to heat the air in the enclosure. In contrast, with an HLF of 0.7, 30% of the total fire heat release is available to heat the air. As a result, raising the HLF from 0.7 to 0.94 meant that only one-fifth as much

---

[2] The NRC reviewed the FIVE methodology during its development in the late 1980s, and a part of that review involved comparing of the FIVE hot layer correlations to experimental data.

heat would go into the hot gas layer and, in turn, the predicted hot gas layer temperature increases would be reduced by 80%. The temperature increases in the plume and ceiling jet, but to a lesser degree and in a less predictable manner. This is because the general hot layer temperature increase is only one of the factors in estimating the plume and ceiling jet temperature increases.

In support of efforts to resolve this concern, a series of validation calculations were performed. These calculations were aimed at assessing the impact of changes in the HLF value on estimated hot gas layer temperature, and comparing the correlation's predictions with large-scale fire experiments [Nowlen, 1987]. The results were obtained through a comparison between the maximum hot gas layer temperature predicted by the engineering correlation using three HLF values (0.7, 0.85, and 0.94) to the maximum temperatures measured during full-scale tests over a range of room elevations.[3]

In all cases, an HLF of 0.94 led to significant underestimation of the measured hot gas layer temperature. Using an HLF value of 0.85 also underestimated the hot gas layer temperature for most cases. In only one case did an HLF value of 0.85 yield a predicted temperature increase that fell within the range of the measured data. Use of the FIVE-recommended value of 0.7, however, led to results that compared quite favorably with the test data. In most cases, using an HLF of 0.7 yielded a temperature that modestly bounded the measured data. In four cases, the predicted temperature increase did not fully bound the measured data but, in all such cases, the prediction did fall within the range of the experimental data.

As a second exercise, the actual heat loss factors experienced during two fire test programs were estimated [Nowlen, 1987 and Cline, 1983]. The HLFs in the tests nominally ranged from 0.5 to 0.7. Some limited cases had HLF as low as 0.3. While these results contain considerable uncertainty, they do illustrate a nominal consistency with the correlation results, as described above.

The revised EPRI guidance directs licensees to two possible approaches for responding to the generic RAI. In general, the guidance recommends returning to the original FIVE HLF value of 0.7. The major exception is for cases where the fire source is assumed to be located at or above 40% of the room height. One factor in the hot gas layer correlation is the assumed hot gas layer volume. FIVE recommends that if the fire source is modeled as being elevated above the floor, such as a fire on top of a panel or transformer, only the room volume above the fire source elevation should be assumed to be involved in the hot gas layer. In effect, reducing the room volume tends to offset an increase in the HLF.

B.4   Modeling of Cable Tray Fire Growth

The growth of fire in a stack of cable trays is a common fire PRA scenario. Past practice has generally relied on predictive fire models such as COMPBRN [Ho, 1991] for this analysis. The FPRAIG introduced an approach to modeling the growth of cable tray fires by extrapolating fire test data. In particular, the approach relied on the fire spread behavior noted in a 1976 NRC-sponsored fire test [Klamerus, 1977] as documented by Nowlen [Nowlen, 1989]. Nowlen's description included the approximate time the fire was observed to spread from tray to tray during the test. The FPRAIG recommended using these reported fire spread times as a general model of cable tray fire propagation.

---

[3] The correlation can also be exercised in a pseudo-transient format that predicts the temperature increase over time. These results are not illustrated, but follow the same overall pattern of behavior.

A concern with this approach was that it effectively assumes that all cable tray fires will follow the behavior observed in a single test. Of particular concern was the fact that the test in question was designed to simulate a self-ignited cable fire. Hence, no external fire source was present during the period of tray-to-tray fire spread. Application of this limited test result to other fire scenarios appeared to be inappropriate and potentially optimistic, especially for fire scenarios that involved exposure to an external fire source. Furthermore, in applying the FPRAIG guidance, a number of IPEEE analysts assumed that the FPRAIG model also predicted fire damage times. That is, licensees assumed that fire spread was the indicator for thermal damage when, in fact, cables can be damaged before they are ignited.

A review of other cable fire tests [Newman, 1983 and Sumitra, 1982] revealed that cable tray fires could spread substantially faster than was observed in the cited 1976 test, particularly under conditions involving exposure to an external fire. However, EPRI demonstrated that the combination of the tray-to-tray spread model and the FPRAIG-recommended fire heat release rate model for each tray did yield reasonable estimates of the total fire heat release rate for a range of fires, including those cited in the generic RAI. Hence, the resolution of this issue involved something of a compromise.

For the purposes of the IPEEE process, use of the fire spread model recommended in the FPRAIG was found to be acceptable, provided that the fire scenario did not involve substantial exposure to an external fire. Furthermore, the model was only to be used to predict fire heat release rates. An independent assessment of cable damage was also required.

B.5   Main Control Room Abandonment

In a fire PRA, it is common to assume that a severe, unsuppressed fire in the main control room (MCR) will lead operators to abandon the MCR and rely on remote shutdown. The FPRAIG recommended using a conditional probability of abandonment given an MCR fire of 3.4E-3. This value was derived by interpreting data from a small number of actual control room fires and from NRC-sponsored electrical panel fire tests [Chavez, 1987 and 1988]. The interpretation was that operators would have at least 15 minutes after detecting a fire to suppress the fire before a forced abandonment would be required. A further assumption was that, because the MCR is continuously manned by well trained staff, fire detection would occur with little or no significant time delay. In particular, it was assumed that operators would smell a fire with an equal level of reliability and as quickly as would fire detectors that had been optimally placed within the fire source panels during the cited fire tests.

The NRC review of the FPRAIG revealed that the recommended approach did not adequately consider MCR-specific design features. The approach was considered optimistic for some MCRs, including those that do not have in-panel smoke detection available. It was also considered potentially optimistic for MCR configurations that use electrical panels as ventilation system return air plenums. In such cases, smoke from a panel fire would likely be drawn quickly into the ventilation exhaust. There, dilution of the small quantities of smoke associated with the incipient fires observed at the time of detection in the fire tests would mean that ventilation duct smoke detectors would likely not actuate. Under such conditions, the prompt detection times indicated by the test would likely be optimistic when detection in practice relies on operators smelling the smoke from the incipient fire.

An additional complication of this particular generic RAI was the fact that some IPEEE analyses also applied "severity factors" to adjust the MCR fire frequency, typically to reflect prompt detection and suppression of

MCR fires. Because the conditional probability of 3.4E-3 directly credited fire detection and suppression, application of an additional fire severity factor was found, in effect, to represent "double counting" the same mitigating behaviors. Using this approach, a number of IPEEEs screened MCR abandonment scenarios as being risk insignificant, and did not assess the plant's remote shutdown capabilities in the event of a challenging MCR fire. Given the insights gained from past PRAs, and the results of other IPEEEs, the screening of MCRs on such a basis was considered to be potentially optimistic and inappropriate.

The accurate treatment of serious MCR fires and subsequent MCR abandonment is a difficult challenge for fire PRA and, in many regards, is beyond the current state-of-the-art for fire PRA. The IPEEE process was specifically not intended to advance the state-of-the-art. Hence, for the purposes of the IPEEE process, the NRC agreed that licensees could apply the conditional abandonment probability of 3.4E-3 as a nominal estimate of the non-suppression/abandonment probability, but should not apply any severity factors. That is, the likelihood of MCR abandonment was to be taken to be the MCR fire frequency (typically assumed to be 1.9E-2) times the conditional abandonment probability (3.4E-3). The NRC, therefore, directed licensees not to screen MCR abandonment scenarios and to provide an assessment of remote shutdown capability and reliability.

B.6   Recovery of Fixed Fire Suppression Systems

Fixed fire suppression systems are widely used to enhance fire safety in United States nuclear power plants. These systems are also important factors in a fire risk analysis. In fire PRA, it is common to find that fixed fire suppression systems offer a substantial risk benefit. Depending on the timing of system actuation versus critical damage, fire scenarios may be of potential risk importance only if a fire suppression system is assumed to fail on demand (for example, as a result of failures in supporting equipment). Licensees commonly apply generic failure rates to assess the likelihood of such failures.

The FPRAIG included an approach for crediting recovery of a failed fire suppression system. Many types of fire suppression system failures are recoverable. For example, a system inadvertently left in manual actuation mode may be recovered (or actuated) by a simple flip of a switch (provided that no damage to the system has occurred). If fire-fighting personnel arrive on the scene of the fire and find that a fixed suppression system has not actuated, they will likely attempt to recover and/or manually actuate that system.

It was noted that the FPRAIG approach did not address some potential dependencies. In particular, attempts by fire fighters to recover a fixed suppression system would likely delay initiation of other manual fire-fighting actions. If the recovery attempts are not successful, the fire, which would have continued to grow, may present a greater challenge to subsequent manual fire suppression.

EPRI, therefore, provided revised guidance directing licensees to re-examine scenarios that credited both recovery of a failed fixed system and manual fire-fighting. Specifically, licensees were asked to consider the impact of the recovery attempts on the timing of subsequent fire-fighting efforts and the potential for additional fire growth while recovery was attempted. In particular, attention was directed to rooms that are protected by CO_2 or Halon systems. In such cases, fire fighters might be especially hesitant to enter the area knowing that an attempt was being made to actuate the fire suppression system.

B.7   Control Systems Interactions

The fire-induced failure of an electrical cable will lead to some type of circuit fault. How a cable failure will be manifested in the circuit depends on the purpose of the cable in the circuit (i.e., power, instrument or control), the circuit design, and the assumed mode of cable failure. For example, conductor-to-conductor "hot shorts" might lead to spurious component actuations, whereas a short to ground on the same conductors might lead to a loss of system power and/or control. These behaviors, and other related issues, are broadly referred to as control system interaction (CSI) issues.

The CSI issues are also interrelated with the question of fire in the MCR as well as MCR abandonment scenarios. Depending on a plant's safe shutdown strategy, MCR abandonment may be initiated as a result of fires in the MCR itself and/or fires in other critical plant areas (the cable spreading room being a common example). It is important that remote shutdown functions be independent of fire damage and the circuit faults that might occur in such areas.

The treatment of fire-induced CSI is a point of both regulatory and PRA interest. In 1989, the Fire Risk Scoping Study (FRSS) [Lambright, 1989] concluded that the then current fire PRA methods did not fully treat the CSI issues. The CSI issues are arguably one of the most difficult challenges currently facing fire PRA. The potential circuit interactions of interest to fire PRA are complex and difficult to analyze [LaChance, 2000]. The methods of analysis available at the outset of the IPEEE process were both limited and subject to debate.

The FPRAIG provided some guidance for resolving the CSI issues. However, the guidance did not consider all potentially important aspects of the CSI issues. Hence, the NRC developed a generic CSI-related RAI and discussed with EPRI. The generic RAI requested that licensees provide additional discussion and analysis of four specific areas of potential importance to fire PRA. In general, the NRC did not expect licensees to advance the state-of-the-art in their IPEEE analyses. Ultimately it was agreed that licensees' ability to fully address the CSI issues in their IPEEEs was clearly impacted by limitations in the state-of-the-art. Furthermore, a range of related regulatory activities are underway to address CSI concerns. Hence, for the purposes of the IPEEE process, licensees were asked to address one specific aspect of CSI, namely, the independence and reliability of remote shutdown. Licensees were directed to provide an assessment of their remote shutdown capability to ensure that it was independent of fire-induced failures in the areas where fires might force an MCR abandonment, and to assess the capability and reliability of the plant's remote shutdown features.

B.8   Other Fire Risk Scoping Study Issues

In addition to the CSI issues discussed above, the NRC requested that licensees address three issues raised in the FRSS, namely, seismic-fire interactions, smoke control and manual fire-fighting, and the adverse impact of fire suppression systems. In its letter accepting the use of FIVE in the IPEEE process, the NRC noted shortcomings in the guidance for verifying the FRSS issues [U.S. NRC, 1991]. The FPRAIG largely adopted the same guidance regarding these issues as in the FIVE methodology, without addressing the shortcomings identified by the NRC. Hence, the NRC developed three additional generic RAIs, one relating to each of these three issues.

In its response, EPRI provided additional guidance to licensees relating to the three issues. For example, in the area of seismic-fire interactions, EPRI's revised guidance recommended that licensees consider the seismic ruggedness of installed fire suppression systems, the potential for spurious actuation of fire suppression systems, the possible impact of an unsuppressed fire following an earthquake, personnel response to spurious fire alarms that might mask a real alarm, and the impact of spurious suppression system actuations on operator actions required to respond to an earthquake. Licensees were also directed to describe the walkdown approach used to address each issue and document the results obtained in those walkdowns.

B.9   Screening of Fire-Induced Special Initiators

As defined in the FPRAIG, a "special initiator" trips the plant and causes loss of a mitigating safety system. Examples include loss of service water and loss of component cooling water. For some plants, an unrecovered special initiator can lead directly to core damage. Hence, special initiators are potentially significant risk contributors if, as in a fire, there is a potential for common mode failure in multiple mitigating safety systems.

One step in the FPRAIG stated that licensees should "consider the need to locate equipment and cables for those special initiators whose (non-recoverable) frequency is greater than 1E-4/yr." This implied that if the initiation frequency was less than 1E-4/yr, the special initiator scenarios could be screened. A concern with this implied screening criterion is that it might lead to premature screening of potentially important fire risk scenarios. In the worst case, a fire scenario leading directly to core damage (i.e., without additional independent equipment failures) with an initiating frequency of 1E-4/yr would clearly represent a dominant fire risk scenario, if not a fire vulnerability. Following discussion of the concerns, EPRI provided revised guidance that deleted this particular step in the analysis. Licensees were directed to re-examine any fire scenarios that might have been screened using the original guidance.

B.10   Screening of Enclosed Ignition Sources

The FPRAIG process for screening ignition sources was founded on an assessment of the potential that each ignition source might lead to propagation of fire to other combustibles. One aspect of this screening was to "eliminate from further consideration situations where ignition sources are fully enclosed, making them unable to ignite other combustibles." The IPEEE reviewers found that licensees were broadly applying this criterion to screen a range of ignition sources.

Therefore, a concern was raised that this approach might prematurely screen some ignition sources. In particular, some ignition sources have the potential to breach their enclosures. The generic RAI cited transformers and electrical panels as example cases. An electrical panel fire, for example, may generate sufficient heat to warp the panel's doors, thereby allowing fire to escape despite the lack of other openings. Fire experience also includes cases where an energetic electrical fault allowed fires to breach an electrical enclosure.

Following discussion of the issue, EPRI provided revised guidance directing licensees to re-examine a number of fire ignition sources to determine if they were prematurely screened. These sources included transformers of greater than 480V, switchgear, any electrical panel of 480V or greater fed by a high-energy source (such as a diesel generator or transformer) and motor control centers of 480V or greater. With certain specific case-by-case exceptions, licensees were to re-evaluate these sources as "open ignition sources."

B - 7

B.11 Electrical Control Panel Heat Release Rates

Fire scenarios involving a fire in an electrical panel that threatened overhead cables were quite common in the IPEEE fire analyses. In assessing fire propagation and/or fire damage associated with such fires, the assumed heat release rate (HRR) of the initial panel fire source can be critical. The FPRAIG recommended that most panel fires could be modeled using an HRR of 65 BTU/s (69 kW). This recommendation was primarily based on interpretation of NRC-sponsored electrical control panel fire tests [Chavez, 1987 and 1988].

IPEEE reviewers found that the recommended panel fire HRR may be optimistic for a number of electrical panels because the cited HRR values did not bound the referenced tests, the referenced tests did not address fires involving electrical distribution panels, and the results of other panel fire tests [Mangs, 1994 and 1996] were not considered. The overall concern was that if panel fires were assumed never to exceed 65 BTU/s (69 kW), a fire risk study might prematurely screen some electrical panel fire scenarios.

In response, EPRI provided revised guidance for licensees to use in assessing the fire potential for electrical panels. First, the guidelines established for when it was appropriate to assume an HRR of 65 BTU/s (69 kW). These guidelines reflected the actual test conditions under which panel fire sizes were indeed so limited, namely, panels containing only qualified cables (per IEEE-383 flame spread testing) and panels where the fuel load was concentrated in individual cable bundles such that fire spread beyond a single cable bundle could be dismissed. Second, for all other panels, licensees were directed to reconsider the risk contribution should the HRR be increased to 190 BTU/s (200 kW). The higher HRR value was largely based on the results of the panel fire tests in Finland [Mangs, 1994 and 1996].

B.12 Screening of Fire Sources Based on Non-Combustible Shields

One criterion that the FRAIG cited for screening fire sources was the presence of a non-combustible shield between the source and key targets. IPEEE reviewers found that this criterion would be overly optimistic for some cases, particularly those cases involving high hazard combustibles (such as large oil sources), where flames might impinge on the shield and where hot gases in the plume or hot layer might move around the shield to expose the targets. As a result, licensees might prematurely screen some fire scenarios.

EPRI agreed with these observations, and provided additional guidance for licensees to use in the treatment of non-combustible shields. Specifically, licensees were directed to reconsider any fixed fire sources that were previously screened using the original guidance. In addition, licensees were directed to reconsider fire scenarios that involved potential plume, ceiling jet, and hot layer exposures that would not be impacted by such shields. The revised guidance also notes that it may be appropriate to limit the fire's "damage zone" associated with radiant heat transfer on the basis of the intervention of such shields between the fire and target. However, licensees were directed to take such credit only "if the shield is designed and maintained to protect against the source-target combination being considered."

B.13 Screening of Transient Combustibles

As a general rule, the FPRAIG recommended screening ignition sources if an analysis shows that the source poses no potential for either propagation to secondary fuels or damage to PRA targets. Furthermore, one passage in the FPRAIG stated that "if all fixed ignition sources in a zone screen, the zone probably will screen." IPEEE reviewers noted that some licensees were interpreting this passage as allowing for direct screening of transient ignition sources if all of the fixed ignition sources screened. When applied in this manner, this passage might lead to premature screening of fire zones.

In discussions with EPRI, it became clear that the intent of the FPRAIG authors was not to establish a transient fire screening criterion, and that some licensees were misinterpreting the guidance. The actual intent of the passage was to convey the likely outcome of the transient fire analysis, not to allow for screening of transients. That is, in many situations, transient fire sources do not represent significant fire threats. This is typically attributable to geometry considerations (for example, cables being located too far above the floor for a transient fire source to threaten). Hence, if the fixed sources screen, one might expect the transient sources to screen as well. However, there are cases where this observation does not apply. In particular, the assessment of target vulnerability based on fixed sources alone would be incomplete for areas where there are no significant fixed fire sources, or where the fixed fire sources are not located near the critical targets. In these cases, transient fire sources, which may occur anywhere in the room, might still represent significant fire risk contributors. EPRI, therefore, developed revised guidance to clarify that a specific analysis of transient fire sources is still needed even when the fixed fire sources have screened or are absent. EPRI also directed licensees to re-examine any fire zones that were screened without considering transient fire sources.

B.14 Fire Suppression Criteria

One additional aspect of the FPRAIG treatment of fire suppression led to another generic RAI. Specifically, the FPRAIG provided probabilistic curves for the likelihood of fire suppression versus time for a number of specific fire types (e.g., transients, welding fires, cable fires, panel fires, etc.). In one passage, the FPRAIG stated that fire suppression efforts could be considered successful if the source fire or any subsequently ignited targets were suppressed. The approach estimated the likelihood of successful suppression before damage as the product of two suppression terms, namely, the likelihood that the fire ignition source was suppressed before damage, and the likelihood that any subsequently ignited materials were suppressed before damage. For example, in a scenario involving a panel fire that spreads to overhead cable trays, an analyst might assess the likelihood for fire suppression within a given time as the product of the likelihood that the panel fire is suppressed times the likelihood that a cable fire is suppressed within that time. In effect, the two suppression probabilities are treated as fully independent when, in fact, the two are highly dependent because there is really only one consolidated fire and fire fighters will attack the overall fire, rather than attacking two separate fires.

EPRI provided revised guidance clarify that there is one consolidated fire that requires suppression. The revised guidance states that if the fire does not spread beyond the fire ignition source, the likelihood of suppression is based on suppression of the fire source. However, if the fire does spread, for example to cable trays, the likelihood of suppressing the larger (cable) fire should be used.

B.15 Cable Ignition Temperatures

One aspect of fire growth modeling, as commonly applied in fire PRA, requires the analyst to establish temperature criteria for the ignition of combustible materials. The criteria for piloted ignition of cables (i.e., ignition of cables in the presence of a pilot flame) is a particularly common question encountered in nuclear power plant fire scenarios.

In 1991, an NRC-sponsored cable damage test program revealed that cable electrical failures and arcing often led to self-sustaining fires in the exposed cables [Nowlen, 1991] This lead to a conclusion that the piloted ignition temperature (the electrical sparks representing the pilot source) for the tested cables was at or below the damage threshold for those cables.

The results of the NRC-sponsored tests were cited in the FIVE methodoloy, which recommended that, for cables, the damage temperature and piloted ignition temperature should be assumed to be the same. The most commonly applied value was 700°F (370°C) given the damage thresholds for IEEE-383 qualified cables. The FPRAIG recommended that 932°F (500°C) be used as the threshold for both piloted and spontaneous (i.e., in the absence of a pilot flame) ignition of cables. The higher value derives from earlier EPRI data extrapolation results [Tewarson, 1979]. However, it has since been shown that those extrapolations do not reflect the actual threshold behavior [Nowlen, 1989].

The NRC, therefore, developed a generic RAI to address this change in the assumptions related to piloted cable ignition criteria. Specifically, the RAI stated that using the higher piloted ignition temperature could lead to premature screening of fire growth scenarios. In response, EPRI issued revised guidance recommending that licensees return to the original FIVE guidance.

B.16 References

Chavez, J.M., "An Experimental Investigation of Internally Ignited Fires in Nuclear Power Plant Control Cabinets, Part I — Cabinet Effects Tests," SAND86-0336, NUREG/CR-4527, Volume 1, U.S. NRC, April 1987.

Chavez, J.M. and S.P. Nowlen, "An Experimental Investigation of Internally Ignited Fires in Nuclear Power Plant Cabinets, Part II — Room Effects Tests," SAND86-0336, NUREG/CR-4527, Volume 2, U.S. NRC, October 1988.

Cline, D.D., W.A. von Riesemann, and J.M. Chavez, "Investigation of Twenty-Foot Separation Distance as a Fire Protection Method as Specified in 10 CFR 50, Appendix R," NUREG/CR-3192, U.S. NRC, October 1983.

Cooper, L.Y., et. al., "An Experimental Study of Upper Hot Layer Stratification in Full-Scale Multiroom Fire Scenarios," Journal of Heat Transfer, Volume 104, pp. 741-749, November 1982.

EPRI, "Fire-Induced Vulnerability Evaluation (FIVE)," TR-100370, April 1992.

EPRI, "Fire PRA Implementation Guide," TR-105928, December 1995.

EPRI, "COMPBRN IIIE: An Interactive Computer Code for Fire Risk Analysis," EPRI NP-7282, May 1991.

Klamerus, L.J., "A Preliminary Report on Fire Protection Research Program (July 6, 1977)," SAND77-1424, SNL, October 1977.

LaChance, J., S.P. Nowlen, F. Wyant and V. Dandini, "Circuit Analysis — Failure Mode and Likelihood Analysis," letter report to the U.S. NRC, SNL, May 8, 2000 (available through the U.S. NRC Public Document Room under memorandum from T.L. King, RES/DRAA, to G.M. Holahan, NRR/DSSA, and M.E. Mayfield, RES/DET, dated June 13, 2000, RES File Code RES-2C-1).

Lambright, J., S.P. Nowlen, V.F. Nicolette, and M.P. Bohn, "Fire Risk Scoping Study: Investigation of Nuclear Power Plant Fire Risk, Including Previously Unaddressed Issues," SAND88-0177, NUREG/CR-5088, U.S. NRC, January 1989.

Lambright, J., and M. Kazarians, "Review of the EPRI Fire PRA Implementation Guide," a letter report to the U.S. NRC, Energy Research Inc., ERI/NRC 97-501, August 1997.

Mangs, J., and O. Keski-Rahkonen, "Full Scale Fire Experiments on Electrical Cabinets," VTT Technical Research Centre of Finland, Publ. 186, Espoo, Finland, 1994.

Mangs, J., and O. Keski-Rahkonen, "Full Scale Fire Experiments on Electrical Cabinets II," VTT Technical Research Centre of Finland, Publ. 269, Espoo, Finland, 1996.

Newman, J.S., "Fire Tests in Ventilated Rooms — Detection of Cable Tray and Exposure Fires," EPRI NP-2751, February 1983.

Nowlen, S.P., "Enclosure Environment Characterization Testing for Base Line Validation of Computer Fire Simulation Codes," SAND86-1296, NUREG/CR-4681, U.S. NRC, March 1987.

Nowlen, S.P., and V. Nicolette, "A Critical Look at Nuclear Qualified Electrical Cable Insulation Ignition and Damage Thresholds," SAND88-2161C, published in Conference Proceedings of the Operability of Nuclear Systems in Normal and Adverse Environments, ANS/ENS, September 1989.

Nowlen, S.P., "A Summary of the U.S. NRC Fire Protection Research Program at Sandia National Laboratories 1975-1987," NUREG/CR-5384, U.S. NRC, December 1989.

Nowlen, S.P., "An Investigation of the Effects of Thermal Aging on the Fire Damageability of Electric Cables," NUREG/CR-5546, U.S. NRC, May 1991.

Siu, N., and H. Woods, "The U.S. Nuclear Regulatory Commission's Fire Risk Research Program — An Overview," Proceedings from International Workshop on Fire Risk Assessment, NEA/CSNI/R(99)26, 2000.

Sumitra, P.S., "Categorization of Cable Flammability Intermediate-Scale Fire Tests of Cable Tray Installations," EPRI NP-1881, August 1982.

Tewarson, A., et. al., "Categorization of Cable Flammability Part 1: Laboratory Evaluation of Cable Flammability Parameters," EPRI, NP-1200, October 1979.

U.S. NRC, "Individual Plant Examination of External Events (IPEEE) for Severe Accident Vulnerabilities," Generic Letter 88-20, Supplement 4, June 28, 1991.

U.S. NRC, Letter from A.C. Thadani, NRC/NRR/DST, to W.H. Rasin, NUMARC, Subject: "NRC's Staff Evaluation Report on Revised NUMARC/EPRI Fire Vulnerability Evaluation (FIVE) Methodology," August 21, 1991 (see letter attachment, paragraph 4).

APPENDIX C - PUBLIC COMMENTS AND NRC RESPONSES ON DRAFT NUREG-1742

C.1 Introduction

The NRC initially issued NUREG-1742, "Perspectives Gained From the Individual Plant Examination of External Events (IPEEE) Program," Volumes 1 and 2, in April 2001 as a draft report for public comment, with the comment period ending on July 31, 2001. At that time, the NRC published notices in the *Federal Register*[1] announcing the availability of the report and requesting comments. The NRC also made the report available on the NRC's web site <http://www.nrc.gov/>. The NRC distributed the report to more than 500 people and organizations.

In response to the request for comments, the NRC staff received four letters. Table C.1 lists the authors and organizations who submitted these comments. All comments received are available from the NRC's Agencywide Document Access and Management System (ADAMS) using the accession number listed in Table C.1.

Table C.1: Submitted comments on draft NUREG-1742

Identification #	Organization	Author(s)	Date received by NRC	ADAMS Accession #
1	Nebraska Public Power District	John H. Swailes, V.P. of Nuclear Energy	7/06/01	011910159
2	Rochester Gas & Electric Corporation	Dr. Raymond H.V. Gallucci	7/30/01	012130238
3	BWR Owners Group	J. M. Kenny, BWR Owners' Group Chairman	8/06/01	012190262
4	Union Electric Company	Dave Shafer, Superintendent, Licensing	8/06/01	012190272

In addition to these comments, as part of the IPEEE review process, the staff discussed the approach and results of draft NUREG-1742 with the NRC's Advisory Committee on Reactor Safeguards on June 22 and July 12, 2001.

The final version of NUREG-1742 addresses all of the comments that the NRC received. Specifically, the comments fell into three broad categories:

---

[1] *Federal Register*, "NUREG-1742, 'Perspectives Gained from the Individual Plant Examination of External Events (IPEEE) Program'; Draft for Comment," Vol. 66, No. 86, Page 22269, May 3, 2001.

(1)   A number of comments were editorial in nature. Such comments are not reproduced in this appendix. However, the NRC corrected the text to reflect these comments where appropriate.

(2)   Some comments reflected a difference between the report's representation of a plant feature and the current plant condition. These comments are not reproduced in this appendix. However, the NRC reviewed the comments. The final report was revised to properly reflect the plant feature and the current plant condition.

(3)   Other comments related to the presentation of findings and perspectives, the potential uses of the findings, and the plant-to-plant comparisons that could be made. The next section of this appendix summarizes these comments and presents NRC staff's responses.

C.2   Specific Comments and Responses

This section summarizes the comments received, and presents the NRC staff's responses.

(1)   **Comment:**   The report inappropriately compares core damage frequencies (CDFs) for internal fires, seismic external events, and HFO events with those for internal events. The comment raised the point that the nature of the process for determining the CDFs for the two analyses is significantly different. In the IPEEEs, a conservative screening analyses was performed to look for potential plant vulnerabilities. Even though some aspects of the IPEEE review used PRA techniques, it was still a screening analysis rather than a full-scope PRA. In many cases, conservative assumptions were used to bound the analysis and show that no vulnerabilities exist. In the IPEs, a less conservative, more realistic, assessment was performed. Thus, it is not appropriate to compare the IPEEE CDFs with the IPE CDFs. (Reference: see Table C.1, #3)

Response: It is true that most of the submittals indicated that the IPEEE results were generated using a more conservative approach than employed in the IPE. However, there were also instances where the staff observed that certain assumptions may have been overly optimistic (i.e., non-conservative). While recognizing the uncertainties with any CDF estimate, the staff believe that general comparisons between the IPEEE and IPE CDFs are reasonable. Therefore, NUREG-1742 does not provide plant-specific comparisons or evaluations, but provides general comparisons (e.g., by reactor type). The format for the figures, predominantly in Chapter 3, have been revised to make it clear that plant-specific comparisons are not intended. The "Scope, Limitations, and General Comments" and the "Uses of IPEEE Information" sections in the summary of this report have been revised to clarify the limitations when comparing quantitative CDF results.

The typical fire assessment approach was to perform an initial qualitative screening. Areas that were qualitatively screened would be expected to be areas that would not lead directly to a fire initiation and would not cause the loss of safe shutdown function. To evaluate areas that did not screen, licensees typically applied a PRA approach with variable amounts of uncertainty, detail, and conservatism. Indeed, licensees used some of the IPE PRA information to evaluate the unscreened areas. Similarly in the seismic area, there were different levels of uncertainty and conservatism applied in evaluating seismic capacities. The amount of conservatism varied between analyses and was influenced by the analyst and the method chosen. The NRC staff did not evaluate the amount of conservatism, and it is not clear what level of conservatism could be generically attributed to the IPEEE submittals.

(2) **Comment:** The IPEEE was intended to be a vulnerability screening analysis, rather than a full-scope PRA and, as such, licensees used only the technical resolution needed to support that objective. NUREG-1742 identifies potential uses of the IPEEE information that would need a higher degree of precision than that presented in the IPEEE. Using the IPEEE (with low technical resolution) to resolve issues needing higher technical resolution could result in inaccurate conclusions. Therefore, using the IPEEE information requires careful consideration of the IPEEE objective and how it could affect the results. (Reference: see Table C.1, #3)

Response: We agree that those who use the IPEEE information need to carefully consider both the objective of the activity and the level of detail and completeness of the IPEEE information. We have revised the "Uses of IPEEE Information" in Section 1.4 of NUREG-1742 to emphasize that care needs to be taken when IPEEE information is to be used. Anyone using this information needs to carefully consider the nature, quality, and completeness of the IPEEE analysis to ensure that the analysis is suitable, reasonable, and robust in the context of the desired application.

(3) **Comment:** NUREG-1742 identifies substantial differences in the IPEEE results, without addressing the many differences between the plants' designs and sites. This could be misleading, and could lead to inappropriate conclusions. (Reference: see Table C.1, #3)

Response: We agree. We have enhanced the discussion of the scope of the IPEEEs and the limitations on using this information in the "Scope, Limitations, and General Comments" in Section 1.3 of NUREG-1742.

NRC FORM 335 (2-89) NRCM 1102, 3201, 3202	U.S. NUCLEAR REGULATORY COMMISSION **BIBLIOGRAPHIC DATA SHEET** *(See instructions on the reverse)*	1. REPORT NUMBER (Assigned by NRC, Add Vol., Supp., Rev., and Addendum Numbers, if any.) NUREG-1742, Vol. 1

2. TITLE AND SUBTITLE

Perspectives Gained from the Individual Plant Examination of External Events (IPEEE) Program

Final Report

3.	DATE REPORT PUBLISHED	
	MONTH	YEAR
	April	2002

4. FIN OR GRANT NUMBER

5. AUTHOR(S)

6. TYPE OF REPORT

Technical

7. PERIOD COVERED *(Inclusive Dates)*

8. PERFORMING ORGANIZATION - NAME AND ADDRESS *(If NRC, provide Division, Office or Region, U.S. Nuclear Regulatory Commission, and mailing address; if contractor, provide name and mailing address.)*

Division of Risk Analysis and Applications

Office of Nuclear Regulatory Research

U.S. Nuclear Regulatory Commission

Washington, D.C. 20555

9. SPONSORING ORGANIZATION - NAME AND ADDRESS *(If NRC, type "Same as above"; if contractor, provide NRC Division, Office or Region, U.S. Nuclear Regulatory Commission, and mailing address.)*

Same as above

10. SUPPLEMENTARY NOTES

Alan M. Rubin, NRC Project Manager

11. ABSTRACT *(200 words or less)*

The NRC requested by Generic Letter 88-20, Supplement 4, and NUREG-1407, that each licensee perform an IPEEE to identify and report all plant-specific vulnerabilities to severe accidents caused by external events. The external events considered included seismic events; internal fires; and high winds, floods, and other external initiating events including transportation or nearby facility accidents and plant-unique hazards. All currently operating U.S. nuclear power plants have completed their assessments.

The objective of the NRC's IPEEE submittal reviews was to ascertain whether the licensees' IPEEE processes were capable of identifying severe accident vulnerabilities to such external events, and implementing cost-effective safety improvements to either eliminate or reduce the impact of those vulnerabilities. The reviews did not attempt to validate or verify the licensees' results.

The purpose of this report is to document the perspectives gleaned from the technical reviews of the IPEEE submittals. These include a description of the overall IPEEE process and findings; conclusions regarding the dominant risk contributors for the major areas of evaluation; an overview of plant improvements; a description of the overall strengths and weaknesses in the licensees' implementation of the IPEEE evaluation methodologies; and an assessment of the overall effectiveness in meeting the IPEEE objectives.

12. KEY WORDS/DESCRIPTORS *(List words or phrases that will assist researchers in locating the report.)*

IPE, IPEEE, Probabilistic Risk Assessment, severe accident, seismic, fire, flood, tornado, earthquake, hurricane, Generic Letter 88-20, NUREG-1407, external events, Fire Induced Vulnerability Evaluation, unresolved safety issue, generic safety issue,

13. AVAILABILITY STATEMENT

unlimited

14. SECURITY CLASSIFICATION

(This Page)

unclassified

(This Report)

unclassified

15. NUMBER OF PAGES

16. PRICE

Printed
on recycled
paper

Federal Recycling Program